A Cruising Guide to the Virgin Islands

*Including
the Spanish Virgin Islands,
the United States Virgin Islands,
and the British Virgin Islands*

SECOND EDITION

by

Stephen J. Pavlidis

Cocoa Beach, Florida

A Cruising Guide to the Virgin Islands

Second Edition
Copyright © 2017 by Stephen J. Pavlidis
ISBN 978-1-892399-35-9
ver. 7.7.2016

Published in the USA by:
Seaworthy Publications, Inc.
2021 N. Atlantic Ave., Unit #226
Cocoa Beach, Florida 32931
Phone 321-610-3634
email orders@seaworthy.com
www.seaworthy.com - Your Bahamas and Caribbean Cruising Advisory

All rights reserved. No part of this book may be reproduced stored in a retrieval system, or transmitted in any form, or by any means, electronic, mechanical, photocopying, recording, or by any storage and retrieval system, without permission in writing from the Publisher.

CAUTION: Sketch charts are not to scale and are not to be used for navigational purposes. They are intended as supplements for NOAA, DMA, or British Admiralty charts and no warranties are either expressed or implied as to the usability of the information contained herein. The Author and Publisher take no responsibility for their misuse.

A publication like this is actually the result of a blending of many people's talents, knowledge, and experiences. I would like to take this opportunity to thank the following for their help in this effort: Gil, Skyler, Kaia, Anspacher and Sandra Romano of the S/V *Kauhalekai*; Captain Lee Bakewell of the S/V *Escape Cay* for his help with the programming; Carlyle Benavent of the S/V *Halben II*; Captain R. Bensen; Ben Botond; Monika Anna Darmstaedter; Todd Duff who contributed so very much, including many of the photos in this book, thank you Todd; Bob Grieser; Clyde Hancock, Michelle Rexach (who provided many photos of the SVI), and Jake of the S/V *Monsita*; Stuart and Natalya Kaydash of the *Vieques Yacht Club*; Capt. Pat Lerocque of the S/V *Instant Karma*; Andy Lowe and Star Droshine; Jorge and Isabel Molina of the S/V *Pursuit*; Chris and Maria Nielson of the S/V *Altamar*; Angel Perez Morales; Filo and Janet Rico; Juan Seda of the M/V *Lumar*; Captain Tom Shepherd; Surfer 1%er Chicago Outlaw, retired National President of the Outlaws M.C.; Bruce and Rosa Van Sant; Dr. Juan M. "Van" Vicens; and last but not least, Collette Marie Wilson. If there is anybody that I have neglected to mention here, rest assured that it is an oversight and I sincerely apologize.

Cover Design by Ken Quant, *Broad Reach Marketing*, Milwaukee, Wisconsin.

Library of Congress Cataloging-in-Publication Data

Pavlidis, Stephen J.
 A cruising guide to the Virgin Islands : including the Spanish Virgin Islands, the
United States Virgin Islands, and the British Virgin Islands / by Stephen J. Pavlidis. -- Second edition.
   p. cm.
 Includes bibliographical references and index.
 ISBN-13: 978-1-892399-35-9 (pbk. : alk. paper) —ISBN-10: 1-892399-35-0 (pbk. : alk. paper)
 1. Boats and boating--Virgin Islands--Guidebooks. 2. Nautical charts--Virgin Islands.
3. Virgin Islands--Guidebooks. I. Title.
   GV776.29.V6P38 2011
   797.109729'72--dc22
                              2011012804

Introduction

This guide covers the waters of what are probably the finest cruising grounds in the world if not the most popular, the Three Virgins; the Spanish Virgin Islands (SVI), the United States Virgin Islands (USVI), and the British Virgin Islands (BVI). Until recently the Spanish Virgin Islands were not as visited as the more popular sites in the USVI and the BVI, but with the U.S. Navy ending the bombing on Vieques, the future for the Spanish Virgin Islands looks bright indeed. Especially since the opening of a charter operation at *Puerto Del Rey Marina* that also has a branch at *Maya Cove* on Tortola in the BVI. You can charter a boat at either location and drop it off at the other. Now that's convenience!

The Virgin Islands are steeped in history having been under the influence of many cultures during their history. The British, the French, the Dutch, the Danes, the Spanish, and even the Knights of Malta had a stake in these islands at one point or another, and you'll find evidence of their occupation everywhere you look from the street names to the architecture and cuisine.

Whatever you're looking for you'll probably be able to find it in the Virgin Islands. Divers will find an undersea Mecca full of beautiful coral reefs alive with all manner of sea life and scores of amazing wrecks such as the famous *HMS Rhone*. For your convenience you'll find mooring buoys at most dive sites. If you're not interested in diving, perhaps you'll like the shopping or the dining out. St. Thomas is a haven for those with money to spend on duty-free items and it's easy to spend hours and hours strolling the shops along the Charlotte Amalie waterfront. On every island you'll find wonderful places to dine out, from mom-and-pop eateries to fine resorts with upscale restaurants that rival the world's best.

Sailing the islands is like voyaging through a Jimmy Buffet song, but if you get tired of the crowds at anchor, head over to Anegada or St. John to get away from it all. Anegada offers some of the finest beaches and reef diving in the islands, and St. John is known far and wide for its laid-back lifestyle. If you're into getting off the beaten path deep into the rainforests and backwoods of these steep, mountainous islands you'll find paths and trails to lead you far away from civilization.

Whether you come here for a two-week charter, a month, or a season, the islands will satisfy your cravings and leave you hungering for more. You, too, might be drawn back again and again, until you give in to the urge and stay here year round. Life can be so difficult, but not here.

Stephen J. Pavlidis

Table of Contents

Introduction **3**

Irma and Maria **7**

The Basics **9**
    Anchoring 9
        BVI National Parks Regulations 10
        USVI National Park Regulations 10
    Caribbean Etiquette 11
    Chartering 11
    Clothing-What to Bring 12
    Currency 12
    Customs and Immigration 13
        British Virgin Islands 13
        SVI and Puerto Rico 14
        United States Virgin Islands 14
    Ports of Entry 15
        Puerto Rico 15
        The Spanish Virgin Islands 15
        The United States Virgin Islands 15
        The British Virgin Islands 15
    Dinghy Safety 15
    Ferries 16
        SVI and Puerto Rico 16
        United States Virgin Islands 16
        British Virgin Islands 16
    Garbage 16
    Holidays 17
        SVI and Puerto Rico 17
        United States Virgin Islands 17
        British Virgin Islands 17
    Hurricane Holes 17
        SVI and Puerto Rico 19
        United States Virgin Islands 19
        British Virgin Islands 20
    Language 20
    Medical Emergencies 20
    Navigation 20
    Phoning Home 21
    Rastafarians 21
    Rum 22
    Safety and Security 23
    Taxis and Buses 25
    Tides and Currents 25
    Time 26
    VHF 26
    VISAR 26
    Weather 27

Using the Charts **30**

Chart Legend **30**

List of Charts **31**

The Spanish Virgin Islands **34**
    Port of Entry: 34
    Isla de Palominos 35
    La Cordillera to Isla de Culebra 37
    Isla de Culebra 41
    Isla de Culebrita 47
    Isla de Vieques 49
        Punta Arenas 52
        Punta Arenas to Isabel Segunda 52
        Bahia Icacos 54
        Ensenada Honda, Isla Chiva 54
        Puerto Ferro 56
        Puerto Mosquito 56
        Ensenada Sun Bay 56

The United States Virgin Islands **59**
    Port of Entry: 59
    A Brief History 59
    Approaching from the Spanish Virgin Islands 63
    St. Thomas 64
        Charlotte Amalie 64
        Historical Charlotte Amalie 65
        Shopping in Charlotte Amalie 67
        Haulover Cut to Krum Bay 70
        Krum Bay 72
        Water Island 72

Table of Contents

- Benner Bay 74
- Christmas Cove, Current Cut 75
- Cowpet Bay 77
- Red Hook 77
- Sapphire Beach Marina 79
- The Northern Shore 82
- Driving Around St. Thomas 83
- St. John 84
  - Moorings at St. John 86
  - Cruz Bay 86
  - Great Cruz Bay 88
  - The Lameshur Bays 88
  - Saltpond Bay 92
  - Coral Bay 92
  - Coral Harbor 94
  - Newfound Bay 94
  - Haulover Bay 96
  - Leinster Bay 96
  - Francis Bay 96
  - Trunk Bay 98
  - Hawksnest Bay 100
  - Caneel Bay 100
  - Driving Around St. John 100
- St. Croix 102
  - Alexander Hamilton and St. Croix 102
  - Approaching St. Croix 103
  - Christiansted 103
  - Buck Island 106
  - Green Cay Marina 107
  - Green Cay to Teague Bay 108
  - Salt River Bay 109
  - Frederiksted 110
  - Krause Lagoon 112
  - Driving Around St. Croix 112

The British Virgin Islands 114

- Port of Entry: 114
- A Brief History 114
- Tortola 117
  - Road Town 117
  - Fort Burt Marina, Road Reef Marina. 122
  - Prospect Reef Resort 123
  - Brandywine Bay 123
  - Maya Cove, Buck Island 125
  - Fat Hog's Bay 127
  - Marina Cay 127
  - Scrub Island 128
  - Trellis Bay, Beef Island 130
  - Guana Island 132
  - Brewers Bay 134
  - Cane Garden Bay 136
  - West End 137
  - (Soper's Hole) 137
  - Nanny Cay 140
  - Sea Cow Bay 142
  - Driving Around Tortola 142
- Jost Van Dyke 145
  - Little Jost Van Dyke 145
  - Great Harbour 146
  - Little Harbour 148
  - White Bay 151
- Norman Island to Virgin Gorda 152
  - Norman Island 152
  - Benures Bay 153
  - The Bight 153
  - Pelican Island and The Indians 156
  - Peter Island 156
  - Little Harbour 157
  - Great Harbour 157
  - Sprat Bay 157
  - Deadman's Bay 159
  - Key Bay 159
  - Dead Chest Island 159
  - Salt Island 159
  - Salt Island Bay 160
  - Lee Bay 160
  - Cooper Island 160
- Virgin Gorda 163
  - The Baths 164
  - Virgin Gorda Yacht Harbour 164
  - Little Dix Bay 169
  - Savannah Bay 169
  - The Dogs 169
  - Long Bay 171
  - North Sound 171
  - (Gorda Sound) 171

- Drake's Anchorage 172
- Prickly Pear Island 172
- Saba Rock 174
- The Bitter End Yacht Club 174
- Biras Creek 175
- Gun Creek 175
- Leverick Bay 175
- Eustatia Sound 176
- South Sound 177
- Driving Around Virgin Gorda 177
- Necker Island.................................... 180
- Anegada 181

Dining in the Spanish Virgin Islands 186

Dining in the U.S. and British Virgin Islands 188

References 189

Appendices 190
- Appendix A: Navigational Lights 190
- Appendix B: Marinas 194
- Appendix C: Service Facilities 196
  - Appendix C1: Spanish Virgin Islands 196
  - Appendix C2: U. S. Virgin Islands..... 201
  - Appendix C3: British Virgin Islands... 207
- Appendix D: Waypoints 211
- Appendix F: A Little Spanish 214
- Appendix E: Metric Conversion 214

Index 218

Notes 224

About the Author 225

Where to Go for Hurricane Season. 226

Irma and Maria

THIS GUIDE WAS WRITTEN IN THE SUMMER OF 2017, AND WAS BEING EDITED WHILE we were witnessing the destruction wrought by Hurricane Irma and Hurricane Maria in The Bahamas and Caribbean. I was shocked at the amount of utter devastation these storms left behind and how some of the holes, so favored by both cruisers and charter fleets for hurricane protection, lost nearly every vessel present, while other holes escaped with little or no damage. I have gone through this guide again since Hurricane Irma and Hurricane Maria passed through the islands and annotated the text to reflect how some of these places survived. The one good thing to take from this is that the people affected will rebuild, it is their way, they have done this for centuries, but the damages from Irma and Maria will set them back for months, some for years.

Irma left a huge path of destruction from Barbuda and Antigua through the Virgins and then right up the middle of Florida. The eye of Irma went over Barbuda which is now little more than a ghost town; everybody has been evacuated off the island and who knows when they will return. Irma then leveled St. Martin, St. Barth's, Anguilla, and the U.S. and British Virgin Islands. However, *North Sound Boatyard* located on Crabbs Peninsula on Antigua, about 25 or so miles south of Barbuda, suffered minor damage and all the boats there were fine. *Jolly Harbour Boatyard* on the western shore of Antigua also suffered little damage.

Irma taught much about the holes that people have been using for years in the Virgins. Paraquita Bay, the safe hole for most of the BVI charter fleet, the safe hole that charges for moorings and lines up the charter vessels in nice, long rows, was decimated and has set the Virgin Islands' charter industry back who knows how long. Nearly every hole in Irma's path suffered with few exceptions. Nanny Cay was wiped out, both the docks and the other infrastructure but they are rebuilding already (they have ordered new docks which should be installed in early 2018). In North Sound, Virgin Gorda, the *Bitter End Yacht Club* is in total ruins and closed for rebuilding.

In the USVI, St. John and St. Thomas were hit hard but Benner Bay (especially the area at the head of the bay known as "The Lagoon"), Flamingo Bay, and Mendahl Bay survived with just a few losses. The small cove north of the airport runway and south of Brewer's Beach on the west side of St. Thomas also proved a valuable hole with its mangroves and 7' depth where boaters survived both Irma and Maria. *Sapphire Bay Marina* suffered some boat losses as well as dock destruction. All in all, St. Thomas had a better survival rate for boats than did Tortola and Virgin Gorda where gusts to 200 mph and tornadoes laid those islands to waste, there was no truly safe place there.

IGY stated that *Blue Haven Marina* on Provo in the Turks and Caicos Islands, *Yacht Haven Grande* on St. Thomas, USVI, *American Yacht Harbor* at Red Hook, USVI, *Yacht Club* at Isle del Sol, St. Martin, and *Simpson Bay Marina* are all closed for repairs, when they will open is anyone's guess. Most marinas in Simpson Bay and Marigot were heavily damaged and will be closed for a while. Gustavia suffered a lot of damage but should be up and running by the time this guide is published. Christophe Harbour on St. Kitts seems to have made it through with little damage. As did *St. Kitt's Marine Works*.

Irma skirted the northern coast of Cuba, heavily damaging the marina and boatyard at Gaviota but leaving *Marina Hemingway* virtually untouched. A few marinas in The Bahamas were damaged but all were up and running within a week of Irma's passing.

Maria appeared to be following in Irma's wake beginning her path of destruction by leveling Dominica and then hitting St. Croix hard before crossing Puerto Rico and knocking out ALL power on the island (even snapping concrete power poles) and leaving few vessels unscathed. *Puerto del Rey Marina* suffered minimal damage and most boats survived with little harm. The damage to local boats in Puerto Rico is sad as many Puerto Rican boaters usually keep an eye out for strong storms and many will simply head south for three days to the ABCs and return after the storm has passed Puerto Rico.

The eye of Maria then passed approximately 35 miles to the east of Grand Turk and North Creek faired as well as can be expected with little damage.

So, what have we learned? We have discovered that some of the best holes are not as safe as many claim them to be. While other, perhaps not so well-known holes did their jobs in two major hurricanes. Bear these lessons in mind when you seek refuge.

All in all, the best protection is not to find yourself in the hurricane zone during hurricane season, call it avoidance. You might wish to consider Panama or Venezuela's offshore islands.

The Basics

Anchoring

In a word, crowded. If you wish solitude, stay in the Spanish Virgin Islands, for in the BVI and USVI you'll rarely find an anchorage all to yourself, there are just too many charter boats and sometimes every anchorage appears as a forest of masts. The truly private anchorages are usually too rolly for a nighttime stay, so you'll just have to get used to having neighbors around.

It is often the case that those who charter boats frequently forget some of the basics when it comes to anchoring so let me take a moment and offer a refresher course of sorts. First, make sure that your choice of anchorage or mooring area is secure and that any predicted wind shifts or northerly swells will not leave you trapped or put you in harm's way. If you are a sailboat start your engine and furl or lower your sails before entering the anchorage and secure your dinghy so that the painter will not entangle your prop. A tangled prop can put you in a very dangerous situation if you have no propulsion and the wind or seas are blowing you onshore or onto a reef.

Never enter an unfamiliar anchorage with the sun directly in your eyes, at night, or in periods of poor visibility such as a squall. A good system of communication is necessary between the helmsperson and whomever is working the foredeck; hand signals signifying forward, starboard, port, reverse, and stop should suffice. And don't forget to put out enough scope. Figure on a 7:1 ratio using the depth of the water plus the distance from the water to your bow roller times 7, and always allow swinging room (difficult in the more crowded anchorages). Always make sure your anchor is set well, either by diving on it, or by using a glass bottom bucket from the dinghy.

You'll find that many of the anchorages here are, in general, deeper than those in places like The Bahamas. In The Bahamas, and the Turks and Caicos as well, if you're anchored in 20' of water you are in a deep anchorage. In the Virgins, 20' can be very shallow, especially in places like *Soper's Hole* where it's best to take a mooring for the waters there, unless you can tuck in close to the eastern end of the harbour, range from 40'-70' in depth. Of course, if you are heading for the Virgins from the lower Eastern Caribbean, you're probably quite used to anchoring in deeper waters. And if you're not used to anchoring in the lee of mountains you will soon learn about that art as well. Here you will encounter a phenomenon called *backwinding*. This is first noticed by the novice when his boat lies 180° from the angle it first lay when he dropped his hook and went below for a nap. If this happens you'll need to set a stern anchor and try to remember that the stronger the trade wind the stronger the backwind.

Anchor choice is basically a personal preference. Some skippers prefer *CQRs*, while others swear by a *Bruce*, a *Mantus*, a *Rocna*, or a *Danforth*. Of the lot, you will find that a *Danforth* holds as well or better than a *CQR* or *Bruce* in sandy bottoms while the *CQR* or *Bruce* is preferred when anchoring in rocky bottoms. Whatever your choice of anchor, you must deploy your anchor correctly and with sufficient scope to hold you when the tide changes, if a front approaches, or if a squall should blow through at 2:00 a.m. (which seems to be the time they choose to blow through). Your anchor should have a length of chain (at least 15') shackled to your anchor to keep your rode from chafing against coral or rocks and to create a catenary curve that helps absorb shock loads while lowering the angle of pull on your anchor. Too high an angle may cause your anchor to pull up and out of the bottom. Some cruisers prefer all chain rodes with a nylon snubber to absorb the shock loads. This is an excellent arrangement but a windlass may be needed unless you prefer the workout involved with hauling in the chain and anchor every time you move.

Always set an anchor light. Some cruisers feel this is unimportant in some of the more isolated anchorages. What they probably do not understand is that many locals run these islands at all hours of the night, even on moonless nights, and an anchor light protects your vessel as well as theirs.

The *Atlantic Ocean* surge seeks out any way it can to round the tips of these islands to cause you seemingly no end of discomfort and here is not much you can do about it except possibly use a second anchor or bridle arrangement to keep your bow or stern into the swell. If using a bridle, set up your line on the opposite side that you wish to turn your vessel. For instance, if you need to turn your bow to starboard to face the incoming swells and make for a calmer ride, run your bridle line from a winch to a block on your port quarter and then forward outside your shrouds to your anchor line. Either tie it to your rode or, if you use all chain, attach it to the shackle where your nylon snubber (be sure to use a long one, at least 10'-20' if you are setting up for a bridle arrangement) hooks to your chain. After your anchor is set, simply crank in your bridle line bringing your bow to starboard and off the wind.

In the winter season, roughly between October through April, you must take into account that northerly swells can and will affect your anchorage choices. Usually caused by a front passing well to the north of the Virgin Islands, swells are generated that create rough conditions on all the north shore anchorages making these anchorages untenable, and these swells can even make some normally calm anchorages rolly.

Never anchor in coral, even with your dinghy anchor. An anchor can do a great deal of damage to these very fragile ecosystems that will take years to recover if it is to recover at all. Besides, sand holds so much better anyway.

Proper anchoring etiquette should by practiced at all times. For instance, if the anchorage is wide and roomy and only one boat is at anchor, do not anchor right on top of them, give your neighbor a little breathing room and some solitude. You would probably appreciate the same consideration should the situation be reversed. All too often cruisers exhibit a herding instinct where they seek the comfort of other nearby cruisers, anchoring much too close at times.

Many boaters, after a long, hard day in rough seas or bad weather, anxiously await the peace and tranquility of a calm anchorage. The last thing they want is noise and wake. If you have a dog aboard that loves to bark, be considerate of your neighbors who do not wish to hear him. They do have that right. At sunset, many cruisers are sitting in their cockpits enjoying cocktails and watching the sun go down and do not want a generator disturbing their conversations, courtesy shown is usually courtesy returned.

You'll find a lot of moorings in use in the USVI and BVI, and in both areas most moorings are available for a daily fee. It would behoove the cruiser venturing to the USVI or BVI to learn the rules and regulations concerning anchoring, mooring, and fishing.

BVI National Parks Regulations

The BVI *National Trust* has installed permanent moorings (most are stainless steel pins set in bedrock) at most major dive sites designated for daytime limited usage with a 90-minute time limit. If you plan to avail yourself of these moorings you must get a permit either from *Customs* when clearing in, or your charter company. The buoys are in several different colors with orange representing non-diving daytime use only. Yellow buoys are set aside for commercial vessels only, while the large yellow buoys may also handle vessels over 55' in length. Blue buoys are for dinghies, and white buoys are for non-commercial vessels for daytime dive use on a first come-first served basis.

Please use your own line through the pennant and be careful not to damage the pennant upon departure by motoring right over it. Vessels that have damaged moorings will be assessed repair costs. All moorings are used at your own risk and you must have a valid permit for their use. For more information you can contact the *National Trust* in Road Town at 284-404-3904. The following dive sites have moorings: The Baths, Blonde Rock, *Carrot Shoal*, the Caves, Cooper Island, Dead Chest Island, The Dogs, Fallen Jerusalem, Ginger Island, Guana Island, The Indians, Norman Island, Pelican Island, Peter Island, the *Rhone's Anchor*, the *Wreck of the Fearless*, and the *Wreck of the Rhone*.

USVI National Park Regulations

1. Use of *National Park Service* moorings is restricted to vessels of less than 61' of length on deck. Vessels of 61' (length on deck), or over may not use park moorings. Park mooring balls are white with a blue stripe. No rafting of vessels or setting of anchors is permitted while on a mooring. Use of more than one mooring by a single vessel is prohibited. Anchoring within 250' of a mooring is prohibited. Vessels using a *National Park Service* mooring can guard against chafe by running their own line through the mooring line.
2. In *Great* and *Little Lameshur Bays*, *Reef Bay*, and *Salt Pond Bay,* mooring use is required and anchoring is prohibited. Anchoring on the southern shore of St. John is prohibited inside the area from *Cocoloba Cay* to White Point to Cabrita Horn Point to Ram Head.
3. Vessels between 126'-210' (length on deck), must anchor only in *Francis Bay*, in sand, in water depths greater than 50'. Vessels longer than 210' on deck may not anchor in *National Park Service* waters.
4. Where a mooring is not available and anchoring is not permitted, anchor in sand only (if you anchor

in coral or on a seagrass bed you are subject to a citation by *National Park Service* rangers.
5. Vessels are not permitted to enter or anchor in any swim area marked by "No Boat" buoys. Anchor at least 250' from all buoys.
6. During rough sea conditions or storms, moorings must not be used.
7. For dinghies, use only the marked channel (red and green markers) to go to the beach. Do not anchor in the marked channel or elsewhere in the swimming area and do not tie your dinghy to any living flora.
8. Water-skiing, boogie-boards, and use of personal watercraft are prohibited in *National Park Service* waters.
9. Spearfishing, the collection of fish and taking or damaging natural resources are not allowed in *National Park Service* waters. No fishing of any kind is allowed in *Trunk Bay*, St. John. Possession of a spear gun within *National Park Service* boundaries is prohibited.

Caribbean Etiquette

Proper etiquette is important when visiting foreign lands; lack of it can be embarrassing at the least and can create serious misunderstandings at its worst. For instance, when greeting people as you board a bus, give a hearty "Good morning" all around (if indeed it is morning) and it will be returned. The rule is greetings first, business later. Not offering a greeting first may be received as rude. If you approach a home that has a fence, stop at the front gate and say loudly "Inside." If you receive no answer, try again. If there is still no answer, the folks are either not at home or do not wish to be disturbed.

And by the way, when two people are speaking, as with good manners everywhere, it is extremely rude to interrupt. West Indians don't do it, neither should you.

Many Americans judge a man by his handshake, which does not work in the Caribbean. Here a soft, gentle hand "embrace" is more the norm. I have heard some folks (Canadians and Americans, never the British) say that they are surprised that West Indians do not smile. This leads to the misconception that the person does not like the cruiser. This is ridiculous. West Indian manners call for a reserved face to be shown, saving the smile for something funny or someone they are familiar with. The lack of a smile should not imply a negative attitude to the visitor unaccustomed to the lifestyle here in the Caribbean.

Now let's discuss a very important subject, it will be a part of a lot that you do here in the Caribbean. Let's take a moment and touch briefly upon the Caribbean pastime of liming. If you're invited to join a group for a drink or a bite to eat, by all means, do! Hang out! You'll be liming! People in the Caribbean can be found liming everywhere, in the streets, in restaurants and bars, at home, or even on your boat. Liming is just chilling, hanging out...get the picture?

I cannot end this section on etiquette without mentioning dress. What we cruisers take for granted in the way we dress while aboard is quite different from what is expected of us in public in the Caribbean. In town, a bathing suit is not acceptable and men should wear shirts as well as shoes. We should all dress as we would in going to our local mall when we go into any town in the Caribbean. Shorts and shirts is fine, bathing gear is not and is considered inappropriate. On some of the islands, particularly the French islands, it is not unusual for women to go topless on the beaches and even aboard their own boats, and yes gentlemen, it is rude to stare!

Chartering

Chartering in the islands is big business, and not very difficult to arrange. Winter is the season for chartering; prices are higher then and reservations should be made well in advance for November through May. Prices from May to November may be as much as 40% lower, but don't fret, the winds will still be steady. The Christmas/New Year's holidays are the busiest, followed by the final two weeks of February, and the Easter holidays. Bookings for these periods may require a year's advance notice.

You can charter just a boat, called a bareboat, or a captained vessel where you do as little or as much work on board as you desire. If you choose to go bareboat, you will likely have to prove to the charter company your skill level, filling out forms and giving an account of your experience on the water. Sometimes you will be asked to go on a check-out sail before the charter company will let you take their expensive toys out on the water all by yourself. Captains can be hired for somewhere between US$100-$150 a day and it is customary to tip them. Some charters are there and back again, while others will allow you to take the vessel downwind where a charter company captain will return it to the base after you fly out. The season is from November through July with rates lower in the midst of hurricane season from August to October with some companies offering discounts from July all the way through December. Bear in mind that if you charter during the latter part of December you might have a week or two of unusually strong and steady winds called the *Christmas Winds*, which generally blow a steady 20-25 knots and sometimes as much as 30-40 knots! During the summer the winds are lighter and a bit more from the southeast.

You usually provision these boats yourself or have the charter company do it for you, the choice is yours. Some folks opt for the convenience of a completely stocked larder courtesy of the charter company, while others prefer the island shopping experience. A good idea is not to plan on having all your meals aboard as there is an abundance of good restaurants ashore that cater to mariners. Check with your charter company and see what plans they offer and perhaps have them send you a sample menu or listing of the stores carried aboard.

Appendix C, offers a partial listing of Virgin Island based charter boats. No matter which charter company you choose, you need to be aware of certain issues before you sign on the dotted line. You need to be aware that some charter companies will not permit you to take their vessel to Anegada, while nearly all forbid night sailing. Some companies will waive these restrictions while others offer flotillas to Anegada.

Know in advance what your charter company's policy is concerning breakdowns. Will your company reimburse you for food spoilage if your refrigerator fails? In other words, read the fine print, especially in regards to taxes and supplementary fees.

Clothing-What to Bring

Okay, if you're a cruiser and you've already arrived in the Virgin Islands, it's useless for me to tell you what to bring, you've got it all aboard your floating home anyway. But if you are coming to these islands to charter for only a week or two, and you have a limited amount of gear that you can bring with you, the following may offer some hints as to what you might need. Remember, most people have a tendency to bring too much.

You will be arriving in a tropical climate where the theme for clothing is light and durable, you'll most likely live in T-shirts, shorts, and bathing suits during your stay. Long pants and sturdy shoes are necessary for hiking in the bush and a good pair of reef/beach shoes is a good idea as well. A sweater or light jacket is advisable for those cool evenings during the winter months if you plan to stay in the mountains. If you intend to dine in any of the finer resorts more formal wear might be required such as a jacket and tie for the men, and slacks or a cocktail dress for the ladies. And don't forget, pack your clothes in soft luggage, something that can be folded up and stored away during your charter. Hard luggage has no place on a boat.

Polarized sunglasses are a must as are suntan lotion (suntan oil has a tendency to get all over everything that comes in contact with you), a wide brimmed hat, bug repellent, and a camera (an underwater camera if you plan on diving). You might wish to bring your own snorkeling or dive gear (not tanks) unless you are content with using what may already be on your chartered boat. If you have any prescription medicines that are necessary you will need to bring enough for your cruise and then some. If you have any specific dietary needs you must also plan accordingly by asking your charter company for their suggestions, as most have dealt with all manner of special needs and are happy to help.

It is important in the Virgin Islands that one dresses accordingly when entering communities. Bathing suits are to be worn only on board or at the beach; it is considered improper to wear beachwear in town, and men, please wear a shirt when not on the beach or onboard, and bare midriffs on ladies are frowned on as well. Violators might be asked by a local to cover up, remember, you are a visitor here and that entails a certain responsibility.

Currency

Everywhere in the Spanish Virgins, the United States Virgins, and the British Virgins, the U.S. dollar is the standard currency. Most establishments will take the major credit cards, but don't leave home without cash as it is good everywhere and is the only method of payment of taxis, some small businesses, and most of the businesses on Anegada. *ATMs* are located on St. Thomas, St. Croix, Culebra, Road Town and West End on Tortola, and on Virgin Gorda.

SVI: There is no sales tax in the SVI.

USVI: There is no sales tax in the USVI.

BVI: In the BVI there is a $.10 stamp duty on all checks and traveler's checks (there is an *American Express* office in Road Town). There is no sales tax in the BVI, but there is a departure tax of $20 if leaving by air, $5 if leaving by private yacht or ferry, and $7 if leaving by cruise ship. Some dining establishments will add a 10%-15% gratuity to your bill so be sure to check it before you decide to leave a tip.

Customs and Immigration

Vessels entering and departing the Spanish, British, and United States Virgin Islands must clear when entering and leaving the territory. U.S. flagged vessels need not clear when leaving the BVI if you are staying in the BVI for less than 72 hours. U.S flagged vessels must clear in at Puerto Rico and the Spanish Virgins when leaving the USVI since St. Thomas is a duty-free port.

eSeaClear has been replaced by *Sail Clear* (https://www.sailclear.com/), in many locales. eSeaClear and Sail Clear are both services that provide vessel operators the ability to submit electronic notifications of arrival to participating *Customs* offices in the Caribbean. Sail Clear is now operating in the Cayman Islands, Grenada, St. Kitts, Nevis, Montserrat, Anguilla, Curaçao, Bermuda, St. Lucia, the BVI's, Dominica, as well as the Turks and Caicos Islands, while eSeaClear is currently only available in Antigua and Barbuda.

Currently registered users can access the eSeaClear and Sail Clear systems via the Internet to enter and maintain information about their vessel and crew. Prior to arrival at a new country the vessel operator simply insures that the information is accurate and submits a new notification. Upon arrival, *Customs* can access the notification information to process your clearance more efficiently and without the need for the Ship's Master to fill out the declaration forms.

British Virgin Islands

Only the Captain may go ashore to clear when arriving in the BVI. Overtime charges may be applied if you clear outside of the normal office hours, including Sundays and holidays. Normal working hours are from 0830-1700 Monday-Saturday and from 0900-1700 on Sundays. If you are carrying firearms aboard, be prepared to turn them over to BVI *Customs* officials for the duration of your stay. You can ask for them just prior to clearing for your departure. If you leave your weapons at Road Town when you clear in and then sail to Virgin Gorda, you'll have to return to Road Town to pick up your weapons, *Customs* will not ship them to Virgin Gorda for you. The BVI charges for harbour dues, ship's dues, and form charges. Cruising permits are $35-$45 per vessel (depending on the size of your boat), and $4 per person per day. If you plan to use the *BVI National Parks Trust* moorings at the dive sites of the BVI, you must obtain a *National Parks Permit* when you clear upon arrival. The fee is approximately $1 per person for each day that you use the park's moorings, or $25 per week. For more information on the moorings, see the previous section entitled *Anchoring*. Never pick up a mooring unless you are sure it is available and not private, and unless you are certain it is secure and safe for use.

U.S. flagged vessels may clear in and out of the BVI at the same time to avoid a second visit to the *Customs* office, however, if you have turned over weapons upon arrival you will need to return to *Customs* to arrange to pick up your weapons.

Visitors to the British Virgin Islands may be granted entry for up to one month at the port of entry, those arriving by air must have an ongoing or return ticket. Visitors wishing to stay longer than one month are permitted to stay for up to 6 months, but must apply for an extension from the *Immigration* office in Road Town, Tortola, or at the *Government Administration Building* on Virgin Gorda.

United States and Canadian citizens may enter with a passport or proof of citizenship such as an authenticated birth certificate and photo identification, just a driver's license will not suffice. Visitors from all other countries will require a passport and some will require a visa. If you have any questions concerning the need for a visa you can contact the *Chief Immigration Officer* at 284-494-3471 or 284-494-3701, extension 2538. A cruising permit is required for all boats in the BVI. From December 1-April 30, all recorded charter boats are charged $2 per person per day, and non-recorded charter boats are charged $4 per day. From May 1-November 30 all recorded charter boats are charged $.75 per person per day, and all non-recorded charter boats are charged $4 per person per day.

Pets are allowed into the BVI only after the *Department of Agriculture* has issued an import permit.

For more information you can contact the *Department of Agriculture*, Paraquita Bay, Tortola, British Virgin Islands, 284-495-2532, fax 284-495-1269. If you plan to visit the BVI it's best to arrange for an import permit a few months before your expected arrival.

Items imported into the BVI on a temporary basis are not subject to duty and most *Customs* duties vary from 5%-20% (although all computers are duty-free). Proper invoices are required for all goods bought abroad and being imported. Since the BVI is not duty-free, U.S citizens may only take home $600 worth of items duty-free as long as their stay in the BVI has been over 48 hours (U.S. *Customs* will place a duty of 10% on the next $1,000 worth of goods). Bear in mind that the term "Duty-free" means that the vendor that sells you the item was not required to pay duty so he is passing that savings along to you. It has nothing to do with your own country's *Customs* regulations. Spare parts may be brought into the BVI duty-free for yachts in transit. You will need the packages clearly marked with your vessel's name and the words *Yacht In Transit* on the face. To obtain clearance from *Customs* you will need your ship's clearance papers, if you cannot produce these papers you will have to pay duty on the parts and apply later for a refund. Duty on marine parts is 5%.

You can obtain a fishing license from the *Department of Conservation and Fisheries* in Road Town, their phone number is 284-494-3429.

SVI and Puerto Rico

There are new regulations concerning clearing *Customs* in Puerto Rico and the Spanish Virgin Islands. All vessels leaving the United States Virgin Islands, or the British Virgin Islands, must clear upon arrival in the Spanish Virgin Islands or at Puerto Rico. Vessels entering outside of normal business hours must phone the *Customs* office in San Juan (787-253-4533) for instructions. You must clear *Customs* in person immediately upon arrival, a $10,000 fine is the penalty for an infraction of this regulation. If you arrive Tuesday morning you must clear on Tuesday, do not attempt to wait until Wednesday.

You must also visit *Customs* to clear out in person when leaving Puerto Rican waters. If you are in Puerto Rico and wish to sail to the Spanish Virgin Islands, you must notify the Fajardo *USCG* district office by phone before departure.

After a vessel has cleared into Puerto Rican waters the master of the vessel must notify *Customs* by phone before leaving one harbor in Puerto Rico for another harbor in Puerto Rico. This means that if you wish to leave Fajardo for San Juan, you must notify *Customs* by phone before departing.

As a side note, cruisers have complained about being hassled about entry into Salinas. It seems a cruiser threw his "foreign" garbage in the dumpster in Salinas and was threatened with a $1,000 fine for this infraction. Apparently there is a "special" dumpster for this in Ponce, even though Salinas IS a *Port of Entry*.

U.S. citizens need a valid passport, or one not over 5-years old, or a birth certificate with a raised seal and a current photo ID. Citizens of all other nationalities will need a passport, and some will require a visa; visas are not required of citizens of Great Britain, Australia, and New Zealand. Failure to enter with a visa may result in a fine of up to $180 and issuing of a visa on the spot is solely in the hands of the *Immigration* officer on site. When entering a United States *Port of Entry* all crew must report in person to *Immigration*. There are no clearance fees in U.S. ports in the Virgin Islands. Depending on where you are arriving from, you might be asked to clear with an *Agriculture* representative.

U.S. citizens are allowed to return with, or mail back, $1200 worth of goods every 30 days including 4 liters of liquor, 5 if one is locally produced, 5 cartons of cigarettes, and 100 cigars. This can be consolidated for a family so if you and mate and three children travel to the USVI you can return with $6,000 worth of duty-free purchases. U.S. citizens may also mail home duty-free gifts totaling $100 every day, but you cannot mail these items to yourself. If you are importing items into the USVI, goods manufactured in the United States are not subject to duty, but goods manufactured in any foreign nation are subject to an import duty of 6% unless specified as free of duty.

United States Virgin Islands

U.S. citizens need a valid passport, or one not over 5-years old. Citizens of all other nationalities will need a passport, and some will require a visa; visas are not required of citizens of Great Britain, Australia, and New Zealand. When entering a United States *Port of Entry* all crew must report in person to *Immigration*. There are clearance fees in U.S. ports in the Virgin

Islands. A dress code is in effect for clearance at *Customs*, shirts and shoes are required, a bathing suit will not suffice. Dress and act accordingly.

Since St. Thomas is a duty-free port, U.S. citizens are allowed to return with, or mail back, $1,200 worth of goods every 30 days including 4 liters of liquor, 5 if one is locally produced, 5 cartons of cigarettes, and 100 cigars. This can be consolidated for a family so if you and mate and three children travel to the USVI you can return with $6,000 worth of duty-free purchases. U.S. citizens may also mail home duty-free gifts totaling $100 every day, but you cannot mail these items to yourself. If you are importing items into the USVI, goods manufactured in the United States are not subject to duty, but goods manufactured in any foreign nation are subject to an import duty of 6% unless specified as free of duty.

Ports of Entry

Puerto Rico

Fajardo - across from the ferry dock Puerto Real
Guanica
Humacao
Mayaguez - the blue and white building at the head of the commercial dock
Playa de Salinas - *Marina de Salinas*
Ponce - *Ponce Yacht and Fishing Club*
Puerto Jobos
San Juan - any marina

The Spanish Virgin Islands

Culebra - Dewey, airport
Vieques - Airport

The United States Virgin Islands

St. Croix - Christiansted (Gallows Bay)
St. John - Cruz Bay
St. Thomas - Charlotte Amalie

The British Virgin Islands

Tortola - Road Town (Government Dock), West End (ferry dock)
Jost Van Dyke - Great Harbour
Virgin Gorda - VG Yacht Harbour, *Gun Creek*

Dinghy Safety

Most cruisers spend a considerable amount of time in their dinghies exploring the waters and islands in the vicinity of their anchorage. It is not unknown for a dinghy engine to fail or a skipper to run out of gas miles away from the mother vessel. For this reason I urge boaters to carry some simple survival gear in their dinghies. First, I would recommend a handheld VHF radio for obvious reasons. If there are any other boats around this may be your best chance for getting some assistance. A good anchor and plenty of line are also high on the list. I do not mean one of those small three pound anchors with thirty feet of line that is only used on the beach to keep your dinghy from drifting toward Puerto Rico or Central America. It may pay to sacrifice the onboard room and use a substantial anchor with a couple of feet of chain and at least 100' of line. Just as you would go oversize on your mother vessel do the same with your dinghy. If you are being blown away from land a good anchor and plenty of line gives you a good chance of staying put until someone can find you. Next, a dinghy should have a supply of flares. Local boaters in the Bahamas often carry a large coffee can with a rag soaked in oil lying in the bottom. If they get in trouble lighting the rag will produce an abundant amount of smoke that can be seen from a quite a distance. A dinghy should be equipped with survival water, a bottle or some small packages manufactured by a company called *DATREX*. It would be a good idea to throw in a few *MREs*. These are the modern, tastier version of K-Rations that our armed forces survived on for years. Each *MRE* also contains vital survival components such as matches and toilet paper. Another handy item that does not take up much room is a foil survival blanket. They really work and take up as much space as a couple of packs of cigarettes.

Please don't laugh at these suggestions. I have seen people forced to spend a night or two in a dinghy and these few items would have made their experience much more pleasant if not entirely unnecessary. I have run out of gas and used flares to attract some local attention even though one of my boat mates was ready to dive in and swim for the nearest island to fetch some help. Now, I never leave in my dinghy without my little survival bag stashed away in my dinghy. It doesn't take much effort to prepare a small bag for your dinghy and it will be worth its weight in gold should you need it. And one more thing, always have a line from the kill switch on your outboard connected to your wrist or body so that if you fall overboard when motoring by yourself you won't harm yourself and you'll be able to grab your

Ferries

The following is a listing of the ferries running in the islands and may not be complete.

SVI and Puerto Rico

Fajardo-Vieques-Culebra: 787-863-0852

United States Virgin Islands

Charlotte Amalie to Caneel Bay: 340-776-6111
Charlotte Amalie to Virgin Gorda
Native Son Ferry: 284-495-4617
(http://www.nativesonferry.com/)
Smith's Ferry Service: 284-494-4454
(http:/www.smithsferryservices.com/)
Speedy's Fantasy: 284-495-5240 (non-stop)
(http://www.bviferries.com/)
St. Thomas to St. John
Transportation Services: 340-776-6282
Love City Car Ferries, Inc.:340-779-4000
(http://www.lovecitycarferries.com/)
Varlack Ventures: 340-776-6412
(http://www.varlack-ventures.com/)
St. John to Tortola
Inter Island Boat Services: 340-776-6597
Smith's Ferry Service: 284-494-4454
(http:/www.smithsferryservices.com/)

British Virgin Islands

Beef Island to North Sound
Beef Island-Virgin Gorda: 284-495-5240
North Sound Express: 284-495-2138
Beef Island to Virgin Gorda
North Sound Express 284-495 2138
Jost Van Dyke to Tortola
Jost Van Dyke: 284-494-2997
Marina Cay
Marina Cay: 284-494-2174
Peter Island
Peter Island Ferry: 284-495-2000
Tortola to Virgin Gorda
Native Son Ferry: 284-495-4617
(http://www.nativesonferry.com/)
Smith's Ferry Service: 284-494-4454
(http:/www.smithsferryservices.com/)
Speedy's Fantasy: 284-495-5240
(http://www.bviferries.com/)
Road Town Fast Ferry: 284-494-2323
(http://www.roadtownfastferry.com/
Tortola to St. John
Inter Island Boat Services: 284-495-4166
(http://www.interislandboatservices.com/)
Tortola (West End) to Jost Van Dyke
New Horizon Ferry 284-495-9278
(http://newhorizonferry.com/)

Garbage

When I first began cruising I had this naive idea that all cruisers lived in a certain symbiosis with nature. My bubble finally burst with the bitter realization that many cruisers were infinitely worse than common litterbugs, so often they have the attitude of "out of sight, out of mind." I sometimes wonder if they believe in supernatural beings, hoping that wherever they dump their trash imaginary garbage fairies come along and take care of the disposal problems for them. One cruiser leaves a few bags of garbage in some secluded (or not so secluded) spot and the next cruiser says "My, what a good spot for a garbage dump. Ethel, bring the garbage, I've found the dump!" This is why you often go ashore on otherwise deserted islands and find bags and piles of bags of garbage. Nothing is worse than entering paradise only to discover some lazy, ignorant, slob of a cruiser (no, I have not been too harsh on this type of person, I can still think of plenty of other adjectives without having to consult a Thesaurus) has dumped his bags of garbage in the bushes. Please do not add to this problem. Remember, your garbage attracts all kinds

(unmoving dinghy and climb back aboard, this may save your life.)

of foul creatures such as rats (and other careless cruisers).

Nobody likes storing bags of smelly garbage aboard but if you cannot find a settlement nearby to take your garbage for free, you will have to make an allowance in your budget to pay for the local garbage disposal service. If you are nowhere near a garbage facility you should stow your trash aboard separated into three groups for easier disposal. First cans and bottles (wash them first to remove any smells while being stored), then into another container stow the organic stuff such as food scraps, rinds, and eggshells, and finally paper and plastic trash. Your food scraps, you can store them in a large coffee can with a lid, should be thrown overboard daily on an outgoing tide. The paper and plastic should be burned completely when necessary and the ashes buried deep and not on the beach. Cans and bottles should be punctured or broken and dumped overboard in very deep water at least a few miles offshore. Cut off both ends of the cans and break the bottles overboard as you sink them. Aluminum cans may also be dropped off for recycling at *Sopers Hole Marina*, West End, Tortola, the *Loose Mongoose*, in Trellis Bay, Tortola, and at *Village Cay Marina* or at *Parts and Power* in Road Town, Tortola.

If you cannot implement a garbage disposal policy aboard your vessel, stay home, don't come to these beautiful islands. Do not abuse what we all use.

Holidays

All the Virgin Islands celebrate the main holidays such as New Year's, Good Friday, Easter Sunday, and Christmas, but there are several holidays that are unique to each island group and they are listed below.

SVI and Puerto Rico

Three King's Day - January 6
Eugenio Maria de Hostos Day - January 13
Martin Luther King Jr. Day - January variable
President's Day - February, variable
Emancipation Day - March 22
Jose de Diego Day - April 14
Memorial Day - late May, variable
Independence Day - July 4
Luis Munoz Rivera Day - July 21
Constitution Day - July 28
Labor Day - September, variable
Columbus Day - October 12
Veteran's Day - November 11
Thanksgiving - November, variable

United States Virgin Islands

Three King's Day - January 6
Martin Luther King Jr. Day - January variable
President's Day - February, variable
Transfer Day - March 31
Memorial Day - late May, variable
Organic Act Day - June, variable
Emancipation Day - July 3
Independence Day - July 4
Hurricane Supplication Day - late July, variable
Labor Day - September, variable
Columbus Day - October 12
Hurricane Thanksgiving Day - late October,
Liberty Day, Hamilton Jackson Day - November 1
Veteran's Day - November 11
Thanksgiving - November, variable
Boxing Day - December 26
Carnival - April/St. Thomas; July 4/St. John's; December/St. Croix

British Virgin Islands

Commonwealth Day - 2nd Monday in March
Easter Monday - Variable in March or April
Whit Monday - variable in late May or early June
Queen's Birthday - June 11, variable
Territory Day - July 1, variable
Emancipation Festival - 1st Monday-Wed. of Aug.
St. Ursula's Day - variable, usually October 21
Birthday Of Heir To The Throne - November 15
Boxing Day - December 26

Hurricane Holes

THERE IS NO SUCH THING AS A HURRICANE HOLE! There is no anchorage so secure that it cannot be decimated by a strong hurricane and a high storm surge. There are no guarantees; there is no Fort Knox to hide in when a named windstorm threatens. Now, with that of the way we can discuss how to protect yourself in those special places that offer the best hurricane protection. Let's begin our discussion with what constitutes protection and pass along a few hints as to how to secure yourself as well as get along with your neighbors.

First, make sure your fuel is topped off and you have enough food and water for an extended period. Also, make sure you have enough cash to see you through as phone lines may be down for a while which would prohibit credit card usage. Once your tanks, lockers, and wallet are topped off, you can head for protection. Some skippers prefer to head to sea when a hurricane threatens. Some will take off at a ninety-degree angle from the hurricane's forecast path, usually heading south to Venezuela. I cannot advise you as to what course to take, but I for one, unless absolutely necessary, will not gamble with racing a storm that is unpredictable (no matter what the forecasters claim).

For protection, most of us would prefer a narrow creek that winds deep into the mangroves where we will be as snug as the proverbial bug-in-a-rug. These creeks are rare, and to be assured of space you must get there early. When a storm threatens, you can bet that everybody will soon be aware of it and the early birds will settle in the best places. Sure, those early birds might have to spend a night or two in the hot, buggy mangroves, but isn't that better than coming in too late and finding the best spots taken and your choices for protection down to anchoring in the middle of a pond with a bit of fetch and no mangroves to offer protection? Hint number one...get to safety early and secure your vessel.

So how do you secure your vessel? Easy! First, find a likely looking spot where you'll be safest from the oncoming winds. Try to figure out by the forecast path of the storm where the wind will be coming from as the storm passes and plan accordingly (remember that the winds blow counterclockwise around the center in the northern hemisphere). If your chosen spot is in a creek that is fine. Set out bow and stern anchors and tie off your vessel to the mangroves on each side with as many lines as you can, including lines off the bow and stern to assist the anchors. Use plenty of chafe gear (I like old fire-hose, leather, and towels) as the lines lead off your boat and rig your lines so that they don't work back and forth on the mangroves as well. If chain can be used to surround the mangroves that will help (not the mangroves of course). If other boats wish to proceed further up the creek past your position, remove your lines from one side of your boat to allow them to pass. Courtesy amongst endangered vessels will add to the safety factor of all involved, especially if somebody needs to come to somebody else's aid later on.

If your only choice is to head into the mangroves bow or stern first, always go in bow first; it stands to reason that if you place your stern into the mangroves serious rudder damage could result. I prefer to go bow-in as far as I can, until my boat settles her keel in the mud (trying to keep the bow just out of contact with the mangroves), tie off well, and set out at least two stern anchors. If other boats will be tying off into the mangroves in the same manner on each side of you, courtesy dictates each skipper assist the other in the setting of anchors (so that they don't snag on each other) and the securing of lines in the mangroves (and don't forget to put out fenders).

If you must anchor in the open, away from the mangroves, place your anchors to give you 360° protection. The greatest danger to your vessel will likely be the other boats around you, and in the Caribbean there's going to be a better than average chance that you'll be sharing your hole with several unattended boats, often times charter boats that are not secured in the best of manners. A good lookout is necessary for these added dangers.

Once secure, your next step is to strip everything off your boat and stow it below. Sails, bimini top, dodger, awnings, rail-mounted grill, wind-generators, solar panels, jerry cans, and anything small and loose that can become a dangerous object should it fly away at a hundred plus miles an hour. And, don't forget to secure your dinghy as well! Keep a mask and snorkel handy in the cockpit, you might need it to stand watch. Also, keep a sharp knife close at hand, you never know when you might need it.

Pack all your important papers in a handy waterproof container, and in the most severe of circumstances, use duct tape to secure your passport, wallet, and/or purse to your body. Plan ahead as you secure your vessel so that you will not have to go on deck if you don't absolutely have to, it is most difficult to move about in 100-knot winds.

The Virgin Islands are some of the finest cruising grounds in the world, but they also seem to be a favorite target of many hurricanes and tropical storms. In recent memory, *Hurricane Luis* hit the islands on September 5, 1995, with winds of 130 mph with gusts to 160 and two weeks later *Luis* was followed by *Hurricane Marilyn* bringing winds of 110 mph on September 15, 1995. When the dust finally settled the two hurricanes caused $3.5 billion in damages to the islands as well as taking six lives on St. Thomas. Let's take a moment and discuss what protection we can find in the waters covered by this guide.

SVI and Puerto Rico

The mainland of Puerto Rico is blessed with some of the finest hurricane protection in the Caribbean. My first choice would be to tie up in the mangroves in Los Jobos. When *Hurricane George* hit here a few years ago no boats in Los Jobos were damaged. Cayo Puerca marks the entrance to the holes at Jobos where the best protection is found by working your way up the mangrove creeks west of Cayo Puerca.

A second choice is at the southern end of Bahia de Boqueron on the western coast of Puerto Rico where you'll find a 7' deep channel leading into *Cano de Boqueron*, the cove where the marine police and the *DNR* have their docks. Follow the stakes in and keep between them as you round the mangroves and head northeast towards the police docks. You'll have a minimum of 7' the entire way though outside the channel the waters shoal rapidly.

There are still some tertiary choices if you cannot reach the protection of the two harbors I just mentioned. Salinas would be my third choice, but unattended boats would be a real concern here. Some folks like the protection that Palmas Del Mar offers, narrow canals amid high condos. Unfortunately, one must know somebody with dock space here that will allow you to tie up for a while. The principle danger here would be a strong storm surge that could wreak havoc in the canals.

Other possible shelters include *Bahia de Guanica*, but I find it far too open and with too much fetch, it might serve better as hurricane protection for larger vessels such as freighters and the like. Deep in the mangroves at La Parguera might be a good spot except for the storm surge, or in Puerto Real on the western shore of Puerto Rico just north of Boqueron. In Fajardo there is one small option. In the small corner of the easternmost island of Cayo Obispo (Chart PRE-4) there is an 8' channel leading in to a 90° turn with mangroves directly ahead. I would put my bow as far as I could into the mangroves and set out a couple of anchors on the shallow bar off my stern. Here you are protected to the east, south, and west by islands, and to the north by a shallow reef. Unfortunately there is only room for one boat here and a strong storm surge could make this spot untenable. I do not consider these places as prime locations, but I mention them as options.

A viable option however is also located in the area of La Parguera. La Parguera is best known for its bioluminescent lagoon called *Bahia Fosforescente* lying just to the east of La Parguera. The best protection here for vessels of 6' draft is in the creek that leads to the northeast and a smaller creek that leads off to the northwest. Vessels drawing 4' or less can take the creek in the northwest section of the bay deep into the mangroves where 6' of water can be found.

If you are in the Spanish Virgin Islands, your best choice, and it is a good one, is in the mangrove creeks at Ensenada Honda, Culebra (Chart SVI-6). Many boats survived fierce *Hurricane Hugo* here and this is as fine a shelter as you'll find in the Caribbean. Remember though, better get here early as other Puerto Rican and Virgin Island boaters will have the same idea as you for seeking shelter in Culebra. Vieques boaters like the protection offered by Puerto Mosquito on the southern shore of Vieques.

United States Virgin Islands

Hurricane Hole, inside the southeastern tip of St. John, USVI, in the *Virgin Islands Coral Reef National Monument*, is regarded as the best hurricane protection in the United States Virgin Islands. Moorings and anchorage spots in *Hurricane Hole* are now assigned by the *Park Service* and must be applied for in advance of the season. You must vacate the area within 48 hours of the passing of the storm. The park wants NO damage to the mangroves; regulations require that you do NOT tie up to the mangroves or through them to other trees. It is illegal to tie ropes to any vegetation on park lands. The park will have staff coming through that will remove any ropes or chains fastened to the mangroves! Sand screws are also prohibited. The park suggests that vessels secure themselves fore and aft with several large anchors in an east/west orientation parallel as the winds tend to funnel though the area in those directions.

In St. Thomas, USVI, *Benner Bay* is the entrance to a mangrove-lined lake with good protection. Follow the markers into *Benner Bay*, then follow the creek leading westward from the marinas, just south of the mainland of St. Thomas. Keep in the deeper water closer to shore until you are in the lake. It can be tricky getting in here, but this route can accommodate about 6' at low water. It will be crowded and tensions high.

Salt River Marina (http://www.jonesmaritime.com/saltrivermarina.htm) on St Croix is the only place on St. Croix that offers any sort of hurricane protection. The entrance can be tricky, but the marina is very secure.

British Virgin Islands

On Tortola, BVI, a bit southwest of Road Town, you can find some protection at *Nanny Cay Marina* (http://nannycay.com/), but I only mention this as a last resort. Just to the west of *Maya Cove* on the eastern shore of Tortola is *Paraquita Bay* (see Chart BVI-3). This bay is often used as a hurricane hole by local boats and it's not unusual to see boats tied up here during the entire hurricane season. The mangrove-encircled bay is shallow and should be sounded by dinghy before entering with the big boat.

I have heard some cruisers mention *Gorda Sound* or *Virgin Gorda Yacht Harbour* as possible hurricane holes. I find that *Gorda Sound* is a bit too open and with too much fetch, and the small basin of *Virgin Gorda Yacht Harbour*, though protected from the seas, appears to me as a spot I would not want to be in the event of a hurricane of any strength.

Language

English is spoken exclusively in the BVI and USVI, and although Spanish is the official language of Puerto Rico and the SVI, many people speak English. It's a good idea if you are visiting the SVI or Puerto Rico, to carry a Spanish phrasebook with you at all times and to practice your Spanish every chance you get. Many people are happy to help you with your Spanish and will often smile and answer you in English removing your fear of being misunderstood. At the very least, learn how to greet somebody in Spanish and ask them if they can speak English (Como esta? Se habla englais?). I've included a section in this guide that will give you a bit of basic Spanish, keep reading, it's near the end of the book.

Medical Emergencies

For medical needs in the BVI, the *B&F Medical Complex* (http://www.bfmedicalcomplex.com/) is located just off the cruise ship dock in Road Town and welcomes walk-ins (it is also a dental clinic). Also in Road Town at the roundabout north of Wickham's Cay, is the *Medicure Pharmacy* (284-494-6189), which has medical personnel on duty as well as an X-ray lab. If you need a true hospital, the *Peeble's Hospital* (284-494-3497; http://www.bvihsa.vg/) is located in Road Town. On Virgin Gorda there is a clinic in Spanish Town (284-495-5337) and another at *North Sound* (284-495-7310). For dental emergencies visit *Dental Surgery* (284-494-3274) behind the *Skeleton Building* in Road Town.

In the USVI you'll find the Juan F. Luis Hospital (340-778-6311; http://www.jflusvi.org/) on St. Croix just outside of Christiansted north of the Sunny Isle Shopping Center on Route 79, and in Frederkisted you can try the Frederiksted Health Center (340-772-0260; http://fhc-inc.net/) on Strand Street. On St. Thomas, the Roy L. Schneider Hospital (340-776-8311x) located at Sugar Estate just east of Charlotte Amalie has a 24-hour emergency room. On St. John, an emergency medical technician is on call at the Myrah Keating Smith Community Health Center (340-7693-8900) on Route 10 a short distance east of Cruz Bay.

Navigation

Cruising in the Virgin Islands is primarily done by sight, anchorages are never far apart and 15-20 miles is a fair day. GPS offers added security to any bit of navigation and waypoints shown in this guide allow users to access the anchorages or passes in the islands easily. Waypoints are intended to place you in the vicinity of your anchorage or pass, not to guide you in, that must be done by eye and you'll soon learn to read the water. Datum used is WGS84.

All of the Virgin Islands, the BVI, SVI, and USVI, all use *IALA* (International Association of Lighthouse Authorities; http://www.iala-aism.org/) *Maritime Buoyage System B*, which is also used in North and South America. You probably know it by the phrase "Red, Right, Returning". This is an easy way to remember that when returning from seaward, the red buoys and lights will be on your starboard side. In system B red buoys with green stripes are to be kept to starboard, while green buoys with red stripes should be kept to port.

All navigational aids are subject to change and may be missing from time to time so keep a sharp eye out when underway.

The waters of the Virgin Islands are very busy with charter boats, ferries (very fast), private yachts, freighters, and cruise ships. All are required to follow the *Rules of the Road*, but it's far simpler to just stay out of everyone else's way because you don't know if the other skipper knows the rules of the road, don't hurry, take it easy, be safe. Night cruising is not recommended unless you are very familiar with the waters, many local boats do not use running lights at night.

Phoning Home

The area code for the BVI is 284, the area code for the USVI is 340, and the area code for the SVI is the same as the area code for Puerto Rico, 787. Most 800 numbers in the United States can be dialed from Puerto Rico and the SVI, but if you have trouble, try dialing from a private phone instead of a pay phone.

Cable and Wireless (West Indies) Ltd. provides digital national and international telecommunications in the BVI featuring full *IDD (International Direct Dialing)* service, fax and data services including *IDAS (International Database Access)* and privately leased circuits. Inbound 800 numbers are accessible from the United States and Canada as well as the rest of the Caribbean. For easy access to U.S. numbers from the BVI, use *USA Direct*, an *AT&T* service that you can access by dialing 1-800-872-2881 from any BVI phone. It is possible to rent cell phones in the islands, get in touch with the local *Cable and Wireless* office for more details or ask your charter company.

If you have friends back home who must get in touch with you, have them call *Virgin Islands Radio* (USVI) at 340-776-8282, or *Tortola Radio* (BVI) at 284-494-4116, and leave a message for your boat's name. The boat will be hailed during traffic hours from 0500-0000 for *Virgin Islands Radio*, and at 0700, 1100, 1500, and 2200 on *Tortola Radio*.

If you need to make a call from your boat, hail *Virgin Islands Radio* (ch. 16). Make sure that you make arrangements prior to or upon your arrival for payment as you will not want to give out your credit card number over the airwaves.

Rastafarians

Everywhere you look in the Caribbean, you will see and meet Rastafarians. The man that sells you fruit and veggies, the boat boy that takes your line, or perhaps the guy that is working on your boat in the yard (such as Kenroy who helped me paint *IV Play* in Carriacou), Rastafarians, Rastas for short, are as much a part of the Caribbean as the trade winds. A goodly number of cruisers on their first voyage to the Caribbean bring preconceived notions with them about these highly religious folks and I strongly urge visitors to these islands to come here with an open mind.

Mention the word Rasta and a vision of dreadlocks, ganja, and reggae music comes to mind, but there is a lot more to these people than that, remember, don't judge a book by its cover. True Rastas maintain certain dietary practices and other religious beliefs that is the hallmark of this particular Christian religion. Sure, there are many folks who you'll meet that sport the dreadlocked look of the Rastafarian, and who will claim to be a follower of *Rastafari*, but who are not what they seem. This book's cover is a false one. Sometimes it is difficult to tell the difference, but if you observe them, the speech, their diet, you will soon learn the difference. This is not to say that there is a clear line between true Rastas and false Rastas, there are all kinds of Rastafarians the same as there are all manner of Catholics, Protestants, or Jews. Some live a life with a strict adherence to their beliefs, while others live a life a bit more relaxed. Some fear Rastafarians feeling that they are involved with drug smuggling and other assorted crimes. Not all are involved with illegal activities, one cannot indict an entire religion for the indiscretions of a few.

Where lie the roots of the *Rastafari*? It is generally accepted that the movement began in Jamaica in the 1930s when Marcus Garvey sought to bring the black race to a higher prominence. Garvey wanted an exodus of blacks from the Americas back to Africa and the establishment of a black nationality. Garvey preached that Africans would someday rise again to their true stature and that a black King would be crowned and he would lead all blacks to freedom. The crowning of Haile Selassie I as Emperor of Ethiopia became Garvey's prophecy fulfilled. Selassie, whose real name was Ras (Prince) Tafari Makonnen, is believed to be the 225th direct descendent of King Solomon and Queen Sheba and is said to be the second Messiah, Jesus in all his Kingly glory.

Rastafari is a religion full of ideals of purity, strength, and freedom from corruption and oppression that plagued black people for centuries. Rastas celebrate their Sabbath on Saturdays and view our modern society as "Babylon", an evil institution that is responsible for that same corruption and oppression. Most Rastas tend to distance themselves from Babylon as much as possible, seeking independence from the evils associated with it. That is why so many Rastas that you meet are self-sufficient, many of them farming, or earning a living from their own talents, such as wood-carving and crafts, preferring to live peaceful, simple, healthy lives. These people are very proud of who they are and are eager to educate others about their beliefs and way of life.

During his reign, Haile Selassie stressed education as the way forward for his people, and as a result, Rastas seek knowledge from the Bible as well as academically. Many are well educated and hold excellent positions. However, because of a lack of understanding, many Rastas are prevented from achieving levels of success they deserve. Without a doubt, a better understanding of the Rastafarian culture will assist in removing the barriers that prejudice has placed in their paths. One of those prejudices stems from the Rasta's use of ganga, marijuana, for religious, meditational, medicinal, and culinary purposes and justified by several quotations from the Bible. The most obvious icon of the Rasta is the dreadlocks, the long locks that are seen as a symbol of strength that also has a basis in the Bible, in the story of Samson. And what discussion of *Rastafari* would be complete without the mention of Reggae music and especially the music of Bob Marley, who helped bring the message of *Rastafari*, of *Jah*, of Haile Selassie, to the world.

Rum

"Yo ho ho and a bottle of rum!" So go the words to that famous pirate chanty, said to have originated when Blackbeard marooned 15 men on Dead Chest Cay in the BVI with nothing but their sea chests and a bottle of rum. Whether or not this is a true story, without a doubt, rum is THE drink of the Virgin Islands.

For some reason, cruising the Caribbean and drinking rum go hand in hand, in fact, when I'm cruising I often have a rum drink in my hand (even when I'm not cruising I can often be found with rum in hand). Most of the islands in the eastern Caribbean will have a rum distillery somewhere on their shores. Some islands such as Guadeloupe, Martinique, or Barbados will have many distilleries, and no visit to these islands is complete without a tour and sampling. One could make a whole day of it, others of us could make a whole week of it, while a few of us choose to make it a lifestyle.

On his third voyage to the New World, Columbus planted sugarcane on Hispaniola and Spanish colonist soon learned that one could produce a sweet liquor by distilling the heavy residue from sugarcane processing called molasses. Cheap to produce and easy to transport, sailors and buccaneers discovered the drink and it became identified with life on the high seas and ruffians in particular.

The term *rum* originated in the West Indies, some say in the taverns along the waterfront in Bridgetown, Barbados, but nobody truly knows for sure. *Rumbullion* is an old English word used in the 1600s to describe an intoxicated individual so when sailors in the West Indies distilled liquor from sugarcane they called it *rum* as it was seen to be *"... laying the locals on the ground asleep."* Still others claim that the term *rum* came from the official name for sugarcane, *saccharum officinarum*.

Rum has had varied uses besides recreational drinking, it has been said that rum was given to slaves as an inducement to keep them productive. It has also been said that parents in the Colonies gave rum to their babies to help them through the "terrible twos" while older children were given sips to ease the stress of exams. Workers sometimes had rum breaks at 1100 and 1600, "elevenses" and "fourses." In 1677, the British Royal Navy introduced the practice of providing sailors with a "*tot*" (½ pint) of rum twice a day to help prevent scurvy, actually, the lime that the sailors added to their rum did more to prevent scurvy than the rum itself. In the last century the rum ration was reduced to 1/8 pint once a day until August 1, 1970, when the practice was abolished on a day known as "*Black Tot Day.*"

The body of Admiral Lord Nelson, who was killed at Trafalgar, was placed in a vat of rum for preservation until the ship carrying the Admiral arrived in England. Upon arrival it was discovered that rum loving sailors drilled a hole in the vat and drained off all the rum, which led to the expression "Nelson's Blood" in describing rum in seaside areas of Britain.

Although probably considered the norm amongst the sailing crowd, rum as a popular drink really didn't catch on until World War II when French soldiers stationed on Martinique discovered its powers and brought it home with them (though I'm sure that Ernest Hemingway and the *Cuba Libre* also had a part to play in the emergence of rum as a popular libation).

Most brands of rum that you find in these islands are available in liquor stores at home, but some rums are truly exotic and cannot be purchased anywhere but the island on which they are distilled. Rum is a natural product of Guadeloupe, Martinique, and Barbados as it's made from genuine sugarcane, the cash crop for so many years on the island's plantations. Some rums, such as those produced in Puerto Rico, Haiti, and some other Caribbean islands are made from molasses or other sugar by-products and some rum connoisseurs consider them inferior. On Martinique in particular, rum has been elevated to a special status. In 1996, Martinician rum was granted an *AOC, Appellation d'Origine Contrôlée*, not an easy award to win and one which guarantees that rum production is as strictly controlled as the production of the great wines of France.

Many of these rums begin their life as sugar cane, which after harvesting is brought to a crushing station where a large water-powered wheel squishes the juice from the cane producing both sugar and byproducts such as molasses. The mixture then moves to the next stage of the process, the boiling room where water is added to the molasses and the mixture pasteurized. Here the cane juice is boiled at different temperatures in different tanks, yeast is added and the fermentation process begins producing alcohol, which in turn kills the yeast and the result is called "dead wash" which is sloughed off to the fermentation and storage areas. After aging the product is distilled and the final product is ready...rum. This is the process in a nutshell, different distillers use different methods, this is only meant to give you an idea of the processes involved. This process is handled a bit differently by the folks at the *Callwood Rum Distillery* in Cane Garden Bay on Tortola in the BVI. Here they distill pure cane juice to make their own brand of rum called *Arundel*. The famous *Cruzan* rums of St. Croix are considered by many to some of the best rums anywhere and the rums of the Virgin Islands are noted for being "overproof," 151 proof, and their potency is legendary.

Now let's discuss the different kinds of rum you'll find and what the labels mean, you may want to look for these classifications on the bottles when you shop, and believe me, you'll find lots and lots of different bottles and brands of rum. Rum that is made from sugarcane juice is given the name *Rhum Agricole* while rum distilled from molasses is referred to as *Rhum Industrial* or *Rhum Traditionnel*. White rum from sugar cane juice (*vésou*) is called *Rhum Blanc Agricole*, is not aged, and has a strong, some say rough taste and is best mixed into a punch such as *Ti-punch* popular on the French islands of Guadeloupe and Martinique. Another favorite is *Planter's Punch*, or *Punch Planteur. Planters Punch*, one of the oldest rum punches dating to the plantation days, can be remembered by this simple little ditty: sour, sweet, strong and weak. This translates to one part sour, lime juice, two parts sweet, sugar, three parts strong, your favorite rum, and four parts weak, water or fruit juice.

What many consider the top of the line rum is *Rum Vieux*, aged rum that ripens in 650 liter oak barrels from 3-15 years or more which gives it its rich, distinctive amber color, although caramel is sometimes added to produce the darker shades of rum that you might see. Rum that is aged 18 months is called *Rhum Paile*, while *Rhum Ambré* is aged three years. Rum aged from 5-7 years is called *Rhum Vieux Traditionnel*, rum aged 8-12 years is called *Rhum Vieux Hors d'Âge vc*.

To learn more about rum, and in particular several brands of rum, visit www.ministryofrum.com. If you'd like a great drinking guide to the BVI pick up a copy of *The Drinking Man's Guide To The BVI*, it offers free food and drinks at 33 restaurants and bars in the BVI.

Safety and Security

One of the greatest concerns of cruisers in the Caribbean is crime. I would love to paint a picture of a tropical Eden, but that would be a lie. Crime does exist here, crimes upon cruisers exist here, but it is a fact of life that we deal with here and simple precautions will usually keep you out of harm's way. Crime in the Virgin Islands is rare, although it can happen. Usually somebody leaves a wallet, purse, or an expensive item lying around and it grows legs and wanders off.

First and foremost, avoid high-risk anchorages, and buddy-boat for safety's sake, currently this is a special concern for vessels transiting the waters off the northern shore of Venezuela between Trinidad and Margarita and hardly a concern in the Windward Islands. You'll learn of these trouble spots by talking to other cruisers or by listening to the *Caribbean Safety and Security Net*, which we'll learn more about in a moment. When leaving your vessel, lock it, all hatches and large ports, don't leave an opening for a skinny child to enter (don't laugh!) and don't leave items on deck that you do not want stolen. At night, you might also wish to lock yourself inside your boat so you don't wake up with an intruder hovering above you. The choice of carrying weapons aboard is strictly a personal one, I prefer to have one and not need it than need one and not have it, but that's just me. Some folks like to keep a flare gun handy as well as a spotlight for blinding intruders in the night. Don't laugh at a flare gun, it can be a very effective weapon.

One of the greatest temptations for a thief is your dinghy, *lock it or lose it* as is the motto of the *Safety and Security Net*. You can usually tell someone who has cruised in the Caribbean, they often have their dinghy hoisted in the air at night. Some of us don't do that, preferring instead to use a wire cable and lock, but either way, a good thief can still get away with your dinghy despite your best efforts it seems.

A lot of cruisers try to make their dinghy look as unappealing as possible by joining in a competition to see who can have the ugliest outboard motor. Thieves tend to concentrate on those nice, new looking outboards, ones that look like they have a long life ahead of them. Here again, *lock it or lose it*. Don't keep anything in your dinghy that you don't want stolen, not that these items will be stolen, just don't take that chance. Another idea is not painting the name of your boat on it such as "Tender To My Boat." This only informs people when you are NOT on your boat. If you plan to travel about on land in questionable areas, and you will learn where they are by talking to other cruisers or listening to the *Safety and Security Net*, do not advertise by wearing a lot of jewelry. Keep your money safe in your pocket or other location. Women, this means that you should keep your cash on your person instead of in a purse or fanny pack as people have been known to sneak up from behind and slice the strap on a purse or fanny pack and make off with it.

If you're attending a major event such as *Jump Up* or *Carnival*, keep your money in your shoe as there may well be pickpockets working the crowd with surgical precision. If you're walking about at night, do so in a group, there is strength in numbers, and ladies, please, never walk around unescorted!

Vessels equipped with SSB receivers can tune in to the *Caribbean Safety and Security Net* on 8104 at 0815 daily. Currently maintained by Melodye and John Pompa on the *S/V Second Millenium*, the *Safety and Security Net*, sometimes jokingly referred to as the *Moan and Complain Net* by its detractors, offers cruisers the latest scoop on what's going on where. If a dinghy has been stolen in St. Vincent, if the Montserrat volcano is acting up, or if somebody was robbed while walking down the streets of some Caribbean town at night, you'll learn about those happenings on the net. What's to gain from this information? Well, you'll learn where to take special security measures and what areas you might wish to avoid. Besides accessing the net on SSB, you can email the net at safetyandsecuritynet@gmail.com.

In most Caribbean anchorages you will be approached by local vendors in small boats (it's a good idea to keep fenders out on both sides of your vessel for just such an event) asking to do your laundry or sell you fruits and veggies, handmade crafts, or offering to get you anything you need from town. If you've already got a boat boy, tell them so and there should be no problem. If you're in some anchorage where there is no boat boy per se, the lady that wants to do your laundry might actually be a good deal if you're tired of washing your clothes in a bucket. It's all a learning experience and you will soon learn to trust your gut instinct about people. Most of these vendors know the difference in charter boats and cruising boats and generally know that the charter boats are the best customers, so if you're chartering, either put out a sign saying that you're not buying anything, or relax and enjoy, it's all a part of the show and certainly gives you something to talk about.

I've found a lot of what I call "land sharks" that abound in the Caribbean, hanging around marinas and scenic overviews wanting to work on your boat or guide you to a certain waterfall or other tourist haunt. Use caution with the guys that want to work on your boat; I've found several, such as Kenroy in Tyrell Bay, Carriacou, that are extremely diligent, hardworking, conscientious laborers who give you a fair day's work for a fair day's pay and who are worth the largest tip you can afford to give them. On the other hand, there are those that have no idea of what they're doing and who then want to borrow every tool you have so they can do the work they've contracted to do. If in doubt, ask around, check with other boaters, check with the local yard or marina office, or question the man to see if he does indeed know what he is talking about.

Taxis and Buses

If you're not walking, riding a bicycle, or renting a car, the chances are you'll be taking a taxi here and there and there are certain things about taxis in the Virgin Islands that visitors not acquainted with "island time" need to know. Taxis can range in size from small cars to vans and even small buses that can carry 20 passengers. It is the custom in the Caribbean to fill a taxi before leaving, whether at the dock or airport where taxis may even wait for the next plane before leaving (it's an economic thing folks, empty seats are a waste of space and fuel translating to lost income). This can be irritating to those not accustomed to waiting, my only advice is to take a chill pill and relax, you'll get there soon enough and the few minutes lost won't make much difference either way and you'll learn something in the process about Caribbean etiquette.

Take a few minutes and talk to the driver or other passengers, you might learn a thing or two about the island you're on. If you have a taxi all to yourself or your party, make sure you agree on a fare before departing to avoid any embarrassment at your destination.

Taxis in the SVI, on Culebra and Vieques, are not metered and fares are set by the number of passengers and the destination. Always agree to a fare BEFORE departing in the taxi.

Taxis in the USVI, either sedans or vans, are easy to recognize by their domed tops and license plates lettered *TP*, *CP*, or *JP* for St. Thomas, St. Croix, or St. John. The taxis are not metered and charge by person and destination. All USVI taxis are required by the *Virgin Islands Taxi Association* to have a rate card in the vehicle and should you have any question about the fare ask the driver to produce it. It's always easier to agree to a fare BEFORE departing in a taxi. There are additional small surcharges for each suitcase or box carried, for trips between midnight and 0600, and for radio-dispatched taxis. In the BVI the taxi system is similar, taxis are not metered and fares are set by the *Ministry of Communications and Works*.

There is no bus system in the SVI, but in the USVI, St. Thomas has a good bus system called *VITRAN* operating between Market Place in Charlotte Amalie and Red Hook as well as the western end of St. Thomas and the airport. These buses come in three styles, open-air, taxi-buses, and closed buses. In St. Croix *VITRAN* runs from Christiansted to Frederiksted. St. John has no bus system so your best bet is to take a taxi or rent a car. In the BVI it may be hard to distinguish a bus from a taxi. Buses tend to be open-air trucks with benches, or large vans on Tortola and Virgin Gorda.

Tides and Currents

Most of the Virgin Islands lie on the southern side of the *Virgin Bank*, a large ocean shelf with abrupt drops in depth near its edges. The bank extends in an east/northeast direction for approximately 86 miles from the eastern end of Puerto Rico. For the first 50 miles the bank extends east and averages about 25 miles in width, and then turning east/northeast as it widens to approximately 32 miles. The *Virgin Bank* ends just beyond the southeast point of Anegada. On the southern edge of the *Virgin Bank* lies a narrow ledge of coral, about 200 yards wide and 60'-120' deep, that extends almost unbroken from *Horse Shoe Reef* at Anegada in the British Virgin Islands, to Isla de Vieques in the Spanish Virgin Islands.

Tides in the British and United States Virgin Islands range only about 1' being diurnal (one high and one low each day) along the Caribbean shores (generally the southern sides of the islands) and semidiurnal (two highs and two lows each day) along the Atlantic shorelines (generally the northern shores of the islands). The currents in the islands vary sometimes from island to island and passage to passage and can be anywhere from .2 knots to 4 knots. I'll do my best to report currents for each passage in the appropriate text. Generally you can allow for the tidal flow to set southeast and northwest while an overall current of about ¼-½ knot sets in a west to northwest direction.

The tides in Puerto Rico are only about 1'-1½', although the actual fluctuations depend largely upon the wind strength and direction as well as other meteorological conditions. The tides are primarily semidiurnal along the northern and western coasts of Puerto Rico, and more or less diurnal along the island's Caribbean coast. Tides in the Spanish Virgin Islands are based on tides at San Juan, Puerto Rico and vary on a day to day and tide to tide basis.

As a general rule of thumb you can use the following: At Fajardo high tide is 10 minutes before and low tide is 30 minutes after San Juan; at Roosevelt Roads high tide is approximately 2 minutes before and the low tide is 20 minutes after San Juan; Culebra's high tide is roughly 2¼ hours before and low tide is only 25 minutes before San Juan; Puerto Ferro, Vieques, has a high tide 2 hours and 10 minutes before and a low tide only 10 minutes before San Juan; and tides at Punta Malas, Vieques, are approximately 15 minutes before San Juan.

In the *Sonda de Vieques* in the Spanish Virgin Islands, there are strong tidal currents over the shoals in the western areas and around Isla Cabeza de Perro. In *Pasaje de San Juan* and *Pasaje de Cucaracha* just north of Cabo San Juan, velocities of over 2 knots have been reported, while in the wider passages between Cayo Icacos and Cayo de Luis Pena the current is less than 1 knot.

From Isla de Culebra the current sets toward Punta Este on Isla de Vieques, around which the tidal currents are strong. On an average you can figure on west/northwest current of about ½ knot in the *Sonda de Vieques*. Just off Culebra, in the *Canal de Luis Pena*, the current is deflected north of *Bahia Tarja* and then sets toward the southern end of Cayo de Luis Peña. The current is weak off the entrance to Bahia de Sardinas and the northwesterly current sets directly through the channel here at about 2 knots.

In the USVI and BVI, currents in the *VI Passage* can run .5 knots setting north and south, while on the eastern side of the passage, around Savanna Island, can run as high as 2 knots. Currents in *Middle Passage* and *Windward Passage* can reach 4 knots.

In *Coral Bay*, St. John, the current sets SW and NE across the entrance at .7 knots. The tidal range in Coral Bay is about 1'.

Vessels heading to St. Croix from St. Thomas or the BVI will usually find a slight westerly setting current of 1-3 knots depending on weather conditions.

Time

All of the Virgin Islands are located in the *Atlantic Standard Time Zone*, which is one hour ahead of *Eastern Standard Time*, the time zone for the eastern United States from New York to Miami. None of the Virgin Islands use *Daylight Savings Time*. To be perfectly honest, the Virgin Islands truly run on *Island Time*, so don't hurry, take it slow and easy, where are you going in such a hurry anyway?

VHF

As with cruising anywhere, VHF is your handle to the world immediately around you. Channel 16 is the international hailing and distress channel; ch. 12 is for port operations and most charter boat companies use this channel for communications with their charterers; ch. 6 and 68 are for ship to ship communication, ch. 27 and 84 are used by *Radio Tortola*; ch. 25, 85, and 87 is used by *Virgin Islands Radio* (*WAH*); ch. 22A is for *Coast Guard* use; and weather can be received on weather channels 3 and 4. Do not use channel 70, it is reserved for digital distress calls. And don't forget, when you have made contact with your party on ch. 16 you must switch to a working channel. Please reserve ch. 12 for port operations.

If you have friends back home who must get in touch with you, have them call *Virgin Islands Radio* (USVI) at 340-776-8282, or *Tortola Radio* (BVI) at 284-494-4116, and leave a message for your boat's name. The boat will be hailed during traffic hours from 0500-0000 for *Virgin Islands Radio*, and at 0700, 1100, 1500, and 2200 on *Tortola Radio*.

VISAR

In November of 1988 *VISAR*, the *Virgin Islands Search and Rescue Association* (http://visar.org/) was created. *VISAR* is a non-profit organization manned by volunteers who risk their lives to rescue mariners in distress. If you are in distress and need assistance in the USVI or BVI, and happen to have a cell phone on board, call 999, 911, or 767 (*SOS*) and you will be connected to *VISAR*. You can also reach *VISAR* through *Radio Tortola*, ask for *Fire and Rescue* and tell them that you need *Search and Rescue*. If you are interested in learning more about *VISAR*, or if you wish to become a supporting member and/or make a donation, you can contact VISAR at 284-494-4357 or email VISAR at visar@caribsurf.com.

Weather

The one thing that most visitors to the Virgin Islands notice is that the islands have a very small difference in average daily temperatures year round. Usually the difference is about 10° with winter temperatures averaging around 75° and summer time temperatures averaging about 85°. The winter brings frequent but short lived periods of rain and low humidity, while summer is frequently drier, less windy, and more humid. In fact, during the summer the normally lush green hills on the islands may take on a brown shading due to the lack of rain.

The outstanding feature for mariners is the steadiness of the easterly trade winds. The trades blow about 80% of the time year round. Winds from the east and southeast are particularly dominant in summer when the *Bermuda High* has shifted north while northeasterlies are more prominent from around November through April and give way to easterly and southeasterly winds in the spring. In the winter months the trade-wind pattern is occasionally interrupted by cold fronts that have survived a journey from the United States. As the cold front approaches, winds shift toward the S, and then as the front passes they gradually shift through the SW and NW quadrants back to the NE.

During the summer months the easterly wave occurs and is characterized by winds out of the east/northeast ahead of the wave and followed by an east/southeast wind. In summer the trades tend to lessen at night and strengthen during the day. This is why it is suggested that sailors plying the southern coast leave their anchorage early in the morning, say around 0300, and get in to their next anchorage by 0800-0900 before the trades begin to pick up. At night, near the coast, a land-sea breeze effect helps exert a diurnal influence on the wind. If the pressure gradients are weak, a land breeze may develop during the night...northeasterly on the southern coast and southeasterly on the northern coast. The sea breeze develops during the morning hours and reinforces the trades on all but the western coast. Along the western coast the land effect opposes the trades and tends to merely weaken them.

During the winter you will experience the *Christmas Winds*, so named because they seem to arrive around that particular time of year. During this period the wind may blow 20-25 knots and sometimes up to 30-40 knots for days on end. While the waters north of the Virgin Islands (Bahamas, Turks and Caicos) experience several frontal passages each winter, it is rare that a frontal passage makes its way all the way down to the Virgin Islands, perhaps one or two fronts a year will bring a westerly wind shift. Gale-force winds are rare, but they can occur with a strong front, thunderstorm, tropical storm, or hurricane.

The rainy season is roughly from May through December (although showers can and do occur at any time during the year), the same as hurricane season, with the heavier showers associated with passing tropical storms or hurricanes. The official hurricane season begins on June 1 and ends on November 30. When a storm threatens all radio stations issue regular updates about every 2-3 hours and if you are somewhere where you can receive TV, say you're at a dock with cable TV, you can pick up *CNN* or the *Weather Channel* for the latest every hour. For info online visit the *National Hurricane Center* website at http://wwwnhc.noaa.gov, the *Weather Channel* website at http://weather.com, and at http://www.caribwx.com.

In the summer, since the Virgin Islands are about due west of the Sahara desert it is not unusual to have a hazy summertime day due to high amounts of Saharan dust in the air that has been carried across the *Atlantic Ocean* by the trade winds.

You can pick up local weather on *WIVI*, 99.5 FM at 0730, 0830, 1530, and 1630, on *WVWI*, 1000 AM hourly from 1000, and on *WSTA*, 1340 AM and *Radio Antilles* on 830 AM. Tortola hosts *ZBVI Radio*, 780 AM with weather forecasts at 0730 and 0805, Monday-Friday, and at 0945 on Sundays; weather is also available on the half –hour from 0730-2130. In St. Croix you can receive weather on *WSTX* at 970 AM. In Puerto Rico you can pick up *WOSO* at 1030 AM with weather reports in English at 6 minutes after each hour, just after the news. You can also pick up local weather forecasts in the Virgin Islands on VHF weather channels 03 and 04. *Virgin Islands Radio* broadcast weather forecasts at 0600, 1400, and 2000 on VHF channels 28 and 85 (I've heard these broadcasts as far away as Fajardo in Puerto Rico) and on the following Marine SSB frequencies: 2506 KHz, 4357.4 (ch. 401), 4382.2 KHz (ch. 409), 6.515.7

KHz (ch. 604), 8728.2 (ch. 804), and 13100.8 (ch. 1201).

The *United States Coast Guard* in Portsmouth, Virginia weather broadcasts can be received on 4428.7 KHz (ch. 409), 6506.4 KHz (ch. 601), 8765.4 (ch. 816), 13113.2 KHz (ch. 1205), and 17307.3 (ch. 1625). Times are 0600, 0800, 1400, and 2200.

Chris Parker's summer schedule, April to October, begins at 0630 EDT on 4.045 or 8.137 MHz, 0730 EDT on 8.137 MHz, 0830 EDT on 8.104 MHz, on 12.359 MHz at 0900 EDT (or when Chris finishes on 8.104 MHz), and 16.531 at 0930 EDT if Chris expects to communicate with any vessel in the Eastern half of the Atlantic that day. Chris' winter schedule, November to March, begins at 0600 EST on 8.137 MHz, then moves to 4.045 MHz at 0630 EST, and then at 0730 EST you'll find Chris on 8.104 MHz, and Chris will finish up on 12.359 MHz at 0800 EST. Quite often during the winter months Chris may be late in getting to the 12 meg and 16 meg frequencies. If 12.359 MHz is busy Chris will use either 12.356 MHz or 12.362 MHz. When severe weather or tropical weather systems threaten Chris will also transmit in the evenings, usually on 8.104 MHz at 2400 UTC (2000 EDT) and Chris will usually announce this on the morning net. Chris begins the net with a 24-48 hour wind and sea summary followed by a synoptic analysis and tropical conditions during hurricane season. After this, Chris repeats the weather for those needing fills and finally he takes check-ins reporting local conditions from sponsoring vessels (vessels who have paid an annual fee for this service).

For those who seek more information about weather, weather patterns, and the forecasting of weather, should pick up a copy of Chris Parker's excellent publication: *Coastal and Offshore Weather, The Essential Handbook* (http://www.mwxc.com). You can e-mail Chris at chris@mwxc.com.

Another well respected forecaster is a ham operator named George Cline, KP2G. George can be found on the *Caribbean Maritime Mobile Net* (http://users.isp.com/kv4jc/) located at 7.250 MHz, lower sideband at 0715 AST, 15 minutes into the net. Daily, except Sunday, George gives an overview of the current Caribbean weather from the Turks and Caicos to Trinidad as well as the western Caribbean basin. During hurricane season George provides weather updates at 7086.0 LSB at 1630 if weather is threatening the islands. During the high season George may return to the airwaves at 1630 AST, on the afternoon cocktail net at 7.086 lower sideband if there are enough listeners. To find weather online go to WeatherCaribe at http://www.weathercarib.com/.

Using the Charts

For the soundings on the charts I use my dinghy (*Afterglow*) with a computer-based hydrographic system consisting of an off-the-shelf GPS and sonar combination that gives a GPS waypoint and depth every 2 seconds including the time of each observation. The software used records and stores this information in an onboard computer. When I begin to chart an area, I first put *Afterglow's* bow on a well-marked, prominent point of land and take GPS lat/longs for a period of at least 10 minutes. I use the average of all these positions to check against the lat/long shown on the topos that I use to create the charts. I also use cross bearings to help set up control points for my own reference. At this point I begin to take soundings.

My first objective is to chart the inshore reefs. Then I'll plot all visible hazards to navigation. These positions are recorded by hand on my field notes as well as being recorded electronically. I rely primarily on my on-site notes for the actual construction of the charts. The soundings taken by the system are later entered by hand but it is the field notes that help me create the basis for the chart graphics. Next I will run the one-fathom line as well as the ten-fathom line and chart these. Here is where the system does most of the work. Finally, I will crisscross the entire area in a grid pattern and hopefully catch hazards that are at first glance unseen. It is not unusual to spend days sounding an area of only a couple of square miles.

Due to the speed of *Afterglow*, each identical lat/long may have as many as ten or twenty separate soundings. Then, with the help of *NOAA* tide tables, the computer gives me accurate depths to one decimal place for each separate lat/long pair acquired on the data run. A macro purges all but the lowest depths for each lat/long position (to two decimal places). At this point the actual plotting is begun including one-fathom and ten-fathom lines. The charts themselves are still constructed from outline tracings of topographic maps and the lat/long lines are placed in accordance with these maps. The soundings taken are shown in feet at MLW, *Mean Low Water*, the average low tide. Since MLW is an average, cruisers must be aware that there are times that there will be less water than shown, particularly on Spring low tides, during the full moon and new moon.

These charts are as accurate as I can make them and I believe them to be superior to any others. However, it is not possible to plot every individual rock or coral head so piloting by eye is still essential. On many of the routes in my guides you must be able to pick out the blue, deeper water as it snakes between sandbanks, rocky bars, and coral heads. Learn to trust your eyes. Never approach a cut or sandbar with the sun in your eyes, it should be above and behind you. Sunglasses with polarized lenses can be a big help in combating the glare of the sun on the water. With good visibility the sandbars and heads stand out and are clearly defined. As you gain experience you may even learn to read the subtle differences in the water surface as it flows over underwater obstructions.

All courses shown are magnetic. All waypoints for entrances to cuts and for detouring around shoal areas are only to be used in a general sense. They are meant to get you into the general area, you must pilot your way through the cut or around the shoal yourself. You will have to keep a good lookout, GPS will not do that for you. The best aids to navigation when near these shoals and cuts are sharp eyesight and good light.

Not being a perfect world, I expect errors to occur. I would deeply appreciate any input and corrections that you may notice as you travel these waters. Please send your suggestions to Stephen J. Pavlidis, C/O Seaworthy Publications, 2023 N. Atlantic Ave. Unit #226, Cocoa Beach, Florida, 32931, or email me at stevepavlidis@hotmail.com.

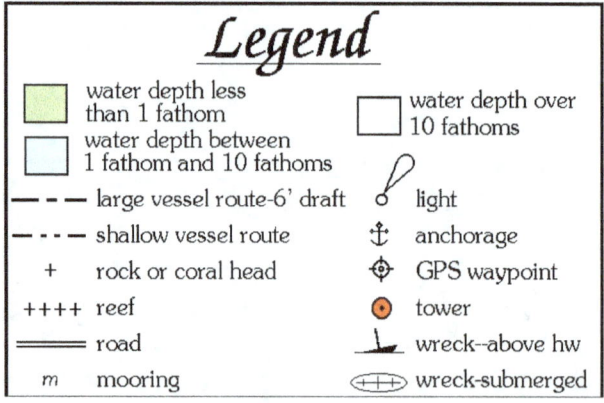

List of Charts

CAUTION:

All charts are to be used in conjunction with the text in this guide and an overall chart of the Virgin Islands (NOAA, DMA, BA, Imray or CYC). All soundings are in feet at Mean Low Water. All courses are magnetic. Projection is *Transverse Mercator*. **Datum** is WGS84. North is always "up" on these charts. The Index charts are designed strictly for orientation, they are NOT to be used for navigational purposes.

The prudent navigator will not rely solely on any single aid to navigation, particularly on floating aids.

Differences in latitude and longitude may exist between these charts and other charts of the area; therefore the transfer of positions from one chart to another should be done by bearings and distances from common features.

The author and publisher take no responsibility for errors, omissions, or the misuse of these charts. No warranties are either expressed or implied as to the usability of the information contained herein. Always keep a good lookout when piloting in these waters.

The Spanish Virgin Islands		
Chart #	Chart Description	Page #
	Spanish Virgin Islands - Index Chart	34
PRE-4	Punta Cascajo to Cabo San Juan	35
SVI-1	Isla Palominos	37
SVI-2	Cayo Lobos	37
SVI-3	Culebra & Approaches	38
SVI-4	Cayo Lobito to Cayo Luis Pena	40
SVI-5	Cayo Luis Pena to Punta del Soldado	40
SVI-6	Punta Soldado to Canal del Sur, Ensenada Honda	42
SVI-7	Cayo Norte to Canal del Sur	45
SVI-8	Bahia Flamenco to Bahia de Oleaje	45
SVI-9	Vieques & Approaches	50
SVI-10	Western Coast, Punta Arenas	52
SVI-11	Desembarcadero Mosquito to Punta Malas, Isabel Segunda	52
SVI-12	Puerto Diablo to Bahia Fanduca, Punta Este	53
SVI-13	Bahia de la Chiva to Bahia Fanduca, Ensenada Honda	55
SVI-14	Bahia Mosquito to Bahia Tapon	55
SVI-15	Puerto Real to Ensenada Sun Bay, Esperanza	57

The United States Virgin Islands		
Chart #	Chart Description	Page #
St. Thomas - Index Chart		64
USVI-1	Approach to Charlotte Amalie	66
USVI-2	Charlotte Amalie	66
USVI-3	West Gregerie Channel, East Gregerie Channel	69
USVI-4	Krum Bay	69
USVI-5	Druif Bay to Flamingo Bay	73
USVI-6	Jersey Bay, Benner Bay	73
USVI-7	Great St. James Island, Current Rock to Christmas Cove	76
USVI-8	Cowpet Bay	77
USVI-9	Red Hook Bay	80
USVI-10	Sapphire Bay Marina	80
St. John - Index Chart		84
USVI-11	Cruz Bay	85
USVI-12	Frank Bay to Great Cruz Bay	89
USVI-13	Great Lameshur Bay	90
USVI-14	Saltpond Bay	91
USVI-15	Coral Bay	91
USVI-16	Coral Harbour	93
USVI-17	Haulover Bay, Newfound Bay	93
USVI-18	Leinster Bay	95
USVI-19	Francis Bay	95
USVI-20	Trunk Bay	97
USVI-21	Hawksnest Bay	97
USVI-22	Caneel Bay	101
St. Croix - Index Chart		102
USVI-23	Christiansted	105
USVI-24	Buck Islans	105
USVI-25	Green Cay to Teague Bay	107
USVI-26	Green Cay Marina	108
USVI-27	Salt River Bay	108
USVI-28	Frederiksted	111
USVI-29	Krause Lagoon Channel, Limetree Bay Channel	111

List of Charts

The British Virgin Islands		
Chart #	Chart Description	Page #
Tortola - Index Chart		117
BVI-1	Road Harbour, Road Town	121
BVI-2	Brandywine Bay	124
BVI-3	Paraquita Bay, Buck Island, Maya Cove	126
BVI-4	Fat Hogs Bay	129
BVI-5	The Camanoe Passages	129
BVI-6	Marina Cay	131
BVI-7	Trellis Bay	131
BVI-8	Guana Island	131
BVI-9	Brewers Bay	133
BVI-10	Cane Garden Bay	135
BVI-11	Sopers Hole	139
BVI-12	Nanny Cay Marina, Sea Cow Bay	139
Jost Van Dyke - Index Chart		145
BVI-16	Little Jost Van Dyke	147
BVI-17	Little Harbour to Great Harbour	147
BVI-18	White Bay	150
Norman Island to Virgin Gorda - Index Chart		152
BVI-13	Norman Island	153
BVI-14	Peter Island	156
BVI-15	Salt Island to Round Rock	161
BVI-15A	Cooper Island, Manchioneel Bay	161
Virgin Gorda - Index Chart		163
BVI-19	The Baths to Round Rock	165
BVI-19A	Big Trunk Bay to Stoney Bay, The Baths	165
BVI-20	Virgin Gorda Yacht Harbour	165
BVI-21	Savannah Bay	168
BVI-21A	The Dogs	170
BVI-22	Long Bay	170
BVI-23	North Sound	173
BVI-24	Eustatia Sound	173
Necker Island		180
BVI-25	Necker Island	180
Anegada - Index Chart		182
BVI-26	West End Anchorage	182
BVI-27	Horse Shoe Reef	184

A Cruising Guide to the Virgin Islands

The Spanish Virgin Islands

Port of Entry:
Culebra
Fuel: Culebra, Vieques
Haul-Out: None
Diesel Repairs: Culebra
Outboard Repairs: Culebra
Propane: Culebra, Vieques
Provisions: Culebra, Vieques

Vessels heading south and east from Puerto to the Virgin Islands will get their first tastes of this paradise in the Spanish Virgin Islands, just off the eastern shore of Puerto Rico. Stretching from Las Cucarachas just off Cabo San Juan eastward to Culebra and south to Vieques, the Spanish Virgin Islands you begin to get your fist sampling of clearer waters than those surrounding the mainland of Puerto Rico, beautiful secluded beaches, free moorings, great snorkeling, and, last but not least...good fishing.

The Spanish Virgin Islands can be broken down into four separate areas, Isla Palominos, the islands and reefs of *La Cordillera*, the islands of Culebra, and the island of Vieques, and we shall explore them in

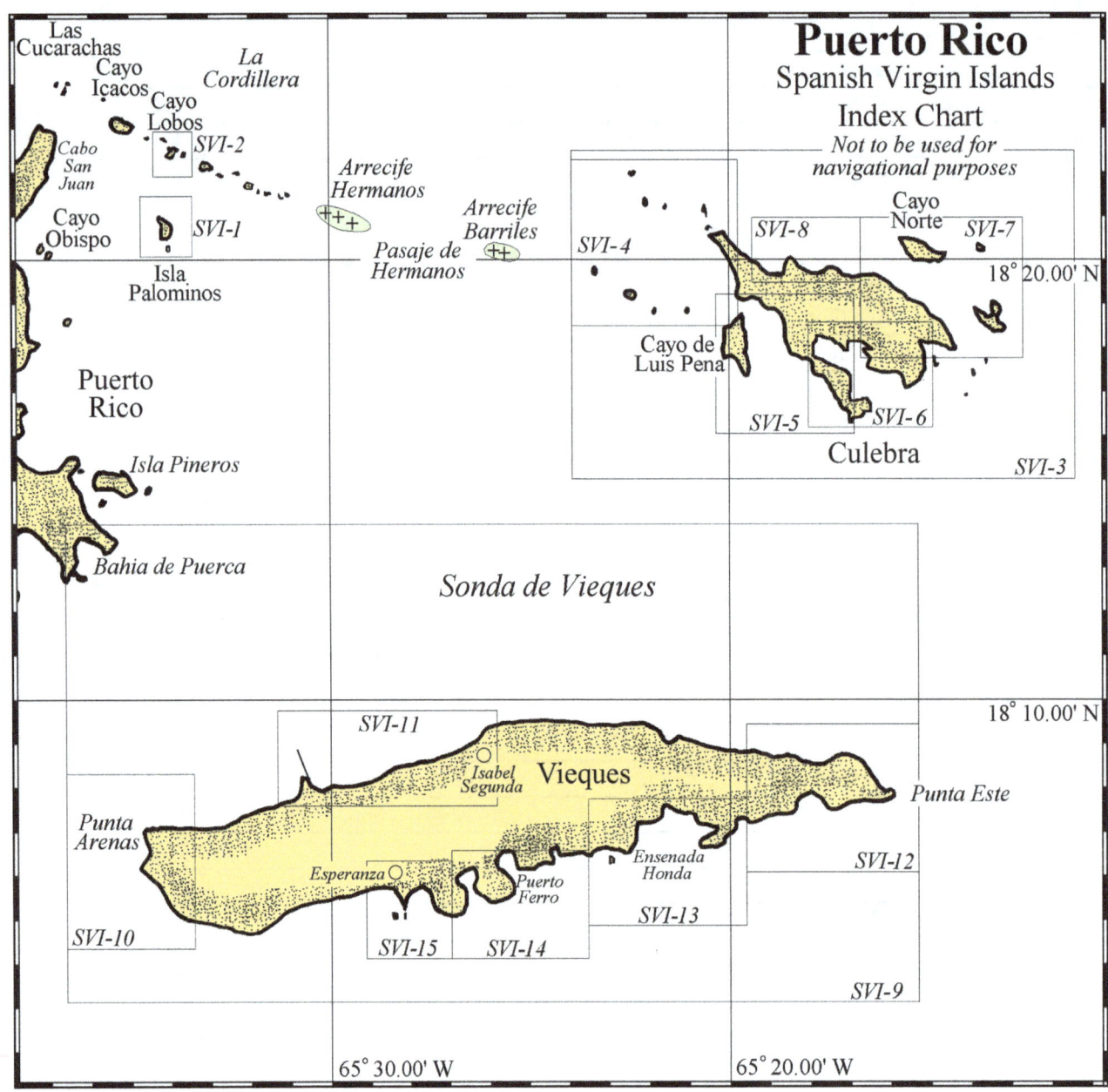

The Spanish Virgin Islands

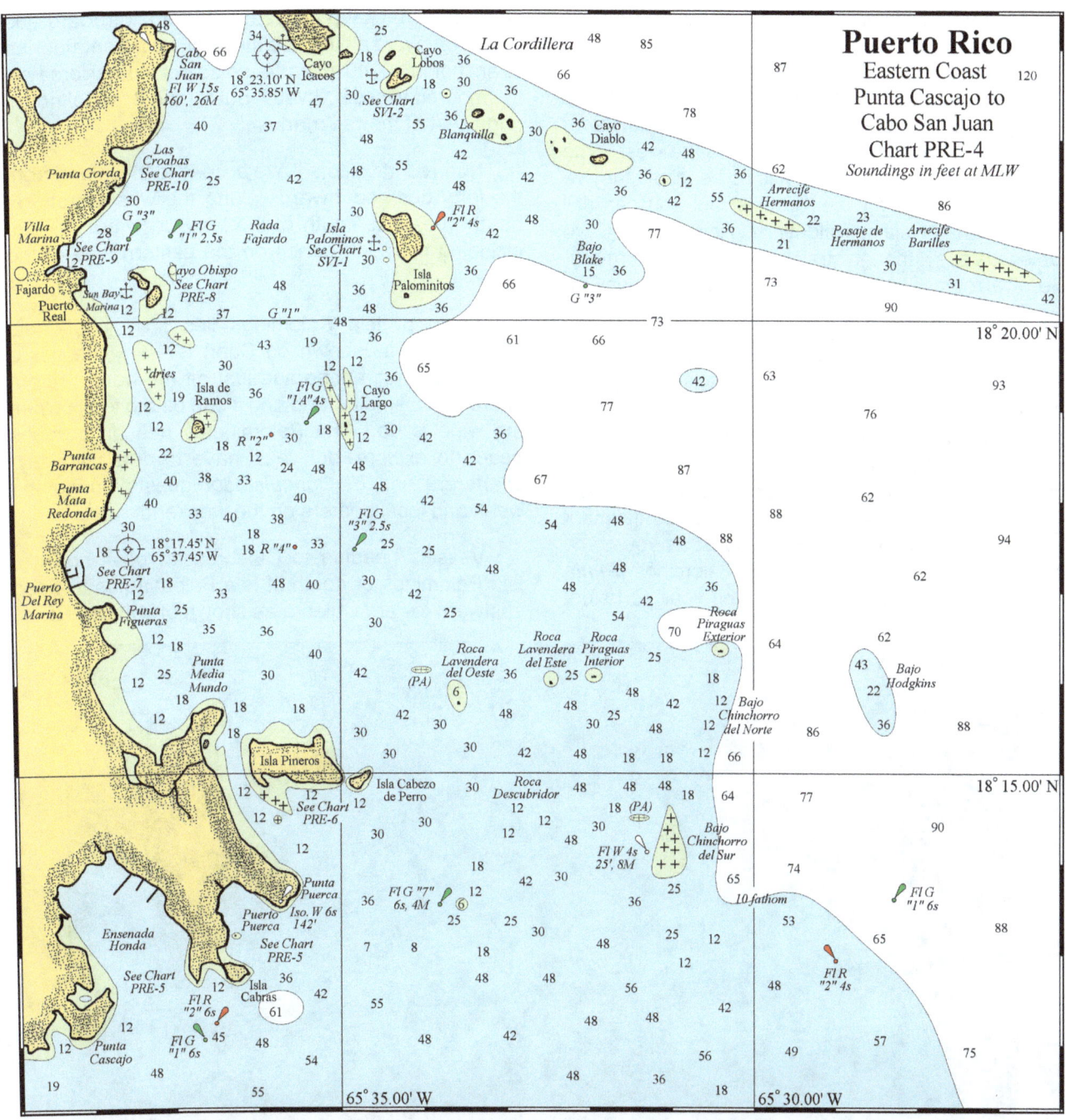

that order. I will not attempt to suggest how you should explore the Spanish Virgin Islands; some cruisers head straight for Vieques or Culebra when rounding Punta Tuna, while others head north to Palmas del Mar, Puerto del Rey, or Fajardo. I prefer to head east from Cayo Obispo to Culebra paralleling the southern edge of *La Cordillera*. You won't get much of a lee here, but I still prefer that route to Culebra. Okay, let's start our voyage to the Spanish Virgin Islands just off Fajardo at Isla de Palominos.

Isla de Palominos

Important Lights
Isla Palominos #2: Fl R 4 sec

Waypoints:
Isla Palominos - ½ nm W of anchorage area:
18° 20.70' N, 65° 34.80' W

A Cruising Guide to the Virgin Islands

Isla de Palominos, Chart SVI-1, lies approximately 3½ miles southeast of Cabo San Juan and is impossible to miss, its high (165') rounded hill is an easy landmark from all directions. Isla de Palominos is a private island leased by the *El Conquistador* resort across the *Bahia de Fajardo* to the west. The huge *El Conquistador* resort has no beach so they've leased the island for their guests, but you can still access parts of Isla de Palominos. Access from Cayo Obispo is easy, though straight to windward normally. Be aware that Isla Palominos is very, very busy on weekends when the locals come out to play.

Navigational Information

As shown on Chart SVI-1, a waypoint at 18° 20.70' N, 65° 34.80' W, places you approximately ½ mile west of the anchorage area on the western shore of Isla Palominos. Head generally eastward or towards the ferry dock just south of east. Ahead of you will be some shoals marked by a red daymark that you must keep to starboard. Just as you come abeam of the northwest tip of Isla Palominos (*Punta Aguila*), you must avoid a 5' spot off your port side.

Once past that keep the red marker to starboard and head northward a bit and either pick up a free mooring or anchor in 20'-40' of water so as not to interfere with the moored vessels. Watch out for the 3' shoal north/northwest of the red marker.

Non-resort visitors have access to the island from the ferry dock northwards along the western shore, but the beaches south of the ferry dock are private, including the nude beach on the eastern side of the island.

South of Isla Palominos lies tiny, lovely Isla Palominotos as shown on Chart SVI-1. There is a small, but snug anchorage just off the northwestern shore of the small island and it can be a bit rolly when the wind is up. Isla Palominotos has a gorgeous beach to explore, but you'll have to deal with day-charterers and *El Conquistador* guests during the week and local boaters on the weekend.

Vessels heading to Culebra can pass north of Isla Palominos or south of Isla Palominotos to head eastward toward Culebra as shown on Chart PRE-4.

Isla Palominos as seen from the Northeast, Isla Palominitos in the background

Photo by Todd Duff

The Spanish Virgin Islands

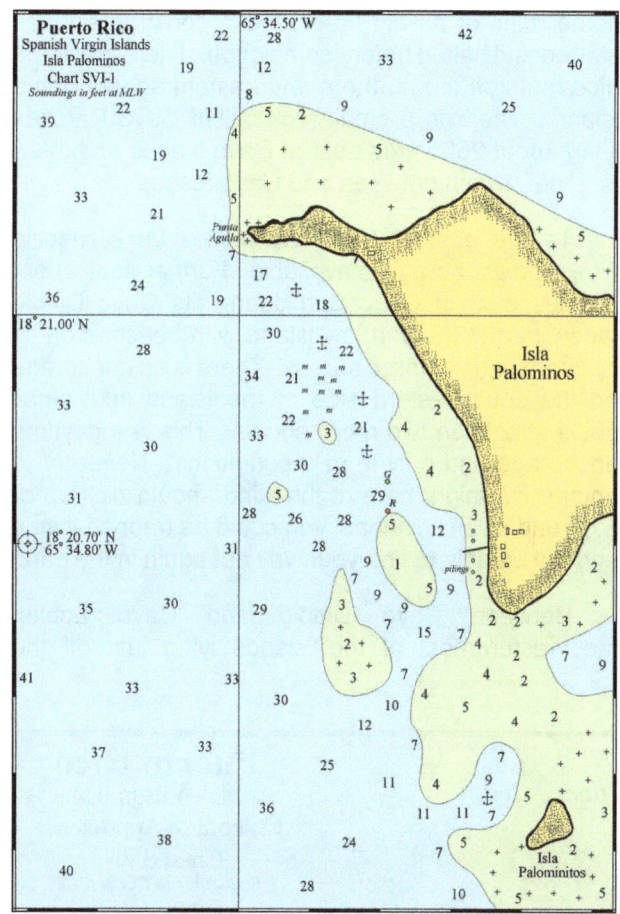

La Cordillera to Isla de Culebra

Important Lights:
Cayo Lobito Light: Fl W 6 sec

Waypoints:
Pasaje de San Juan - ½ nm NE of C. San Juan:
18° 23.28' N, 65° 36.50' W

Cayo Icacos - ½ nm SW of anchorage:
18° 23.10' N, 65° 35.85' W

Cayo Lobos - ½ nm SW of anchorage area:
18° 22.60' N, 65° 34.65' W

Cayo Lobo - ½ nm SW of:
18° 19.50' N, 65° 23.00' W

Cayo de Luis Pena - ½ nm NNW of:
18° 19.10' N, 65° 20.30' W

La Cordillera is a small chain of rocks, reefs, and small islands beginning approximately 1½ miles north of Cabo San Juan at Las Cucarachas and extending east/southeast approximately 12 miles to the small islands lying west of Isla de Culebra. There are several passages between the rocks and reefs and mariners are advised to give these islands a berth of at least a mile when transiting this area at night (NOT recommended) and ½ mile in the daytime when the shoals are visible and usually breaking.

Navigational Information

The northwesternmost point in *La Cordillera* is Las Cucarachas, a small group of rocks rising up about 15' out of the water a mile north of Cabo San Juan. The ¾ mile wide channel (30'-65' depths) between Cabo San Juan and *Las Cucaraches*, *Pasaje de San Juan*, is a main entrance into the *Sonda de Vieques* (*Vieques Sound*) from the northern shore of Puerto Rico. About ¾ mile east of *Las Cucarachas* are *Los Farallones*, a group of rugged bare rocks 30' high. Deep water lies close along their northern and western sides. *Pasaje Cucaracha* lies between *Las Cucarachas* and *Los Farallones* and has depths of 17'-23'. A breaking reef lies .2 mile south of *Los Farallones* and continues to almost ½ mile west of the northwestern tip of Cayo Icacos.

The first of the islands of *La Cordillera* that offers an anchorage is Cayo Icacos (see Chart PRE-4), a part of the *Cordillera Reserve* and administered by the *Department of Natural* Resources. A 40' high island covered with scrubby growth, Cayo Icacos is

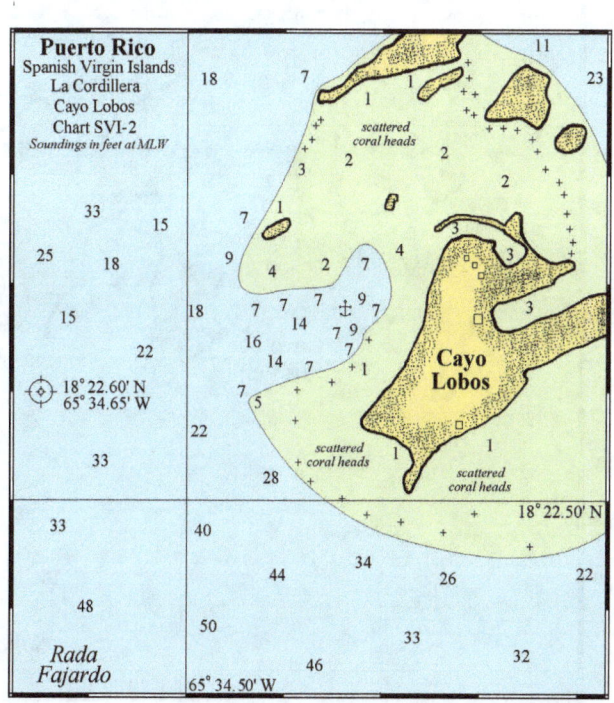

A Cruising Guide to the Virgin Islands

the second largest island in the chain. A small wharf and the ruins of a former limestone quarry are near the southwest point of the island and a prominent tower lies almost in the center of the island.

As shown on Chart PRE-4, a waypoint at 18° 23.10' N, 65° 35.85' W, will place you approximately ½ nautical mile southwest of the anchorage area just off the beach on the southwestern shore of the island.

It may be a bit rolly, but in settled conditions, it can be comfortable enough for an overnight stay.

A half-mile east of Cayo Icacos is a favorite stop for cruisers and local boaters alike, Cayo Lobos. As shown on Chart SVI-2, a waypoint at 18° 22.60' N, 65° 34.65' W, will place you approximately ½ mile southwest of the anchorage in the small cove on the western shore of the island just off the concrete pier. A nice though rolly (at times of strong southeast winds) anchorage, the island is private and the anchorage untenable with a northerly swell running. Ashore are some ruins of an old hotel whose construction was started and halted before completion. There are some nice reefs off the northern and eastern shores of the island. There is a small rock called Cayo Ratones lying about 250 yards east of Cayo Icacos and there is a reef awash between and Cayo Icacos.

To the east of Cayo Lobos lies La Blanquilla where no anchorage is available. Further east, about 5 miles east of Cabo San Juan, sits Cayo Diablo (see Chart PRE-4), a low island with beaches on its northern and southern shores. There is an anchorage on the southwestern side of the island in a small pocket between two rocky shoals. This is a daytime anchorage and only in mild conditions! Never try to anchor overnight here; if the wind should pick up or a ground swell develops, you could be trapped inside and not be able to find your way out again in the dark.

Between Cayo Diablo and Cayo Lobito, the westernmost of the islands lying just off the

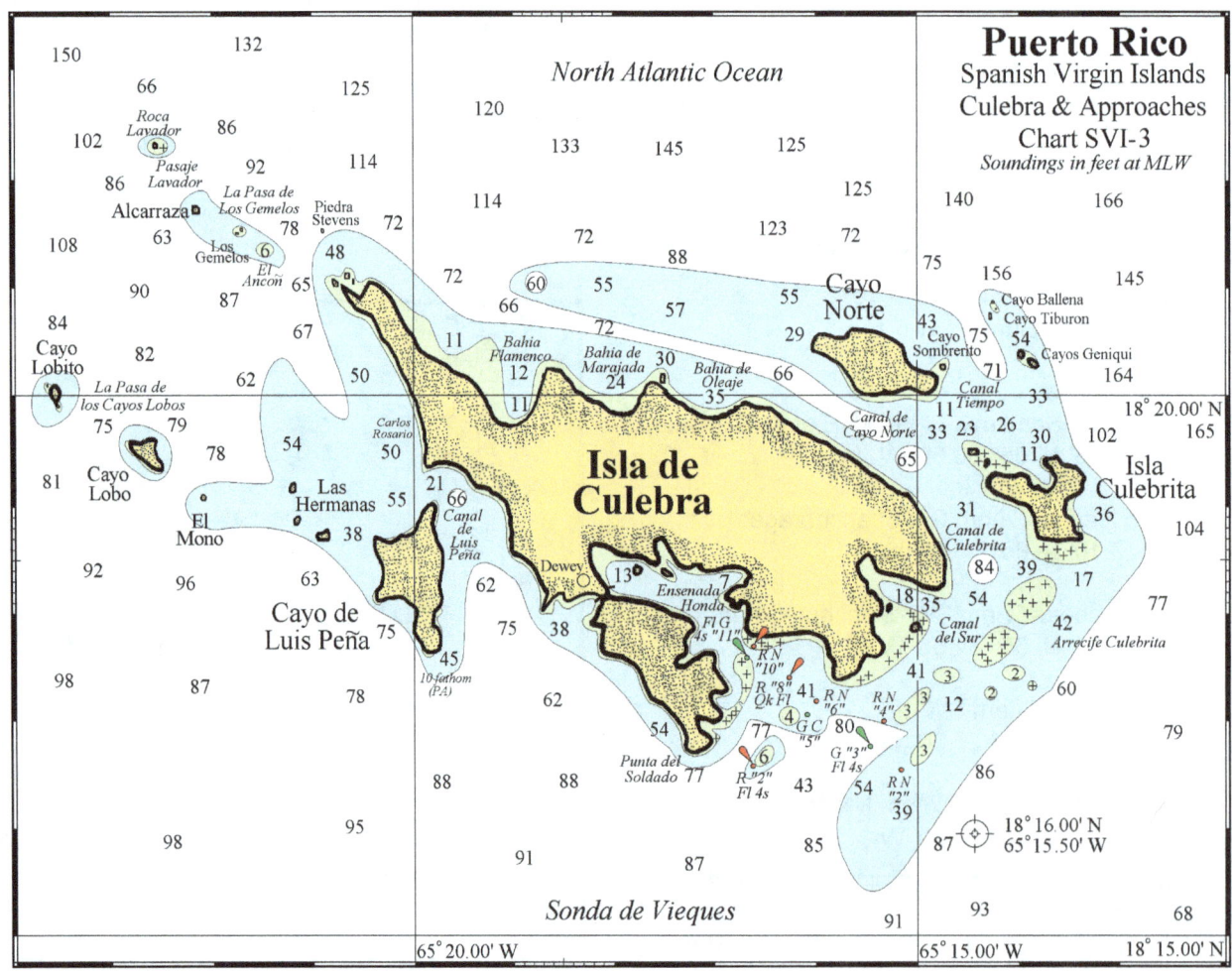

38

northwestern tip of Culebra, are two groups of rocks 2'-15' feet high known as *Arrecife Hermanos* and *Arrecife Barriles* as shown on Chart PRE-4. Small vessels can pass between these shoals using *Pasaje de Hermanos* or *Pasaje de Barriles*. Large vessels have been known to take advantage of *Pasaje de Barilles*. These reefs, while offering no place to anchor, make for good diving on settled days with no swell running.

Just east of *Arrecife Barilles* you will begin to enter the Culebran archipelago made up of 23 islands and rocks and we will begin our exploration of them at their western terminus at Cayo Lobito.

Cayo Lobito lies approximately 13 miles east of Cabo San Juan and is the westernmost of the chain of islands that extend for over 3 miles northwest to Isla de Culebra as shown on Chart SVI-3 and in greater detail on Chart SVI-4. There is a small and deep anchorage on the northwestern shore of the island in a deep pocket between Cayo Tuna and Cayo Lobito. The anchorage should be used only as a daytime stop as it is quite rolly in prevailing conditions.

At the south end of Cayo Lobito is the very conspicuous 75' pinnacle called *Roca Columna*. *Cayo Lobito Light* rises 110' above the water atop a skeleton tower with a red/white diamond/shaped daymark.

The next island in the chain is the larger Cayo Lobo, about ¾ mile southeast of Cayo Lobito across the 10 fathom deep *La Pasa de los Cayos Lobos*. As shown on Chart SVI-4, a waypoint at 18° 19.50' N, 65° 23.00' W, will place you approximately ½ mile west of the island. There is a small anchorage on the northern side of the island in a deep cove, but be advised that it is rolly and untenable with northerly swells running. Both Cayo Lobito and Cayo Lobo are good snorkeling and diving sites.

Approximately ½ mile southeast of Cayo Lobo lies tiny El Mono, a small irregular 15' ledge with several heads and something to definitely avoid.

There are several small islands between El Mono and Cayo de Luis Pena called *Las Hermanas*. Made up of Cayo Yerba, 66' high, Cayo Raton, the smallest at 46' high, and Cayo del Agua, the lowest at only 39', their only claim to fame is some fair snorkeling.

The last stop before reaching Isla de Culebra is well worth investigating. Cayo Luis Pena is named after the second owner of the island and is now a *U.S. Fish and Wildlife Refuge*. The area in the *Luis Pena Channel* from is designated a no-take zone. Cayo Luis Pena has several beautiful beaches and good snorkeling abounds, especially of the beach on the southwest side of the island. The island itself rises to a peak near the center with the southern and northern ends joined by low necks. Punta Cruz, the southwestern tip of the island, is a prominent white cliff.

As shown on Chart SVI-4, a waypoint at 18° 19.10' N, 65° 20.30' W, will place you approximately ½ mile north/northwest of an anchorage on the northern shore of Cayo de Luis Pena. The same waypoint places vessels bound though the *Canal de Luis Pena* for Punta Soldado on Isla de Culebra ½ mile west/southwest of the entrance to the canal between Cayo Luis Pena and Punta Tamarindo Grande as shown on Chart SVI-5.

The anchorage on the northern shore of Cayo Luis Pena should only be used in settled prevailing conditions; it can be quite rolly. Vessels can anchor in sand patches and shallower draft vessels can work their way further in between the reefs. There is a fair lee anchorage on the western shore of the island as shown on Chart SVI-5 just north of Punta Cruz. This anchorage can be used in prevailing conditions, but not with northerly swells running. There is now a mooring here for your use as well as south of Punta Cruz in *Lana's Cove*.

Vessels bound for Dewey on Isla de Culebra, or headed for Punta Soldado (round the point to head to *Ensenada Honda*) can pass north or south of Cayo de Luis Peña. In the *Canal de Luis Peña* beginning just north of the island, currents can be strong, up to 2 knots at times. The current is weakest at the mouth of *Bahia de Sardinas* on Culebra and is deflected somewhat by Punta Melones and sometimes flows towards the southern end of Cayo de Luis Peña and not through the *Canal de Luis Peña*.

A Cruising Guide to the Virgin Islands

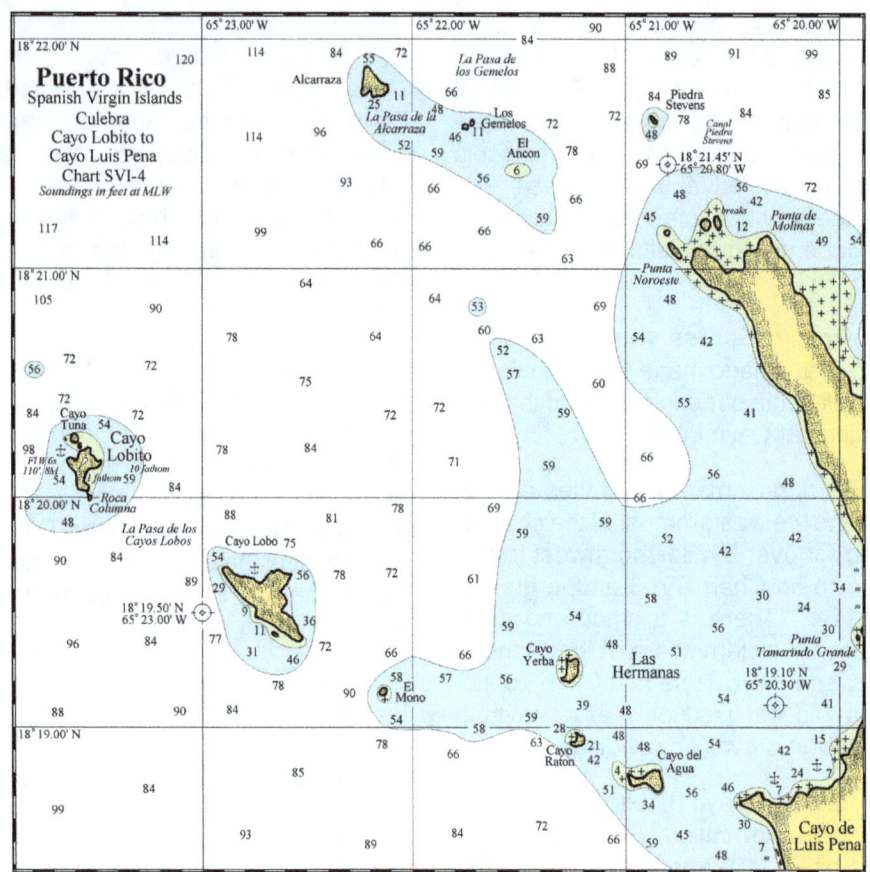

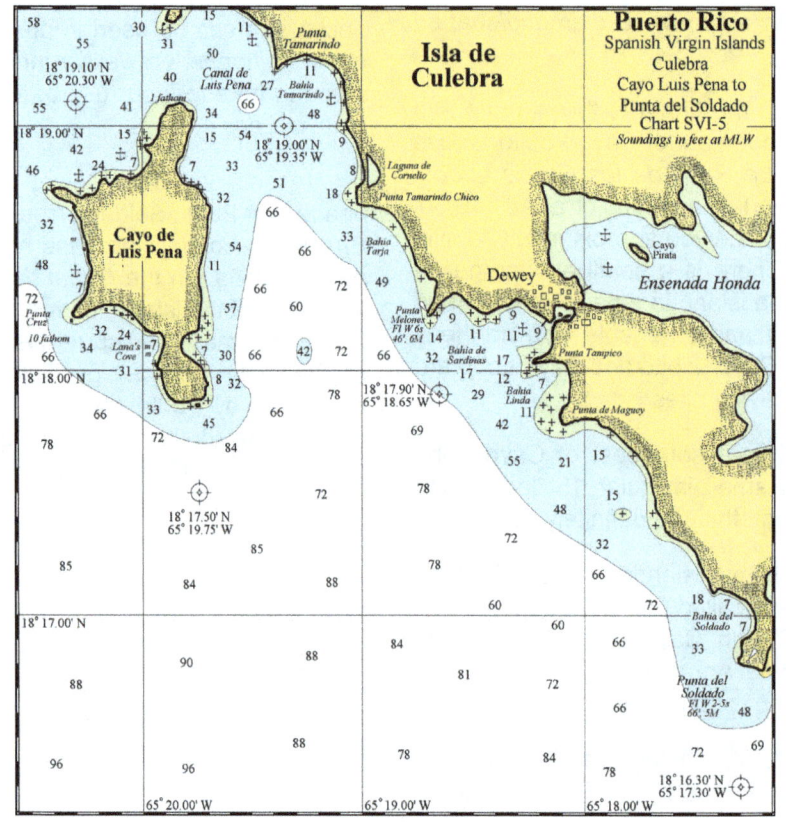

Isla de Culebra

Important Lights:
Punta Melones Light: Fl W 6 sec
Punta del Solado Light: Fl W 2.5 sec
Bajo Amarillo #2: FL R 4 sec
Cabezas Crespas #3: Fl G 4 sec
Bajo Snapper #8: Q R
Punta Colorada #9: Fl G 4 sec
Bajos Grampus #2: Fl R 4 sec

Waypoints:
Bahia Tamarindo - ¼ nm SW of:
18° 19.00' N, 65° 19.35' W

Bahia de Sardinas - ½ nm SW of:
18° 17.90' N, 65° 18.65' W

Puerto del Manglar - ¼ nm SE of anchorage:
18° 18.05' N, 65° 14.50' W

Cayo de Luis Peña - ½ nm S of:
18° 17.50' N, 65° 19.75' W

Ensenada Honda - 1 nm SE of marked entrance:
18° 17.33' N, 65° 16.35' W

Punta del Soldado - ¼ nm S of point:
18° 16.30' N, 65° 17.30' W

When the Spanish began their decimation of the *Tainos* on Puerto Rico, many fled to Culebra as a last refuge. The first non-Indian to visit Culebra was *The Admiral of All Oceans*, Christopher Columbus, in 1493, on his second voyage to the New World. Later, Sir Henry Morgan and other pirates allegedly used the island as a hideout; legend has it that some of their booty is still buried there.

Although part of Puerto Rico, Culebra's flavor is more like the Virgin Islands to her east. *Culebra* means *snake* in Spanish and the name describes the shape of the island itself; the 7 mile long by 3 mile wide island was first shown on Spanish charts as *De la Culebra* in 1886 and the English called the island *Pasaje Island* in the 1800s. When authority of the island transferred to the U.S. in 1898, the U.S. government specified that these islands be used for their "highest and best use." Five years later Roosevelt surrendered the islands to U.S. Navy control. In 1911, after a change of heart, Roosevelt ordered the islands serve the secondary purpose of providing a breeding ground for native seabirds. The island of Culebra and her surrounding islets encompass over 7,000 acres of which over 2,800 are designated as a part of the *U.S. National Refuge System*. Hence there is little development and the land and waters are a sanctuary for indigenous plants and animals. In 1936, the U.S. Navy began using some 2,000 acres of Culebra for bombing exercises until 1975.

The island of Culebra is home to about 2,000 permanent residents and crime is not a problem, you'll be safe walking around the center of Culebra, the town of Dewey, day or night. Dewey was originally *Pueblo Viejo* and quite a ways from where it is now; in fact, some old-timers still call it "*Pueblo.*" In 1903, the U.S. military decided the town needed to be closer to the water and they moved Pueblo Viejo and its inhabitants to the current location and changed its name to "Dewey" after the famous Admiral. The lift-bridge in town was originally built for two local fishing boats that are no longer in existence. The bridge today is unused, though quite a sight.

We'll begin our exploration of Isla de Culebra at *Canal de Luis Peña* and circumnavigate the island discovering several good anchorages, an excellent hurricane "hole," and many irresistible beaches.

Navigational Information

Heading southeast along the southeastern shore of Culebra from the *Canal de Luis Pena*, you'll find a couple of fair anchorages. The first is just inside *Canal de Luis Pena* at *Bahia Tamarindo*. As shown on Chart SVI-5, a waypoint at 18° 19.00' N, 65° 19.35' W, will place you approximately ¼ mile southwest of the bay. Simply head into the bay and anchor wherever your draft allows. Be prepared to have a rolly night if the winds are up at all. Again, as in all lee anchorages in Puerto Rico and the Spanish Virgin Islands, do not anchor if northerly swells are imminent. There is good snorkeling just off the point at Punta Tamarindo Grande.

Proceeding southeastward, you will soon come to *Bahia de Sardinas*, the small bay that lies to the west of Dewey. As shown on Chart SVI-5, a waypoint at 18° 17.90' N, 65° 18.65' W, will place you approximately ½ mile SW of the anchorage area. Head NE toward the town dock avoiding the shoal to starboard off Punta Tampico and anchor wherever your draft allows. I much prefer to anchor on the other side of town in *Ensenada Honda*, it's much calmer there and not as rolly.

If you choose to anchor in *Bahia de Sardinas*, please don't block the dock as the ferry from Fajardo

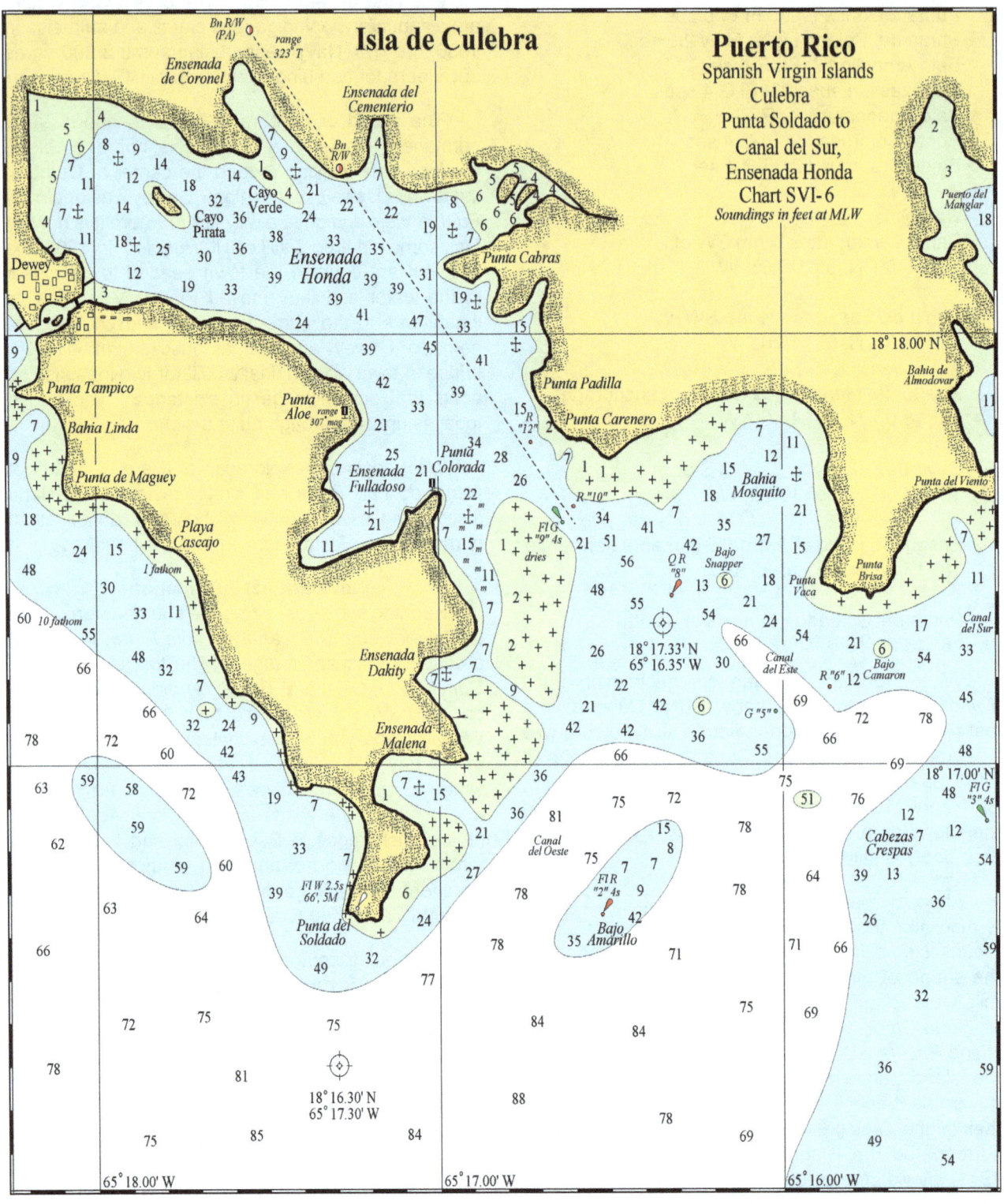

The Spanish Virgin Islands

The bridge in Dewey, Culebra
Photo by Michelle Rexach

Beach scene, Culebra
Photo by Michelle Rexach

Culebra as seen from Culebrita
Photo by Michelle Rexach

uses it on a daily basis. The ferries to Culebra leave Fajardo Monday-Friday at 0930 and 1500, while the ferry leaves Culebra for Fajardo at 1100 and 1630. On Saturday and Sunday the ferries leave Fajardo ½ hour earlier and leave Culebra at 0700 (Saturday only), 1400, and 1730. For more information on the ferries call the *Fajardo Ports Authority* at 863-0705 (https://ati.pr/en/routes-and-maps/).

Continuing towards Punta Soldado, the only hazards are the shoals off Punta de Maguey as shown on Chart SVI-5 and Chart SVI-6. As a point of reference, a waypoint at 18° 16.30' N, 65° 17.30' W, will place you ¼ mile south of Punta Soldado where you'll pick up a bit of current and seas if the winds are east or north of east. Good snorkeling can be found just off Punta Soldado about 50 yards off the point where the reef drops from 10'-30' and then gently on to 50'. Punta Soldado is named for an event that happened there a couple of centuries ago when a deserter from the Spanish army was found here. Closer to town, the beach by Punta Melones offers good snorkeling also where you'll find some coral heads just off the end of the beach in 8'-10' of water.

From the waypoint south of Punta Soldado, head northeastward towards the entrance to *Ensenada Honda* or to *Ensenada Malena*, if that is what you prefer. Just a bit northeast of Punta Soldado lies *Ensenada Malena* (as shown on Chart SVI-6), a fair anchorage, but not in prevailing conditions as surge can be expected.

If headed for the entrance to *Ensenada Honda* from Punta Soldado, head for a waypoint at 18° 17.33' N, 65° 16.35' W (see Chart SVI-6), keeping the very visible reefs to port and R "2" (marking *Bajo Amarillo*) to starboard. Never attempt this route at night! When you reach the waypoint you'll see R "8" (marking *Bajo Grouper*) in front of you, keep the light to starboard and turn to port to pass between the markers, G "9" and R "10" that define the channel between the reefs into *Ensenada Honda*. In the distance you'll see a range bearing 323° T consisting of two daymarks at the northern end of the 1½ mile long by ½ mile wide harbour. The reefs at the entrance are easily seen and dry at low water in places. Once inside keep the red buoy R "12" to starboard.

Vessels arriving in Culebra from the USVI or BVI will find a well-marked channel leading in to *Ensenada Honda*, but you must use caution. Head to a waypoint at 18° 16.00' N, 65° 15.50 W, which places you in deep water ½ mile southeast of RN "2" as shown on Chart SVI-3 (whatever you do, do not attempt to pass north/northeast of RN "2" as you'll just go up on *Arrecife Culebrita*). Bear in mind that RN "4" is more prominent (larger and more visible) than RN "2" so make sure that you're not heading to it instead as you'll pass right over the reef on that courseline. Keep RN "2" to starboard and steer generally NW to pass between G "3" and RN "4" (see Chart SVI-6). Keep G "3" to port and as shown on Chart SVI-6, head for the passage between G "5" and RN "6" and then head onwards keeping R "8" to starboard. From there follow the above directions to enter the harbor at *Ensenada Honda* (while vessels leaving *Ensenada Honda* for the Virgin Islands should follow the above directions in reverse). In addition, upon entering *Ensenada Honda* from RN "4" you'll see a range (307° mag-orange and white daymarks) at Punta Colorada and Punta Aloe.

There are several places to anchor in *Ensenada Honda*. A favorite of mine is just behind the reef in the channel that leads to *Ensenada Dikity*. As shown on Chart SVI-6, once inside the entrance round the end of the reef to port and work your way southward to anchor behind the reef where you'll have plenty of wind and little if any sea. Skippers can even work their way further south to anchor in the small reef protected *Ensenada Dikity*. There are new moorings in the anchorage at *Ensenada Dikity* for your convenience. Intermittent *Wi-Fi* is available to vessels in *Dikity*.

Continuing northward in *Ensenada Honda*, anchorages abound. To port you can anchor in *Ensenada Fulladosa* while to starboard you can anchor northwest of Punta Padilla or north of Punta Cabras at the mouth of the mangrove lined creeks that are excellent hurricane holes and worked so well during *Hurricane Hugo*. Most boats tend to anchor off Dewey north and west of Cayo Pirata.

What You Will Find Ashore

Cayo Pirata was originally constructed to give shelter to pirate ships. It was to be turned into a museum, but funding ran out before completion. All that remains of this plan is a dock and some picnic tables that you can make use of if you choose to dinghy over and explore the island. The El Batey Dinghy dock is in a sad state of disrepair, however, *El Batey* is an excellent place to eat. You can tie up to the Dewey town dock or at the *Dinghy Bar* to visit town.

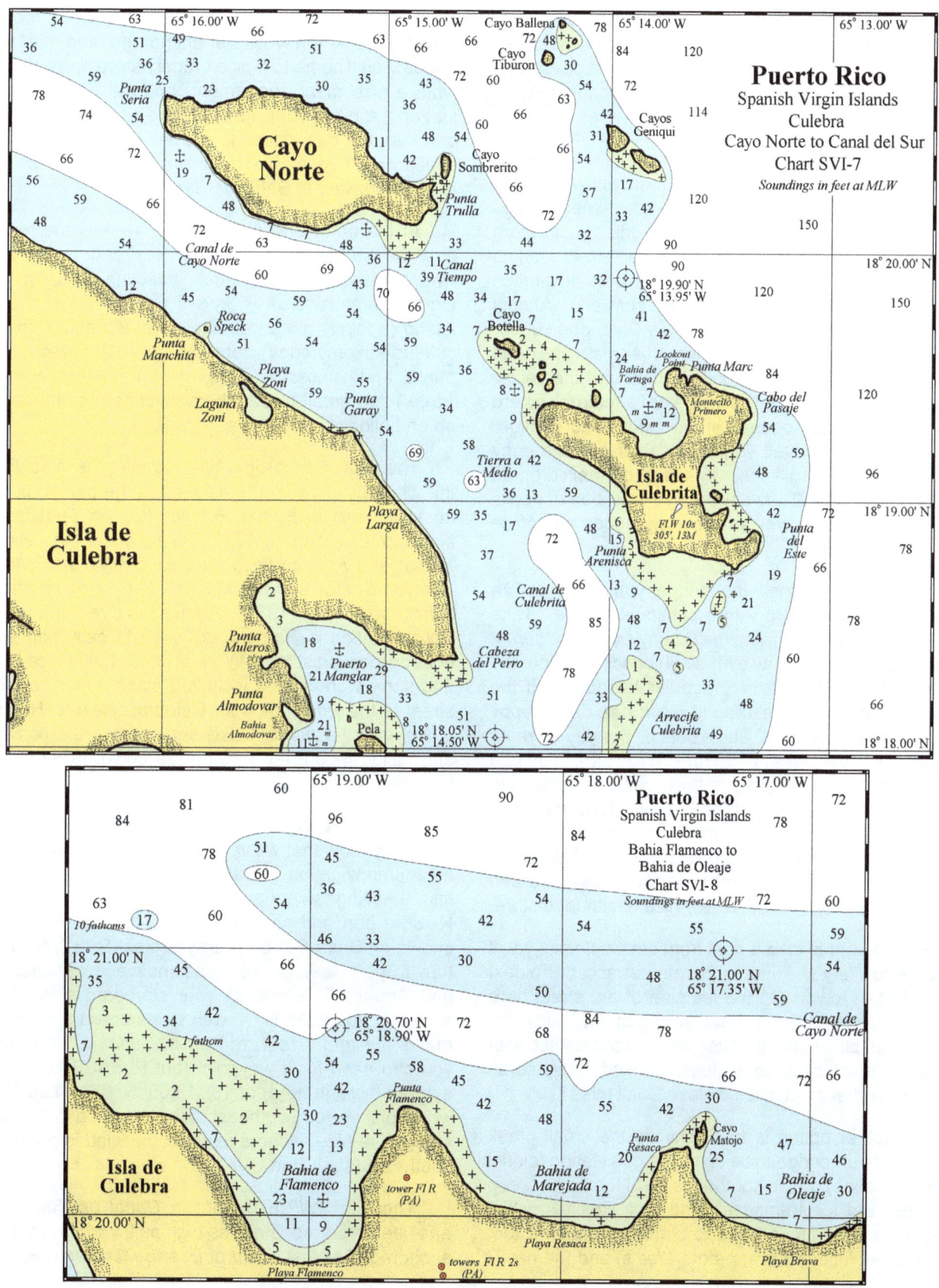

Boats anchored in the bay have access to Wi-Fi (for a fee), a service that can best be described as intermittent. This *Wi-Fi* can also be accessed by boats in *Bahia Almodovar* and the *Dikity* anchorage

Take a walk up the hill and you'll come to *The Barefoot Contessa*, a nice little art and gift shop. Here, too, you'll find *La Loma* for more gifts and such. At this point you are on the main road where, if you take a left, you'll come to the lift-bridge. Just before the lift bridge, on the right, is a small street leading to *Mamacita's*, another popular Culebra institution (http://www.mamacitasguesthouse.com/). Almost next to *Mamacita's* is *Mrs. Rosita's Cafe*, open 0600-1800. Continue on past to where this small road dead ends, take a left and immediate right and the yellow building on your right is home to *eXcetera*, where you can use the phones in air-conditioned comfort, surf the net, or avail yourself of their fax and copy services, shipping services, and even their drop-off laundry service! They have a nice selection of books and magazine as well as some dry goods and office products.

When you cross the bridge you'll find a *Fire Station* on your right with a public telephone. Take the first left and you'll find the *Dinghy Dock Restaurant and Bar* (yes, it has its own dinghy dock and you can tie up there also), a very popular hangout with the cruising crowd. The *Dinghy Dock* has daily happy hours from 1500-1800 and a special Sunday morning cruiser's breakfast at 0800 (free *Wi-Fi* too). You can also get free *Wi-Fi* at the town center and library. Across from the library is the *El Eden Restaurant* with fresh baguettes and homemade lasagna (http://www.eledenculebra.com/). Across from the *Post Office* and next to the veggie market (open Tuesdays and Fridays) is *Vibra Verde*, a very nice health food store.

If you opt to take a right from the *Contessa*, you'll come to *Rafy's*, a nice supermarket and the oldest building in town. On the left side of the street here keep an eye out (and have your camera ready) for the small pink cement house whose yard is filled with hundreds of ceramic statues, painted tires, coral, rocks, and even plastic gorillas. Don't miss it!

Another option is to dinghy up the small creek under the lift-bridge to tie up by the gas station (diesel and gasoline) on the southern side of the creek (keep an eye out for *Mamacita's* and *Mrs. Rosita's* docks right on the water's edge to starboard). Here, too, is a great little hardware store (*Joe's*) and the newly opened *El Pescador*, a good spot for local food. Walking back towards the anchorage and the lift bridge, you'll come to a nice grocery store on your left (with a nice meat department) and the *Fire Station* just up the hill to your right. On the same side of the creek as the gas station is a small haul-out yard for shallow draft vessels and small sailboats. Entrance is from the west at *Bahia de Sardinas*.

At the outer end of the small creek is the ferry dock for the ferry from Fajardo. Next door is *Ricky's* where you can get groceries, gasoline, and liquor. On the same road as *Ricky's* is *Culebra Diver's*, *On Island* (a lovely gift shop), the *Hotel Kokomo* (http://culebra-kokomo.com/), and *Marta's Al Fresco* for drinks and snacks. Across the street (*Mayaguez Street*) is a small plaza where local bands often set up on holidays and special occasions.

The Dewey municipal building is in the *Alcaldia*, the white building on the hill next to the plaza. Just up from here is *Banco Popular* (closed Tuesdays and Sundays) with an *ATM*. Take a left at the *Police Station* and you'll come to the *Civic Center*, the *Felipe Serrano Center* and the *Medical Clinic* (rebuilt after Hurricane Hugo in 1989). Across the street from the *Police Station* is *Hart's Oasis* with its gaily painted door by local artist Mark Wilken. *Hart's* has a nice bar and serves great food including pizza. Just up the street is the *Post Office* for Culebra. Next to *Hart's* is *Ramona Fashion*. *Oasis* serves up great pizzas and Italian food, their small pizza could easily pass for large.

Navigational Information

Okay, now that we've explored Dewey, let's take a circumnavigation of Culebra and see what we can find. Leaving the entrance to *Ensenada Honda* keep R "8" to port and pass between G "5" and R "6" as shown on Chart SVI-6. After you clear R "6" you can turn to port pass between the mainland of Culebra and *Arrecife Culebrita* off your starboard side. Be sure that you keep R "4" well to starboard also as it marks the reef. You are now in *Canal del Sur* and you can head for a waypoint (but PLEASE keep an eye out through here) at 18° 18.05' N, 65° 14.50' W, which places you southeast of the entrance to *Puerto Manglar*, a nice anchorage when the wind is north of southeast (see Chart SVI-7).

There is SW/NE current in *Canal del Sur* that has been reported to run as high as 2 knots. A great anchorage lies just south of *Puerto Manglar* in *Bahia*

Almodovar as shown on Chart SVI-7. From Bahia Manglar head towards the western shore of the bay and parallel it south in 10' of water inside the tiny island shown as Pela. You can anchor in a very calm little cove in 11' of water over sand or pick up one of the moorings there. Sometimes there are red and green markers here, but they are unreliable; the last time I anchored there they were missing. Intermittent *Wi-Fi* service is available here.

Continuing around Culebra give the rocks off Cabeza del Pero a wide berth and you will be entering the Canal de Culebrita and see Isla de Culebrita just off your starboard bow. You can anchor in the lee of the island on its western shore, but this is generally a settled weather anchorage only as there always seems to be a bit of surge between Culebra and Culebrita and Cayo Norte. South of Cayo Botella is a small cove, actually little more than a pocket in the rocks to the east, where you can make a short stop for snorkeling in settled weather.

You can round Cayo Botella, the small island lying northwest of Isla de Culebrita, and head to the anchorage inside the small cove at the northern side of the island called *Bahia de Tortuga*. Keep well off Cayo Botella and the reefs between it and Isla de Culebrita and head southeastward into the small cove as shown on Chart SVI-7. If you're not comfortable with this, head to a waypoint at 18° 19.90' N, 65° 13.95' W, and then southward into the anchorage. This is a great anchorage (not tenable in northerly swells). There are several free moorings available in *Bahia de Tortuga*.

Isla de Culebrita

Important Lights:
Isla Culebrita: Fl W 10 sec

Waypoints:
Isla de Culebrita - ¾ nm N of anchorage:
18° 19.90' N, 65° 13.95' W

Canal de Cayo Norte - 1 nm NW of:
18° 21.00' N, 65° 17.35' W

Bahia Flamenco - ½ nm N of:
18° 20.70' N, 65° 18.90' W

Navigational Information
Continuing around Culebra and paralleling the shore, you'll enter the *Canal de Cayo Norte* separating Cayo Norte and Isla de Culebrita. There are only two anchorages of note off Cayo Norte, the first is in a small cove behind the reef on the southeastern end of the island as shown on Chart SVI-7. You should anchor in the patch of white sand in 15' of water either north or south of the southernmost dock. Don't anchor in the darker water to the west, it is a reef and you'll only destroy it. In light prevailing conditions this can be used as an overnight stop, but the other anchorage off the western shore should only be considered for daytime use in light prevailing conditions.

What You Will Find Ashore
Isla de Culebrita, a wildlife refuge, is one of the most beautiful islands surrounding Culebra and is open to the public for daytime use. There are 6 beaches ringing the island including *Tortuga* at the northeastern tip of the island. *Tortuga* is home to *The Jacuzzis*, an area of dark boulders and natural pools. *The Jaccuzzis* are filled with water that works its way through the rocks on the NE tip of the island, forced into the pool by seas from the east.

A stop at Isla de Culebrita would not be complete without a hike up to the century old lighthouse (built in 1880) to sample its impressive view. Sitting 305' above the water, the light sits atop a stone-colored cylindrical tower with red trim. You can't miss it folks, it's the only one there. Currently the lighthouse has a fence around it so entry is not permitted.

There's good snorkeling off *Playa Zoni* which you'll find on Culebra directly south of Cayo Norte as shown on Chart SVI-7. You'll find good beachcombing in the large cove on the eastern shore of Isla de Culebrita. If you'd like a guided snorkeling tour of Isla de Culebrita, Culebra, Cayo Luis Pena, and Carlos Rosario, call Capt. Pat Lerocque at 787-501-0011. Capt. Pat has a glass bottom boat called *Tanama* and she'll be happy to share her special knowledge of Culebra with you.

Navigational Information
Leaving Cayo Norte and heading northwestward along the shoreline of Culebra you will come to several small bays with beaches, the absolute best one however is *Bahia de Flamenco* and it should not be missed. As shown on Chart SVI-8, a waypoint at 18° 20.70' N, 65° 18.90' W, will place you approximately ¼ mile north of the entrance to the bay. Entrance is fairly straightforward passing between the reef off Punta Flamenco to port and the huge reef to starboard. Once inside head as far in as you can to anchor off the beach in 7'-15' of water.

The anchorage at Bahia de Tortuga, Isla de Culebrita — Photo by Michelle Rexach

Cruisers enjoying *The Jaccuzzis*, Bahia de Tortuga, Isla de Culebrita — Photo by Michelle Rexach

The Spanish Virgin Islands

What You Will Find Ashore

Flamenco Beach, unforgettable and gorgeous, is named after the pink flamingos that once nested in the nearby cove. If you don't feel like taking your boat there, or if a northerly swell makes the anchorage untenable, you can take a publico from

Dewey. Either way, when you arrive be sure to explore the two wrecked tanks, reminders of the U.S. military occupation of the island. *Flamenco Beach* was closed to swimming temporarily in 1993 because many mainland Puerto Ricans were coming over and getting drunk and stoned and the locals put a stop to this after a teenage girl was raped. But, that was then and this is now, what happened almost a decade ago is no longer a problem...do not miss a trip to *Flamenco Beach*. As a side note, the anchorage can be a bit rolly, even uncomfortable at times.

Navigational Information

Continuing towards the northwestern tip of Isla de Culebra, give Punta de Molinas a wide berth as you round the small off-lying islands past Punta Noroeste as shown on Chart SVI-4. *Carlos Rosario Beach* on the northwestern side of Culebra (just north of Punta Tamarindo Grande as shown on Chart SVI-4) is one of the best snorkeling spots on the island. There are several new moorings here that are available for your use. Also known as *Impact Beach*, snorkelers will find a natural channel that slices through the reef at the right side of the beach creating a vertical wall of coral 15' down to a white sand bottom. But possibly the best snorkeling in all of Culebra is a place called *The Wall*, a mile of blazing colors that begins ¼ mile past Carlos Rosario and heads toward Punta Flamenco.

Off the northwestern tip of Culebra lie several small islands such as Alcarraza, Piedra Stevens, and Los Gemelos (see Chart SVI-4). Alcarraza, a 144' high, bare, rounded rock with perpendicular sides and a whitish appearance is very conspicuous.

What You Will Find Ashore

The U. S. Navy advises that since Isla de Culebra and the islands in the vicinity were once used as naval sea and air weapons targets, unexploded ordnance remaining from previous target practice presents a hazard in the area of the northwestern peninsula of Isla de Culebra. The areas of concern lie north of a line running between 18° 19.90' N, 65°18.95' W, and 18°19.50' N, 65° 14.50' W, and within the immediate offshore vicinity including Alcarraza, Cayo Botella, Cayo Lobo, Cayo Tiburon, Cayos Geniqui, Los Gemelos and Cabo del Pasaje. Divers are advised to exercise extreme caution in the area.

As a final note on Culebra, though I don't show it on my charts, roughly 2-4 miles from the southeast extremity of Isla de Culebra you will find *Bajos Grampus*, a group of coral heads rising from a bank of 60'. The bank has a least depth of about 23' and is an excellent spot for fishing.

Isla de Vieques

Important Lights:
Puerto Rico to Vieques
Isla Cabras, range-F, 025.4°: Q W
Isla Cabras, range-R, 025.4°: Iso W 6 sec
Pasaje de Vieques, buoy #2: Fl R 2.5 sec
Pasaje de Vieques, buoy #3: Fl G 2.5 sec
Pasaje de Vieques, buoy #6: Fl R 2.5 sec
Radas Roosevelt, buoy #11: Fl G 4 sec
Radas Roosevelt, buoy #10: Fl R 4 sec
Radas Roosevelt, buoy #9: Fl G 4 sec
Radas Roosevelt, buoy #8: Fl R 2.5 sec
Radas Roosevelt, buoy #7: Fl G 6 sec
Radas Roosevelt, buoy #6: Q R
Radas Roosevelt, buoy #5: Q G
Radas Roosevelt, buoy #3: FL G 2.5 sec
Radas Roosevelt, buoy #2: Fl R 4 sec
Radas Roosevelt, buoy #1: Fl G 6 sec
Vieques, Naval Pier lights (2): F R
Vieques, Naval breakwater light: Q R
Vieques, Punta Mulas light: Oc R 4 sec
Vieques, Punta Este light: Fl W 6 sec
Vieques, Punta Conejo light: Fl W 6 sec
Vieques, Puerto Ferro light: Fl W 4 sec

Spanish Virgin Islands to St. Thomas
Sail Rock #1: Fl G 6s
Savana Island Light: Fl W 4s

Vieques (Chart SVI-9) is sometimes called *La Isla Nina* (*Daughter Island*-referring to its relationship with the larger island of Puerto Rico). The name Vieques actually comes from the Arawak (Taino) Indian word *bieques* meaning *small island*. The Spanish called Vieques and her neighboring islands *Las Islas Inutiles, The Useless Islands*.

The little that we know about Vieques' pre-Columbian inhabitants is derived from archaeological findings at La Hueca, where artifacts made in amethyst, agate, turquoise and jadeite were found. The most remarkable ones were shaped like South American condors (remember, the *Tainos* originally ventured northward through the Caribbean from their origins in Venezuela). When the Spanish arrived, conquering and enslaving the *Tainos*, two brave brother *Caciques* (Chiefs) in Vieques, Cacimar and Yaureibo, lead separate revolutions against the Spaniards, but they were soon defeated and killed and what was left of the *Taino* population was reduced to slavery and taken to Puerto Rico.

After the Tainos were removed from Vieques, a succession of periods of colonization began. The English, French, and Dutch attempted to set up colonies on Vieques, but were thwarted by the Puerto Rican Spaniards. Vieques was allegedly also used by pirates as a re-supply stop for their vessels as there was an abundance of fish, birdlife, and timber here at that time.

The Spaniards decided to colonize Vieques in the early 1800s. In 1843, the construction of the fort was begun and Vieques had its first governor, Don Teofilo Jaime Maria LeGuillou, a Frenchman. At the time, Vieques was independent from Puerto Rico. Puerto Rico annexed the island in 1854 and during the latter part of the 19th century, Vieques saw a great economic boom in the sugar industry as black slaves were brought in from the neighboring British islands and several sugar mills began operations. Their names of these sugar mills were eventually adopted for the barrios: Playa Grande, Santa Maria, Puerto Real, Esperanza. Then, by the time the United States took over Vieques in 1898, there were 4 big *centrales* (major sugar mills). As was the story throughout the Caribbean at that time, sugar made a few families rich while most of the population of Vieques worked on the fields in oppressive conditions.

In 1898, the American gunboat *Yale* arrived with Lt. Cont and his men. The locals feared that the crew of the *Yale* would eat their babies, and when they realized that the crew were not cannibals tensions eased. When asked to surrender the fort, the Commander told Lt. Cont that he could not surrender without firing a shot, so Lt. Cont graciously allowed him to fire a volley into the air. In 1941, the U.S. Navy arrived on Vieques. At that time Vieques had 10,362 inhabitants and those people produced over 8,000 tons of sugar that year. The U. S. Navy immediately purchased over 2/3 of the island of Vieques including most of the land used for farming. *La Central Playa Grande* did its last milling that year as the sugar industry waned.

During the first couple of years after the Navy arrived, there were plenty of jobs in Vieques in the construction of the bases as folks came from all over Puerto Rico and the Virgin Islands to work in Vieques.

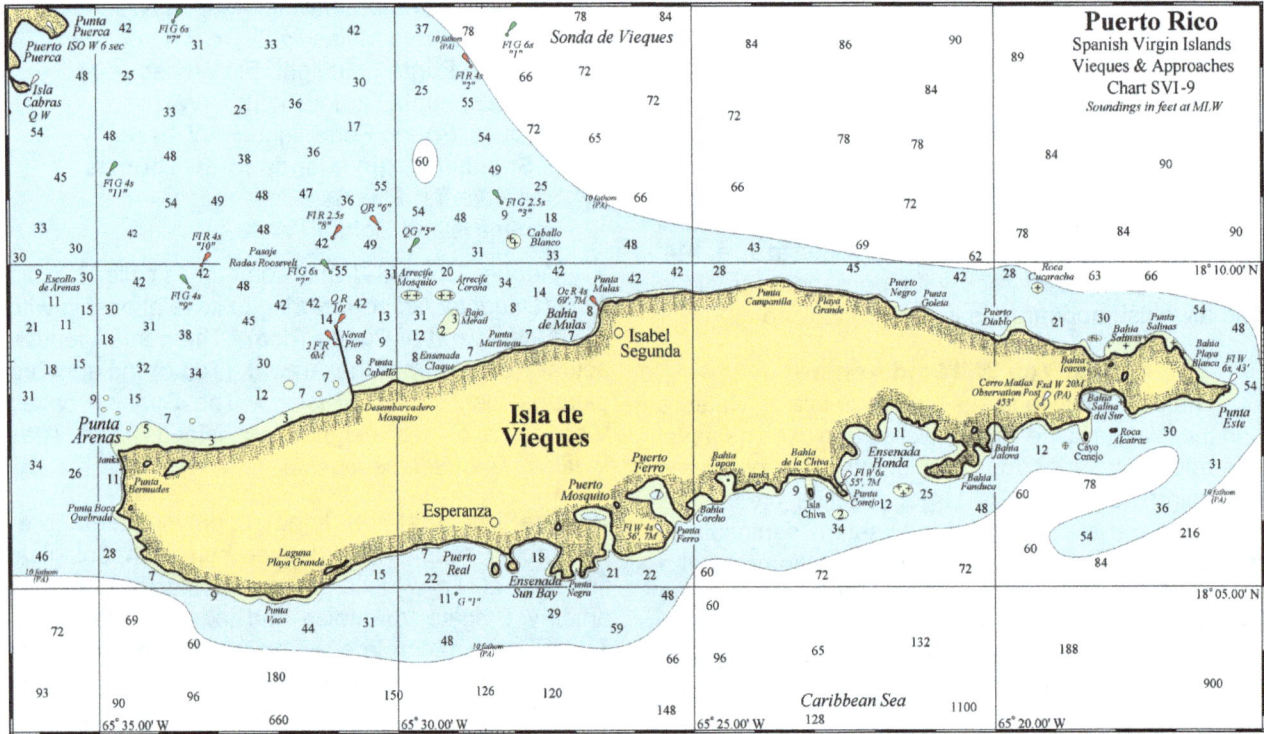

When the dust from the rapid construction settled, some 3,000 of the inhabitants of Vieques had been relocated to St. Croix. The rest were settled in the areas of Santa Maria and Monte Santo in Vieques. The economy was in a shambles as there was no sugar and no construction. The government of Puerto Rico valiantly tried to re-establish an agricultural based economy on the island between 1945 and the mid-1960s in the civilian sections of Vieques, but to no avail. A bit of an economic boost occurred when *General Electric* opened a plant there in 1969.

For the last couple of decades Vieques has been quite a hot topic in Puerto Rico, thanks to the United States military. The U.S. Navy continued to occupy and use the area for aerial and naval bombardment. There was a constant battle between the U.S. military and those that oppose the misuse of Vieques and demanded that all military actions cease. In 2001, the U.S. Navy reconsidered, and in 2003 the bombing on Vieques ceased.

What You Will Find Ashore

The island of Vieques is approximately 21 miles long and 3½ miles wide at its middle region. A range of hills runs the length of the island with a prominent hill at each end; Monte Pirata is at the western end and Cerro Matias is near the eastern end. The principal products are horses and cattle while vegetables and tropical fruits are grown mostly for local consumption. Today the population of Vieques hovers around 10,000 and unemployment is high. The tourism industry is in some early stages of development and offers promise.

Vieques lies roughly 7 miles off the eastern shore of Puerto Rico, but is quite further away in ambiance, Vieques is quite laid back. Where as Puerto Rico can be hustle and bustle, Vieques feels barefoot and manana. If you wish to explore the island by land, the distance is short between the two main towns, Isabel Segunda in the north, and Esperanza in the south, but beware when driving, you'll share the road with chickens, horses, and goats. What you won't find in Vieques is *McDonald's*, *Wal Mart*, *KFC*, traffic lights, and all the other trappings of civilization on the Puerto Rican mainland. What you will find is several exquisite beaches, drivers who stop to greet other drivers, wild horses, a bioluminescent cove, rolling green hills, and the last fort built by the Spanish in the New World (*Fort Conde de Mirasol*, which has been totally restored and is now a museum), the *Esperanza Museum*, and three art galleries.

Getting around on Vieques is not difficult, there are several car rental companies on the island (see *Appendix C*), as well as *publicos* and a couple of bicycle rentals available as well (*DYMC* at 316-2617, and *La Dulce Vida* at 617-BIKE). There are no taxis per se in Vieques and the *publicos* are quite inexpensive. The fares are (as of this writing), $2 one-way anywhere in the civilian area, $5 one-way anywhere in the military area, and $5 for a tour of the lighthouse, the fort, and *Sun Bay Beach* in Esperanza. You can make arrangements with any of the drivers to pick you up at specified times.

If you wish to keep your mother vessel in Fajardo and visit Vieques another way, you can catch the ferry from the docks at Puerto Real on the mainland of Puerto Rico. The ferries to Vieques cost $2.00 per person, one-way. Monday through Friday the ferries leave Puerto Real (Fajardo) at 0930, 1300, and 1630 and leave Vieques for Puerto Real at 0700, 1100, and 1500. On the weekends they leave Puerto Real at 0900, 1500, and 1800, and depart Vieques at 0700, 1300, and 1630. You can also transport a car on the ferry, but for the price involved it would be cheaper to visit Vieques and rent a car there. For more information you can phone the *Fajardo Port Authority* at 800-981-2005, or in call the port in Vieques at 741-4761.

CAUTION: As of this writing, Summer of 2016, the beaches on the E end of Vieques on the N and S coasts are off limits to cruisers due to ordinance removal.

Navigational Information

Now that we've gotten the basics out of the way, let's explore Vieques. We'll start from the western end of the island as it lies only about 7 nautical miles southeast of Fajardo. We'll then visit the northern shore, the eastern point, and save the southern shore for last. If you intend to circumnavigate the island from Puerto Rico, this is the way to do it, heading with the prevailing winds and currents along the more exposed southern shore...although the northern shore takes a pounding during the season of winter northers and northerly swells.

A Cruising Guide to the Virgin Islands

Punta Arenas

Waypoints:
Punta Arenas - 1¼ nm NW of point:
18° 07.80' N, 65° 35.70' W

Punta Arenas - ½ nm W of anchorage:
18° 06.80' N, 65° 35.00' W

A waypoint at 18° 06.80' N, 65° 35.00' W, will place you approximately ½ mile west of the western shore of Vieques. Pick a spot to anchor and settle in. The only hazard on this route is *Escollo de Arenas* that stretches north/northwest of Punta Arenas for about 1½ miles. At the northwestern tip of this shoal the ater can be 9' deep, but closer in, generally south of 18° 08.00' N, you'll find several spots that only have 5'-6' of water over them. Scattered shoals stretch eastward for miles to Punta Mulas along the northern shore and up to almost 1 mile offshore to the north. If heading eastward along this shore, give it a wide berth, about 2 miles. The waters of the shoal are generally un-sounded and there are several wrecks and a lot of debris to contend with, it is better to just avoid it completely. I usually head to latitude 18° 09.00' N - 18° 09.50' N before turning to the east, but that's just me, I like to avoid trouble if I can. Bear in mind that there is a good bit of current off the northern end of *Escollo de Arenas* that sets southwest.

The best anchorage on the western coast of Vieques is just off the lovely beach known as *Green Beach*, about ½ mile south of Punta Arenas (good diving can be found off the beach). Another good spot is south of the old dock. The bottom holding is iffy here, grass interspersed with rocky ledges, but the water is quite clear and it's easy to see your anchor.

Punta Arenas to Isabel Segunda

Waypoints:
Isabel Segunda - 1 nm NW of Bahia de Mulas:
18° 09.80' N, 65° 27.50' W

Navigational Information

As you head generally east/northeast for Punta Mulas (see Chart SVI-11) from the northern tip of *Escollo de Arenas,* you'll notice several buoys marking the deep ship channel of *Radas Roosevelt* as shown on Chart SVI-11 (the tide in this passage floods southwest and ebbs northeast at about .7 knot). The prudent mariner would likely follow these markers until past G "5" when you can take up a course to the waypoint 1 mile northwest of Punta Mulas at 18° 09.80' N, 65° 27.50' W (shown in greater detail on Chart SVI-9). On this route you'll notice the long concrete naval pier jutting northward from Vieques far out into *Sonda de Vieques*. This 300' long finger pier was built to shelter the English fleet in the event England should fall to Germany in World War II. The jetty was once used to load sugar cane for transport to Puerto Rico and is now used to bring supplies over from *Roosevelt Roads*. Archeological digs are now being conducted near the pier. Twelve feet can be taken to the outer end of the pier with depths of 4' and more the entire length of the pier.

From the waypoint, head generally southeast keeping Punta Mulas on your port bow as you head towards the dock at Isabel Segunda. Anchor wherever your draft allows south of the ferry dock, but don't block the ferry dock. Be advised that this can be an extremely rolly anchorage and decide whether or not you wish to stay here and explore or anchor later off Esperanza and take rent a car or take a *publico* from there for your exploration. Tie up the dinghy to the small fishing dock to the north or simply land it on the beach to avail yourself of the facilities here.

The Spanish Virgin Islands

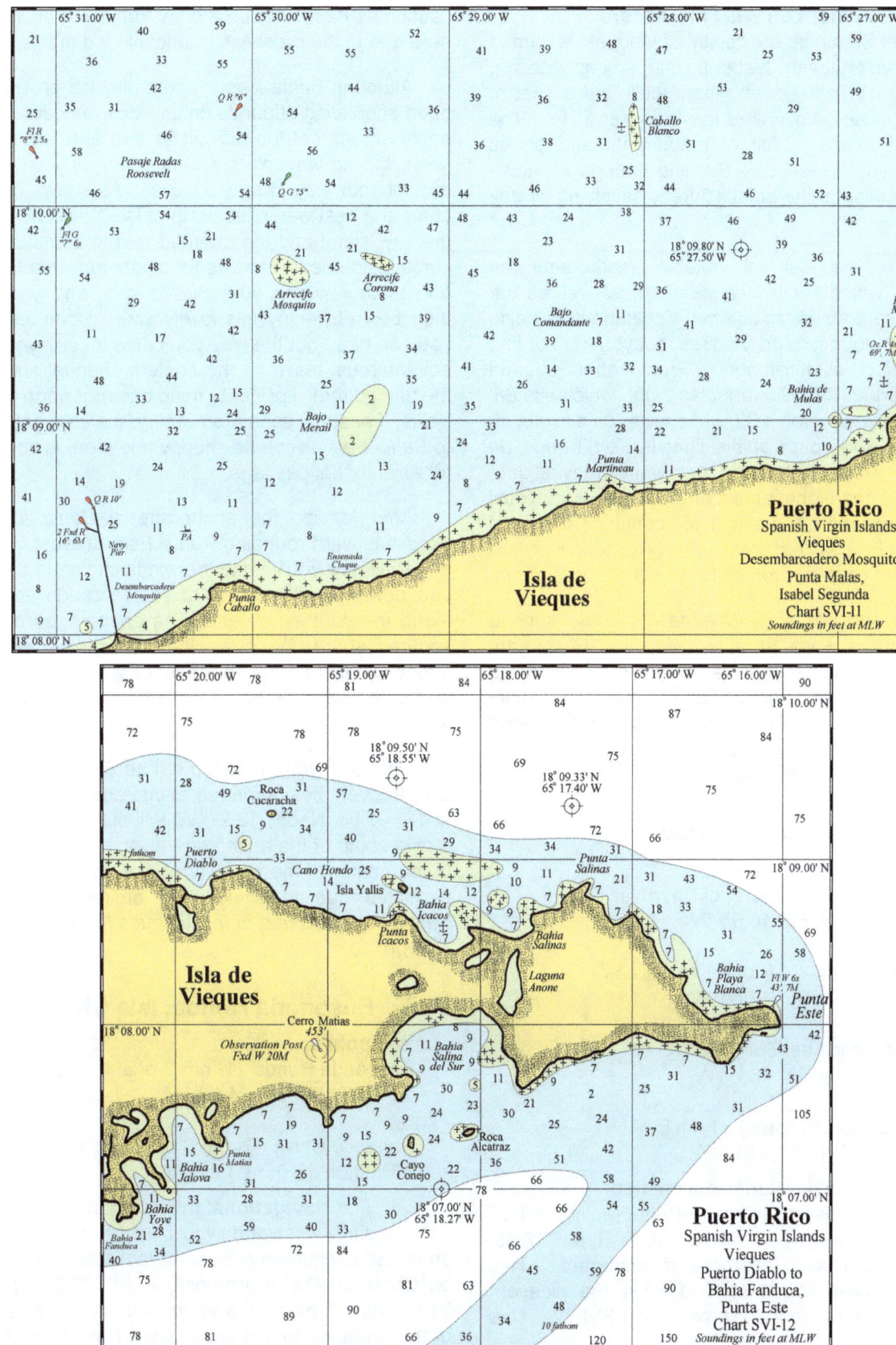

53

What You Will Find Ashore

Isabel Segunda, the capital of Vieques, is named after Spain's Queen, Isabel II, and is simply oozing with charm. In the town plaza you'll find a bust of Simon Bolivar who visited the island in 1816. The traditional plaza is full of restaurants and shops awaiting your presence. Strolling through the town and marveling at the architecture is satisfying by day or night.

There are several notable restaurants on Vieques, which serve local seafood, as well as the ever-present American cuisine. Vegetarians can also find sumptuous fare on Vieques, but you will not find any fast food establishments. From Isabel Segunda it's a short walk to *Punta Mulas Light*, which sits 68' above the water atop a 32' white tower on a low bluff. About ½ mile south of the light is *Fort Conde de Mirasol*. Treasure hunters may want to investigate *Mt. Pirata*, the highest point on Vieques. Here you'll find a cave where it is said a 16th century *Taino* chief hid his tribe's sacred treasures. The roar that you hear in the cave is rumored to be is the chief's ghost.

Near the plaza is *Taverna Espanola* serving ethnic dishes while *St. John's Bar and Restaurant* has seafood and daily specials. *Nelson's Cafe* serves tacos and burritos and *El Palomar* offers a special Sunday breakfast. The *Crow's Nest* sits on a forested hillside about 1½ miles east of Isabel Segunda and offers good food with a view.

Bahia Icacos

Waypoints:
Bahia Icacos - ¾ nm N of Cayo Yallis:
18° 09.50' N, 65° 18.55' W

Bahia Icacos - ½ N of Punta Salinas:
18° 09.33' N, 65° 17.40' W

Bahia Salina del Sur - ½ nm S of:
18° 07.00' N, 65° 18.27 W

Punta Este (Vieques) - 1 nm E of:
18° 08.10' N. 65° 14.90' W

Navigational Information

Heading east again round Punta Mulas well off and head for a waypoint at 18° 09.50' N, 65° 18.55' W, keeping Roca Cucaracha to starboard. This waypoint gives you a start to enter the pleasant anchorage in *Bahia Icacos* (see Chart SVI-12). Use caution as there may be a buoy forbidding anchoring here due to the presence of unexploded ordinance.

Although *Bahia Icacos* offers only fair protection, good snorkeling abounds on all sides. Access to the anchorage is not too difficult as the reefs are easily seen, but no waypoints will be given as you'll have to pilot your way in on your own. As shown on the chart, the best water lies north of Isla Yallis, between the tiny island and the unamed reef to its northeast. Once inside head towards the shore in *Bahia Icacos* and anchor where your draft allows and you can then begin to enjoy this lovely spot. Upon leaving, you can head out the way you came in, or if you feel adventurous, leave by the eastern channel south of the named reef. I prefer to head back out north of Isla Yallis, if easterly seas are running, the east entrance to *Bahia Salinas* can be choppy and there is no room for error in that passage.

After leaving the anchorage at *Bahia Icacos*, head eastward rounding Punte Este at least ¼ mile off. Until now you've had the winds and seas against you, now they will help you as you proceed westward along the southern coast. The anchorages on the southern shore of Vieques offer great spots to ride out strong winds from the northeast-east as are common during the winter months. Northerly swells will not affect you here.

Normally, your first stop will be *Bahia Salina del Sur*, a lovely beach-fringed anchorage. A waypoint at 18° 07.00' N, 65° 18.27' W, will place you roughly 1 mile south of the anchorage area, however a buoy in the center of the bay warns that anchoring is not permitted due to unexploded ordinance! *Bahia Salina del Sur* is part of the *Vieques National Wildlife Refuge*.

Ensenada Honda, Isla Chiva

Waypoints:
Ensenada Honda - ½ nm S of entrance:
18° 06.05' N, 65° 21.90' W

Bahia de Chiva - ¼ nm S of entrance:
18° 06.05' N, 65° 23.35' W

Navigational Information

Heading westward you'll come to the well-protected anchorage at *Ensenada Honda*. As shown on Chart SVI-13, a waypoint at 18° 06.05' N, 65° 21.90' W, will place you approximately 1 mile south of the entrance to this large bay. The entrance will

The Spanish Virgin Islands

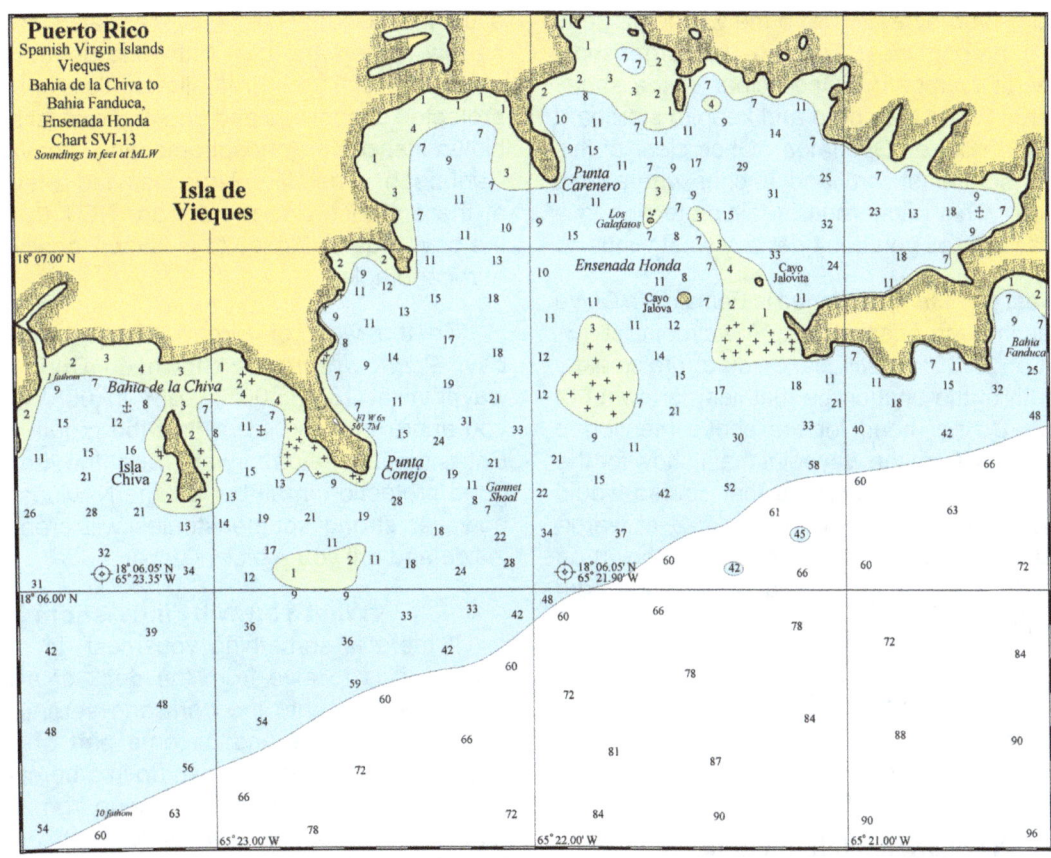

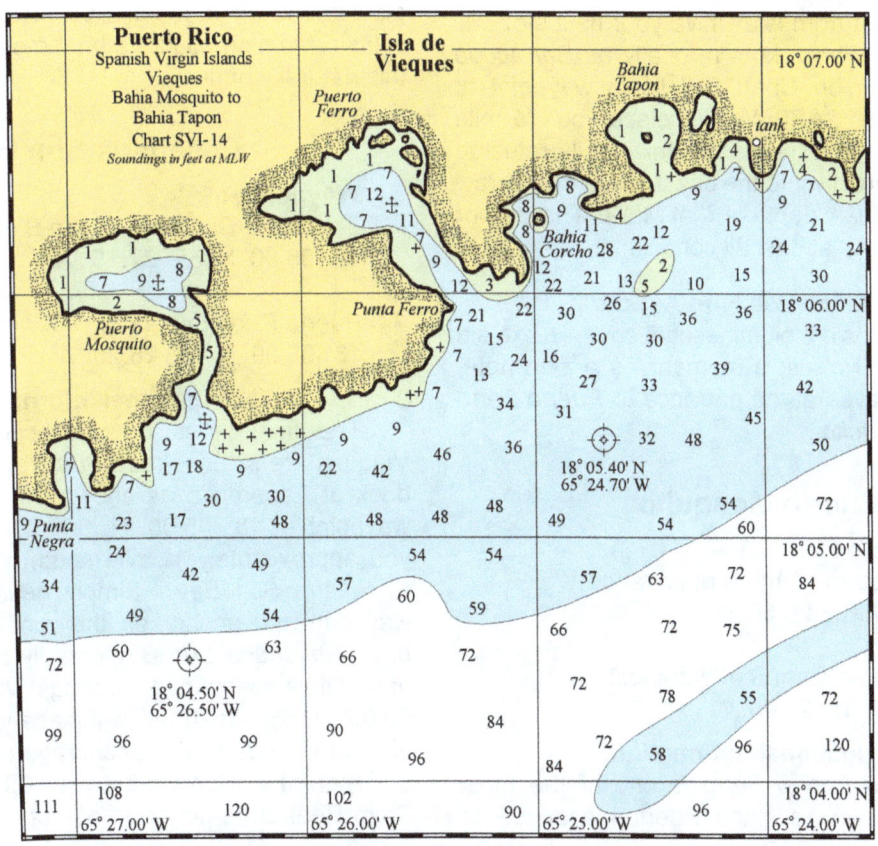

55

have to be piloted by eye. From the waypoint, head generally north/northwest keeping the large shoal shown well to starboard. Once clear of the shoal, head towards Punta Carenero and keep to starboard the shoal north of Los Galafatos. Once clear of this shoal head southeastward and anchor wherever it pleases you. This anchorage is fair protection in a hurricane as long as you don't get any west winds.

Just west of *Ensenada Honda* is *Bahia de la Chiva* with two anchorage possibilities. A waypoint at 18° 06.05' N, 65° 23.35' W, will place you approximately ½ mile south of the anchorage that lies northwest of Isla Chiva. Do not head for the above mentioned waypoint directly from the waypoint that I show for the entrance to *Ensenada Honda* as that course would take you right over a shoal with only 1'-2' of water. You can also anchor east of Isla Chiva as shown on the chart. Both anchorages are good in winds from west through north to southeast.

Puerto Ferro

Waypoints:
Puerto Ferro - ½ nm SE of entrance:
18° 05.40' N, 65° 24.70' W

Navigational Information
Heading west from Isla Chiva your next stop will likely be *Puerto Ferro*, known locally as *Barracuda Bay*. As shown on Chart SVI-14, a waypoint at 18° 05.40' N, 65° 24.70' W, will place you ½ mile southeast of the entrance to this well-protected harbor. Head directly into the bay through the narrow entrance with a least depth of 7' at MLW. This harbor offers protection in almost all conditions.

What You Will Find Ashore
Puerto Ferro is a bioluminescent cove, I'll explain what that means in just a moment. s a side note, check out the caves at the entrance to *Puerto Ferro* and *Puerto Mosquito*.

Puerto Mosquito

Waypoints:
Puerto Mosquito - 1 nm S of entrance:
18° 04.50' N, 65° 26.50' W

Puerto Negro - ¼ nm S of entrance:
18° 05.00' N, 65° 27.00' W

Navigational Information
Just west of *Puerto Ferro* is one of the most spectacular bays on the island, Puerto Mosquito. As shown on Chart SVI-14, the entrance is through a narrow dogleg and the controlling depth is almost 5' at MLW. But if your draft allows, it's a beautiful, well-protected anchorage and one of the most spectacular bioluminescent (phosphorescent) bays in the Caribbean. The *DPNR* has installed a few moorings at the entrance and motors are NOT to be used in the bay. Puerto Mosquito is known locally as a good hurricane hole.

To the west of *Puerto Mosquito* is a smaller bay, *Puerto Negro* as shown on Chart SVI-15. A waypoint at 18° 05.00' N, 65° 27.00' W, will place you approximately ¼ nm S of the mouth of the bay. Entrance is straightforward and the harbor offers good protection in all but southerly winds and seas, however strong southeasterlies will create a surge inside and roll you a bit.

What You Will Find Ashore
If there is something you must do during your lifetime, it is to dive from the deck of a boat on a moonless night into the dark and serene waters of one of these bays and become part of the magic. You will see the water splash up in a burst of millions of lights as if fireworks were sent up from the depths. As you glide through the water you develop and eerie glow and when you resurface, thousands of sparkling lights remain on you for a brief moment. Do not miss this natural wonder.

Ensenada Sun Bay

Waypoints:
Ensenada Sun Bay - ¼ nm S of:
18° 05.00' N. 65° 27.75' W

Puerto Real, Esperanza - ¼ nm S of entrance:
18° 05.00' N, 65° 28.28' W

Navigational Information
The final stops on your circumnavigation of Vieques are in *Ensenada Sun Bay* and off the town dock at Esperanza as shown on Chart SVI-15. A waypoint at 18° 05.00' N, 65° 27.75' W, will place you approximately ¼ mile south of the entrance to *Ensenada Sun Bay*. Simply head north from the waypoint and anchor on the windward side of the bay. *Ensenada Sun Bay* proudly boasts a new set of privately maintained moorings. A waypoint at 18° 05.00' N, 65° 28.28' W, will place you ¼ mile south of the entrance to the anchorage off the town dock at Esperanza. Head in between Cayo de Tierra and Cayo Real and anchor so as not to block the dock.

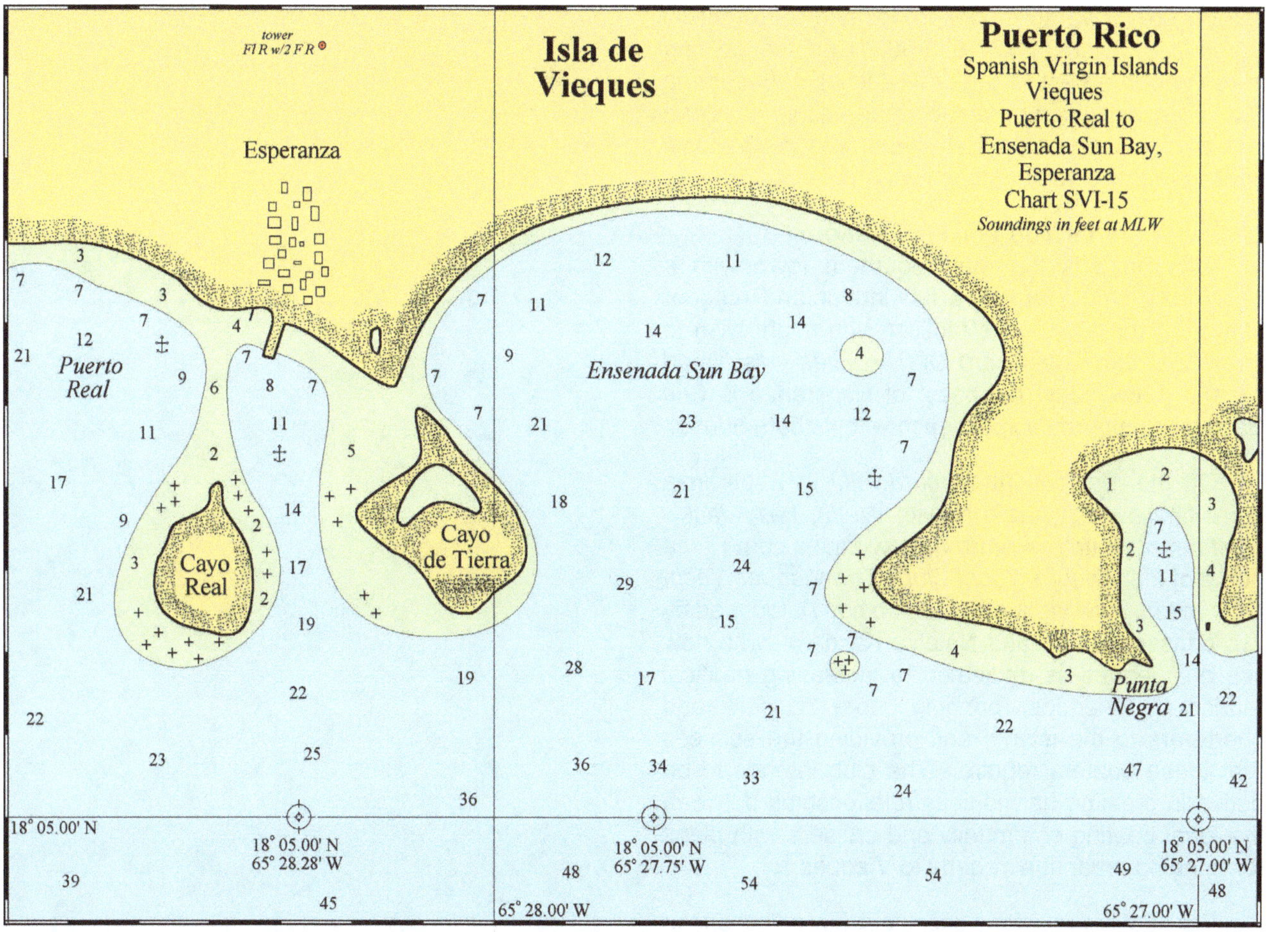

The Spanish Virgin Islands

Explosive ordinance sign, Vieques
Photo by Michelle Rexach

The beach at *Ensenada Sun Bay*, Vieques

THere are several moorings located here(phone Chrstina or Glen at 787-930-0831) as the holding here is not the best. I prefer to anchor in *Ensenada Sun Bay* and dinghy over to Esperanza. You can also anchor west of Cayo Real just west of the town dock though it's sometimes rolly here.

What You Will Find Ashore

Esperanza is the main southern town with a beachfront strip that offers fun indoor and outdoor dining. If the area looks familiar, you might wish to know that the movie *Lord Of The Flies* was filmed here in 1963. Just northeast of Esperanza is *Sun Bay Beach*, the municipal beach with its bath house.

On the *Malecon (*the *Boardwalk)* in Esperanza you'll find a great pizzeria (with *Wi-Fi*), *Lazy Jack's Restaurant* (http://www.lazyjacksvieques.com/), the home of the *Vieques Yacht Club*. The *Vieques Yacht Club* (http://www.viequesyachtclub.com/), founded by two cruisers, Stuart and Natalya Kaydash, who now live on Vieques, is dedicated to increasing nautical tourism in Vieques, bringing more cruisers and charterers to the island, and providing the services that these boaters require. The club intends to be active in creating harmonious relationships between the local boating community and cruisers with plans for bringing an annual regatta to Vieques.

For quality provisions check out *Buen Provencho* on the main street, about a block from *Banco Popular*. On Wednesday's and Fridays there is a fresh produce market on the N side of *Nale's Ferretería*. If you need help with provisioning call Christina at 787-930-0831 for help or for an overnight mooring. In town is a large *Morales* grocery store. *Lydia's* also has groceries and is located on a side street just down from the *Trade Winds Restaurant* (http://www.tradewindsvieques.com/).

By the dinghy dock you will find *Bili* (http://bilirestaurant.com/), a very nice restaurant owned by Miguel and Evita, a couple of avid boaters. For provisioning visit Pablo's *Green Store*. If you are in *Sun Bay*, Pablo will be happy to give you a ride to and from the bay. If you need someone to work on your boat or handle jerry jugs of fuel for you, look up Sharkey.

The United States Virgin Islands

Port of Entry:
St. Croix - Christiansted
St. John - Cruz Bay
St. Thomas - Charlotte Amalie
Fuel: St. Croix, St. John, St. Thomas
Haul-Out: St. Croix, St. John, St. Thomas
Diesel Repairs: St. Croix, St. John, St. Thomas
Outboard Repairs: St. Croix, St. John, St. Thomas
Propane: St. Croix, St. John, St. Thomas
Provisions: St. Croix, St. John, St. Thomas

The United States Virgin Islands are made up of some 60 islands, cays, and rocks, with the largest and most populated being St. Thomas, St. John, and St. Croix well to the south. With a population of over 105,000, the USVI are far more densely populated than the Spanish Virgin Islands and the British Virgin Islands together.

St. Thomas and St. John are characteristic volcanic islands complete with sharp peaks, deep valleys, and very indented shorelines. St. Croix on the other hand, lying some 40 miles to the south of the main grouping of islands and separated from them by a deep ocean trench, is less rugged with a few mountains, some rolling hills, and a relatively gentle shoreline.

Most of the Virgin Islands lie on the southern side of the *Virgin Bank*, a large ocean shelf with abrupt drops in depth near its edges. The bank extends in an east/northeast direction for approximately 86 miles from the eastern end of Puerto Rico. For the first 50 miles the bank extends east and averages about 25 miles in width, and then turning east/northeast as it widens to approximately 32 miles. The *Virgin Bank* ends just beyond the southeast point of Anegada. On the southern edge of the *Virgin Bank* lies a narrow ledge of coral, about 200 yards wide and 60'-120' deep, that extends almost unbroken from *Horse Shoe Reef* at Anegada in the British Virgin Islands, to Isla de Vieques in the Spanish Virgin Islands.

Some will argue that St. Croix really is not part of the Virgin Island archipelago because it lies so far south and is not located on the *Virgin Bank*. And while some geologists go so far as to say that St. Croix is not volcanic in origin, politically, St. Croix is indeed part of the United States Virgin Islands.

A Brief History

Although archaeologists have discovered traces of the *Ingeri* (*Ancient People*) civilization in the Virgin Islands dating back to 3,000 B.C., the first real settlers of these islands were the *Arawaks* (the *Tainos*) who inhabited these islands from 650 A.D. until 1450 A.D. Around the early 1400s, the fierce, cannibalistic *Caribs* arrived in the Virgin Islands and wiped out the *Arawaks* becoming the local inhabitants when the Europeans arrived.

As is so often the case in the eastern Caribbean, the first European to sight the Virgin Islands was Christopher Columbus, the *Viceroy of the Indies*, set sail on his second voyage to the New World with a fleet of 17 ships arriving at Dominica and working his way to the northwest along the chain of islands in the eastern Caribbean. After being blown off course by southwesterly winds, Columbus anchored off St. Croix, which he named *Santa Cruz (Holy Cross)* on November 14, 1493, on his second voyage to the New World.

Columbus sent a party ashore, the only landing Columbus and his men would ever make on U.S. soil, and the men of the landing party found only *Arawak* slaves inhabiting the village. Columbus' men promptly stole a slave from the *Caribs* and fled back to their ship.

But hot on their heels were the enraged *Caribs* who sent a war party out to attack the *Niña* in a canoe. When it was over one Spaniard and one Carib lay dead and Columbus, happy to have survived the attack, sailed northeast exploring the United States and British Virgin Islands on his way to Puerto Rico. Columbus named the area *El Cabo de Las Flechas*, the *Cape of the Arrows* for it was a poisoned arrow that killed his crewman, and when Columbus turned his bow to the northeast, lo and behold, he discovered the United States and British Virgin Islands.

Columbus named the numerous islands that lay before him *Las Islas Virgenes* (some scholars say *Las Once Mil Virgines*) for St. Ursula and her 11,000 martyred virgins. Ursula was a Princess, the beautiful daughter of the King of Brittany, who lived sometime in the 3rd - 4th centuries A.D. Her father's kingdom was threatened by a group of Huns and their

Prince asked her father for Ursula's hand in marriage. Ursula, who had taken a solemn vow of chastity and had no intention of marrying the pagan prince, agreed to the union in order to save her father's kingdom, but with one stipulation. She would gather 11,000 virgins from the two kingdoms and live with them for a period of three years. Legend has it that Ursula used those years to train the virgins as an army. The Princess and her 11,000 virgins went on a pilgrimage to Rome to pledge their allegiance there while the angry Hun Prince went to Cologne to await Ursula and her army. Again asking for her hand in marriage, and Ursula again refusing, the Prince and his Huns killed Ursula and her 11,000 virgins companions creating the martyrs for which these islands are named. St. Ursula is the patron saint of maidens and her feast day, though no longer celebrated except in the Virgin Islands, is October 21.

Columbus claimed the islands for Spain who cared little for the islands, preferring instead to concentrate on the richer islands of Puerto Rico and Hispaniola. Even the British passed the islands by for half a century, considering them too dangerous for navigation. However, for the very reasons the Spanish and British shunned the islands, another group found them quite adequate for their needs. The pirates were happy with the hiding places the islands offered just off the shipping routes and many islands in the archipelago bear piratical names.

Little Thatch Island received its name from Blackbeard, Edward Teach, and Norman Island was also the namesake of a buccaneer who is said to have buried Spanish gold on the island. Jost Van Dyke and Bellamy Cay in the British Virgin Islands are also both named after pirate figures.

For over two centuries after Columbus' discovery of the Virgin Islands, the islands themselves were fought over by the Spanish, French, Danes, Dutch, British, with even the *Knights of Malta* having a stake in the Virgin Islands at one time.

In 1625, English and Dutch settlers set up small communities on Santa Cruz, but invading Spaniards drove off the settlers in 1650. The Spanish soon left leaving the island to Lt. General de Poincy of the *French West Indies Company*, who claimed Santa Cruz for the French and renamed it St. Croix. In 1653, St. Croix went bankrupt under the *French West Indies Company* so the French Governor, who had virtually transformed the island into his own private game park, invited the *Knights of Malta* to settle on the island and run her affairs. The *Knights of Malta* in turn soon sold the island back to the French who had all but deserted the island by 1695.

In 1666, the Danes claimed St. Thomas under the auspices of the *Danish West India and Guinea Company*. Within two years, after being ravaged by a hurricane, disease, and English privateers, the colonists returned to Denmark only to return again to St. Thomas in 1671 with a group of 200 settlers, most of whom were prisoners and indentured servants. Almost half of the colonists who set out for St. Thomas died along the way and within six months of their arrival the colony was down to about 30 hardened, strong settlers who established a foothold here and refused to budge.

In 1674, *Fort Christian* had been built and the Danes named their first settlement *Taphaus*, but you know it by its current name, Charlotte Amalie. The Danes quickly set about importing slaves to work on their plantations and in 1685, seeking to import more and more slaves, the Danes signed a treaty with the Dutchy of Brandenburg to allow the *Brandenburg American Company* to establish a slave-trading post on St. Thomas. Dutch planters soon joined their Danish counterparts on St. Thomas as well as settlers from Ireland, England, and Scotland.

The early 18th century saw dramatic growth of the Dutch colony in the Virgin Islands. By 1718, the Danes expanded their settlements to St. John and a fort was constructed in *Coral Bay* by a group of 40 settlers, and in 1733 the *Danish West Indies and Guinea Company* purchased St. Croix from France. The Danes originally attempted to settle in St. John around 1694 when they formally claimed the island, but the British on nearby Tortola prevented any colonization for years.

Within three decades there was to be a massive slave rebellion on St. John, which left the island in the hands of the slaves for over six months. By 1733 there were over 100 plantations on St. John, up from 40 a just a decade earlier, and the slave population then stood at over 1,100, which greatly outnumbered the whites on the island. Several factors contributed to the uprising in 1733. A drought in 1725-1726 caused dissent when water was diverted to the cane fields and plantation homes and away from the slaves quarters and the slave's own little gardens, so important to the slave's survival. Many slaves were left to starve to death and some plantation owners gave their slaves a day off to tend to their gardens which actually gave them time to plot uprisings. Over the following years slaves plotted while other slaves turned in the plotters for cash rewards. A series of natural disasters followed, another drought, a hurricane, a plague of ravenous insects, all of which destroyed the precious little food that the slaves were allowed to grow for themselves.

Faced with starvation slave leaders conspired and on November 23, 1733 a group of slaves innocently approached the garrison at *Coral Bay* and once inside the fort took control killing the seven soldiers with cutlasses hidden in the firewood that they were carrying, but missing one trooper who escaped and carried word of the rebellion to St. Thomas. The slaves at the fort fired a cannon three times as a signal to other slaves to act as well. Within hours bands of armed slaves roamed St. John murdering plantation owners, overseers, and their families as more and more slaves joined the revolt.

For weeks thereafter St. John was wild, in a state of anarchy, and the fear of rebellion spread to other islands. Governor Gardelin of St. Thomas sent a force of 18 soldiers to St. John to halt the rebellion, but although somewhat successful, failed to do any damage to the majority of the rebels, some 100 or so. By Christmas, reinforcements arrived from St. Thomas and 600 French troops from Martinique lured with the promise that they could keep 80% of the slaves they captured. By late winter, outnumbered and demoralized, their numbers dwindling, some slaves surrendered while others committed suicide by shooting themselves or jumping off the cliffs near Mary Point.

By August only 15 rebels remained at large and on a promise of pardon gave up only to be executed. The final count had 150 slaves participating in the rebellion, nearly all of whom were killed. If you wish to learn more about the St. John slave rebellion, pick up a copy of *Night of the Silent Drums* by John Lorenzo Anderson; you can pick one up at *MAPes MONDe* in Charlotte Amalie. John Michener devotes a chapter in his epic *Caribbean* to the rebellion on St. John. It is based on fact with a few fictional characters thrown in to the mix and is quite informative.

Around this same time the pirates discovered the Virgin Islands and the early governors of St. Thomas gave their approval for the use of their island as a pirate refuge, which would benefit the local merchants who would profit from the open sale of pirate loot on the city streets. In fact, the famous pirate Bartholomew Sharp is said to have retired from the *Sweet Trade* in 1696 and settled on St. Thomas to become a planter. Sharp later wound up serving life in prison for his deeds after his "retirement."

By the mid-1700s the pirate business was declining and legitimate trade was taking its place in the shops along *Main Street*, then called *Dronnigens Gade*, in Charlotte Amalie, and in 1764, St. Thomas was declared a free port by Danish King Frederick V. Charlotte Amalie was originally established in 1691 by the Danes and named *Taphaus*. The town was renamed Charlotte Amalie after the coronation of King Christian V in 1730 in honor of the new Queen of Denmark.

The late 1700s found St. Croix one of the wealthiest islands in the Caribbean. Her massive, and numerous (around 400) sugarcane plantations brought great wealth to the immigrant planters from Barbados, England, and Denmark. By 1802, there were over 30,000 slaves on St. Croix that over the following years revolted several times before gaining their freedom in 1848. In 1801, the British wrested control of St. John from the Danes for a period of one year and returned again in 1807 to reclaim the island, this time for 7 years.

As St. Thomas began an era of free trade with piracy ceasing to be part of the island's economy, the slave trade rolled right along. The British banned the slave trade in 1802 and by 1814 most European countries had done the same. Emancipation in the British lands came about in 1834, while on July 3, 1848, General Peter Von Sholten, under pressure from slaves led by Gottlieb Buddhoe, freed the slaves in the Danish Virgin Islands. Today, July 3, *Emancipation Day*, is still celebrated as heartily as July 4.

In 1839, Charlotte Amalie became the Caribbean base for the *Royal Mail Steam Packet Company*, which brought many visitors to the shores of St. Thomas every year. A huge shipyard on Hassel Island was built and St. Thomas became of hub of Caribbean shipping and American Civil War blockade running with the resulting economic boost, but this financial boom would not last long.

Without slave labor the plantation owner's profits dropped considerably changing the entire economic outlook of the Virgin Islands. To make things worse, the advent of steam ships ended the need to stop in the Virgin Islands, and in particular Charlotte Amalie's deep harbor. In the mid-1900s, St. Thomas was ravaged by a cholera epidemic, a hurricane, an earthquake, and a harbor destroying tidal wave, all of which contributed to the end of a very prosperous era for St. Thomas. But sad as the economy was the strategic location of these islands did not go unnoticed as World War I approached. On March 31, 1917, the United States bought the Virgin Islands, now called the United States Virgin Islands, from Denmark for $25 million in gold to prevent the islands from being used as an Axis submarine base and to protect American's Panama Canal interests. The U.S. quickly named Charlotte Amalie as the capital of the USVI and developed parts of St. Thomas into a military base. A decade later the United States conferred citizenship upon the Virgin Islanders and the *Organic Act* of 1936 granted a bit of self-rule to the U.S. Virgin Islands and gave the islanders the right to vote.

The depression years at the beginning of the 1930s plunged the economy of the U.S. Virgin Island into despair causing Herbert Hoover to declare them an "effective poorhouse." As the fifties came around the islands were being discovered by cruise ships and the tourism industry, the boon and the bane of the islands.

Today, St. Thomas is a tourist mecca and the old Danish warehouses are now filled with boutiques and restaurants, part of Charlotte Amalie's duty-free shopping zone. St. John is much more laid back than

Approaching Sail Rock from the SVI, St. Thomas in the background.

Photo by Todd Duff

St. Thomas, in part due to Laurance Rockefeller who feared the island would be overrun by development and donated 5,000 acres of land to the *National Park* system in 1956. Today 2/3 of St. John is under the protection of the *Virgin Islands National Park*. The once mighty plantations of St. Croix are now mostly just ruins preserved as historic sites. The rainforest on St. Croix is not to be missed as is the diving and snorkeling off Buck Island.

The future of the USVI is still to be written, some islanders want independence, some opt for statehood, and some are happy with the way things are. But for us boaters, the USVI are, and will remain, part of the greatest sailing archipelago in the world, a charterboat paradise and an unforgettable destination.

Approaching from the Spanish Virgin Islands

Important Lights:
Sail Rock #1: Fl G 6s
Savana Island Light: Fl W 4s
Buck Island: Fl W 4s

St Thomas lies approximately 35 miles east/ northeast of Puerto Rico, and when approaching St. Thomas from the Spanish Virgin Islands your course will be to windward and you will be bucking a westward setting current as well. The 8-mile wide *Virgin Passage* lies between Savana Island in the United States Virgin Islands and Isla Culebrita in the Spanish Virgin Islands. Depths in the *Virgin Passage* range from about 60' to over 100' and the passage is clear from dangers with the exception of *Bajos Grampus* on the southwest side of the passage and Sail Rock on the southeast side.

Tidal currents in the *Virgin Passage* run about ½ knot and set south and north. On the eastern side of the *Virgin Passage*, in the vicinity of Savana Island, the current is usually stronger, about 2-3 knots. If you're heading eastbound you should stay south of Savana Island to avoid the north setting current inshore.

Savana Island lies approximately 2 miles west/ southwest of the western tip of St. Thomas and is home to the *Savana Island Light* (Fl W, 4s, 300', 7 M). There are some detached rocks lying over 200 yards south of Savana Island and on the southeastern tip of the island is a crag with twin steeple-shaped pinnacles that resemble a cathedral.

On the eastern side of the *Virgin Passage*, about 7½ miles east/southeast of Isla Culebrita is Sail Rock, called that because it resembles a vessel under sail. There is a rock awash about 200 yards west of Sail Rock and a lighted buoy (Fl G, 6s, 4 M) is located approximately ½ mile west of Sail Rock.

Little St. Thomas is a low, grass-covered peninsula connected to the western end of St. Thomas by a sandspit. Off the southwestern point of Little St. Thomas is the *Mermaid's Chair*, a 15' high rock that has the shape of a chair. *Big Current Hole* is the name of the passage separating West Cay from Little St. Thomas and there are rocks awash here extending east from West Cay and strong currents and heavy tide rips make this passage difficult at best. *Big Current Hole* is not advised for usage, but if you are passing through it from the south, head for Drum Rock and leave it close on your port side.

Off the southeastern shore of St. Thomas there are several islands and rocks extending southeast for about 2 miles. The current rips through here at 4 knots at times in the vicinity of Dog Island. Approximately ¾ mile southwest of Long Point is *Packet Rock*, a coral reef about 100 yards in length that lies within 5' of the surface at low water. Use caution here as the sea breaks in this location but usually only in heavy weather. There is a buoy about 300 yards southeast of *Packet Rock* to warn of its location. South of Packet Rock, between St. Thomas and Buck Island and Capella Island, the tidal current is not very strong, only about ½-2 knots at most times. The tidal current between the Flat Cays and Saba Island off the southwestern shore of Water Island sets east/southeast and west/northwest at a speed of approximately 1 knot.

St. Thomas

Busy St. Thomas is the cultural and political center of the United States Virgin Islands, though I'd bet the folks on St. John and St. Croix might argue that remark. When Columbus discovered St. Thomas for the Spanish he named the island San Tomas and its name has changed little over the centuries, the name surviving its Anglicization. St. Thomas is approximately 13 miles long and it varies in width from 1-4 miles, with a total area of about 28 square miles. Most of the population of over 50,000 live predominantly in and near Charlotte Amalie, the capital of St. Thomas. Aviators will be interested in knowing that in 1929, two years after setting the solo transatlantic record in *The Spirit of St. Louis*, Charles Lindbergh landed his famous aircraft on St. Thomas and returned later that year in a *Sikorsky* seaplane.

Charlotte Amalie

Waypoints:
Charlotte Amalie - 1 nm SSE of entrance channel
18° 18.50' N, 64° 55.40' W

Charlotte Amalie (pronounced ah-MAHL-yah), is one of the most colorful towns in the Caribbean, her charming harbor is a flurry of activity with cruise ships, private yachts, and island traders coming and going at all hours of the day and night. *Signal Hill* sits about a mile northwest of St. Thomas Harbor and is the second highest peak on St. Thomas. A ridge extends east/southeast from *Signal Hill* and passes about ½ mile north of Charlotte Amalie and the town is built upon three spurs that extend south of that ridge. *Frenchman Hill* is on the western spur, *Berg Hill* is on the center spur, and *Government Hill* is on the eastern spur.

The tides in *St. Thomas Harbor* at Charlotte Amalie are chiefly diurnal with a range of almost 1' and there is a noticeable tidal current at the entrance to the harbor.

Navigational Information

Entrance to the harbor at Charlotte Amalie is straightforward although you really cannot see the harbor from the south; you'll only see the cruise ship docks at Havensight. As shown on Chart USVI-1, a waypoint at 18° 18.50' N, 64° 55.40' W, will place you

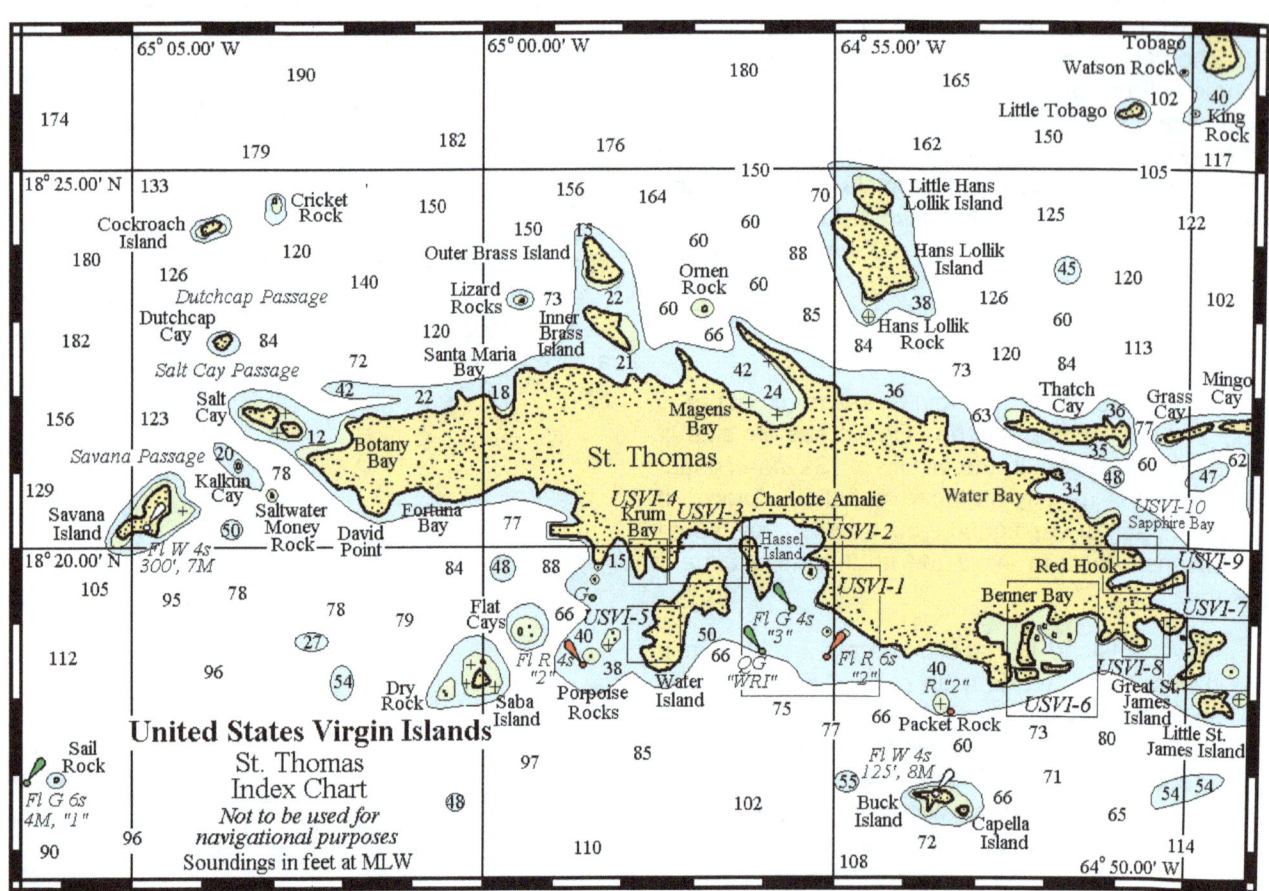

approximately 1 mile south/southeast of the marked entrance channel. If you're approaching the waypoint from the east you must pass south of Flamingo Point on Water Island, and if approaching from the east you must pass well south of Long Point and Packet Rock which only has about 4' over it at low water, and *Barrel of Beef* which is shown on Chart USVI-1.

From the waypoint head generally north/northwest following the markers. The first green marker you come to is the light on Scorpion Rock and the red marker that sits on the edge of *Rhoda Bank* as shown on Chart USVI-1. Continue north/northwest past the shoals off Rupert Rock, the red marker #6, and the red light at the end of the cruise ship dock at Havensight, just north of Rupert Rock (see also Chart USVI-2). You are now in the harbor at Charlotte Amalie.

The most popular anchorage is north of Havensight and the cruise ship dock towards the eastern end of the harbor near *Yacht Haven Grande Marina* (although you can anchor almost anywhere inside the harbor). Do not pick up any moorings in the harbor, they are all private. There is a very nice anchorage along the eastern shore of Hassell Island, *Careening Cove*, but it's usually crowded (see Chart USVI-2).

At the northern end of the harbor is the city's waterfront section where you can tie stern-to the dock. Beware of the surge here, besides being dangerous it is extremely uncomfortable and it's usually crowded with boats catering to the tourists. Inside *King's Wharf* is a *Coast Guard* station and a dinghy dock that allows access to the shopping that is available along the waterfront. Use a stern anchor here; the wall is rough.

What You Will Find Ashore

If you need to clear *Customs* and *Immigration* their office is located by the ferry dock at the western end of the harbor at Charlotte Amalie north of Hassell Island. Office hours are from 0800-1200 and 1300-1630 Monday through Saturday with no fee for clearance. Office hours on Sundays and holidays are from 1000-1800 and you can expect an overtime fee of $25 maximum per vessel if you clear at this time. There is no other *Port of Entry* on St. Thomas; if you don't clear here, you'll need to clear at *Cruz Bay* on St. John, or at *Gallows Bay* in Christiansted on St. Croix. Please remember that all persons aboard must visit *Customs* and *Immigration* along with the skipper.

Yacht Haven Grande Marina (758-452-0185, or, yhgst@igymarinas.com), formerly known as *Yacht Haven Marina*, lies in *Long Bay* (see Chart USVI-2) at the eastern corner of the harbor at Charlotte Amalie, is designed for mega-yachts and offers slips that can accommodate vessels from 80' to 656' in length with drafts to 18' deep. The marina offers full electric (including 3-phase) along with water, ice, showers, telephone and cable TV hookups, *Wi-Fi*, high-speed fueling right at your slip, and 24/7 security. On site you will find several restaurants, a laundry, a florist, a provisioning stop, and a complex full of small but upscale shops. There are dinghy docks on the eastern and western sides of the marina and ample car parking. The western dinghy dock has issues with theft so if you choose to utilize that dock bring a good lock and don't leave anything of value in your dink.

Historical Charlotte Amalie

Most people know of Charlotte Amalie's reputation as a duty-free port, but few know how deeply she is steeped in history. Much of Charlotte Amalie was destroyed by devastating fires in 1802 and 1804 and today's architecture dates back to French, British, and Danish influences after these fires. Charlotte Amalie is listed in the *National Register of Historic Places* for the city's history and architecture, so many of the building that you see were built from the ballast rocks left behind by ships taking on cargo for their homeward voyage.

The oldest building in town is *Fort Christian*, a *National Historic Landmark* on *Waterfront Highway* at the northern side of the harbor. Construction first began on the fort in 1666, and was completed in 1672. The fort was named after King Christian V of Denmark and was used as a jail from 1874-1983. Today it houses several very nice exhibits pertaining to the more recent history, within the last two centuries, of Charlotte Amalie. Across the street from the fort is the *Legislative Building*, once a barracks for Danish troops of three centuries ago and U.S. troops of a half-century ago.

Off *Main Street* just east of the *Post Office* is the *Frederick Evangelical Lutheran Church*, at one time the official church of the islands (at that time Lutheranism was the official religion of Denmark since 1536), it was built in 1666 and lost to fires in 1750

A Cruising Guide to the Virgin Islands

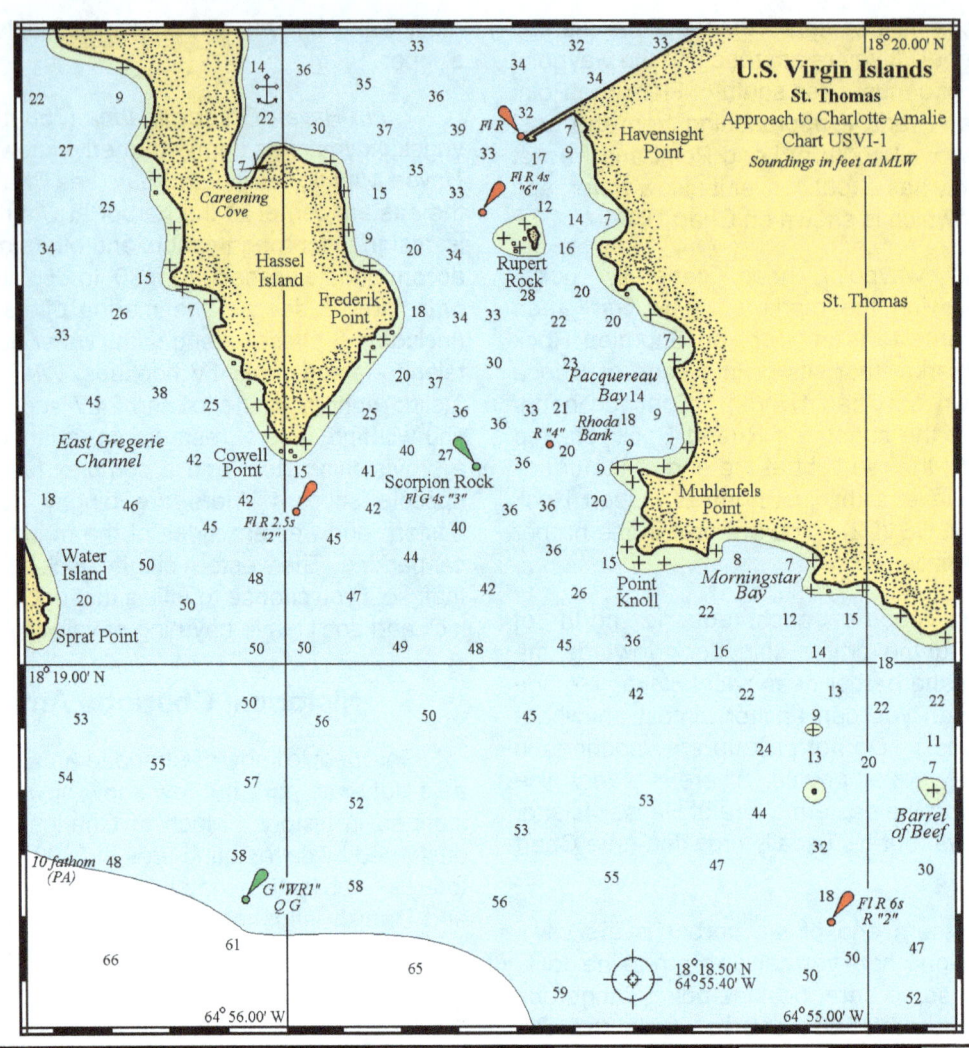

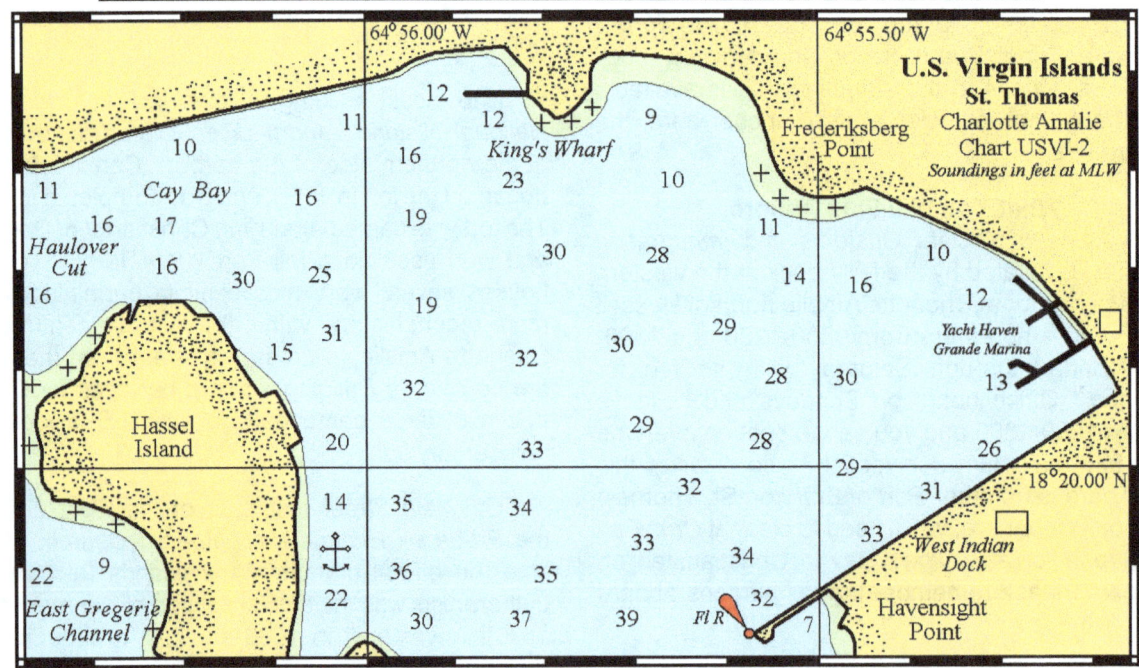

and 1789. The present structure was completed in 1826, gutted by a fire in 1829, and refurbished again a few years later. Just north of the *Vendor's Plaza* is *Emancipation Square* dedicated to the emancipation of the slaves in the Virgin Islands on July 3, 1848.

Continuing on *Main Street* past *Government House* you'll come to the *Seven Arches Museum*, a piece of history from the Dutch era reflecting life of the times. Nearby, just off *Kogen's Gade*, you'll find the *99 Steps*, which date back to the mid-1700s. The steps were built with bricks brought from Denmark that served as ballast for incoming ships. The steps were built to connect the streets of Charlotte Amalie, which were built in a grid pattern designed by Danish engineers who failed to take into account the steep terrain of the city. I believe that whoever named the steep *99 Steps* never actually counted them, there seem to be quite a few more than 99. On one of my more cardiac testing moments I came up with a count of 103, but of course that was going downhill. On *Crystal Gade* you'll find the *Jewish Synagogue* built in 1796, the oldest Hebrew house of worship under the U.S. flag and one of the oldest in the Western Hemisphere (the oldest synagogue in continuous use in our hemisphere is located in Curacao).

Located east of downtown Charlotte Amalie is *Bluebeard's Tower*, a 17th century watchtower that was said to have been the home of the pirate of the same name. Here you can get a bite to eat at *Fergie's*, serving breakfast, lunch, and dinner with a Monday evening pool party. The tower sits on the grounds of *Bluebeard's Castle Hotel* (http://www.bluebeardscastles.com/) on *Bluebeard's Hill*, also called *Frederiksberg*, and is said to have been the hangout of the famous pirate who built the tower for the love of his life, Mercedita. Mercedita apparently strayed from Bluebeard's embraces and the pirate killed her in a jealous rage then sailed away into obscurity. Another tale, that is not nearly as interesting, claims that the tower was built in the late 1700s to help *Fort Christian* guard the harbor.

Now let's discuss what so many people enjoy doing in St. Thomas, shopping!

Shopping in Charlotte Amalie

The road along the northern shore of the harbor at Charlotte Amalie where the ferry docks are located is called *Waterfront Highway*, also called *Route 30*, *Veteran's Drive*, and *Kanal Gade*, and is the seaward edge of the main shopping area. St. Thomas is a duty-free port and shops in this area, as well as street hawkers, abound, as do the crowds of shoppers. Many of the shops here are set in old warehouses and buildings dating back to the 19th century.

Running parallel to the *Waterfront Highway* is *Main Street*, also called *Dronningens Gade*, and between the two are many small streets and alleys where all the stores and malls that entice shoppers into parting with so many of their dollars. The best way to find your way around here is to pick up a copy of *St. Thomas This Week* (http://www.virginislandsthisweek.com/) or one of the other similar publications where page after page are devoted to ads for the various shops. I cannot possibly describe all the shops here, so I'll just touch on those that might interest the cruiser in you, not the shopper, mind you, but the cruiser.

Located in the *Grand Hotel* complex at the eastern end of *Main Street*, north of *Vendor's Plaza* and *Emancipation Park*, the *Island Newsstand* offers just about any U.S. periodical and major newspaper you might desire as well as books, greeting cards, soft drinks and pastries. If you enjoy antiques the *Carson Co. Antiques* is located at the *Royal Dane Mall*. Inside the *A.H. Riise Mall* (http://www.ahriise.com/) is *Calypso Ltd.*, a tea and cappuccino bar where you can pick up all sorts of locally produced sauces, jellies, health care products as well as music and jewelry. Nearby is the *Pusser's Company Store* (https://www.pussers.com/t-shop.aspx), several of which are found throughout the USVI and BVI. *Jen's Island Café and Deli* (http://jensislandcafe.com/) is also located in the *Grand Hotel*.

If you are seeking name brands try the *Tommy Hilfiger* store at the *Royal Dane Mall*, nearby *Janine's Boutique* on *Palm Passage* handles selections from *Christian Dior, Pierre Cardin, Valentino, Louis Ferand, Cacharel*, and *YSL*. East of the *Royal Dane Mall*, *A Chew or Two* is a chocolate lover's paradise. What a selection of gourmet chocolates they have here! Just go! Sample and buy, you won't be disappointed! The *Tavern on the Waterfront* (http://www.tavernonthewaterfront.com/) is located upstairs on the *Waterfront Highway* at the *Royal Dane Mall* and features beer from around the world. A spacious restaurant with an inspiring view of the harbor, the cuisine is some of the best to be found on St. Thomas.

Also at the mall is *Rio Cigars* for cigar aficionados who enjoy their smoking and a glass of wine or champagne as well. Also on the *Waterfront Highway* is *King's Caribbean Coffee Café* between *The Green House Restaurant* and *Blazing Photos*. Here you can sample and purchase many flavors of coffee as well as freshly baked pastries and rolls. *The Green House Restaurant* (http://www.thegreenhouserestaurant.com/) is popular for their live music on Wednesday nights. The *Green House* also offers *Margarita Mondays* as well as numerous other bar events especially during sporting events. West of the mall is *Shipwrecker's Antiques*, a must stop for anyone with any love of things nautical. Here you'll find a fascinating collection of nautical memorabilia (the owner also owns a salvage company) as well as maps, books, and lively, talkative parrots. On the waterfront at the *International Plaza* is the *Hard Rock Café* serving late into the evening with *Rock & Roll* memorabilia all around you. Next door is the *Ice Cream Shoppe* and I'm sure you can guess what they sell there.

On the eastern edge of downtown Charlotte Amalie stands the *1829 Hotel* overlooking *Government Hill*. The hotel was built by a French sea captain as a gift for his bride in 1829; it has been a hotel since 1907 and is now a *National Historic Site*. Long known as one of St. Thomas' best restaurants, the *1829 Restaurant* begins the day with a breakfast buffet and only gets better culminating with elegant dinners compete with cigar humidors and the finest of caviar. At *Government Hill*, upstairs from the *Post Office*, wine lovers will want to visit *Herve* where deeply upholstered chairs line a wide bar that serves over 20 different types of wine.

Just off *Main Street* at *Nye Gade* is the *St. Thomas Apothecary* if you need *OTC* or prescription drugs as well as sundry items. On the waterfront between *Raadet's Gade* and *Hibiscus Alley* is *Lover's Lane*, a shop dedicated to love and featuring exotic swimwear, lingerie and gifts for lovers. Close by is *West Indies Coffee*, a wonderful, unassuming little cappuccino and espresso bar. If you're tired of the same old CDs, or if you just want to pick up some fine island music, visit the *Parrot Fish* on *Back Street* at *Stortvaer Gade*. Nearby is *So Soup Me*, the place for those whose palate prefers soups and absolutely scrumptious pastries.

If you want music from back home, visit *Sam Goody's* on *Main Street*, above the *Leather Shop*, the spot for fine leather goods at prices less than you'll find in the United States. And if you get tired of all the endless shopping (sometimes we all need a break), stop in at the *Visitor's Hospitality Lounge* at the *Grand Hotel Complex*. You can relax here, read a brochure about what to do on St. Thomas, buy a book, or just sit and have a cold beverage while you rest your feet. At the western end of *Main Street* is *Market Square*, an old iron-roofed structure that was once a slave trading center and today houses a produce and gift market. The best day to visit the market is early on a Saturday morning, it's alive, vibrant, you'll love it. Next door is the public library.

Havensight is another area for duty-free shopping located on the southern side of the harbor. Havensight, built to facilitate shopping for the cruise ship passengers who preferred not to travel to the other side of the harbor at *Waterfront Highway*, sits off the cruise ship docks on the south side of the harbor. Here, four long buildings at the back of the cruise ship docks house the many shops located here and many of the shops from the *Main Street* area are represented here as well. There is a new walkway from *Yacht Haven* (close to the dinghy dock), to Havensight. There is also a *Post Office* located at Havensight.

Just across from Havensight is the *Paradise Point Tramway* (http://www.ridetheview.com/) where Swiss-built gondolas take you to the top of *Flagg Hill* some 700' above the water. Here at the cruise ship docks you can take your seat on the air-conditioned *Submarine Atlantis* for a 1½ mile long underwater tour through the *National Wildlife Preserve* of Buck Island. Just past Havensight is the *Al Cohen Mall* on *Rt. 38*, home to a pair of nice art galleries, several smaller shops, great pizza at *Pizza Amore*, and *PC Paradise*, where you can get warranty repairs on *Apple*, *Lenovo* and *HP*.

Up the road northward from Havensite (just a short walk) is *Lockhart Mall* with a small *Kmart*. A *Pueblo* grocery store is along this road as well. A Hospital is just beyond *Kmart* while across from *Kmart* is *The Fruit Bowl* which is very good for produce shopping and many grocery items.

Mall shoppers who delight in the bargains at such places will want to visit the *Tutu Park Mall* (http://www.tutuparkmall.com.php53-27.dfw1-2.websitetestlink.com/) on *Rt. 38* east of Charlotte Amalie. Here you can find a *K-Mart*, a *Cost U Less* wholesale club (great for massive provisioning; http://www.costuless.com/), and on the road to *Tutu Park Mall*, a *Plaza*

The United States Virgin Islands - St. Thomas

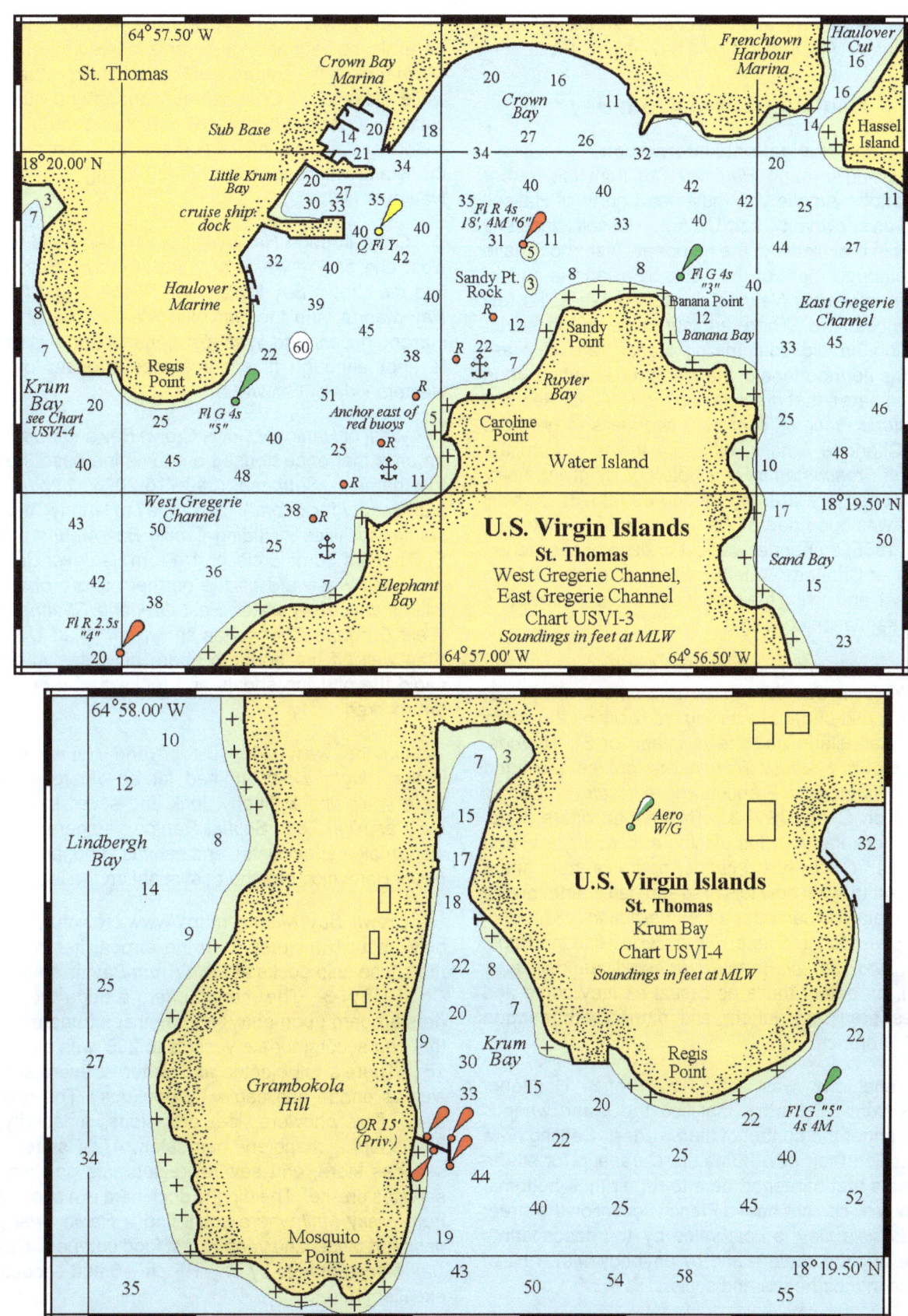

Extra Supermarket, and tons of other shops including a bookstore, *McDonald's*, and a *Domino's Pizza*.

Haulover Cut to Krum Bay

Navigational Information

Passing through *Haulover Cut* from the harbor at Charlotte Amalie you must head north of Hassell Island as shown on Chart USVI-2. Hassell Island sits almost in the middle of the harbor at Charlotte Amalie and although most of the 135-acre island is part of the *Virgin Islands National Park* there are still a few residences here. There are four spots on the island, including an old coal mining station and shipyard near the northern end of the island (use caution when walking here), that are listed on the *National Register of Historic Places*. There are two ways to get here from Charlotte Amalie, either by the ferry from the *Marriott Frenchman's Reef Hotel*, or by giving Larry a call, *Launch with Larry*, at 340-690-8073. Hassell Island was once part of the mainland of St. Thomas, but in 1865, a channel was cut to ease access to the harbor at Charlotte Amalie making entry easier from the west, and giving the harbor a better flow alleviating many sanitation concerns.

What You Will Find Ashore

Haulover Cut, though narrow, is not a challenge, just stay mid-channel avoiding the rocks off the shore of Hassell Island and the mainland of St. Thomas. *Frenchtown Harbour Marina* lies on the mainland of St. Thomas, in Frenchtown, at *Haulover Cut* as shown on Chart USVI-3. The marina offers deep-water dockage with full electric and water, ice, and showers. *CYOA* has a charter operation here and if you want to learn how to sail so you can charter one of their boats you can attend the *International School of Sailing* also located here. On site you'll find the *Hook, Line, and Sinker* (http://www.hooklineandsinkervi.com/), an eatery that's as casual as they come and serves breakfast, lunch, and dinner with a good Sunday brunch.

Frenchtown was settled by French Huguenot exiles from St. Barth's that fled the island when it came under the control of the Swedes. Settling here they called their new home the *Carenage* for all the sailboats that careened here to repair their bottoms. Today, you can still hear a French accent on the street and *Bastille Day* is celebrated by the descendants of the original settlers and by anybody with a bit of France in their hearts and souls.

Frenchtown is a hub of activity and night life with several nice bars and restaurants located here. *Café Normandie* is the standard of French dining in the area while *Alexander's Café* serves German and Austrian cuisine. *Oceana* (http://www.oceanavi.com/), in the historic *Villa Olga,* offers some of the best food on the island with beautiful open-air dining overlooking *Haulover Cut*.

Once through *Haulover Cut* you can head to the west and on the western shore of *Crown Bay* you'll find the *Crown Bay Waterfront*, *Subbase* and *Crown Bay Marina*, and the *Haulover Marine Center*. The current in *East* and *West Gregerie Channel* is about ½ knot although it is sometimes stronger on the western side of *Crown Bay*.

West of *Haulover Cut* is *Crown Bay* and *Subbase*, an area that once housed a submarine base, hence the name. *Subbase* (340-776-2078; http://www.subbasedrydock.com/) is home to many marine service facilities including *Crown Bay Marina* and is St. Thomas' commercial port. From *Haulover Cut* you can head westward off the northern shore of Water Island, which separates *East Gregerie Channel* and *West Gregerie Channel* as shown on Chart USVI-3. Stay well off the northern shore of Water Island to avoid the off-lying shoals and rocks, some of which are marked.

On the west side, just beyond *Haulover Cut*, is the *Dinghy Dock*, named for an old restaurant. Here you'll find a dinghy dock and several services such as *High Tech Scuba*, *Reefco* (refrigeration and watermaker specialists), and canvas shop, and *Enkai Sushi Bar* which has the best sushi on the island.

Crown Bay Marina (http://www.crownbay.com/), only about 5 minutes from the airport, lies north of the cruise ship docks at *Little Krum Bay* as shown on Chart USVI-3. The marina offers a huge fuel dock (to starboard upon entry) and almost a hundred slips that can accommodate vessels to 200' with a draft of 15'. There's full electric and water at every slip as well as phone and cable TV hookups. The marina also offers showers, ice, provisions, a laundry, a dive shop, a chandlery, hair salon, *AT&T* store, mail services store, and several restaurants and marine services on site. The dinghy dock here is a short walk from *Nisky Mall* where you'll find a *Radio Shack*, a passport office, and various fast food eateries. *Crown Bay Marina* stands by on VHF ch. 16 and security is excellent here.

The United States Virgin Islands - St. Thomas

QEII entering Charlotte Amalie — Photo by Todd Duff

Havensight, Charlotte Amalie — Photo by Todd Duff

Water Island, *Flamingo Bay* in foreground — Photo by Todd Duff

Charlotte Amalie with Hassel Island and Water Island in background — Photo by Todd Duff

Benner Bay (*The Lagoon*), *Jersey Bay*, and the Cas Cay anchorage in the foreground — Photo by Todd Duff

Chef Romeo's barbecue is located at *Subbase* and is considered by many to be the best BBQ on the island and the best breakfast on St. Thomas may well be at *Tickles Dockside Pub* (http://www.ticklesdocksidepub.com/) at *Crown Bay Marina*. If you need propane you can get your tanks filled at *Marine Warehouse* or at *Antilles Gas* at *Subbase*. *Marine Warehouse* is a chandler and can also help with your outboard and diesel problems. *Crown Bay Maritime* is an *OMC* and *Westerbeke* dealer and can handle repairs on all manner of drive gear, *Universal* and *Perkins* diesels, and *Lima* generators. *Gourmet Gallery* (http://gourmetgallery.net/) is the place for provisions here. If you need to take care of some laundry, visit *Swash It Laundry*. Nearby, along the *Crown Bay Waterfront* east of the marina, is *Bayside Canvas*, *Island Marine Supply* (in *Crown Bay Marina*), and *Radio One*, *WSVI* radio, 1000 on the AM dial, with their very conspicuous antenna that is visible for miles.

At the southwestern end of *Crown Bay*, northeast of Regis Point (see Chart USVI-3), is the *Haulover Marine Center*, a full-service boatyard with a 300-ton drydock, a 100-ton crane, and a yard full of marine services such as *Awlgrip* specialists, machine and fabrication shops, a wood shop, a fiberglass repair shop, and *Island Rigging and Hydraulics*, dealers for *Harken*, *Navtec*, *Barient*, *Lewmar*, *Edson*, *Hood*, *Maxwell*, *Sta-Lok*, and *New England Ropes*. Here, too, are *Banks Sails,* and *A&J Power Systems* selling and servicing *Onan* and other brands of marine generators. Also located here is *Offshore Marine*, dealers for *Yamaha* outboards, *Yanmar* diesel engines, and *Caribe* inflatables.

There is a *Puerblo Supermarket* in the *Subbase* area just a few blocks from *Crown Bay*.

Krum Bay

Navigational Information
As shown on Chart USVI-4, *Krum Bay* lies northwest of Water Island just across the *West Gregerie Channel*, and just around Regis Point from *Subbase*. It is primarily a commercial and industrial district, but I've included a chart of the bay in case someone needs to seek shelter inside.

What You Will Find Ashore
There is a dinghy dock in here and it is walking distance to two propane filling stations, *St. Thomas Gas* and *Antilles Gas*. The public works yard accepts waste oil but you must leave the oil in a disposable container. There is a good woodshop in this area as well.

Water Island

Waypoints:
Druif Bay - ¼ nm W of
18° 19.02' N, 64° 57.75' W

Water Island lies less than ½ mile off the southern shore of St. Thomas and most people don't realize that it is in fact the fourth largest U.S. Virgin Island. Water Island officially achieved that status on December 12, 1996 when the *U.S Department of the Interior*, which looks after the administration of the USVI, transferred Water Island to the Government of the U.S. Virgin Islands. The *Department of the Interior* received title to Water Island from the U.S. Army in 1952 after Water Island was abandoned as a strategic military base from World War II.

Water Island received its name from the freshwater ponds that refilled many a cask on sailing ships centuries ago; many of these ships were pirate vessels as the island was once a refuge for buccaneers. Water Island is about 2 miles long and from 400 to 600 yards in width, encompassing some 492 hilly acres with its highest point being 294' above sea level. Although there are a few residences on the island, and one small hotel, the *Limestone Reef Terraces*, there are no stores or restaurants on Water Island except for a small deli up the hill from the ferry dock. This is a nice island for long walks on quiet roads.

You can catch the ferry to Water Island west of St. Thomas at *Crown Bay Marina* located near Frenchtown. There are anchorages along the northwestern shore of Water Island at *Ruyter Bay*, *Caroline Bay*, and *Elephant Bay* as shown on Chart USVI-3. These are best used as daytime anchorages (the bay is very deep and most vessels here are on private moorings), but a bit further south you'll find the more popular anchorages of *Flamingo Bay* and *Druif Bay*.

Navigational Information
Flamingo Bay and *Druif Bay*, also called *Honeymoon Bay*, are two nice anchorages on the western shore of Water Island. As shown on Chart USVI-5, *Druif Bay* lies just south of Providence Point and *Flamingo Bay* just a bit further south past Druif Point.

The United States Virgin Islands - St. Thomas

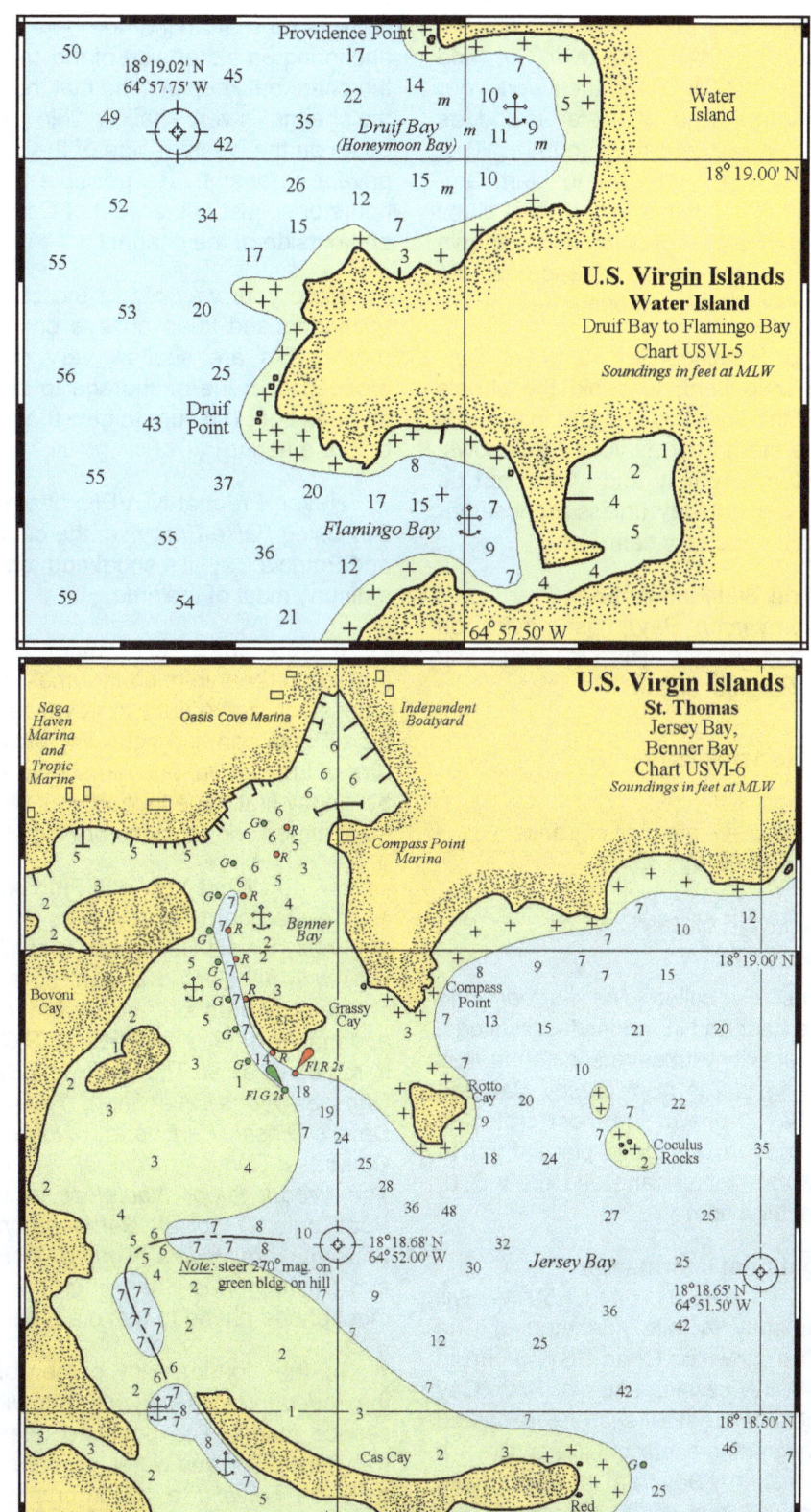

If headed to *Druif Bay* from Charlotte Amalie, pass north of Hassel Island via *Haulover Cut* (see Chart USVI-2 and Chart USVI-3) and then work your way around the northern end of Water Island as you turn to head southwest and then south in *West Gregerie Channel* leaving *Krum Bay* to starboard. A waypoint at 18° 19.02' N, 64° 57.75' W, will place you approximately ¼ mile west of *Druif Bay* as shown on Chart USVI-5. From the waypoint head east into *Druif Bay* to anchor or pick up a mooring.

When headed for *Flamingo Bay* from *Druif Bay*, give Druif Point a wide berth to avoid the shoals there. Once clear of the point you can turn to the east to anchor as far into the harbor as your draft allows. *Flamingo Bay* is often very rolly and should not be considered for an overnight stay unless the weather and seas are forecast to be very calm.

What You Will Find Ashore
Druif Bay, (Honeymoon Bay) has movies on the beach every Monday night. Here too you'll find *Heidi's* food truck for a great snack.

Benner Bay

Waypoints:
Cas Cay Anchorage - .2 nm E of entrance
18° 18.68' N, 64° 52.00' W

Jersey Bay - ¼ nm NE of Cas Cay
18° 18.65' N, 64° 51.50' W

Benner Bay, usually called *The Lagoon* and sometimes listed as East End in marine facility's ads, is a hive of boating activity with several nice marinas and boatyards. Lying just in from *Jersey Bay* and Cas Cay, *Benner Bay* is one of the most protected harbors on St. Thomas, a very good place if you're seeking protection from a hurricane and draw 6' or less (7' can get in at high tide).

Navigational Information
A waypoint at 18° 18.65' N, 64° 51.50' W, will place you approximately ¼ mile northeast of Cas Cay in *Jersey Bay* as shown on Chart USVI-6. From the waypoint head WNW passing south of Rotto Cay where you should be able to get a visual on the marked entrance channel beginning south of Grassy Cay. If you are approaching *Jersey Bay* from the west, make sure that you keep well east of the shoals off Red Point on Cas Cay, a green buoy marks the western end of this shoal. Follow the markers northward around the western shore of Grassy Cay. Although there is no real anchorage here, you will see boats anchoring on either side of the channel as shown on the chart, but keep in mind that the area to the east of the channel is very shallow, 2' in many places. Some boats on the western side of the channel are lying to private moorings. It's possible to anchor for a few hours or so just to the west of *Compass Point Marina* and outside of the channel.

Ease your way out of the channel slowly when anchoring and keep an eye on your depthsounder (both sides are shallow very quickly). You can proceed past the anchorage to avail yourself of the marinas here (be sure to give them a hail on the VHF before entering).

Never, I repeat NEVER, attempt to enter *Jersey Bay* using *False Entrance*, the cut between Cas Cay and Patricia Cay, it's shoal and rocky, tough for even a dinghy most of the time.

If you come to *Benner Bay* for hurricane protection, bear in mind that most marines will be full unless you arrive days in advance. If you draw less than 6' you can find your way back into the western arm of the lagoon, but you should sound your way in by dinghy first. The lagoon gets very crowded during these times and tensions are high.

What You Will Find Ashore
To starboard as you pass the anchorage north of Grassy Cay is *Compass Point Marina* offering 100 slips with full electric and water, a pump out facility, showers, and on site are several charter companies and marine service facilities. *VIP Charters* is located here as well as *St. Thomas Yacht Sales and Charters, Chris Sawyer's Dive Shop, T&J Outboard Repairs, Dave's Diesel (Perkins* and *Northern Lights* dealer), *Compass Canvas, Coki of St. Thomas* (canvas), *The Wood Shop, Nautelect Inc., Compass Point Boatworks, Tropical Refrigeration, Water Wizard Watermakers, Skip's Rigging, Dottie's Front Porch,* and *Davis Marine Surveying.* If you want a slip you must phone ahead to make a reservation.

In the northeastern corner of *The Lagoon* is the *Independent Boatyard* (http://ibyvi.com/), a full-service marina and boatyard offering over 80 slips with full electric and water, propane fills, showers, ice, a 50-ton *Travelift*, a 10-ton crane, and a fine group of marine services. Bruce Merceed's *Marine Repairs* can handle all your prop and shaft repairs as well as your fabrication needs while *Electro Nautical Systems* takes care of your electronic and electrical needs.

Here too is Mike Sheen's *Fiberglass Shop*, *Phillips Ouutboard Marine Sales*, and Tim Peck *Enterprises* who can handle your *Awlgrip* applications. There is now a branch of *Budget Marine* located here and the staff is very knowledgeable and friendly

Carigas is a great place to meet and eat, offering several specials for your pleasure; Wednesday is *Spaghetti Night* with live music; Thursday is *Texas Night* with BBQ ribs, chicken, and chili; and Sunday is *Open Mic Night* so step up and let's hear what you've got (sometimes it's *Movie Night*). The bar is constructed from the remains of *HMS Pinafore* that sank here in 1974. The boat was dragged ashore and the stern became a bar (you'll notice the original mast sticking up out of the kitchen). Once called the *Poor Man's Bar*, it was renamed *Bottom's Up* by the current owner, Tina Roberts, in 1982. Just up the road is *Fabian's Landing* another spot that's popular with the cruising community.

Located next to the *Independent Boatyard*, *East End Boat Park* offers haul-out and dry storage for vessels under 25' in length. *Caribbean Inflatable Services* is located here and they sell and service inflatables and life rafts.

At the northern end of The Lagoon, on the western shore, across from the Independent Boatyard, is *Ocean Cove Marina*. The marina is still in a construction phase but slips have been built and they offer electricity, potable water, *WiFi*, a gourmet restaurant, and 24-hour security. Future plans include a dive center, a retail shop, and boat trips and island tours. The marina can be reached by phone at 340-244-0442, or you can reach them by email at oasiscovemarina@icloud.com.

West is *Saga Haven Marina* offering 50 long-term slips (featuring 50' and 75' skirted finger piers and a select number of slips for catamarans) with electric (50-amp) and water, but liveaboards are not permitted. The fuel dock is open but is shallow, 4' at MLW. This is an important consideration since the only other fuel dock on the eastern side of St. Thomas is at *American Yacht Harbor* in Red Hook.

Near the head of the *TIP* docks is the *Schnitzel and Strudel Restaurant*. *Wrapped and Unwrapped* offers pre-packaged meals, just heat and eat.

Upstairs at *Saga Haven Marina* is a wonderful little sushi bar, *Sushi by Sato*. Here too is the famous *Paddy O'Furniture's Irish Brew Pub* featuring four varieties of locally brewed beers including *Blackbeard's Ale*, *Captain Kidd's Golden Ale*, and *Pit Bull Irish Stout* which is made from four different malts.

One of the best anchorages in the *Jersey Bay/Benner Bay* area is found in the lee of Cas Cay as shown on Chart USVI-6, unfortunately, anchoring here is no longer permitted by the *DPNR (Department of Planning and Natural Resources)* To me, this is sad since this is such a wonderful anchorage, we'll just have to see what time brings. In the hope that the anchorage will reopen someday, I will give entrance guidelines.

The entrance can be daunting and must be taken just before high tide to allow for any error (you can take 5' through here), straying too far north or south of the entrance will result in your going aground on a sand bottom, so take it easy through here and keep an eye on the range and the depthsounder. What range you ask? A waypoint at 18° 18.68' N, 64° 52.00' W, will place you approximately .2 mile east of the entrance to this anchorage, and from this waypoint if you look west, you'll see a large, green building high on a hill, it looks like it might be some sort of concrete plant or the like. Take up a course of 270° on this building and proceed westward over the sandbar as shown on Chart USVI-8. If all goes as planned you will be heading towards a point of land on the eastern shore of Bovoni Cay and you can steer to port to enter an area of deeper water, about 7' at low tide. Continue heading for a point just west of the northwestern tip of Cas Cay to enter the deeper water lying west of Cas Cay. This is a wonderful anchorage! If you look south you'll see the *Caribbean Sea* with a reef stretching from Cas Cay to Patricia Cay that gives you wonderful protection even when the trades are up.

Christmas Cove, Current Cut

Important Lights:
Current Rock Light: Fl W 6s
Waypoints:
Current Cut - .1 nm NNE of
18° 19.00' N, 64° 49.97' W

Current Cut - ¼ nm SSW of
18° 18.70' N, 64° 50.05' W

Christmas Cove - .1 nm WNW of
18° 18.70' N, 64° 50.05' W

A Cruising Guide to the Virgin Islands

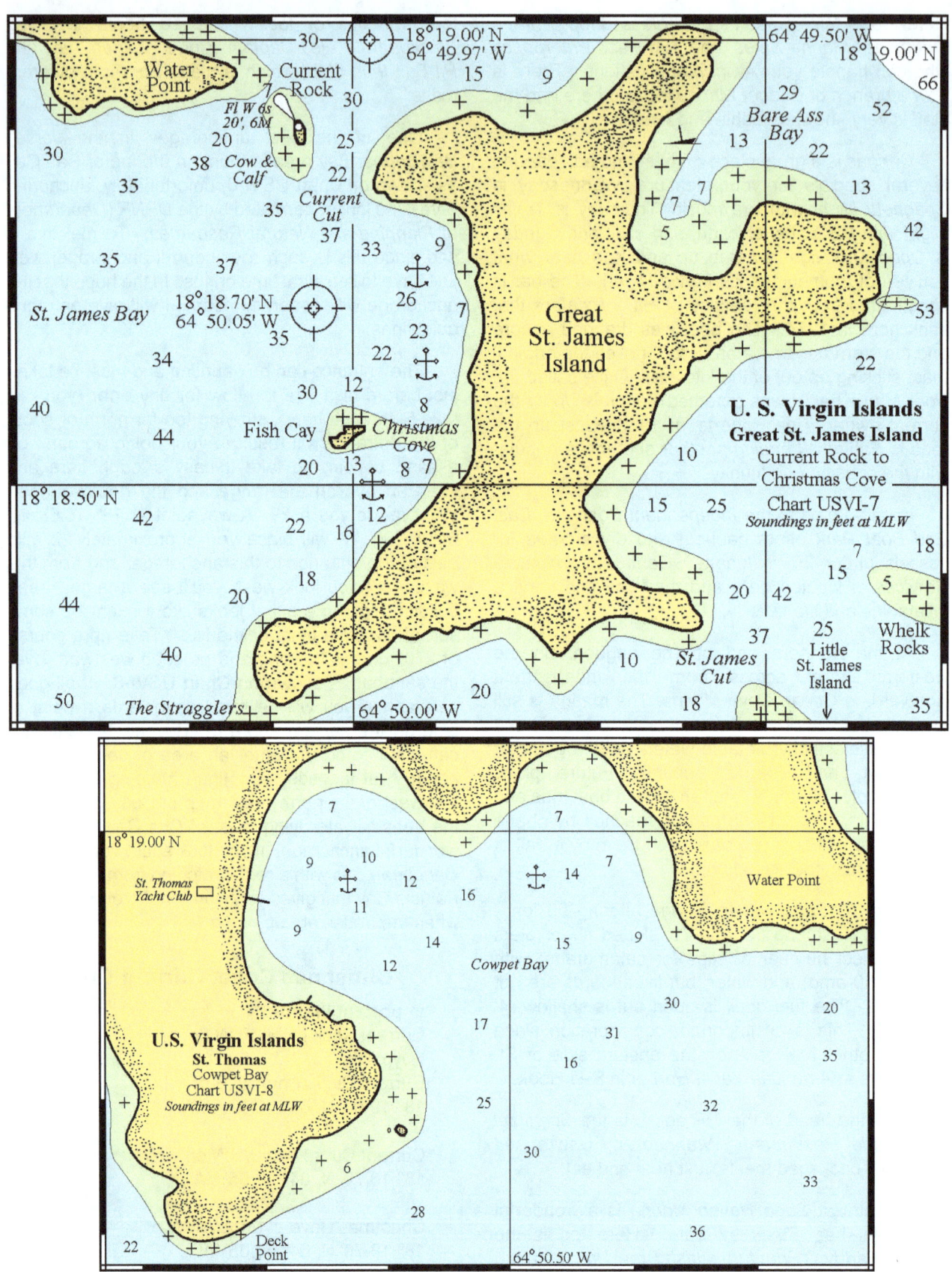

76

The United States Virgin Islands - St. Thomas

Navigational Information

Christmas Cove on the western shore of Great St. James Island is a delightful and well protected anchorage in prevailing conditions. Off the northwestern tip of Great St. James Island is the appropriately named *Current Cut*. *Current Cut* lies between Current Rock and Great St. James Island as shown on Chart USVI-7 and is a main thoroughfare for vessels entering and leaving *Pillsbury Sound* from the southern coast of St. Thomas. For instance, if you wish to go to Red Hook from Charlotte Amalie, *Current Cut* saves a large detour around Great St. James Island. The approximately 100' wide *Current Cut* will carry over 20' at low water and the tidal current here reaches 3-4 knots setting north and south through the cut. Never, I repeat NEVER, attempt to go between Current Rock and Water Point. There is a 7' channel through here, but it is narrow and a slight error in navigation will put you on some nasty rocks.

If you are passing south of Great St. James Island you may pass south of Little St. James Island and then turn to the northeast to head across *Pillsbury Sound* to St. John. If you wish to pass between Little St. James Island and Great St. James Island through *St. James Cut* you must avoid *The Stragglers* off the southwestern tip of Great St. James Island, the rocks that are awash about 150 yards northwest of the northeastern tip of Little St. James Island, and the rocks and shoals surrounding Whelk Rocks, as shown on Chart USVI-7.

If you are approaching from St. John or Red Hook, a waypoint at 18° 19.00' N, 64° 49.97' W, will place you approximately ¼ mile north of *Current Cut*. From the waypoint head mid-channel between Current Rock and Great St. James Island as shown on Chart USVI-7, taking care not to turn to the west too soon, you must avoid the *Cow and Calf*, a group of rocks southwest of Current Rock. If you are heading from Charlotte Amalie to Red Hook or St. John via *Current Cut*, head for a waypoint at 18° 18.70' N, 64° 50.05' W, which is also the waypoint for the entrance to the *Christmas Cove anchorage*. From this waypoint head through *Current Cut* keeping mid-channel.

To access *Christmas Cove* from the waypoint, head east and anchor either north or south of Fish Cay as shown on the chart. Here you'll find 10'-20' of water but don't try to pass between *Fish Cay* and Great St. James Island. If you choose to anchor north of *Fish Cay* try to tuck in as close as possible to the shore of Great St. James Island to avoid the current that flows through *Current Cut*. This is one of the best anchorages in the Caribbean except for the ferry wakes (and during periods of westerly winds). You cannot anchor here but there are 20 new moorings that are free for up to 10 nights.

What You Will Find Ashore

There are no facilities ashore here, but there is good snorkeling to be found around the shoreline and south of Great St. James Island at *The Stragglers*, at Little St. James Island, and Dog Island.

Cowpet Bay

Navigational Information

To the northwest of Great St. James Island is *Cowpet Bay*, home of the *St. Thomas Yacht Club* (http://www.styc.club/), as shown on Chart USVI-8. Members of accredited yacht clubs are welcome to enjoy reciprocal privileges at this exclusive establishment. You might remember the *Virgin Island's America's Cup Challenge*; it was brought by the *St. Thomas Yacht Club*. Members are invited to add their club burgees to the collection in the club's bar. Mariners are welcome to use the docks and phone in an emergency, but are asked not to abuse this privilege. There are moorings off the club in *Cowpet Bay*, but they are private. The *St. Thomas International Regatta* is traditionally held at the *St. Thomas Yacht Club* on Easter weekend.

From Great St. James Island simply head northwest into *Cowpet Bay* passing southwest of Water Point and *Current Cut* as shown on Chart USVI-8. You can anchor on the eastern side of the bay or off the yacht club.

Red Hook

Waypoints:
Red Hook Bay - .1 nm NE of entrance channel
18° 19.77' N, 64° 50.50' W

Navigational Information

Red Hook offers a relief from the hustle and bustle of Charlotte Amalie, but it's still quite a busy place with ferries arriving and departing hourly for St. John. A waypoint at 18° 19.77' N, 64° 50.50' W, will place you approximately .1 mile northeast of the marked entrance channel leading into Red Hook as shown on Chart USVI-9. If you're approaching from *Current Cut* give the tip of Cabrita Point a wide berth before heading for the waypoint. If approaching from

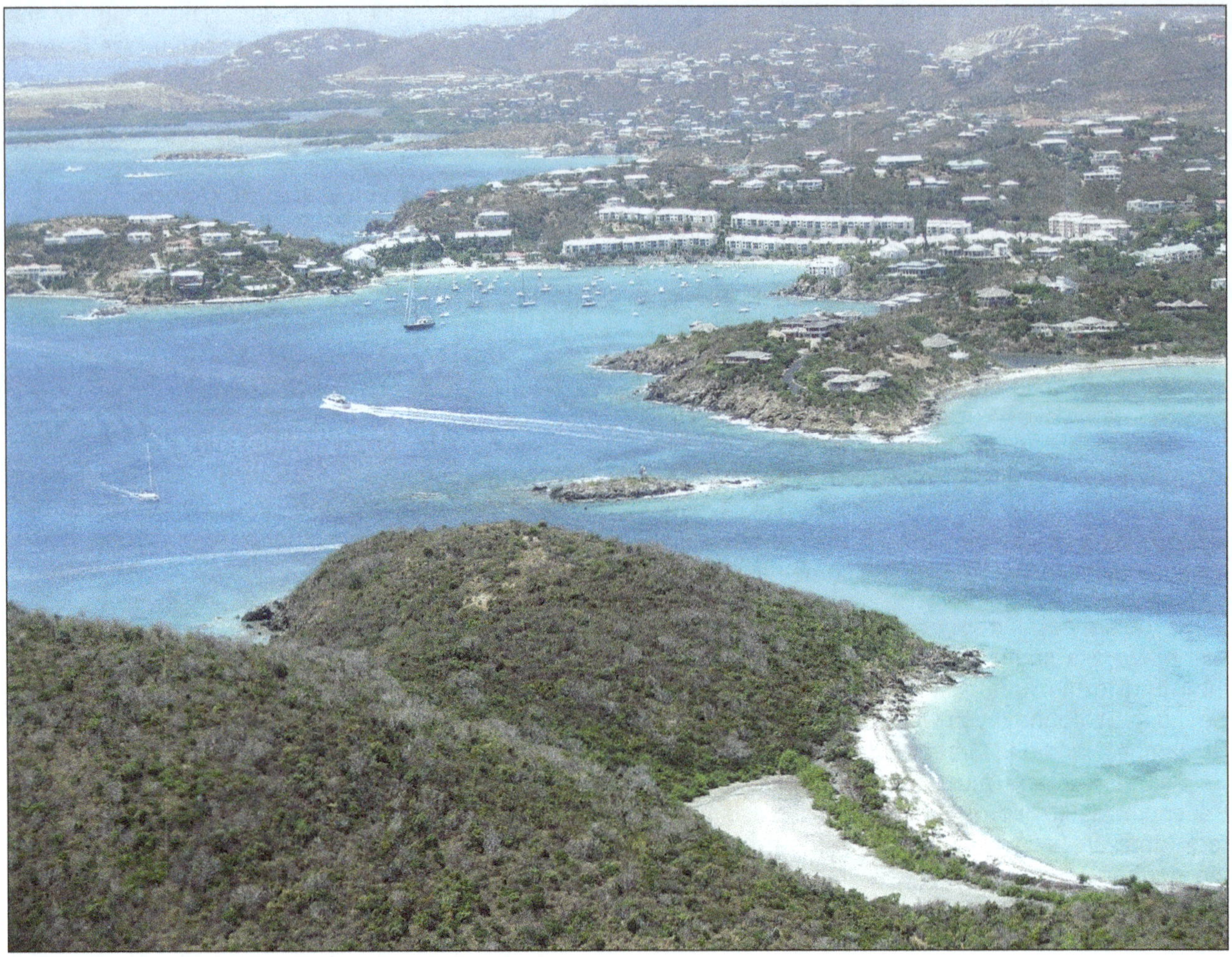

Current Cut, *Cowpet Bay* in background Photo by Todd Duff

Cowpet Bay, Red Hook in background Photo by Todd Duff

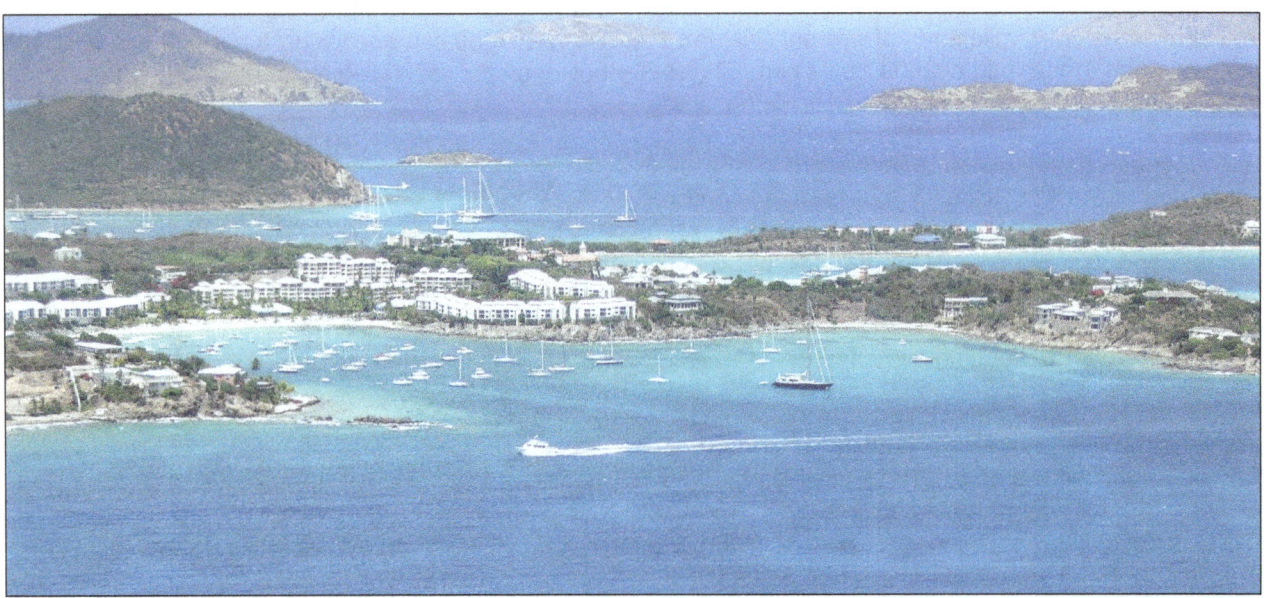

The United States Virgin Islands - St. Thomas

Cruz Bay, St. John, pass the northern tip of Steven Cay and head for the waypoint.

From the waypoint head southwest following the marked channel and avoiding any ferry traffic you might encounter. You can proceed all the way into *Vessup Bay* to anchor or turn south of the channel to anchor in *Muller Bay* as shown on the chart; you can also get a slip in one of the marinas here. *Muller Bay*, since it is so exposed to windward, often gets a good chop built up in the anchorage, but the holding is good and the neighborhood friendly and geared for boaters.

What You Will Find Ashore

On the northern side of *Vessup Bay*, just past the ferry dock as shown on the chart, is the *American Yacht Harbor* complex and on the southern side of the bay is the *Vessup Point Marina*. *American Yacht Harbour* (http://www.igy-americanyachtharbor.com/), look for their trademark red-gabled roofs, offers 104 slips with full electric and water. The marina can accommodate vessels of 110' LOA with drafts to 10'. The marina also offers fuel, showers, a laundry service, a pump-out station, *UPS* and *FedEx* service, car rentals, and all sorts of marine related businesses, gift shops, and restaurants nearby. Coffee lovers should stop in at *Lattes in Paradise* for the best coffee on the island served on a deck above the slips.

Here you'll find *Island Yachts*, a *Yanmar* dealer specializing in the sales and service of diesel engines. *All Island Marine* can handle all of your welding and fabrication needs and if you need to replenish your supply of lures visit *Neptune Fishing Supplies*. *Red Hook Dive Center* (http://www.redhookdivecenter.com/) sells dive gear as well as swimwear and postcards.

Across *Vessup Bay* is the *Vessup Point Marina* with only one finger pier these days. The marina can accommodate one yacht of 120' in length with a maximum 15' draft in comfort with full electric and water, showers, ice, storage locker rentals, and a thriving charter business (both *American Yacht Harbor* and *Vessups Point Marina* are home to several charter operations). The marina is home to what is probably the best cruisers bar around, *Latitude 18*.

The *American Yacht Harbor* is bursting at the seams with good places to eat such as the extremely popular *Molly Malone's Dockside Irish Pub* serving breakfast, lunch, and dinner, *Amigos Mexican Food*, *Lotus Sushi*, *East End Café* (Italian food), and the *Big Bambooz* burger joint and bar. The *Caribbean Saloon Steakhouse and Bar* (http://caribbeansaloon.com/) offering steaks and seafood daily from 1130-0400 and feature a big screen TV for watching videos and sporting events. Usually crowded, the Saloon boasts 12' wooden sculptures of banana trees and palm trees that act as a backdrop for mirrors and colorful fish mobiles, but ambiance aside, this is a great place for steak! *A Amigos* overlooks *American Yacht Harbor* and is a great spot for dinner. *Island Time Pub* (http://islandtimepub.com/) is upstairs at the marina, and *Fish Tails* features a large open terrace for dining with a fine view of the harbor. For a treat try *Haagen Dazs Bakery & Ice Cream*, the *American Yacht Harbor Deli*, and *The Bake Shoppe*.

Across the street from *American Yacht Harbor* is *Red Hook Plaza* where you'll find the *XO Bistro* (http://www.xobistro.net/), an intimate place featuring wine and champagne by the glass as well as a fully stocked bar. A block away is the *Marina Market*, a great place to provision offering only the freshest produce and name brand grocery items. The market has a quality butcher who is glad to take custom orders. It also offers spirits, and a deli that serves food to go or eat there. Next door to the market is the *Saki House Thai and Japanese Restaurant*. Elizabeth James sells very special jewelry and clothing while the *Color of Joy* offers lots of great little items from clothing to artwork. *Rhiannon's* is a New Age store with all the goodies you'd expect to find in one, including a *Tarot* reading if you're up to it. *Duffy's Love Shack* (http://www.duffysloveshack.com/) celebrates *Taco Tuesdays* with free cockroaches in every drink while their *Chicks Rule Wednesdays* are popular with singlehanders who also love loud *Rock & Roll*.

North of Red Hook on *Smith Bay Road* is *Smuggler's Steak and Seafood Grill*, famous for their *Sunday Brunch* and their "Make Your Own Bloody Mary Bar."

Sapphire Beach Marina

Waypoints:
Sapphire Beach Marina - .1 nm ENE of entrance
18° 20.05' N, 64° 50.75' W

Navigational Information
Sapphire Beach Marina lies just "around the corner" from Red Hook. When leaving Red Hook clear Red Hook Point and head to a waypoint at 18° 20.05' N, 64° 50.75' W; it will place you approximately 0.1 mile east/northeast of the entrance to *Sapphire*

A Cruising Guide to the Virgin Islands

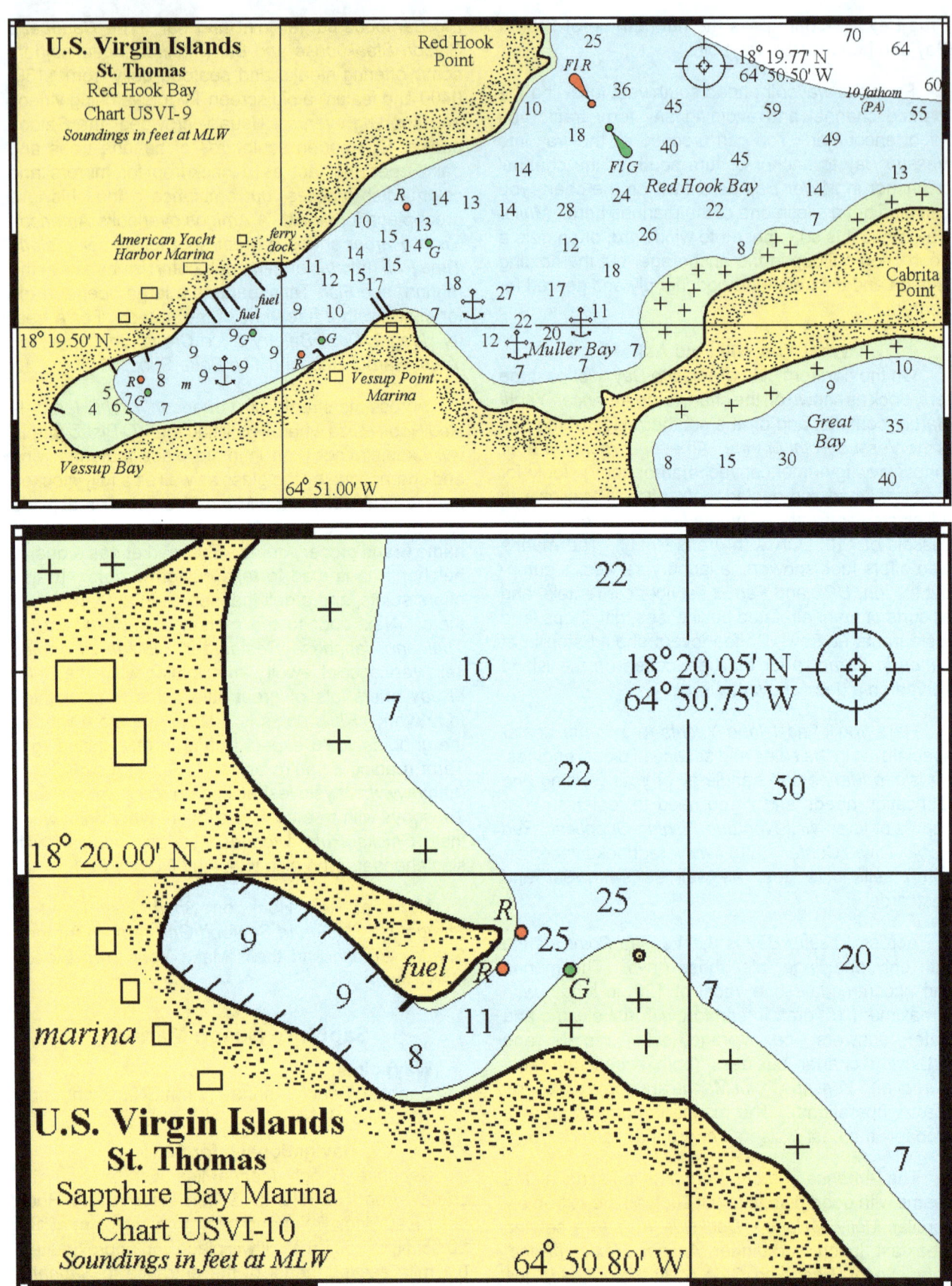

The United States Virgin Islands - St. Thomas

Christmas Cove, Current Cut in background   Photo by Todd Duff

Sapphire Beach Marina   Photo by Todd Duff

Megan's Bay, northern coast of St. Thomas   Photo by Todd Duff

Red Hook, St. Thomas   Photo by Todd Duff

Anchorage at south end of Hans Lollik Island   Photo by Todd Duff

Water Bay, Coki Point   Photo by Todd Duff

Mandal Point Harbor   Photo by Todd Duff

Beach Marina as shown on Chart USVI-10. From the waypoint head southwest to pick up the markers leading into the marina, favor the point of land on the northern side of the channel as a shallow reef lies to the south of the marked entrance channel. Notify the marina prior to entering the harbor on VHF ch. 16 or 12 for a slip assignment or directions to the fuel dock (to starboard near the entrance). There are no moorings available and anchoring is not permitted in the basin. However you can tie up to the marina for a short visit and pay a small fee which allows you use of the marina's amenities.

What You Will Find Ashore

The *Sapphire Beach Resort & Marina* (http://www.sapphirebeachmarina.com/) has 67 slips available with full electric and water, cable TV and phone hookups, a telephone, a swimming pool, a tennis court, provisions, a deli, and car rentals. At the time of this writing the marina's fuel dock was closed.

Just to the north of *Sapphire Beach Marina* is *Water Bay* and Coki Point where you'll find a lovely settled weather anchorage (see photo).

The Northern Shore

Navigational Information

As you will learn more about in the next section entitled *Driving Around St. Thomas*, *Magens Bay* lies on the northern shore of St. Thomas and is easily accessible by car, which is good, for if you bring your boat in here you'll probably find yourself rolling uncomfortably from the surge. At the northeastern tip of *Magens Bay* is Picara Point and there is a submerged rock, Ornen Rock, with less than 6' over it lying about ½ mile northwest of Picara Point. If you intend to anchor in *Magens Bay* watch out for the shoal as you enter and anchor in the northeastern corner of the bay in 12-25' of water. At the northwestern tip of *Magens Bay* is Tropaco Point where you'll notice several gray square buildings constructed atop a 50' cliff at the end of the point. Never attempt to enter or anchor in *Magens Bay* when northerly swells are running. When the seas are up you must avoid Ornen Rock, giving it a wide berth as it often does not break. Two small coves on the western shore of *Magen's Bay*, *Reseau Bay* and *Lerkenlund Bay* are used by local fishing boats.

To the northeast of *Magen's Bay* and Picara Point is Hans Lollik Island on whose western shore can be found a small gravelly beach. On the southeastern side of the island, at *Coconut Bay*, is a small beach protected by the off-lying *White Horseface Reef*. Only enter here in settled weather. There is a small channel southwest of the reef that you will carry you into the bay where you can anchor in 9'-12' of water over a sandy bottom (see photo). Ashore you'll find the ruins of an old plantation. Keep a sharp eye out for Hans Lollik Rock, awash and usually breaking, it lies a bit over ¼ mile east/southeast of the southern tip of Hans Lollik Island.

Just west of Tropaco Point are Inner Brass Island and Outer Brass Island separated by *Brass Channel* (good depths but stay mid-channel). On the southeastern shore of Inner Brass Island is a small anchorage that should only be used by small vessels in settled weather. Anchorage can be found southwest of Tropaco Point in *Hull Bay*, but you can expect quite a bit of roll here. Watch out for coral heads further in and take note that seas break on the reef west of *Hull Bay*. *Cave Cove* lies on the western shore of Outer Brass Island with a large cave opening up into it. Lizard Rocks lie about ¾ mile north of St. Thomas about a bit more west of Inner Brass Island. This small group of rocks is often awash on the tide.

Further west are two small bays that are quite subject to roll, *Santa Maria Bay* and *Botany Bay*. These coves should only be considered as a lunch stop in settled weather with no swells running.

About 3¼ miles to the north/northwest of St. Thomas' western tip, is a small cay named Cockroach Island. Southwest of Cockroach Island are *The Visibles* (not to be confused with *The Invisibles* east of Necker Island in the BVI), a large system of canyons and ledges covered with corals and sponges and teeming with marine life. This reef comes to within 10' of the surface atop a massive pinnacle that rises up 80' from a sandy bottom.

About 3 miles east of Picara Point is *Mandal Bay*, the bay is shoal and has a small beach at its head. There is an unmarked channel west of Mandal Point (on the eastern side of the bay) that leads through some reefs and a jetty into a small dredged harbor (4' depths at jetty). This should be visited by shoal draft vessels only.

Further east, north of Red Hook, are Thatch Cay and Grass Cay, separated by *Middle Passage* where the current can reach a strength of 4 knots. There is a small rock awash about 150 yards west of the western end of Grass Cay and it is easily seen in good visibility. The north and south sides of Lovongo Cay have day moorings and are nice stops for snorkeling. Carval Rock has amazing snorkeling and usually 2 day moorings.

Driving Around St. Thomas

Don't forget, even though these islands are known as the United States Virgin Islands, you must drive on the left. And don't be surprised if you encounter a traffic jam, especially in the area of *Tutu Park Mall* on *Route 38*. If all you need is a simple island tour, it might be best to hire a taxi and take advantage of the driver's knowledge.

Let's begin by heading east from Charlotte Amalie on the *Waterfront Highway* (*Veteran's Drive*), *Route 30* passing Havensight and several small bays and beaches as well as *Morningstar Bay* with the huge *Frenchman's Reef* and *Morning Star* resorts. It is possible to take *Route 38* directly to Red Hook, but you'll miss quite a bit of the southern shoreline of St. Thomas by doing that. Turning more to the northeast now, about halfway to Red Hook you'll come to the intersection with *Route 32*. Actually *Route 30* ends here and *Route 32* continues eastward to Red Hook and also heads off northward into the interior of St. Thomas, *Anna's Retreat* (sometimes called *Tutu*) and nearby *Tillett Gardens* (http://www.tillettgardens.com/) at the intersection of *Route 32* and *Route 38* near the *Tutu Park Mall* (remember what I said about a traffic jam here). *Tillett Gardens* is the 1960-ish creation of London born artist Jim Tillett and is a collection of art shops, boutiques, dance and music recitals, and restaurants, all worth the time it takes to stop and enjoy. You can dine here at *Polli's Mexican Restaurant* from their vegetarian menu.

Red Hook is the second city of St. Thomas and is described in its own section previously. From Red Hook you can take *Route 38* northwestward to *Anna's Retreat* (see above). If you take a right on *Route 388* you'll come to Coki Point and *Coral World* (http://coralworldvi.com/) where you can tour the underwater observatory to see a reef up close and personal. The *Predator Tank* houses barracuda and sharks, and on the tamer side you can pet a baby shark in the *Shark Shallows* or feed stingrays in the *Stingray Pool*.

From *Route 38* take *Route 40* to work your way northwestward toward *Drake's Seat*. But first, if you turn on *Route 42*, *Mahogany Run Road*, you'll come to the *Mahogany Run Golf Course* (http://www.mahoganyrungolf.com/), a fine 18 hole, par 72, 6,022 yard course, and then at the intersection of *Route 35*, you can continue northwest to its end at beautiful *Magens Bay*. Off *Route 40* near the *Magen's Bay* intersection is *Drake's Seat* where it is alleged that Sir Francis Drake used this spot as a lookout when searching for Spanish ships. *Route 35* takes you from Charlotte Amalie to *Magens Bay*, but you'll want to stay on *Route 40* (the *St. Peter Mountain Road*) heading west to the *Estate St. Peter Greathouse and Botanical Gardens* (http://www.greathousevi.com/). On the site of an old plantation, the 150-acre site boasts an observation deck at 1,000', a mini-museum, a small aviary, and the botanical gardens.

Route 40 runs into *Route 33* near *Mountain Top*, 1,550', where you'll find several shops and a restaurant atop *St. Peter Mountain* and what has been described as one of the top ten best views in the world. It is alleged that the *banana daiquiri* was invented here, I can't say for sure, but I suppose stranger things have happened.

At *Route 301*, continue westward and you will eventually meet *Route 30*, which runs from the western tip of St. Thomas eastward back to Charlotte Amalie (remember, we took *Route 30* eastward when we left Charlotte Amalie). Nearby, on *Route 301*, is *Crown Mountain*, St. Thomas highest point at 1,556', just a few feet higher than *Mountain Top*, I suppose one good hurricane could change that.

As you work your way back towards Charlotte Amalie on *Route 30*, you'll pass the *University of the Virgin Islands* and the *Reichhold Center for the Arts* (http://www.reichholdcenter.org/), which offers cultural and folklore performances throughout the year. Further east you will come to the area known as Frenchtown, which is covered in a previous section.

St. John

St. John, named San Juan by its discoverer, Christopher Columbus, is approximately 8 miles long and 4 miles wide at its widest point, and is about 19 square miles in area, roughly the same size of Manhattan. The central and western portions of the island are comprised of irregular hills and peaks of which Bordeaux Mountain is the highest at 1,277'. Much of the island, some 5,650 acres, is part of the Virgin Islands National Park and is untouched and pristine, there's not even an airport on the island. The lush, green land for the park, home to over 800 plant species and 30 species of tropical birds, was donated by the Rockefeller family and opened in 1956 and in 1962, more than 5,500 underwater acres were added to the park. The park has also been designated a biosphere reserve, part of an international network of natural areas established to demonstrate the value of conservation. The Virgin Islands National Park has installed moorings and established protective zones around several of the more sensitive reef and sea grass areas to prevent damage caused by boat's anchors. As of 2002, the National Park Service has decreed that all commercial vessels over 125' are not be allowed to anchor inside the park's boundaries, however, private vessels between 125'-210' are allowed to anchor in *Francis Bay* in sand, 1,000' from the exclusion buoys. For more information, such as the locations of hiking trails, check in at the National Park Visitor Center across from Mongoose Junction in Cruz Bay.

St. John is home to over 5,000 people, but where St. Thomas is all hustle and bustle, St. John is just the opposite. To say this island is laid back would be an understatement, actually it would be misnomer, the ambiance of St. John is far beyond the simple term "laid back," in St. John you are practically in another dimension. You might think you've wandered into a paradise where many of those free spirits of the 1960s and 1970s have settled. Hark back to days

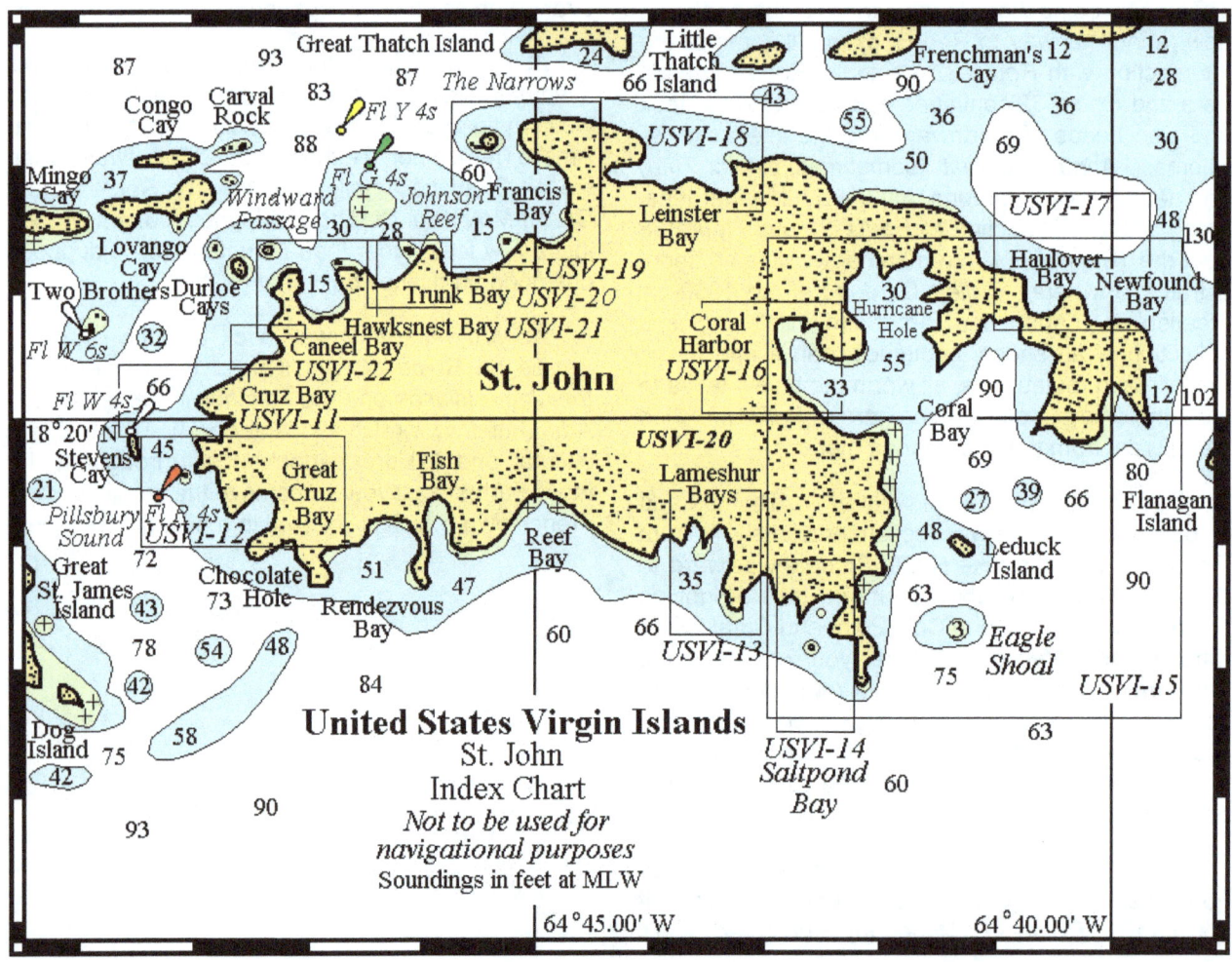

The United States Virgin Islands - St. John

Cruz Bay, St. John

Photo by Todd Duff

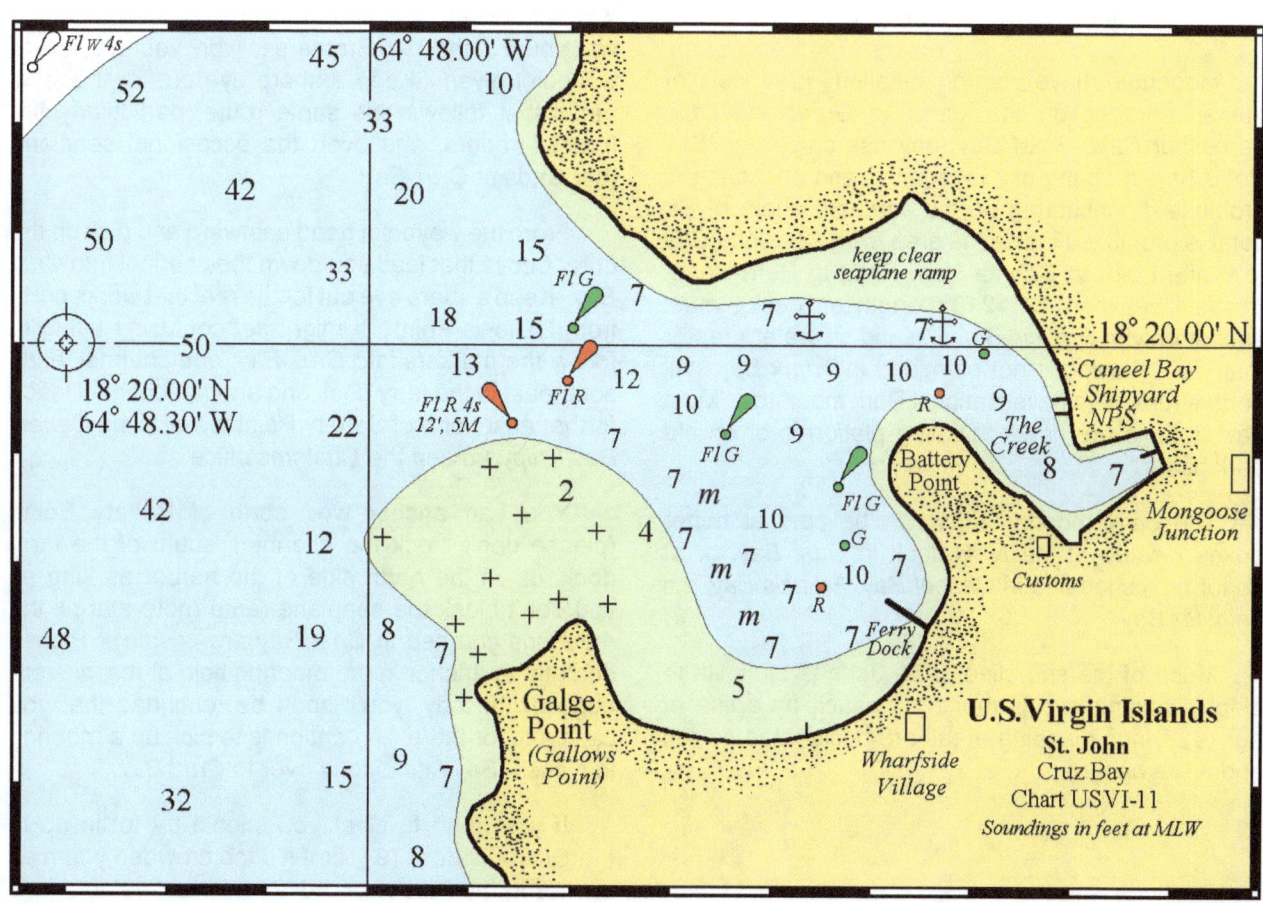

of old and enjoy the ambiance, you are on an island of free thinkers, of artists, writers, creative people all, you'll feel it as you move about, you'll absorb it, you might even enjoy it and then where will you be?

If you wish to visit St. John from St. Thomas, or vice versa, say you wish to dine in Charlotte Amalie or Red Hook and return, you can take one of the hourly ferries that ply the waters of *Pillsbury Sound* between Red Hook and *Cruz Bay*. The trip takes about 20 minutes, but if you're in a hurry, take the *Dohm's Water Taxi* (http://www.virginislandswatertaxi.com/), fast power catamaran that gets you there in 15 minutes for $15. By the way, the last ferry leaves Red Hook for *Cruz Bay* at midnight, and the last ferry from *Cruz Bay* leaves for Red Hook at 2300, so don't miss it. Ferries from Charlotte Amalie leave for *Cruz Bay* regularly and take about 45 minutes for the trip.

Let's begin our circumnavigation of St. John from *Cruz Bay* and head east along the southern shore to *Coral Bay*, and then westward along the northern shore of St. John, through the narrows, and then down the western shore back to *Cruz Bay*.

Moorings at St. John

Moorings have been installed in most of the anchorages on St. John. In *Great* and *Little Lameshur Bays*, *Reef Bay* (day use only), and *Salt Pond Bay*, mooring use is required and anchoring is prohibited. Anchoring on the southern shore of St. John is prohibited inside the area from *Cocoloba Cay* to White Point to Cabrita Horn Point to Ram Head. Vessels between 125'-210' (length on deck), must anchor only in *Francis Bay*, in sand, in water greater than 50'. Fishing is not permitted in *Trunk Bay*. All north shore bays have National Park moorings. Most pay stations are now at floating platforms or on old park boats.

The daily mooring fees can be paid at honor boxes located at the *NPR* dock in *Cruz Bay*, or at honor boxes located in *Caneel Bay, Francis Bay,* and *Leinster Bay*.

Much of the shoreline of St. John is off limits to dinghy landing and is marked as such by a line of buoys. Dinghy landing areas are designated by red and white buoys.

Cruz Bay

Important Lights:
Two Brothers Light: Fl W 6s
Stevens Cay Light: Fl W 4s
Cruz Bay Sea Buoy: Fl W 4s

Waypoints:
Cruz Bay - ½ nm W of entrance channel
18° 20.00' N, 64° 48.30' W

In the mid-1800s, *Cruz Bay* was little more than a military outpost for Danish soldiers. Shortly after the U.S. purchased the islands in 1917, *Cruz Bay* came into its own for its proximity to St. Thomas as the tourism industry developed.

Navigational Information

A waypoint at 18° 20.00' N, 64° 48.30' W, will place you approximately ½ mile west of the marked entrance channel leading into *Cruz Bay* as shown on Chart USVI-11. Approaching from St. Thomas, either from Red Hook or from *Current Cut* at Great St. James Island, you must cross *Pillsbury Sound*, the body of water that separates St. Thomas and St. John and where the tidal current can attain a velocity of 2 knots. You will have to pass north of Stevens Cay, keeping well south of the Two Brothers to work your way to the waypoint given. Keep a sharp eye out for the local traffic that follows this same route, particularly the ferries, traders, and even the occasional seaplane that lands at *Cruz Bay*.

From the waypoint head eastward and pick up the outer buoys that lead you down the channel into *Cruz Bay*. Keep a sharp eye out for the reef that works north from Gallows Point. It might get confusing trying to follow the markers into *Cruz Bay*; one channel leads southeast to the ferry dock and another channel leads further east north of Battery Point towards the *Caneel Bay Shipyard* and the *Customs* office.

You can anchor well north of Battery Point, (please don't block the channel), south of the ferry dock, or on the north side of the harbor as long as you don't block the seaplane ramp (note that all the moorings you see in *Cruz Bay* are private). Please don't try to anchor in the mooring field at the western edge of the bay, you'll soon be reminded that you can't anchor there. An option is to pick up a mooring in *Caneel Bay* and dinghy over to *Cruz Bay*.

If you need to clear you should try to tie up to the *Customs* dock (9'), or if it's too crowded you may anchor in the harbor and dinghy in to *Customs* (this is sometimes acceptable, make a good effort to tie up to the dock first, and if your vessel is registered at over 5 net tons you will be assessed a dock fee by the *Cruz Bay Port Authority*). Vessels may anchor in *The Creek* for a maximum of 3 hours while clearing or provisioning. It is also permissible to anchor or moor in *Caneel Bay* and dinghy into *Cruz Bay*.

What You Will Find Ashore

Across from *Customs* is the *Caneel Bay Shipyard* where you can haul out (check first as I'm told they are doing this intermittently), have your hull repaired or painted, have your sails or refrigeration repaired, and pick up ice, water, and fuel. Some marine supplies are available at *Paradise Lumber & Hardware St John*.

About half of the area north and west of Battery Point is part of the *Virgins Islands National Park* with the boundary line running approximately mid-channel. Remember that anchoring is limited to a 14-day maximum in any one spot in the *Virgin Islands National Park*. The park service has a dock in *The Creek*, but it has a time limit of 15 minutes so load or unload quickly here. There are some dumpsters across the street so please don't use the smaller trash cans that you see near the dock.

Ashore you'll find that there are two main shopping areas in *Cruz Bay*, *Mongoose Junction*, just north of the ferry dock, and *Wharfside Village* on the waterfront south of the ferry dock. As I did in the St. Thomas section, I will not list every store here, but I can give you some highlights, besides, walking around and exploring is part of the fun of this.

Let's begin at the ferry dock (you'll find small dinghy docks on both sides of the ferry dock near the shore; dinghies are not permitted on the beach) and walk northward to *Mongoose Junction* (http://www.mongoosejunctionstjohn.com/). Next to the ferry dock on Battery Point is *The Battery*, built in 1735 as a fortification after the slave revolt of 1733, which now houses a small museum where jails cells once stood. Nearby is the *Fish Trap Restaurant* (http://www.thefishtrap.com/) at *Raintree Court,* and *Morgan's Mango* just across from the National Park dock. *Morgan's Mango* offers a Thursday *Margarita Night* with live music, and of course one of everybody's most popular places is *Cheeseburgers in Paradise* serving what else? Cheeseburgers…and other stuff too. Nearby is a Laundromat and if you need to surf the net you can get Internet access at *Connections* where you can also send and receive faxes, send or receive money via *Western Union*, or make use of their notary service. *Connections* monitors VHF ch. 72.

If you're hungry visit the *Gecko Gazebo*, a charming little outdoor bar tucked in between two shops, or head for the stone walls and French doors of *Paradiso*, a large, elegant, and upscale restaurant that is open for dinner only. If these choices don't suffice, try the *Mongoose Restaurant* located just south of *Mongoose Junction* (just past the *National Park Service Center*) serving fine Mexican cuisine with a vegetarian twist. *Fred's* offers live reggae music on Wednesdays and Fridays and inexpensive West Indian fare. Another good choice is *The Ocean Grill Restaurant* or the *Deli Grotto*.

For groceries try *Starfish Market* (http://www.starfishmarket.com/), *Marina Market*, or the *Dolphin Market* located in the *Boulon Center*.

By now you're probably wondering what a mongoose is doing in the Virgin Islands. The mongoose was introduced to the Virgin Islands by sugarcane growers to attack the huge population of cane rats that devastated their crops. Soon the mongoose turned to other prey such as chickens, fish, crabs, turtle eggs and other island creatures and is still the bane of farmers and conservationists. On the good side, the mongoose has all but eliminated the snake in the Virgin Islands.

At the three-story *Wharfside Village* there are many choices for shopping and dining including *Panini Beach Trattoria, Rumbalaya Caribbean Bar & Grill, Dizzy D's Pizza and Tacos, Cafe Wahoo,* and the *Paradise Cafe*.

Across from *Wharfside Village* is the *Stone Terrace*, an upscale eatery that is open only for dinner. Near the southern end of *Wharfside Village* is the *Fish Trap*, a casual and very popular spot with the locals as well as visitors that is open for dinner only.

Two blocks in from the ferry dock is the *First Bank*, and cross from *First Bank* you'll find *La Tapa* (http://www.latapastjohn.com/) where you can listen to jazz while sampling their Spanish cuisine, dinner only. To the right of the bank is the *Pink Papaya* (http://pinkpapaya.com/) featuring the works of local artist M. Lisa Etre. *Silverlining* is a tiny shop offering some very lovely handcrafted jewelry. If you need a newspaper fix check in at *Sparky's* were you can also pick up a paperback book, film, and spirituous libations.

The *Ivan Jadan Museum* is located on *Genip Street* in *Cruz Bay*. Jadan was one of the greatest Russian tenors and spent the last 40 years of his life on St. John where he died in 1995. His loving wife created this museum as a tribute to her husband's life and love of music. The *Elaine Ione Sprauve Library and Museum* was built in 1757 as the great house of a plantation and today it is a library and museum of boating artifacts from pre-Columbian and Colonial periods. Further on is the old *Parish Hall Estate* and the ruins of *Estate Caterineberg*, one of the earliest plantations on St. John.

Great Cruz Bay

Important Lights:
Mingo Rock: Fl R 4s

Waypoints:
Great Cruz Bay - ¼ nm SW of entrance
18° 19.07' N, 64° 47.80' W

Navigational Information

Great Cruz Bay lies southeast of *Cruz Bay* and is a very popular anchorage as you'll notice by the number of boats in the harbor. If you are approaching *Great Cruz Bay* from *Cruz Bay* you must clear the harbor mouth at *Cruz Bay* and the shoals off Gallows Point (see Chart USVI-11) before turning your bow south to pass between Gallows Point and Skipper Jacob Rock. Continuing south you will pass *Frank Bay* on St. John and come to Moravian Point, see Chart USVI-12. You can pass between Moravian Point and Mingo Rock, or pass west of Mingo Rock and the flashing red light shown as #2 before heading to the waypoint for *Great Cruz Bay*. Watch out for two wrecks shown in the waters southeast and southwest of Mingo Rock. If you are approaching from Red Hook on St. Thomas, you must make sure that when heading to the waypoint you will pass south of Skipper Jacob Rock.

A waypoint at 18° 19.07' N, 64° 47.80' W, will place you approximately ¼ mile southwest of the entrance to *Great Cruz Bay* as shown on Chart USVI-12. From the waypoint you can head a bit north of east to enter the wide mouth of the bay to anchor as far in as your draft allows. There are a few moorings available here if you don't wish to anchor.

What You Will Find Ashore

On shore is the *Westin Resort* with its *Snorkel's Pool Bar & Grill* featuring a Sunday barbecue and a Monday *Surf & Turf Night*. The *Lemongrass Restaurant & Bar* offers a Wednesday *Caribbean Buffet* and a Sunday evening *Ladies Night*.

East of *Great Cruz Bay* are several anchorages that are rarely frequented by cruisers, but deserve a mention (see photos). As shown on the *St. John Index Chart*, *Rendezvous Bay* is primarily used by local boaters in settled weather while nearby *Chocolate Hole* is well protected and has a sandy bottom that makes for good holding. The problem here is that the bay is usually filled with local boats leaving little or no room to anchor and no public moorings are available.

A bit further east is *Fish Bay* and then *Reef Bay* where there is one *National Park Service* mooring available and anchoring is prohibited. There is another private mooring in the harbor, you'll recognize it, it is white with a red stripe while the park moorings are white with a blue stripe. The entrance to *Reef Bay*, actually the anchorage area is in *Genti Bay*, is between two reefs that are awash at low water. *Fish Bay* has better protection than *Reef Bay*, but its protection is so far inside that for the most part the bay is too shallow for all but shoal draft vessels. These anchorages that lie east of *Great Cruz Bay* can be quite rolly when the wind goes just south of east and should never be considered if the wind is from the south.

The Lameshur Bays

Waypoints:
Great Lameshur Bay - ½ nm SSW of
18° 18.30' N, 64° 43.70' W

Navigational Information

Great Lameshur Bay, and *Little Lameshur Bay*, both offer good protection except in times of southerly winds. As you approach *Little Lameshur Bay* you'll notice some prominent 150' high white cliffs that stretch ½ mile to the west of the bay. A waypoint at 18° 18.30' N, 64° 43.70' W, will place you approximately ½ mile south of *Little Lameshur Bay* and the same distance south/southwest of *Great Lameshur Bay* as shown on Chart USVI-13. From the waypoint you can head north to enter *Little Lameshur Bay* by keeping Yawzi Point to starboard, or to enter *Great Lameshur Bay* by keeping Yawzi Point to port.

Anchoring is not permitted in both *Little Lameshur Bay* and *Great Lameshur Bay* so you'll have to pick

The United States Virgin Islands - St. John

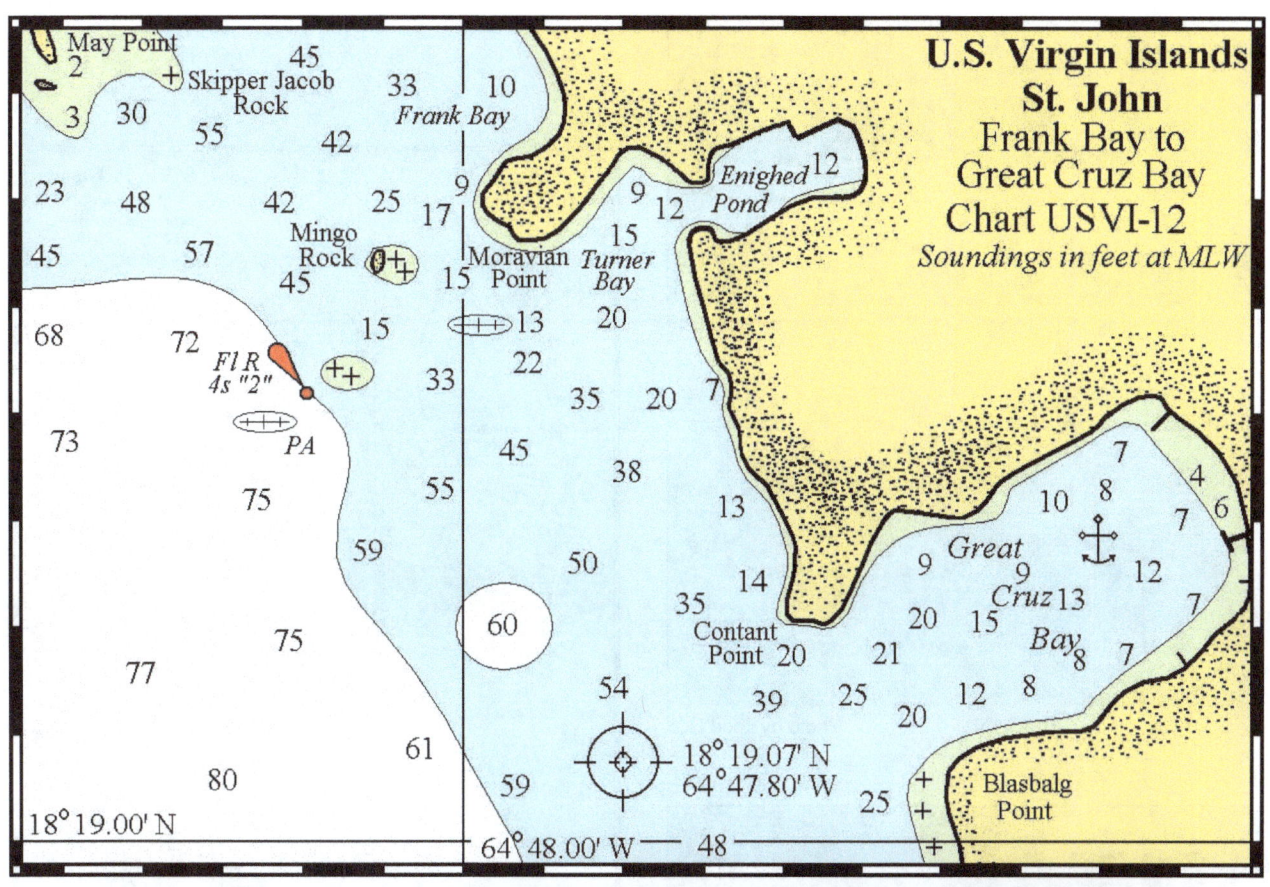

Great Cruz Bay, St. John   Photo by Todd Duff

A Cruising Guide to the Virgin Islands

Chocolate Hole, St. John — Photo by Todd Duff

Rendezvous Bay, St. John — Photo by Todd Duff

Fish Bay, St. John — Photo by Todd Duff

Reef Bay, St. John — Photo by Todd Duff

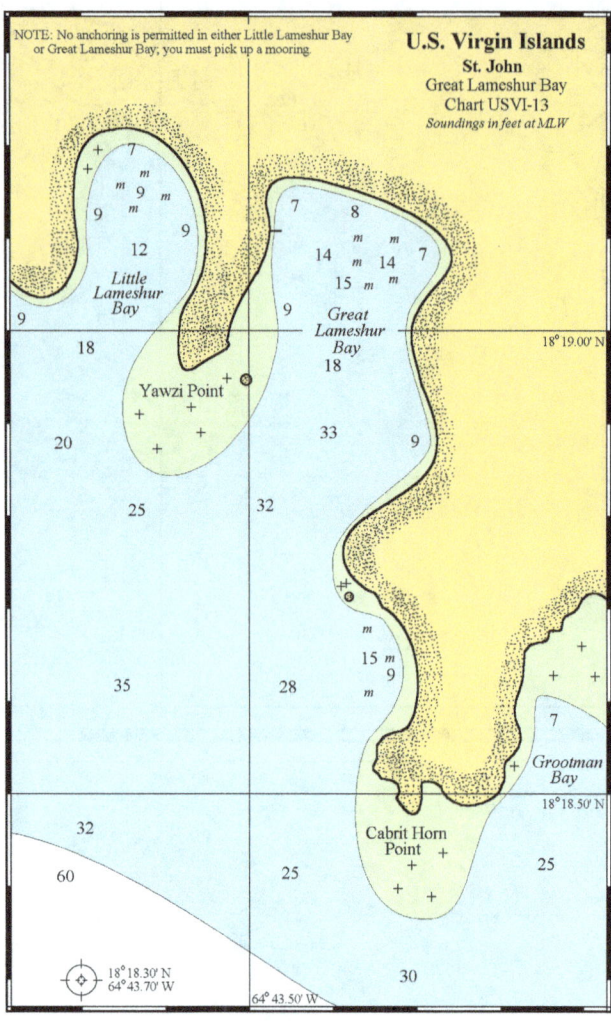

Great Lameshur Bay and *Little Lameshur Bay*, St. John — Photo by Todd Duff

The United States Virgin Islands - St. John

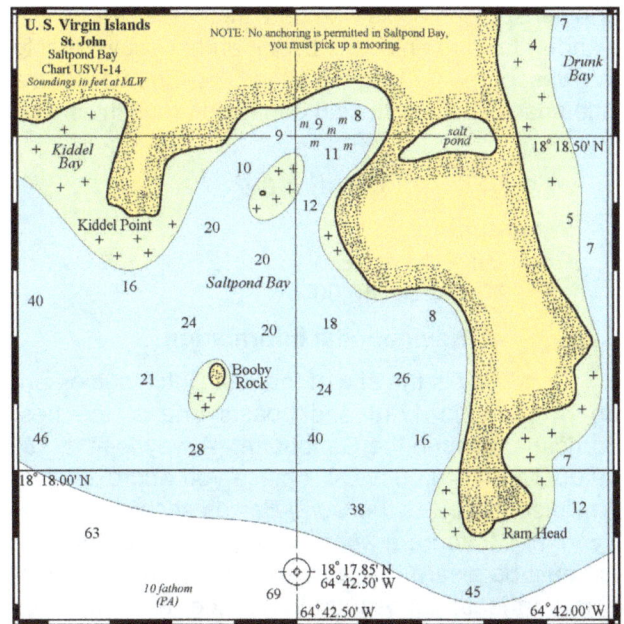

Saltpond Bay with *Coral Bay* in background, St. John
Photo by Todd Duff

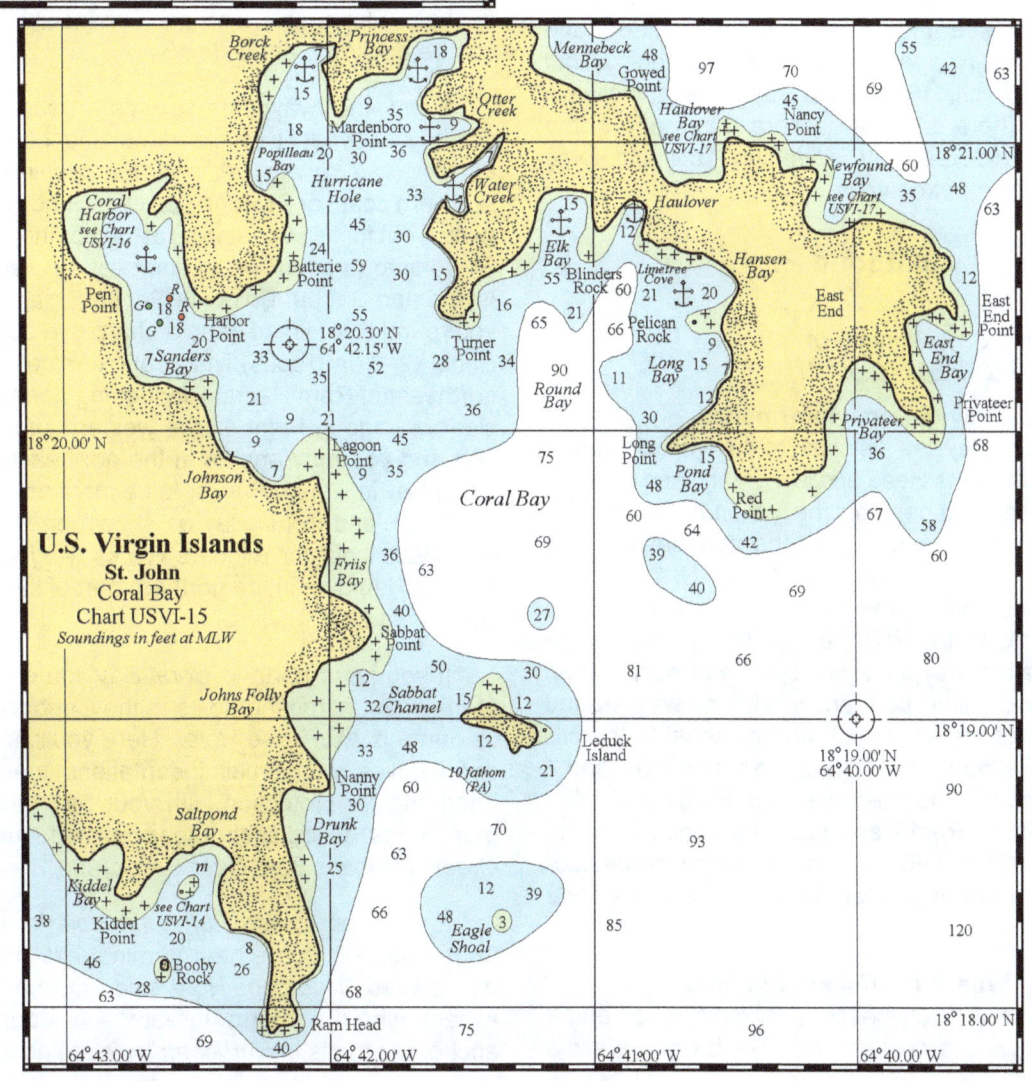

91

up a mooring. In *Great Lameshur Bay* there are nine moorings and a *National Park* dock in the northwestern part of the bay. Dinghies are allowed to tie up on the north side of the dock near shore, but you must keep the rest of the dock open for Park vessels and don't block the *Park Ranger* boat. The southern side of the dock is reserved for vessels belonging to *VIERS*, the *Virgin Islands Environmental Resource Station* a facility that is part of the *University of the Virgin Islands*. The white building on the shore is a lab for *VIERS*. There are some trash cans ashore where you may dump your garbage although the bins are small and the park requests that boaters deposit their trash in bins in either *Cruz Bay* or in *Coral Harbor*.

What You Will Find Ashore

Little Lameshur Bay has several moorings available and anchoring is not permitted here. There are picnic tables and trash bins on the shore courtesy of the *National Park Service* and if you look up on the hill you'll see a radio tower that is located at the *National Park Ranger Station*. The rangers do not monitor VHF ch. 16 and the station is not always manned. There is a path ashore that leads to the ruins of the old *Reef Bay Estate* sugar mill and some pre-Columbian petroglyphs.

Saltpond Bay

Waypoints:
Saltpond Bay - ½ nm S of
18° 17.85' N, 64° 42.50' W

Navigational Information

Saltpond Bay lies just west of the western end of *Coral Bay* at Rams Head and is a great place to moor, you cannot anchor here, but the *National Park Service* has placed some moorings in the northeastern part of the bay. A waypoint at 18° 17.85' N, 64° 42.50' W, will place you approximately ½ mile south of the entrance into *Saltpond Bay* as shown on Chart USVI-14. From the waypoint you can head north, keep Booby Rock well to port, and work your way around either side of the small rock and its shoal to the NE pocket of *Saltpond Bay*. There are 6 moorings, and 2 day moorings on the western side of Ram Head. You can hike up to Ram Head from the beach or up to the *Concordia Eco-Resort* (http://www.concordiaeco-resort.com/) where you can enjoy a lunch in their fine restaurant.

What You Will Find Ashore

Ashore is a lovely beach with picnic tables and a garbage bin at the western end. The beach here is a popular spot for locals who park their cars nearby and wander down to enjoy the beach and the bay. Just to the west of the parking lot is the *Stop Culture Stop*, a little snack shack with cold drinks and munchies.

Coral Bay

Waypoints:
Coral Bay - 1 nm SE of
18° 19.00' N 64° 40.00' W

Navigational Information

Coral Bay is the site of the first Dutch settlement on St. John in 1718 and boasts one of the best hurricane holes in the Caribbean. A waypoint at 18° 19.00' N, 64° 40.00' W, will place you approximately 1 mile southeast of the *Coral Bay* as shown on Chart USVI-15. If you are approaching *Coral Harbor* from the east be aware that a tidal current sets southwest and northeast across the entrance to *Coral Bay* between Flanagan Island and Privateer Point, and it can be as strong as 1½ knots.

From the waypoint you can head northwest passing between Leduck Island and Long Point to enter *Coral Bay* proper. If approaching from the southern coast of St. John you can round Rams Head (watch out for fish traps here) at the southeastern tip of St. John to turn northward and pass between Leduck Island and Sabbat Point via *Sabbat Channel*. When you round Ram Head keep a sharp eye out for *Eagle Shoal* (2'-3' in places) lying approximately ½-¾ mile northeast of Ram Head. Proceeding northward keep clear of Lagoon Point on the western shore of *Coral Bay* and you may anchor in the northeastern part of *Coral Bay* in *Round Bay*, or to be more precise, at the Haulover, and in *Elk Bay* as shown on Chart USVI-15. Watch out for Blinders Rocks lying well off the point at Haulover in the northern part of the bay, west of *Hansen Bay*.

If you head north in *Coral Bay* you come to one of the finest hurricane holes in the Caribbean, in fact its name is *Hurricane Hole*. Here you'll find several deep coves with small indentations that you can head into for protection with your bow safely in the mangroves. Good anchorages can be found at *Borck Creek*, *Princess Bay*, *Otter Creek*, and *Water Bay*.

If you plan to use *Hurricane Hole* for protection from a named storm, bear in mind that this spot will be crowded! *Hurricane Hole* is now closed to vessels except when a storm threatens. Moorings and anchorage spots in *Hurricane Hole* are now assigned

The United States Virgin Islands - St. John

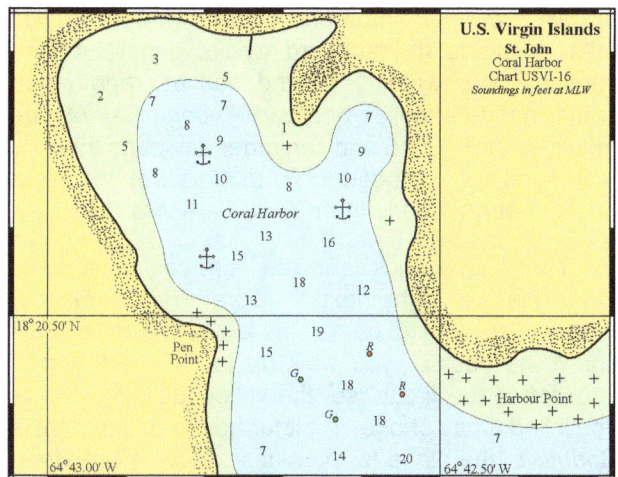

Coral Harbor, St. John — Photo by Todd Duff

Hurricane Hole, Coral Bay, St. John — Photo by Todd Duff

Haulover, Coral Bay, St. John — Photo by Todd Duff

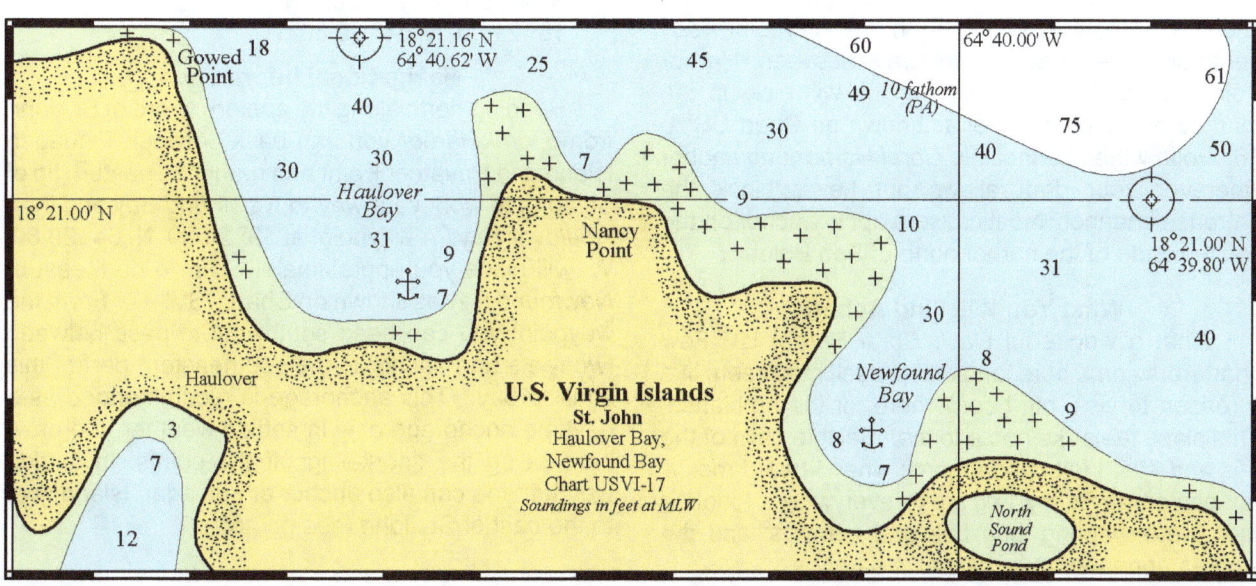

93

by the *Park Service* and must be applied for in advance of the season. You must vacate the area within 48 hours of the passing of the storm. The park wants NO damage to the mangroves; regulations require that you do NOT tie up to the mangroves or through them to other trees. It is illegal to tie ropes to any vegetation on park lands. Mangroves are recognized as an endangered species and are protected by federal and territorial law. The park will have staff coming through that will remove any ropes or chains fastened to the mangroves! Sand screws are also prohibited. The park suggests that vessels secure themselves fore and aft with several large anchors in an east/west orientation parallel as the winds tend to funnel though the area in those directions. There are day use moorings here that make for a pleasant stay before heading back to *Hansen Bay* for the night.

Coral Harbor

Waypoints:
Coral Harbor - ½ nm E of entrance
18° 20.30' N, 64° 42.15' W

Navigational Information

Coral Harbor lies in the northwestern corner of *Coral Bay* and it is the center of boating activity on the eastern shore of St. John. From the waypoint at the entrance to *Coral Bay*, head northwestward passing south of *Hurricane Hole* between Turner Point and Lagoon Point, and then working your way westward to a spot midway between Harbor Point and *Sanders Bay* as shown on Chart USVI-15. A waypoint at 18° 20.30' N, 64° 42.15' W, will place you approximately ½ mile west of the entrance into *Coral Harbor* as shown on Chart USVI-15. From the waypoint head generally west passing midway between Harbor Point and *Sanders Bay* where you will pick up the marked entrance channel as shown on Chart USVI-16. Follow the channel into *Coral Harbor* and anchor wherever your draft allows but never block the entrance channel. Most cruisers opt to anchor on the western side of the harbor north of Pen Point.

What You Will Find Ashore

What a wonderful place *Coral Harbor* is! Few charterers come here, and that in itself may seem like a reason to visit, but I come here for the ambiance. This place feels like home to me. Being a child of the 60s and 70s, I felt right at home when I heard rock & roll played at *Skinny Leg's* and everywhere I looked men were wearing long hair and earrings, and the women appeared quite casual in sarongs.

Ashore you'll find *Coral Harbor Marine Service* offering engine and outboard repairs, general marine services, ice, water, sail and canvas repair, and some marine supplies and parts. *Coral Bay Marine* monitors VHF ch. 16 and can order any parts that you may need. If you need to go to *Cruz Bay* there are buses that run hourly from *Coral Harbor* to *Cruz Bay*.

The dinghy dock is in the northeastern area of *Coral Harbor*, right next to *Coral Harbor Marine*. Please use a long painter here as everyone must share the dock. If you walk up to the road, just to your left is the firehouse, the yellow building, where you'll find a pay phone. A bit further up on the right is *Sputnik's*, the place for breakfast. Across the street is a school and a dumpster for your garbage. If you take a left on the road as you leave the dinghy dock you immediately come to the *Wallstreet Complex* where you'll find one of the best bars to be found in the Virgin Islands, *Skinny Legs Bar and Restaurant* (http://www.skinnylegsvi.com/), which also happens to be the clubhouse of the *Coral Bay Yacht Club*.

Nearby are the ruins of the old *Emmaus Moravian Church* built on the ruins of the old *Estate Carolina*. It is said that the ghost of a ram haunts the area and can be seen on full moon nights. On the lower road are the ruins of an old battery that was built in the 1800s when the British ruled here for a short while. Atop the hill at the harbor's mouth are the ruins of *Fort Berg*.

Newfound Bay

Waypoints:
Newfound Bay - ¼ nm NE of
18° 21.00' N, 64° 39.80' W

Navigational Information

Heading north along the eastern shore of St. John from *Coral Harbor* you can pass between Flanagan Island and Privateer Point and round the eastern tip of St. John to work your way to *Newfound Bay* and then *Haulover Bay*. A waypoint at 18° 21.00' N, 64° 39.80' W, will place you approximately ¼ mile northeast of *Newfound Bay* as shown on Chart USVI-17. From the waypoint you can head southwest to pass between two reefs and anchor in the southeastern part of this shallow bay. This anchorage is recommended as a daytime anchorage only in settled weather, the draw here being the snorkeling off the points. In settled weather you can also anchor at Flanagan Island, just to the east of St. John (see photo).

The United States Virgin Islands - St. John

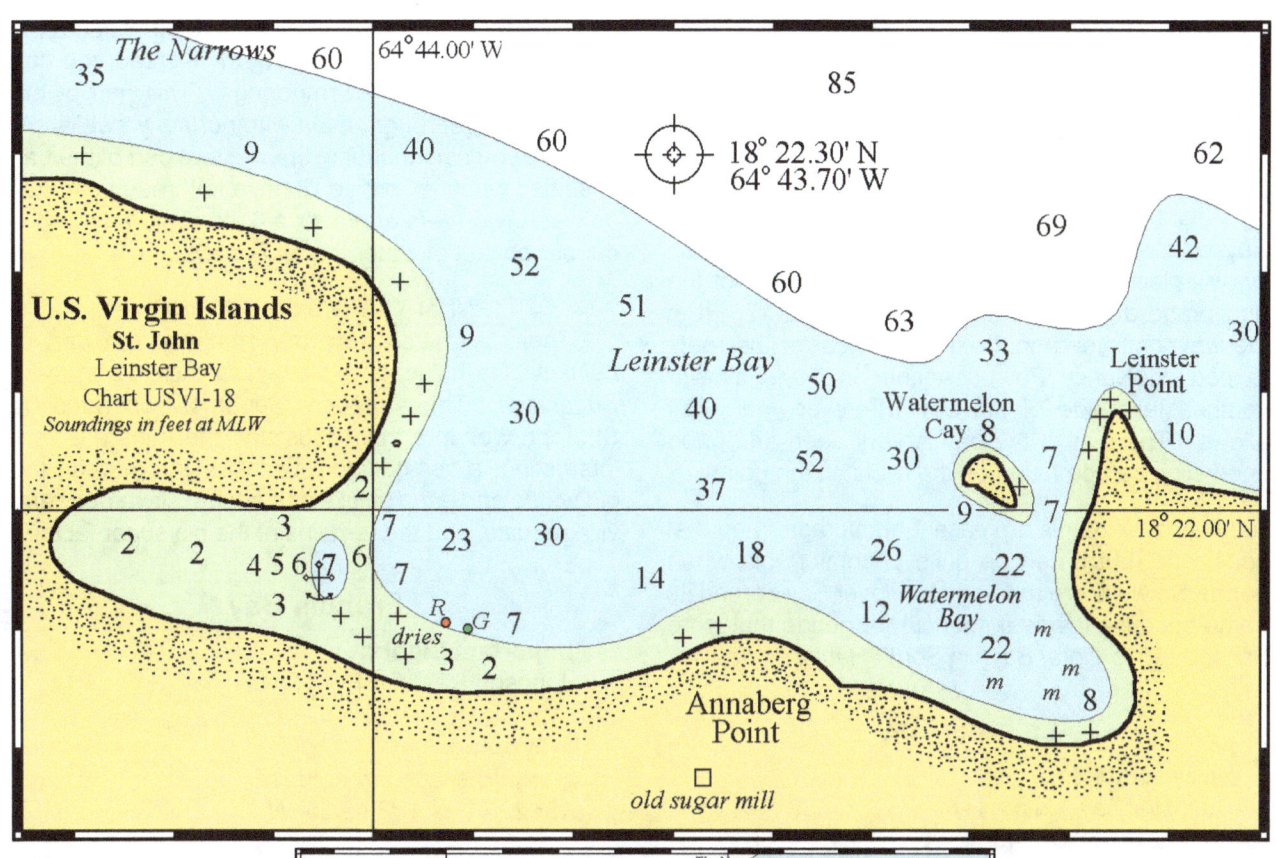

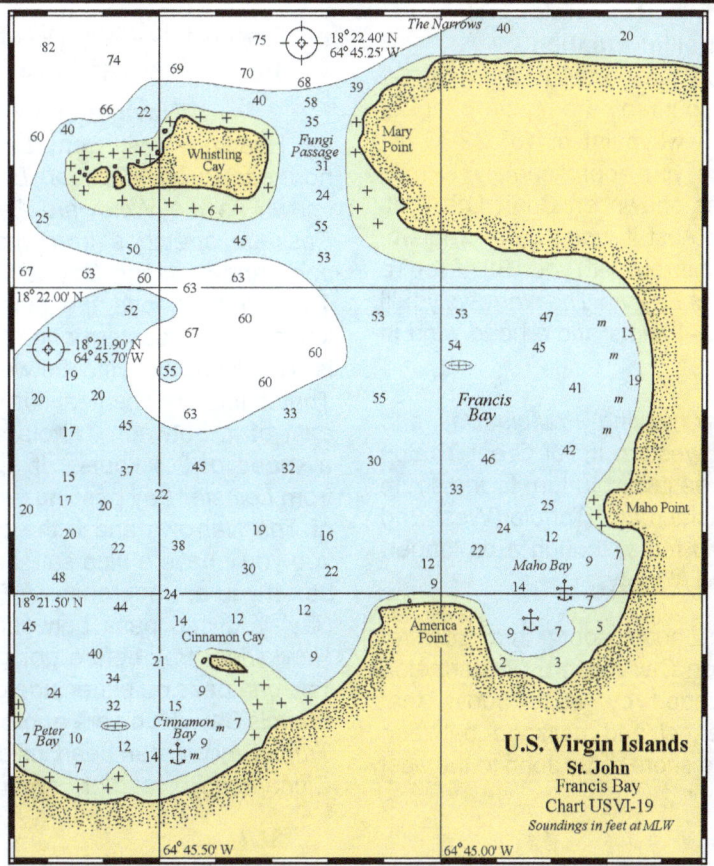

Haulover Bay

Waypoints:
Haulover Bay - ¼ nm N of anchorage area
18° 21.16' N, 64° 40.62' W

Navigational Information

About ½ mile west of *Newfound Bay* is *Haulover Bay* where a waypoint at 18° 21.16' N, 64° 40.62' W, will place you approximately ¼ mile north of the anchorage area as shown on Chart USVI-17. From the waypoint head south keeping clear of the reefs to port off Nancy Point. Anchor in the shallower southeastern side of the bay wherever your draft allows. The rest of the bay is very deep and good snorkeling can be found on the reefs off the points.

Haulover Bay is a pleasant anchorage in normal conditions, but it can be quite uncomfortable when northerly swells are running. *Haulover Bay* earned its name because it was a shortcut for goods that were transported to *Coral Bay* via *South Haulover Bay*.

Leinster Bay

Waypoints:
Leinster Bay - ¼ nm N of
18° 22.30' N, 64° 43.70' W

Navigational Information

Leinster Bay lies on the northern shore of St. John, almost directly south of the eastern tip of Great Thatch Island. A waypoint at 18° 22.30' N, 64° 43.70' W, will place you approximately ¼ mile north of *Leinster Bay* as shown on Chart USVI-18. If approaching from the east it won't be a problem, you'll have the wind and current with you. But if you're approaching from *Francis Bay* via *The Narrows* you'll be fighting a current of 2-4 knots and a head wind in normal conditions.

Some sailors prefer leaving *Francis Bay* and heading north past the western tip of Great Thatch Island and then turning eastward to turn to the south between Great Thatch Island and Tortola (West End and Soper's Hole). This route, though a bit longer, avoids the current in *The Narrows*.

From the waypoint head south into *Leinster Bay* keeping Watermelon Cay to port. Watermelon Cay is usually surrounded by white buoys that mark a snorkeling channel and passage between Watermelon Cay and the shore of St. John to the east is prohibited.

Watermelon Bay is a great spot to spend the night but no anchoring is allowed. Instead you can pick up one of the *NPS* moorings. This part of the bay doesn't get rough, even with northerly swells. At this time you can anchor in the western part of the bay in settled weather, but you'll have to thread your way between two reefs and over a 6' bar before finding a deeper pocket of water that is 7' deep.

What You Will Find Ashore

There is a trail from the southwestern part of *Leinster Bay* that leads to the ruins of the old *Annaberg Sugar Mill*. The *Annaberg Sugar Mill* operated on St. John well into the 1800s and the ruins are very interesting, a self-guided tour takes you through the old *wattle and daud* (sticks and adobe) slave quarters, village ruins, and the remains of the old sugar factory.

Francis Bay

Important Lights:
Johnson Reef #1JR: Fl G 4s

Waypoints:
Fungi Passage - ¼ nm N of
18° 22.40' N, 64° 45.25' W

Francis Bay - ¾ nm W of
18° 21.90' N, 64° 45.70' W

Navigational Information

Heading west from *Leinster Bay*, or heading northeast from *Caneel Bay*, you'll enter what's known as the *Windward Passage*. The *Windward Passage* stretches from the western shore of St. John and Lovango Cay to Great Thatch Island and *The Narrows*, and the currents here can reach 4 knots. At the eastern end of the *Windward Passage* is *The Narrows* lying between St. John and Great Thatch Island. The tidal currents in *The Narrows* and east of it, between Tortola and St. John can attain a speed of 2-4 knots. If approaching *Francis Bay* from *Leinster Bay* passing through the narrowest part of *The Narrows* and if the current and wind is with you you'll have a nice sail, or motor as the case may be. If you are approaching *Francis Bay* from *Caneel Bay*, you can pass between the Durloe Cays and *Hawksnest Bay* before going around *Johnson Reef*. You can pass on either side of *Johnson Reef* to enter *Francis Bay*. If you are approaching *Francis Bay* from *Trunk Bay* you can head inside *Johnson Reef* to enter *Cinnamon Bay* and/or *Francis Bay*.

The United States Virgin Islands - St. John

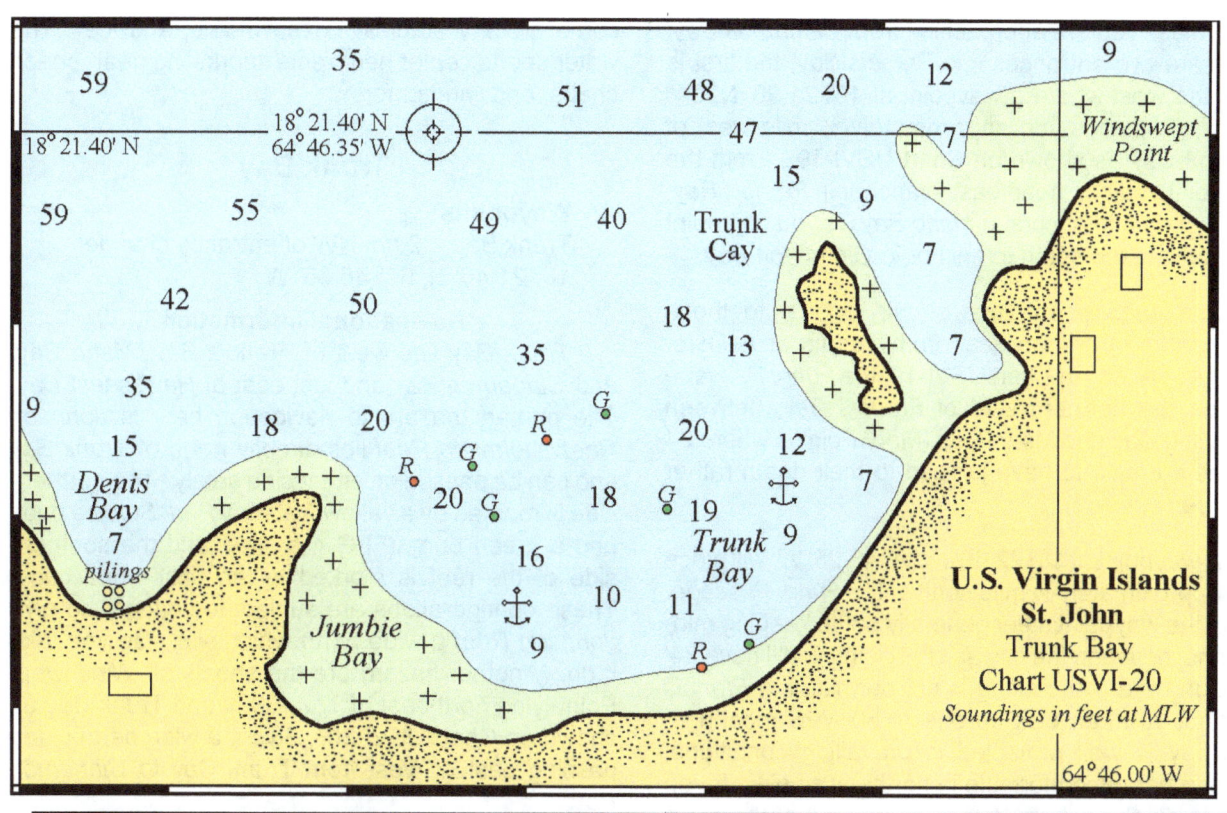

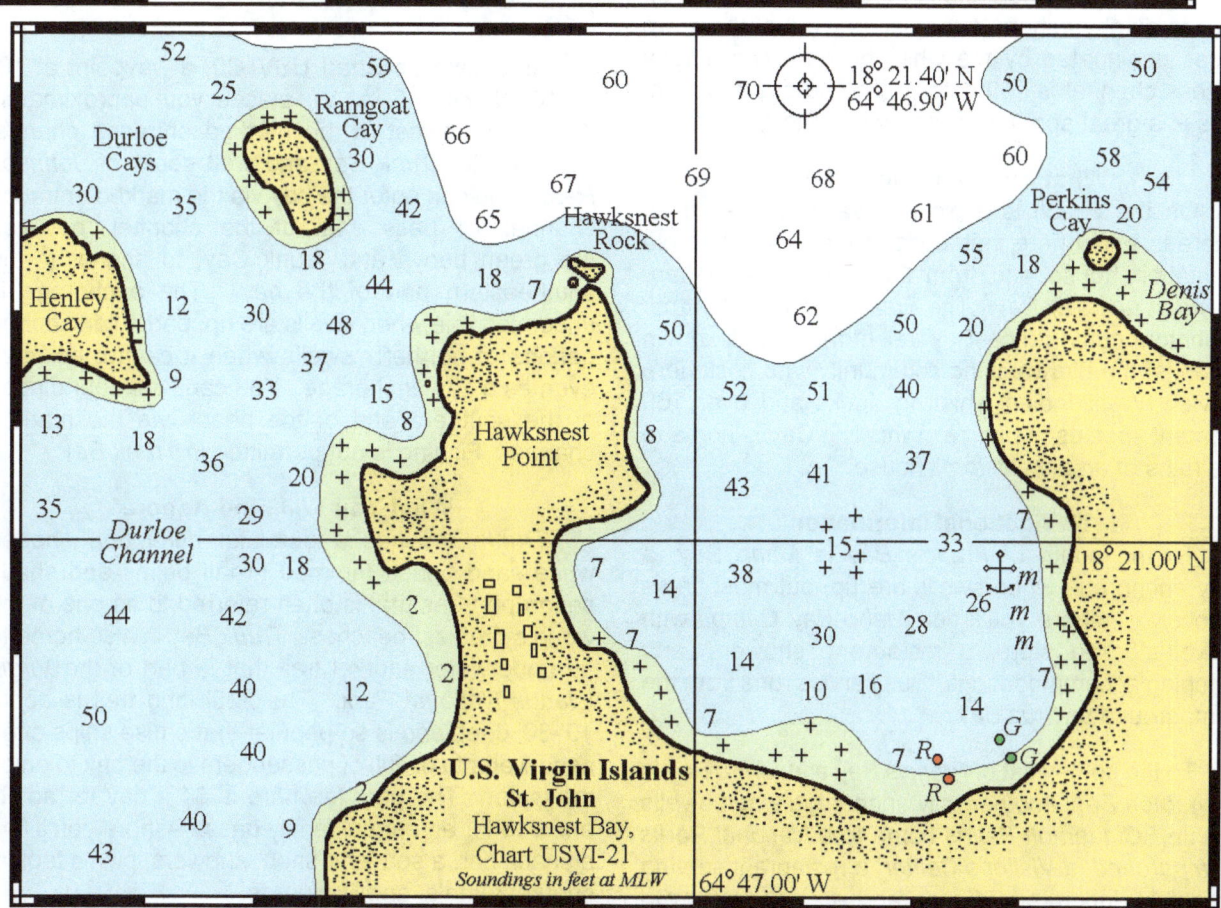

A Cruising Guide to the Virgin Islands

Unless you are approaching from *Cinnamon Bay*, there are two entrances into *Francis Bay*, the first is from the west where a waypoint at 18° 21.90' N, 64° 45.70' W, places you approximately ¾ mile west of *Francis Bay* as shown on Chart USVI-19. From the waypoint you can head east to anchor in *Francis Bay*, south of east to anchor in *Maho Bay*, or you can point your bow to the south to anchor in *Cinnamon Bay*.

The second entrance should appeal to those approaching from the east, from Tortola or *Leinster Bay*. As shown on Chart USVI-19, the *Fungi Passage* lies on the northern side of *Francis Bay*, between Whistling Cay and Mary Point (Mary Point is where 24 slaves are said to have jumped to their death rather than be captured).

A waypoint at 18° 22.40' N, 64° 45.25' W, will place you approximately ¼ mile north of the *Fungi Passage*. From the waypoint steer generally south keeping mid-channel between the cay and the point, you'll have 24' through here. Anchoring is not permitted in *Francis Bay* but you can pick up one of 50 *NPS* moorings. The bay is well protected in prevailing conditions, but can get uncomfortable in northerly swells. If you plan to dinghy ashore you must stay out of the swim areas designated by the white buoys. The dinghy access channel is at the southern end of the beach. This is a great spot for vessels with wind generators.

What You Will Find Ashore

On the beach is a picnic area with trash bins. There is a trail here that leads to the ruins of an old plantation house and from there to the *Annaberg Ruins* at *Leinster Bay*. The *Francis Bay Trail* (http://stjohntour.com/FrancesBayTrail.htm) is well-known amongst the birdwatching community who flock here to view West Indian whistling ducks and over 160 different species of birdlife. Whistling Cay is home to the ruins of an old *Customs* house.

Navigational Information

To the south of *Francis Bay* is *Maho Bay*, a rolly anchorage when swells are up, but most times is lovely. Ashore you'll find *Maho Bay Camps* with a well-stocked store, a restaurant, showers, and camping accommodations. Bus service runs from the campground to *Cruz Bay*.

To the southwest of *Francis Bay* and *Maho Bay* is *Cinnamon Bay*, another rolly anchorage when swells are up. *Cinnamon Bay* is home to a *National Parks Campground*, a *Visitor's Center*, a restaurant serving breakfast, lunch, and dinner, and a small store with some grocery staples, frozen meats, and ice. The water sports center here rents snorkeling gear, beach chairs, and windsurfers.

Trunk Bay

Waypoints:
Trunk Bay - .2 nm NW of entrance channel
18° 21.40' N, 64° 46.35' W

Navigational Information

Trunk Bay lies west of *Francis Bay*, *Maho Bay*, and *Cinnamon Bay* and just east of *Hawksnest Bay*. The primary hazard to navigation here is *Johnson Reef*. *Johnson Reef* lies directly north of *Trunk Bay* and can be passed on either side safely. The northern side is marked by a yellow *National Park Service* buoy and a green buoy (Fl G 4 s, 4M), and the southern side of the reef is marked by an unlit white buoy. These configurations are subject to change, so give *Johnson Reef* a wide berth whichever side you take it on. Another hazard are the shoals off Windswept Point lying northeast of *Trunk Bay* and Trunk Cay as shown on Chart USVI-20. Give it a wide berth when passing east or west from Trunk Cay to *Cinnamon Bay*.

As shown on Chart USVI-20, a waypoint at 18° 21.40' N, 64° 46.35' W, places you approximately .2 mile northwest of the marked entrance channel leading into *Trunk Bay* and well south of *Johnson Reef*. You can enter the bay via the marked entrance channel, or pass east of the channel, between the green buoys and Trunk Cay, to anchor in the southeastern part of the bay. The anchorage is uncomfortable when swells are up, particularly during periods of northerly swells when it cannot be used even as a day anchorage. You can land your dinghy at the southern end of the beach via the marked channel. Fishing is not permitted in *Trunk Bay*.

What You Will Find Ashore

Trunk Bay has a beautiful half-moon shaped white sand beach trimmed in tall palms and shady seagrape trees that is often referred to as one of the world's prettiest beaches. *Trunk Bay* is also home to an underwater snorkel trail that is part of the *Virgin Islands National Park*. The 225' long trail is about 10'-30' deep and is so popular that cruise ships often send water taxis full of passengers to the bay to enjoy the water. The park fee here is $4 a day for adults and $15 for an annual family pass. Ashore you'll find a snack bar, a souvenir shop, showers, picnic tables, snorkel rentals, and lifeguards.

The United States Virgin Islands - St. John

Leinster Bay, St. John — Photo by Todd Duff

Flanagan Island, east of St. John — Photo by Todd Duff

Francis Bay and *Maho Bay*, St. John — Photo by Todd Duff

Francis Bay and Maho Bay, St. John — Photo by Todd Duff

Anchorage between Lovango Cay and Congo Cay, northwest of St. John — Photo by Todd Duff

Caneel Bay, St. John — Photo by Todd Duff

Hawksnest Bay

Waypoints:
Hawksnest Bay - ¼ nm N of entrance
18° 21.40' N, 64° 46.90' W

Navigational Information

Hawksnest Bay lies northeast of *Caneel Bay* and caution must be exercised if approaching from that direction. Approaching from *Caneel Bay* you will pass through *Durloe Channel* lying between the Durloe Cays and Hawksnest Point as shown on Chart USVI- 21. Keep mid-channel and don't try to sail through here eastbound, keep the motor running. Once clear of Hawksnest Rock you can proceed into *Hawksnest Bay*. If approaching from the east you will have to pass either north or south of *Johnson Reef* as discussed in the previous section on *Trunk Bay*.

A waypoint at 18° 21.40' N, 64° 46.90' W, will place you approximately ¼ mile north of the entrance to *Hawksnest Bay* as shown on Chart USVI-21. From the waypoint head south into *Hawksnest Bay*. For the most part, *Hawksnest Bay* is for swimmers and snorkelers and much of the shoreline is designated for that purpose. The anchorage area lies on the eastern side of *Hawksnest Bay* near the three *National Park Service* moorings that lie there. Watch out for small patch reefs and seagrass beds that lie outside the designated swimming areas and avoid anchoring in them. Dinghies can be landed at the southern end of *Hawksnest Bay* at the end of the marked channel. The *National Park Service* beach lies at the end of the dinghy channel and other areas are private and visits there must be by invitation only.

At the northeastern tip of *Hawksnest Bay*, at *Peace Hill*, are the ruins of the old *Denis Bay Plantation* sugar mill. There is good snorkeling to be found on the reefs south of the dinghy channel.

Caneel Bay

Waypoints:
Caneel Bay - ¼ nm W of entrance
18° 20.60' N, 64° 47.60' W

Navigational Information

Just north of *Cruz Bay* on the western coast of St. John is *Caneel Bay*, home to the *Caneel Bay Resort*. A waypoint at 18° 20.60' N, 64° 47.60' W, will place you approximately ¼ mile west of the entrance to *Caneel Bay* as shown on Chart USVI-22. From the waypoint head generally east and you'll pick up the red and green markers that designate the entrance channel leading into the resort's dock. Anchoring is not permitted in *Caneel Bay* but there are moorings available here just off the entrance channel. The resort requests that boaters not use their dock, keep the noise to a minimum, and to please refrain from hanging laundry to dry on your lifelines.

What You Will Find Ashore

The swank *Caneel Bay Resort* (http://www.caneelbay.com/) is built on the site of an 18th century sugar plantation and boasts 4 restaurants, a pool, bar, 11 tennis courts, and 7 beaches. The office has Internet access and fax services while the gift shop at the resort is worth a stop for all manner of resort and swimwear as well as paperback books. The *Caneel Bay Terrace* features excellent buffets for breakfast, lunch, and dinner, and these are not your average all-you-can-eat troughs, the cuisine here is only first rate and very well prepared and is available to cruisers with advance notice. The *Caneel Bay Bar & Grill* is open from 1130-2330 daily and the *Equator*, which is open for dinner only during the season, is built atop the ruins of an old sugar mill. Also check out *ZoZo's at the Sugar Mill*.

North/northwest of *Caneel Bay* are a small string of cays, Grass Cay, Mingo Cay, Lovango Cay, and Congo Cay, and in between is a narrow body of water called the *Windward Passage* where the currents can run from 2-4 knots at time setting northeast and southwest. Between Mingo Cay and Grass Cay there is a narrow, shallow passage with several small rocks in the middle. The channel between Lovango Cay and Mingo Cay is only about 300 yards wide and the tidal current is strong here. North of Lovango Cay is Congo Cay separated by a channel with only about 2 fathoms of water. You can anchor in the channel between Lovango Cay and Congo Cay as shown in the photo, just make sure your anchors are set well. There are a few day moorings here.

Driving Around St. John

Driving on tiny St. John is easy, there are three main roads that leave *Cruz Bay*, and the island is only about 20 square miles so it won't take forever to get where you're going. *Route 20* is the *North Shore Road* and it leaves *Cruz Bay* and quickly climbs into the heights above the northern shore offering some fine panoramas and photo opportunities. Once past *Maho Bay* the *North Shore Road* bears south to meet up with the *Centerline Road*, and you can bear left and continue your journey along the *Leinster Bay Road*, which will take you past the ruins of the *Annaberg Sugar Mill* on Mary Point and on to *Route10*. *Route 10*, the *Centerline Road*, is the main thoroughfare between *Cruz Bay* and *Coral Bay* and travels along the central mountainous spine of the island. Here, near *Camelberg Peak*, one of the highest points on the island at 1,193', you'll discover the ruins of the *Catherineberg Sugar Mill*, an 18th century plantation and mill. A bit east and you'll come to *Bordeaux Mountain*, St. John's highest peak at 1,277'. Here you can dine at the impressive *Chateau Bordeaux*, with an absolutely gorgeous view in an archipelago known for its gorgeous views. A bit further east *Route 107* heads southeastward towards *Salt Pond Bay* and then northward to *Coral Bay*. Further east still on the *Centerline Road* is the junction of the *Centerline Road* and the *North Shore Road*; here the *North Shore Road* ends and the *Centerline Road* continues on to *Coral Bay*.

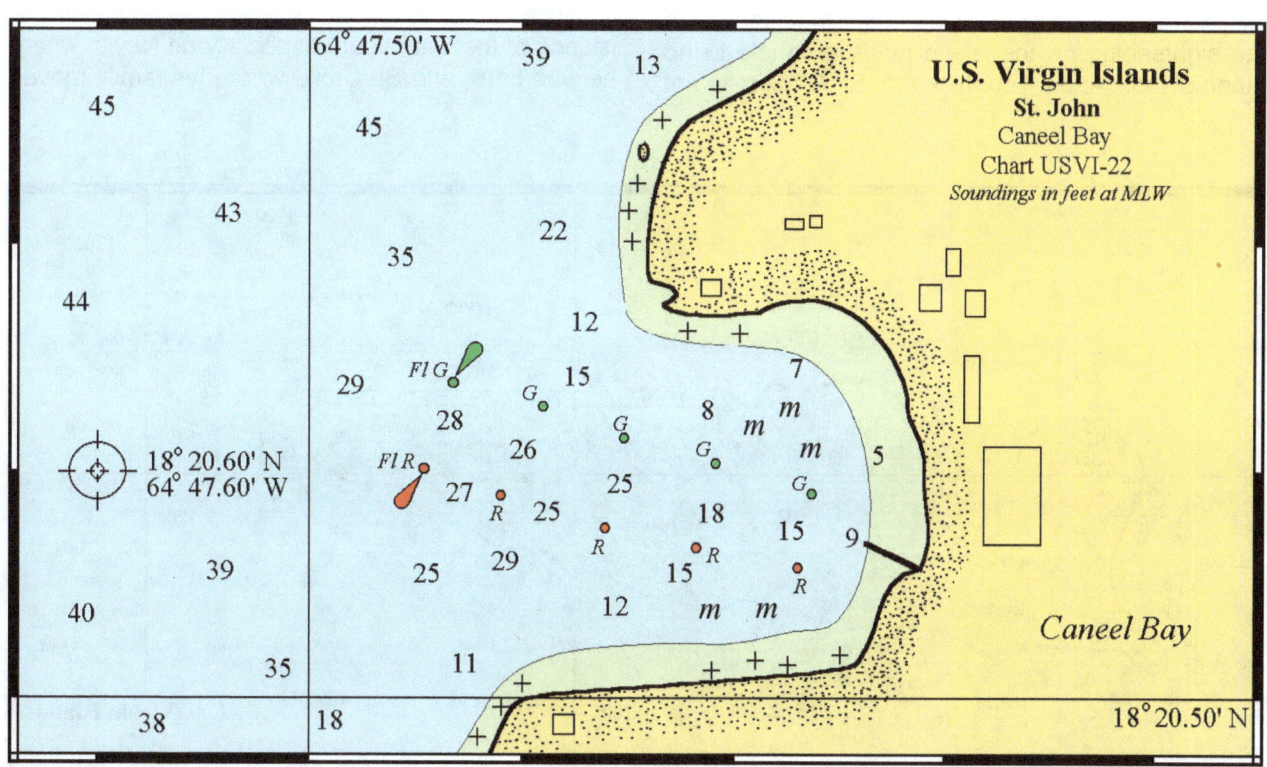

St. Croix

St. Croix, the largest of the United States Virgin Islands, is approximately 28 miles long and 7 miles wide. The northern side of St. Croix is somewhat mountainous, particularly in the western part where you'll find *Mount Eagle*, the highest point on St. Croix at 1,165', about 5 miles from the western end the island. South of the mountain region the land is composed of fertile undulating valleys while the southern shore is nearly straight and generally low.

St. Croix is often described as an island unto itself and it does indeed have its own irresistible charm. It does not share in St. Thomas' financial hustle and bustle and governmental duties, nor does it share St. John's very popularized laid-back lifestyle, rustic St. Croix is a bit different, indescribable, yet felt. St. Croix is an island of history, many of the old Danish government buildings in Christiansted are on the *National Register of Historic Places*, and the shopping, though not up to St. Thomas' frenetic standards, is comfortable and unhurried, St. Croix has been described as the best of Denmark in the New World. The restaurants you find on St. Croix will rival the best anywhere in the Virgin Islands, and the sightseeing on the island holds a candle to no other island. And if you think that St. Croix may not be as lovely as her sister islands to the north, try to remember the enticing beach scenes at the end of the movie *The Shawshank Redemption*, they were filmed on St. Croix.

The Caribs called St. Croix *Cibuquiera, stone land*, and archeological findings at *Salt River Bay* teach us that St. Croix was a major cultural center for various Amerindian groups for many years prior to Columbus' arrival in 1493. There are currently about 52,000 people living on St. Croix and they're known as *Cruzans*, or *Crucians* depending to whom you speak, and an estimated 42% of the *Cruzans* speak Spanish due mainly to the many ex-pat Puerto Ricans living here.

St. Croix is generally off limits to nearly all the USVI and BVI charter boats. The problem is not so much the shoal waters along the northern shore, but rather the logistics involved with servicing a boat 40+ miles from its home base.

Alexander Hamilton and St. Croix

Alexander Hamilton is a well-known figure in American history, but he is also well-known in the islands of the Caribbean, especially on Nevis, where he was born, and St. Croix, where his family moved

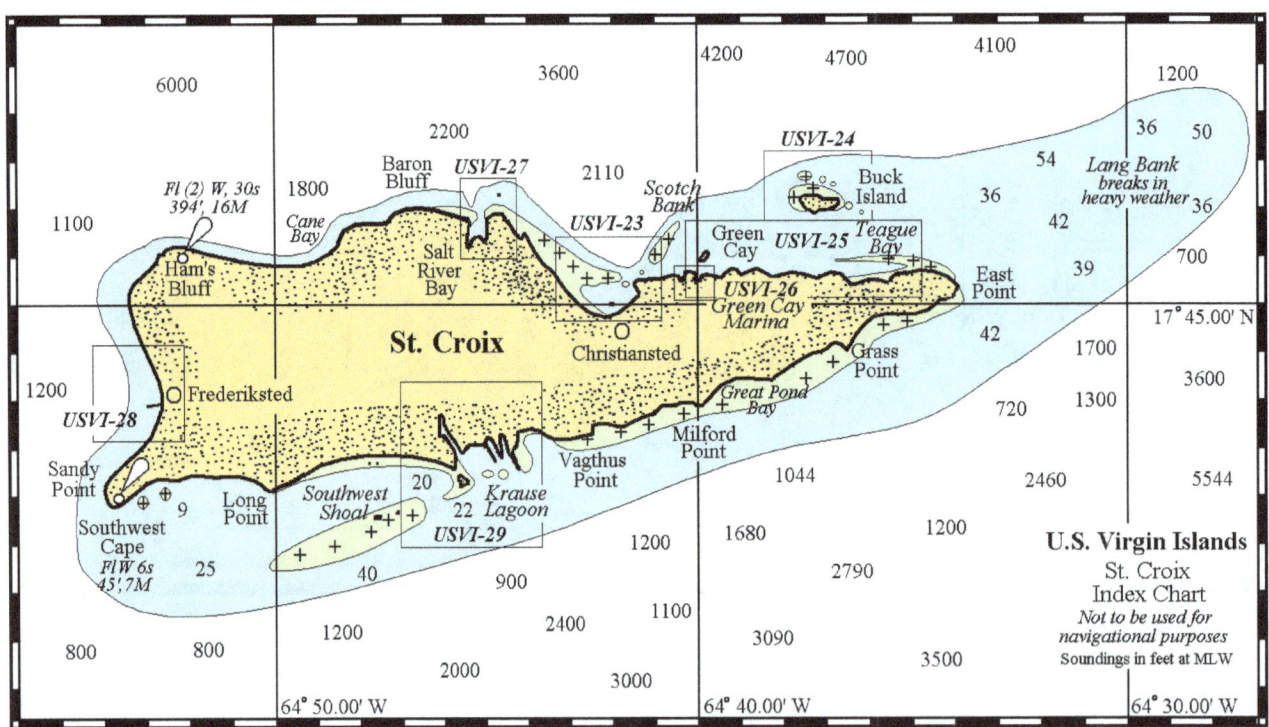

in 1763. Upon arrival the family settled into the *Shoy Plantation*, once owned by Charles Martel of the *Knights of Malta* in 1653 and now the site of the *Buccaneer Hotel*. It was not long after the Hamilton's arrival that Alexander's father, Scottish trader James Hamilton, left the family leaving Alexander's mother, Rachel Levine, who had never married James, to raise the young boy. Rachel contracted yellow fever and passed away when Alexander was only 13 so Hamilton had to find a way to support himself. Taking up accounting he hooked up with a local trader, Nicolas Cruger, who was so taken by the young man's talent with numbers that he financed a higher education for the boy sending him to the American colonies where Alexander sought entry to *Princeton*. Young Alexander Hamilton was denied entry into *Princeton* because of his illegitimate status (James and Rachel never wed), but Hamilton was finally able to secure entry to *King's College* in New York, now known as *Columbia University*.

Alexander Hamilton served in the American *War of Independence*, became a lawyer, and in 1789 was appointed *Secretary of the Treasury* by President George Washington. Hamilton's undoing came about byway of the presidential election of 1800 between Thomas Jefferson and Aaron Burr, who had each received an equal number of electoral votes. Hamilton lobbied many members of the *House of Representatives*, which aided Jefferson's winning the election, but which also enraged Aaron Burr. To further enrage Burr, Hamilton assisted in Burr's defeat in a New York gubernatorial election a few years later and a furious Burr challenged Hamilton to a duel. Hamilton, whose son had been killed in a duel just three years prior, accepted and as we all know, was killed by Burr. The *Steeple Building* in Christiansted houses a small display honoring this son of St. Croix.

Approaching St. Croix

Important Lights:
Ham's Bluff Light: Fl (2) W 30s
Southwest Cape Light: Fl W 6s

St. Croix, located 35 miles south of the other Virgin Islands, about 40 miles south of St. Thomas, has an area of 84 square miles, 28 miles east-to-west and seven miles north to south at its widest point.

The tides at St. Croix are chiefly diurnal and small, the range being only about .8'. Between St. Thomas or St. John and St. Croix you can expect a westerly setting current of about ½ knot. There is no perceptible current at *Christiansted Harbor*, but there is a moderate westerly flow outside the light at *Fort Louisa Augusta* at the eastern side of the harbor entrance. Off East Point, tidal currents of about 1 knot set northwest and southeast in calm weather, but when the trades are up the flow is greater to the northwest and lesser to the southeast. When the trades are blowing you can expect a strong westerly setting current around East Point and through *Buck Island Channel*. Off Southwest Cape you can expect a strong northwesterly setting current and a westerly setting current of about 1-1½ knots along the southern shore of St. Croix with a counter current inside the reef along the shore.

Beware of the *Lang Bank*, an extensive bank from 3-5 miles wide stretching 9 miles northeast from the eastern end of St. Croix. Although much of the bank is from 30'-60' deep, the shallower parts can be very rough in heavy weather.

If you want to visit St. Croix from St. Thomas you can take the QE 4 Ferry (http://www.qe4ferry.com) (340-473-1322, or info@qe4ferry.com), that runs between St. Thomas and Gallows Bay on St. Croix twice daily.

Christiansted

Important Lights:
#1 Christiansted: Fl G 2.5s
Round Reef Light: Fl (2+1) G 6s

Waypoints:
Christiansted - .1 nm NW of entrance channel
17° 45.80' N, 64° 41.90' W

Christiansted is the commercial and cultural center of St. Croix. The harbor area is called *King's Wharf* and is where most of the historic sites, shops, and hotels are located along the small boardwalk facing the sea. This colorful city offers a duty-free shopping arcade featuring colonnaded archways and open-air balconies overflowing with brilliant tropical flora.

Navigational Information
The entrance into Christiansted should never be attempted at night or with strong northerly swells running. There is no perceptible current at *Christiansted Harbor*, but there is a moderate westerly flow, about ½ knot, outside the light at *Fort Louisa Augusta* at the eastern side of the harbor entrance. A good visual landmark when approaching from the

north is the center of the "saddle" formed by *Recovery Hill* and *Lang Peak*. If you don't have a GPS head in on this "saddle" until you can pick up the *WSTX* radio tower at *Fort Louise Augusta*. To the north/northeast of the harbor entrance is *Scotch Bank* leading off to the northeast, give this shoal a wide berth, it often breaks in any kind of swell. *Long Reef* lies across the harbor entrance and the entrance channel into the harbor at Christiansted is at the eastern end of the bay near the point at *Fort Louise Augusta*. As you get closer you'll pick up the entrance range on the point at *Fort Louise Augusta*.

A waypoint at 17° 45.80' N, 64° 41.90' W, will place you approximately .1 mile northwest of the marked entrance channel as shown on Chart USVI-23. From the waypoint pass green buoy "1", the Christiansted sea buoy, and follow the channel southward as it approaches the point at *Fort Louise Augusta*. As you approach the point you'll notice that the marked channel splits at *Round Reef* and yachts drawing more than 10' must take round reef to port and follow the *Schooner Channel* into the harbor. Vessels drawing less than 10' can pass on either side of *Round Reef* though most pass between *Round Reef* and the point at *Fort Louise Augusta*. If you're having trouble negotiating the entrance give a hail to *St. Croix Marine* and they will be happy to talk you through it.

Most vessels anchor in the lee off the southwestern shore of Protestant Cay, but do not pick up any moorings you might see vacant here, they are private. The anchorage here is small and usually crowded so two anchors are suggested as there's a bit of current at times. The harbor at Christiansted can get rolly in strong north or northeasterly winds. Protestant Cay is home to *Hotel on the Cay*, the only beach in Christiansted. At the northern end of the islands are the ruins of *Fort Sofia Frederika*. You can also head into *Gallows Bay* to anchor, although all vessels over 50' in length must anchor to the east of Protestant Cay off *St. Croix Marine* or get a slip.

What You Will Find Ashore

If you need to clear *Customs* their office is a short walk from *St. Croix Marine* and their hours are from 0900-1700, Monday through Friday. If you arrive on the weekend you must telephone the *Customs* officers at the airport (340-778-0216) for instructions. To clear *Immigration* you must phone them at 340-778-1419 for instructions whether you're clearing on the weekend or not.

St. Croix Marine (http://www.stcroixmarine.com/) is a full-service marina offering dockage for vessels to 200' in length with drafts to 10'. All slips have full electric and water and the marina also offers showers, laundry, ice, fuel, a boatyard with a 300-ton railway, a 60-ton *Travelift*, fiberglass repair, painting, mechanical and electrical repairs, and refrigeration and AC repairs. If you need marine supplies the *Island Marine Supply* store is located on the premises. The *Baggy Wrinkle* serves breakfast, lunch, and dinner, and nearby you'll find all manner of places to provision, shop, and dine. You can get your propane tanks refilled at *Al's Marine* and at *Antilles Gas*, both in Christiansted. Nearby is *Cruzan Hardwoods* at the *Gallows Bay Marketplace* and *Gallows Bay Hardware* (http://gbhardware.com/).

The *Silver Bay Dock* has slips with full electric and water for vessels up to 70' in length and drafts to 9'. Their dock is in Christiansted next to the *Caravelle Hotel* and their *Rum Runners Deck Bar* (http://www.rumrunnersstcroix.com/). The *Annapolis Sailing School* occupies the westernmost dock and has three moorings available with occasional dock space, water, ice, electricity, showers, and a dinghy dock.

Jones Maritime Company offers 15 slips with water and full electric, showers, a courtesy car, laundry service, ice, 5-dog security, and managers that live on site. *Jones Maritime*, at the western end of the boardwalk also offers a sailing school, yacht management services, and charters. The marina can be reached by phone at 340-773-4709, or by email at sailing@jonesmaritime.com (http://www.jonesmaritime.com/).

Dinghying ashore in Christiansted access is easy. There are dinghy docks located in front of the Brew Stx restaurant on the boardwalk (use a stern anchor to keep your dink from ending up under the boardwalk), and at St. Croix Marine. From the dinghy dock at Brew Stx you are only minutes away from Market Square, and at the St. Croix Marine dock you are a short walk away from the Customs office located at the commercial dock, the Gallows Bay Marketplace, Chandlers Wharf, and the Schooner Bay Market. Schooner Bay Market is a gourmet shop with a great deli, the Grab N' Go, on site. Brew Stx is open Mon-Sat from 1100-2100, and Sun from 1100-2000. Happy Hour is Tues-Fri from 1600-1800.

If you need a taxi you can pick one up along the waterfront at *King's Wharf*, or at the *Old Market*

The United States Virgin Islands - St. Croix

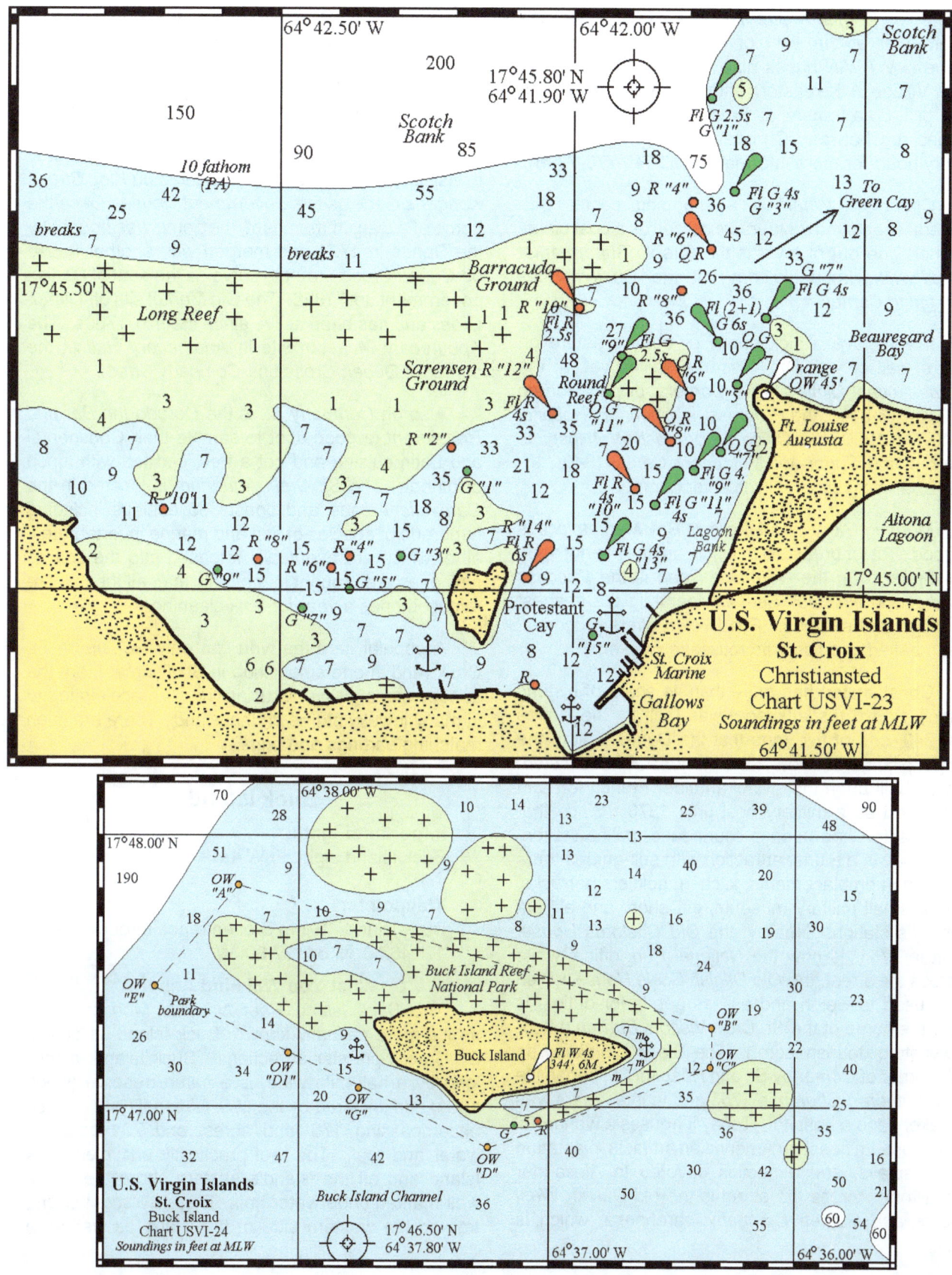

Square on *Company Street* (there's a *U.S. Post Office* nearby) or at the east of *King Street* (*Koningens Gade*). VITRAN buses also run through town from Tide Village to the eastern end of *La Reine* where you can pick up a transfer to Frederiksted or the airport. Buses run between Christiansted and Frederiksted every hour (for more information call 340-773-7746).

Chandlers Wharf is a shopping center with several shops and restaurants as well as a post office. A short ride out of town is the *Pueblo Supermarket* (http://www.wfmpueblo.com/) at the *Golden Rock Shopping Center*.

If you have a sick puppy or other creature on board, call or visit Dr. Hess, the sailing vet, at the *Island Animal Clinic at Five Corners,* or phone them at 340-718-3106, the *Progressive Veterinary Hospital* (340-718-1256, or *Office@ProgressiveVetHospital.com,* or the *Sugar Mill Veterinary Center* (340-718-0002, or info@sugarmillvetcenter.com).

Morning Glory in the *Gallows Bay Marketplace* is a good spot for breakfast or lunch, but they're not open for dinner. On the *Northside Road* is the *Princess Market* and *Princess Seafood* featuring the freshest produce and seafood. *Food Town* offers groceries, fresh baked goodies, and rotisserie chicken.

Christiansted has more than its share of historic sites. *Fort Christiansvaern* was built by the Danes in 1749, one of five forts that the Danes built in the Virgin Islands, to protect the harbor at Christiansted. It was built upon the site of an older French fort and was used as a military post until 1878. Since that time the fort has been a courthouse, police station, and today is a tourist attraction with self-guided tours of the gun emplacements, kitchen, soldiers barracks, and a small military museum, gift shop, and a *Park* ranger's station. Nearby, the *Old Customs House*, built in 1751, is now the *National Park* office, while across the street, the *Old Danish Scale House*, which was used to weigh and assess goods for duties, is now the home of the *St. Croix Visitors Bureau* (http://www.stcroixtourism.com/). The *Steeple Building* on the corner of *Company St.* and *Hospital St.*, began life as a *Lutheran Church* in 1753 and in later years was a bakery and a hospital. Today it houses a wonderful little museum boasting Amerindian artifacts, plantation era displays, and a section devoted to Alexander Hamilton. Across the street is the old *Danish West Indies and Guinea Company* warehouse, which is now home to the *Customs* office, the *Post Office*, a police station, and public restrooms.

Also on *Company St.* is the large, open-air *Christian Hendrick's Market Square* (in the same spot since 1735) where vendors sell their produce and crafts on Wednesdays and Saturdays, the best time to visit is Saturday mornings. Located on *King Street*, *Kongens Gade*, is the *Government House*. Once the home of a Danish merchant, the home was bought by the Danes in 1771 and merged with another house on *Queen Cross Street* to serve as the seat of Danish government until 1826. The *Old Market* sits off *Queen Cross* and has been active since the mid-1700s. The *Apothecary Museum* sits in *Apothecary Hall* at the corner of *Queen Cross* and *Company Street*.

Also on *Company St.* is the *Dorado Inn Bar and Restaurant*, a good spot to sample their Continental and Latin cuisine and get a free iced tea with lunch or dinner. The *St. Croix Aquarium* is located in the *Caravelle Arcade* and boasts 35 exhibits including hundreds of species of fish and marine invertebrates, all of which are eventually released into the sea as new ones are brought in, not only that, all the fish are released once a year for tank cleaning.

A popular item that you can only pick up on St. Croix (and in one small shop in St. Thomas), are the famous sterling silver Crucian "hook" bracelets found in many jewelry stores on the island. There are even matching earrings and rings.

Buck Island

Important Lights:
Buck Island Light: Fl W 4s

Waypoints:
Buck Island - ½ nm S of entrance through reef
17° 46.50' N, 64° 37.80' W

What You Will Find Ashore
The Buck Island Reef National Monument, or as it's more casually known, Buck Island, is one of St. Croix's premier attractions. Buck Island, a mile long by a half-mile wide, is a nature reserve (since 1961) administered by the *U.S. National Park Service* encompassing 176 land acres, and 704 acres of water and reef. The reef practically encircles Buck Island and off the island's eastern shore there is a well-marked underwater trail. There's also a walking trail on the western side of the island as well as a

The United States Virgin Islands - St. Croix

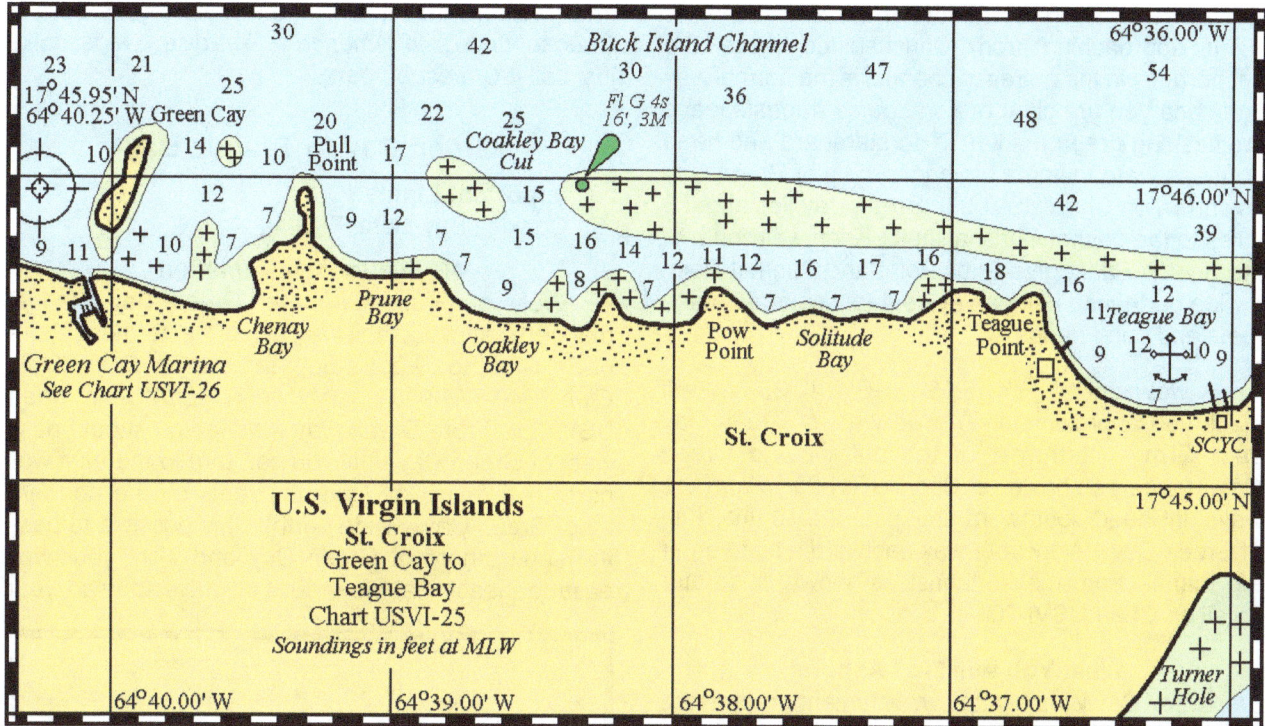

beautiful long beach with picnic areas, grills, and restrooms.

Navigational Information

A waypoint at 17° 46.50' N, 64° 37.80' W, will place you approximately ½ mile south of the entrance channel through the reef as shown on Chart USVI-24. If you are approaching from Christiansted leave the anchorage via the entrance channel in the normal way and once you are clear of *Fort Louise Augusta* leave the flashing green marker "7" to starboard and head northeastward towards Buck Island keeping the northern tip of Green Cay to starboard. Keep well south of the *Scotch Bank* and give Shoy Point and Punnett Point a wide berth and keep an eye out for scattered patch reefs and coral heads. Another alternative is to exit *Christiansted Harbor* and when clear of the sea buoy, green "1" you can turn to starboard to skirt the *Scotch Bank* and then head westward towards Buck Island. Two white buoys mark the extreme western end of the reef system lying west of Buck Island and, along with some white buoys lying south and east of Buck Island, designate the *Buck Island Reef National Park* boundary.

From the waypoint you head northward to anchor in the lee of Buck Island off the beach as shown on the chart. This is a rolly anchorage, but it is suitable for temporary use by vessels drawing more than five feet. Another anchorage lies to the east of Buck Island, from the waypoint head northeastward towards the white park boundary buoy and pass over the reef between the red and green markers (red, right, returning), you'll even see a *National Park Service* sign on the reef here to starboard of the entrance. This route carries almost 5' at low water over the reef so a vessel with a 6' draft won't be able to make it inside even on a high tide. If you have any doubts sound the passage with your dinghy first. Once inside you'll come into some deeper water that you can follow around to the eastern end of Buck Island in the lee of the reef where you'll find several *National Park Service* moorings available. If the moorings are full, you can anchor in a small pocket to the west/northwest and away from the reef and the channel. Please do not drop your anchor on coral.

If you can't or don't want to take your vessel to Buck Island, there are day trips to the park from *Christiansted*, *Green Cay Marina*, and from the *St. Croix Yacht Club*.

Green Cay Marina

Waypoints:
Green Cay Marina - ¼ nm NW of marina
17° 45.95' N, 64° 40.25' W

Navigational Information

If approaching from Christiansted leave the anchorage via the entrance channel in the normal way and once you are clear of *Fort Louise Augusta* leave the flashing green marker "7" to starboard and head northeastward towards the northern tip of Green Cay as shown on Chart USVI-23. Green Cay lies about 3 miles to the east of Christiansted. Keep well south of the *Scotch Bank*, give Shoy Point and Punnett Point a wide berth, and keep an eye out for scattered patch reefs and coral heads.

A waypoint at 17° 45.95' N, 64° 40.25' W, will place you approximately ¼ mile west of Green Cay and ¼ mile northwest of the entrance to *Green Cay Marina* as shown on Chart USVI-25. From the waypoint head southward until past the southern tip of Green Cay. Work your way eastward a bit to enter the marina from the northeast as shown in greater detail on Chart USVI-26.

What You Will Find Ashore

Green Cay Marina (http://www.tamarindreefresort.com/marina-en.html) has 154 slips with full electric and water, showers, laundry, ice, fuel, a restaurant and a hotel. *The Galleon* restaurant, located next to the marina office, if one of the finest dining establishments on St. Croix featuring French and Continental cuisine for dinner daily except Sundays while the *Deep End Bar & Grill* (http://www.newdeepend.com/) offers a poolside bar for drinks and snacks with a gorgeous view of the Caribbean.

If leaving the marina by road, take a left (heading east) instead of a right (leading into town), and you'll soon come to the extremely popular *Cheeseburgers in Paradise*, now known as the more legally correct *Cheeseburgers in America's Paradise*. Most folks just call it *Cheeseburgers*.

Green Cay to Teague Bay

Important Lights:
Coakley Bay Light: Fl G 4s

Navigational Information

West of Green Cay and *Green Cay Marina*, mariners can work their way along the northern shore of St. Croix to *Teague Bay* and the *St. Croix Yacht Club* (340-773-9531), shown as SCYC on Chart USVI-25. From *Green Cay Marina* you should pass west of Green Cay until you can turn to the east well north of Green Cay (give the reefs off the northern tip of Green Cay a wide berth). It is possible to pass the south shore of Green Cay and work your way east/northeast that way, but you have to wind your

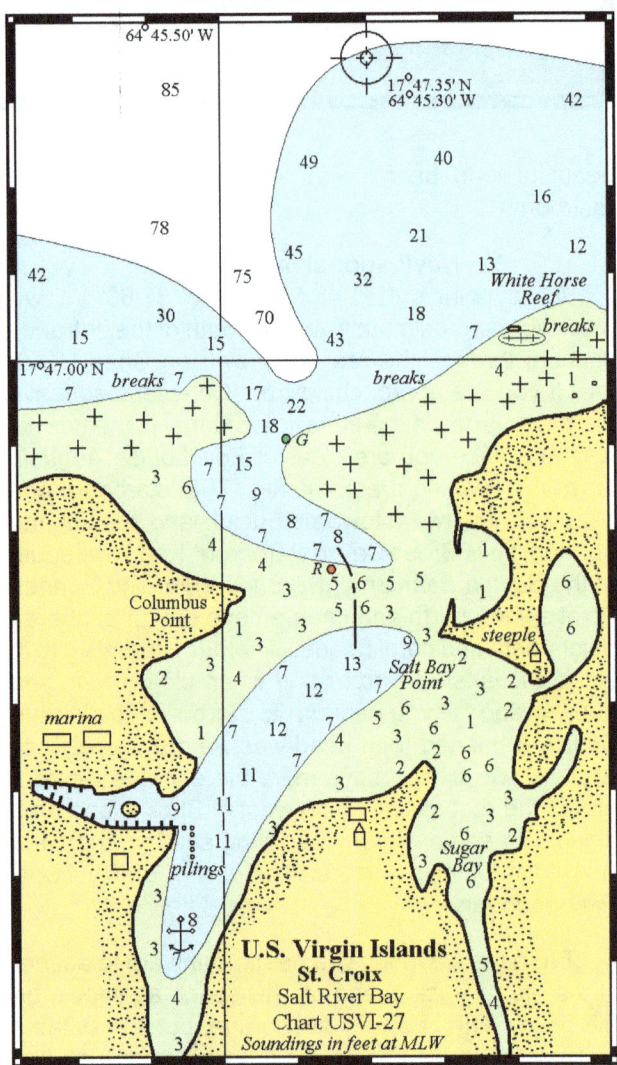

way among scattered patch reefs and coral heads, passing west and then north of Green Cay is far safer and easier on the nerves of captain and crew.

Approximately 1½ miles east of Green Cay, north/northeast of *Coakley Bay*, is a green lighted buoy (Fl G, 4s, 16', 3M) that marks the western tip of a continuous barrier reef at *Coakley Bay Cut*. Keep this buoy to port and head toward the windmill on shore until you can turn to port to pass south of the conspicuous reef, paralleling the reef eastward until you can round Teague Point and enter *Teague Bay* to anchor off the yacht club. Never attempt this route at night or during periods of poor visibility. Heavy northerly swells can also make this trip dangerous, especially in the vicinity of the green buoy. This route has a controlling depth of 11', there is a second entrance called *Cotton Valley Cut* northeast of Teague Point that only carries 7', but the *Coakley Bay Cut* route is much safer and easier.

What You Will Find Ashore

St. Croix Yacht Club welcomes members of accredited yacht clubs and even has some transient slips available with electric and water. You can pick up ice at the marina as well as drop off your garbage and take a shower. The marina monitors VHF ch. 16 and can help offer advice on the entrance into *Teague Bay* and they can assist you with an anchoring location. You will see moorings here, but they are private. Check with the manager when you come ashore (they have a dinghy dock to the east of the main dock) to receive a guest card and make your visit official. St. Croix Yacht Club monitors VHF ch. 16, and can also be reached at (340-773-9531, or scycsailing@gamil.com).

Duggan's Reef Restaurant (http://duggansreef.com/) is nearby and they serve breakfast, lunch, and dinner, and just down the road is a well-stocked little convenience store. Also in *Teague Bay* is the *West Indies Laboratory* of *Fairleigh Dickinson University*.

Salt River Bay

Important Lights:
Salt River Bay NOAA: Q W

Waypoints:
Salt River Bay - ½ nm N of entrance channel
17° 47.35' N, 64° 45.30' W

Salt River Bay, the site where Columbus and his crew landed on November 14, 1493, is now *The Salt River Bay National Park*. The entrance can be quite daunting and if you need assistance call the *Salt River Marina* on VHF ch. 16 for advice and/or assistance. The anchorage inside is delightful and very protected, and the *Salt River Marina* and the surrounding waters should be considered if you happen to be in need of hurricane protection and draw 6' or less.

Navigational Information

Use caution when approaching from Christiansted. Once clear of the sea buoy at the Christiansted entrance channel take up a course to place you at the very least, ½ mile north of Salt River Point, and I heartily suggest that you aim for a spot 1 mile north of the point. You are seeking to avoid *White Horse Reef*, a large reef system that lies north and west of Salt River Point. The sea is usually always breaking over *White Horse Reef* so the reef is not too difficult to discern, but use the utmost caution when transiting this area. Although you can pass between White Horse Rock and Salt River Point, it's safest to pass north of White Horse Rock to proceed to a waypoint at 17° 47.35' N, 64° 45.30' W, which places you approximately ½ mile north of the entrance channel. The entrance through the reef as shown on Chart USVI-27, is marked by privately maintained aids that may or may not be there when you need them to be. Never attempt this passage at night or in periods of poor visibility or heavy northerly swells, and at all times keep one eye on your bearings and the water in front of you, and one eye on the depthsounder.

The end of the reef on the eastern side of the entrance is marked by a green stake. Keep the stake to port as you enter and once past the stake and visible reef turn back to port to parallel the southern side of the reef as you put your bow on the conspicuous steeple and follow that heading. Keep an eye out for the red marker that marks the channel over the shallow sandbar, if you miss it you'll wind up aground on the same sandbar. The channel lies almost midway between Salt Bay Point and Columbus Point. A good range is the small beach house and peaked roof at the southern end of the bay. Once over the sandbar turn to starboard to work your way into the marina and anchorage at the southwestern tip of the bay.

What You Will Find Ashore

The *Salt River Marina* offers slips with full electric and water, showers, and ice. Advance notice is requested if you wish to tie up here, space is limited; if you need fuel, that will require 24-hours notice.

The marina carries some basic marine supplies and has a dive shop on site. The *Columbus Cove Restaurant* serves up breakfast, lunch, and dinner and specializes in seafood, chicken, and steaks, it's a good spot to eat and meet other cruisers and local folks. Christiansted is just a short taxi ride away if you need provisions.

Frederiksted

Waypoints:
Frederiksted - ½ nm W of anchorage S of pier
17° 42.65' N, 64° 53.70' W

Few cruisers call at Frederiksted, the town is primarily geared for the cruise ship visitor. The water here is deep and the only places to anchor are south of the dock and as close to shore as possible. This is a lee anchorage that is subject to some surge in prevailing conditions and most cruisers opt to visit Christiansted and take a taxi or bus to Frederiksted.

Navigational Information

A waypoint at 17° 42.65' N, 64° 53.70' W, will place you approximately ½ mile west of the anchorage south of the pier as shown on Chart USVI-28. From the waypoint head in towards shore to anchor as close in as you can south of the cruise ship dock. The Frederiksted harbor pilots report that here is a westerly setting current (225° to 315°) of about 1-2 knots well off the western end of the cruise ship docks. There is also an almost ever-present counterclockwise current beginning about ¼ mile off the docks with an initial set to the south and then a final set to the north when abeam of the end of the dock.

What You Will Find Ashore

While Christiansted is the center of commercial activity on St. Croix, and the hub of the island, Frederiksted is the island's deep water port and it is here that the cruise ships disgorge their passengers for shuttles to Christiansted's shopping arcade even though Frederiksted has its own, albeit smaller, waterfront arcade and shopping area.

Frederiksted is home to the *Annual St. Croix Blues and Heritage Festival*, which started in 1996. Here you might catch a glimpse of performers like The Fabulous Thunderbirds, Bonnie Raitt, and Maria Muldaur (anybody remember her?). For more information call 800-524-5006.

Every other Friday night is *Harbor Night* at the docks in Frederiksted when the docking of a major cruise ship is celebrated with a street party, a good time to sample homemade foods, pick up some locally made crafts, or dance your cares away until the wee hours.

Frederiksted was built in 1752 as a commercial port and a military post to offer protection to the planters on the western end of St. Croix. Named after King Frederik V, the port's warehouses on *Strand Street* were wiped out by a large tidal wave in 1867 and by the time they had been rebuilt, the plantation economy was crumbling. When planters realized they could not pay their laborers, and contract negotiations broke down, riots broke out and parts of Frederiksted were burned in 1878. When troops were sent in from Christiansted to quell the uprising, the rioters took to the surrounding countryside and for the next five days burned and looted their way across St. Croix. Known as the *Fireburn*, this event actually helped in bringing about better working conditions for workers in all of the Virgin Islands.

Frederiksted suffered a loss of some of its heritage through fire and storms but was rebuilt with quaint, Victorian style gingerbread structures among the surviving Danish masonry work and today *Strand Street* is the center of Frederiksted's bustling waterfront where its northern end intersects with the cruise ship docks at the *Frederiksted Pier*. Here you'll find the *Visitors Center* and the *Old Customs House*, while on the northern side of the pier you'll find the centerpiece of the town, *Fort Frederik*.

Historic *Fort Frederik*, was completed in 1760 (you'll see the date above the entrance) and is said to have been the first foreign post to salute the new United States of America by firing a cannon salute in October of 1776. It was at the fort that the Governor of the West Indies declared the slaves free in 1848, and next door is the brick-paved *Buddhoe Park* where slave leader Gottlieb Buddhoe announced the emancipation of he and his fellow slaves. If you need a taxi you can find one at *Fort Frederik*.

The *Market Place* is located between *Market* and *Queen Streets* and bustles just like it did when it was created in the 1750s. And as you know by now, the best time to visit any sort of open-air market in the Caribbean is bright and early on a Saturday morning. *Turtle's Deli* (http://www.turtlesdeli.com/) is located on *Strand Street* just across from the waterfront, and they offer sandwiches, fresh baked goods, and all sorts of delicious deli products. Nearby, *Café du*

The United States Virgin Islands - St. Croix

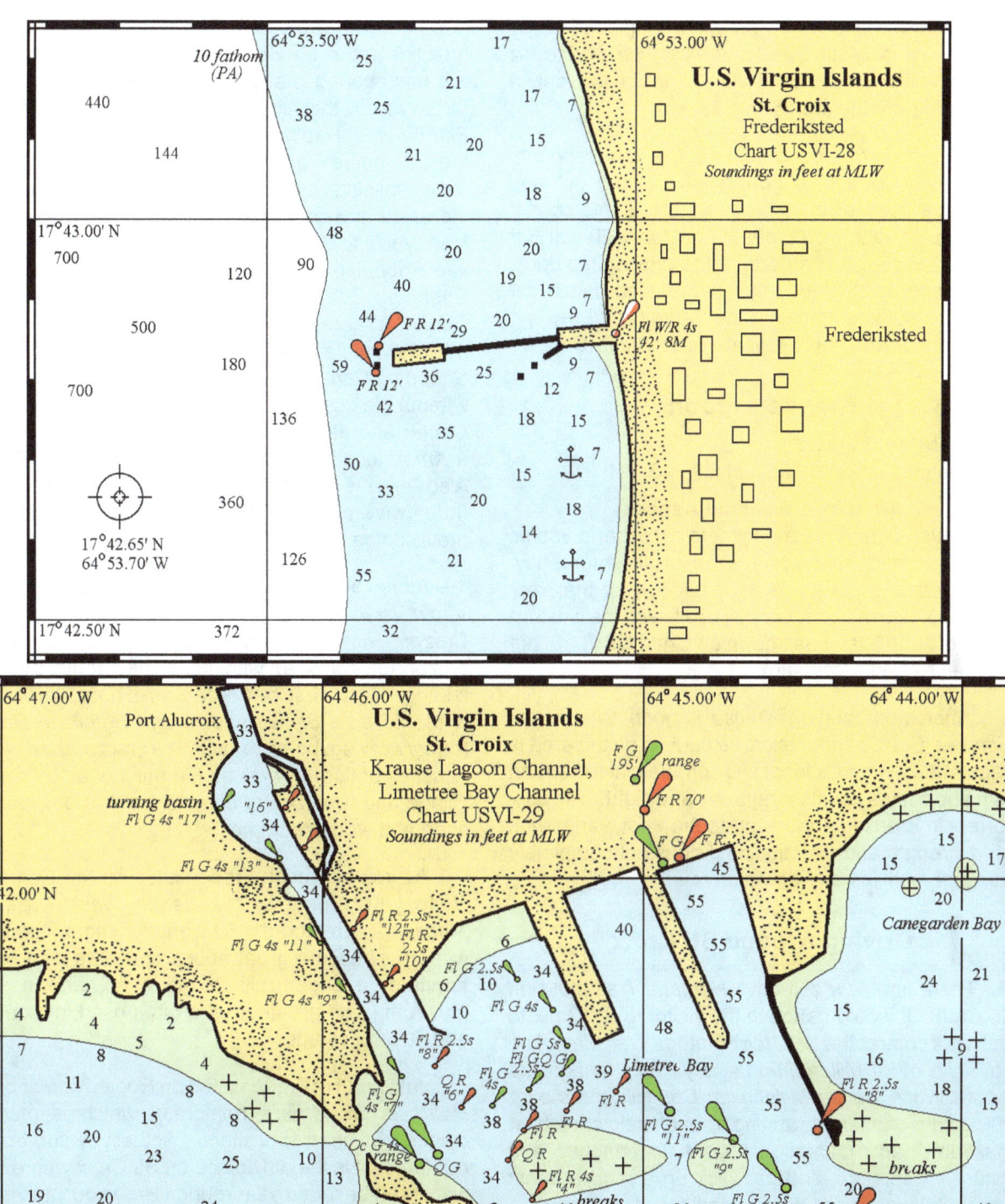

Soleil offers and ocean view while dining and they also have a fantastic *Sunday Brunch*. *Le St. Tropez* offers fine French cuisine while at *The Saloon*, only a few yards from the cruise ship dock.

On the north side of town is the public beach, *Frederiksted Beach*, a good spot to hang out and meet local folks or frolic on the public tennis courts. Here you'll find the *Changes in L'attitudes Beach Bar and Grill* about ¼ mile north of the cruise ship dock, a good spot to chill and enjoy some good beach-bar fare. Just outside of town is the *Santa Cruz Brewery*, producers of St. Croix's favorite beer, *Santa Cruz*.

Krause Lagoon

Important Lights:
Channel Junction Light: Fl (2+1) G 6s

What You Will Find Ashore

Krause Lagoon is a commercial port and yachts are not permitted except in case of an emergency. I've included a chart of *Krause Lagoon* for that very reason. You can anchor in a bit of a lee off the western shore of Ruth Island as shown on Chart USVI-29, but you can expect some surge.

When approaching *Krause Lagoon Channel* or *Limetree Bay Channel* exercise caution as the area is frequented by recreational and commercial fisherman using both lines and fish traps day and night. The tidal current in *Krause Lagoon* sets to the west, varies with wind strength and direction, and does not completely dissipate until inside *Port Alucroix*.

Driving Around St. Croix

There is a new self-drive *Heritage Trail* route on St. Croix. It would behoove the visitor to St. Croix to pick up a copy of the *St. Croix Heritage Trail Map*. The trail, one of 50 *Millennium Legacy Trails* recognized by the *White House Millennium Council*, offers over 200 points of interest ranging from historic churches, museums, and plantation houses to beaches and nature preserves. You can pick up a map at most car rental agencies, hotels, and tourist information centers and it will guide you far better than I can.

St. Croix has a very nice road system, and the only congestion you will encounter will likely be in the Christiansted area. Let's begin our travels in Christiansted and take the *Melvin H. Evans Highway*, *Route 66*, south where we'll pass the giant *Hess* refinery south of Christiansted. *Hess* provides hundreds of jobs on the island as well as keeping gasoline rates on St. Croix far below her those of her neighboring islands and the mainland U.S. Not far away are the *Alexander Hamilton Airport* and the *Flamboyant Racetrack* (horse racing). *Route 70*, the *Centerline Road*, breaks off *Route 66* and heads west passing several small malls boasting such stores as a *Kmart* and several large supermarkets. Here you'll find such shopping delights as the *Sunny Isle Shopping Center, Sunshine Plaza, Scion Farm Shopping Center*, and the *Villa la Reine Shopping Center*. There is a large *Plaza Extra Supermarket* (http://www.plazaextrawest.com/) at the *Sion Farm Shopping Center*, a *Pueblo Supermarket* (http://www.wfmpueblo.com/) at the *Villa La Reine Shopping Center* and at the *Sunny Isle Shopping Center*, and a *Kmart* located at the *Sunny Isle Shopping Center*. Also on the *Centerline Road* is a *Cost U Less* (http://www.costuless.com/), a great spot for bulk provisioning.

Along here you will pass the *University of the Virgin Islands* and one of my favorite stops, the *Cruzan Rum Distillery* (built in 1760; http://www.cruzanrum.com/lpa) with its guided tours and rum tasting. Just west of *Cruzan*, at *Estate St. George*, is the 16-acre *St. George Village Botanical Garden* (http://www.sgvbg.org/) with its more than 1,000 varieties of flora as well as the ruins of a 19th century village and rum factory complete with a blacksmith's shop and worker's homes.

As you approach Frederiksted on the *Centerline Road* you'll come to the *Estate Whim Plantation Museum*, a restored 18th century sugar plantation with its awesome great house complete with period furniture, a sugar mill, a gift shop, and a small museum. The greathouse is often used for concerts and cultural events.

Just north of Frederiksted on *Route 76*, *Mahogany Road*, is St. Croix's rainforest, which is privately owned but open to visitors. Actually a sub-tropical rainforest, it is the only place on St. Croix where fresh water can be found year round. Here you can visit *St. Croix Leap*, an open-air gallery and workshop full of woodcarvers and other artisans practicing their art.

If you have a four-wheel drive vehicle you can take *Route 473* and then take the cutoff at the *Scenic Road* (which also meets up with the *North Shore Road*) or the *Creque Dam Road*, which take you to the northwestern coast and the *Caledonia Rainforest*.

Estate Mt. Washington is home to the remains of an old sugar plantation that was buried in the rainforest until recently. And when you're in the rainforest you must visit the *Mt. Pellier Domino Hut* where you'll find beer-drinking pigs and the best rotis in the rainforest.

For a unique horseback tour of the St. Croix's rainforest visit Jill Hurd and Judy Caldwell at the *Sprat Hall Plantation*, a 1600s French great house in the hills on *Hams Bluff Road* outside Frederiksted. The two sisters have guided tourists on horseback through the rainforest for as long as they can remember. For more information and reservations call *Paul and Jill's Equestrian Stables* at 340-772-2880 (http://www.paulandjills.com/). The stables were started when the sister's mother, Joyce Hurd, began paying $5 per horse to save the creatures from the slaughter house.

Staying on *Route 76* you can take a left on *Route 69*, which takes you north to *Route 80*, the *North Shore Road* where you'll find St. Croix's nest of resorts, restaurants, golf courses, and scenic beaches. In a few minutes you'll come to the *Salt River National Park*, the place where it is said Columbus landed, and which was dedicated as a park on the quincentennial of his landing in 1993.

Okay, now we're back in Christiansted, perhaps having a bite of lunch, and we're getting ready to explore the eastern end of St. Croix. Leaving Christiansted we'll take *Route 82*, the *East End Road*, and pass many hotels and lovely residences. Just a few minutes east of Christiansted is the *Buccaneer Resort* (http://www.thebuccaneer.com/) where you can use their beach and changing facilities for $5. This historic hotel was built on the ruins of an 18th century rum distillery and offers a great view. A few miles east of Christiansted is *Cheeseburgers in Paradise* where you can order a really large burger or have a burrito with chips and salsa, and of course... margaritas!

At the far eastern end of St. Croix you'll come to *Cramer's Park* with its lovely beach, camp sites, and changing facilities, but as of this writing there were no fresh water showers. If you have a 4WD vehicle you can continue on to Point Udall, the easternmost point in the United States and visit the new millennium monument placed there. On the way here you'll pass the huge radio-telescope at the *National Radio Astronomy Observatory*. The telescope, 82' in diameter and weighing in at over 260 tons, was built as part of a network of 10 similar telescopes strategically placed from St. Croix across the continental U.S. all the way to Hawaii.

The British Virgin Islands

Port of Entry:
Tortola, Virgin Gorda, Jost Van Dyke
Fuel: Tortola, Virgin Gorda
Haul-Out: Tortola, Virgin Gorda
Diesel Repairs: Tortola, Virgin Gorda
Outboard Repairs: Tortola, Virgin Gorda
Propane: Tortola
Provisions: Tortola, Virgin Gorda, Jost Van Dyke, Anegada

Lying approximately 60 miles east of Puerto Rico, and 1,150 miles southeast of Miami, the British Virgin Islands officially consider themselves as the "True" Virgin Islands, taking on the "British" in their name for geographical and political clarity. With a population of some 20,000 (most of whom live on Tortola) spread over 59 square miles, the 50 or so islands, cays, and rocks of the BVI would hardly be considered crowded, though it may feel like it during the charter season when every harbor seems to be a forest of masts.

The islands of the British Virgins, with the exception of Anegada, which is of a coral origin, are volcanic in nature, part of a mountainous range stretching from Venezuela in an arc through the eastern Caribbean to Puerto Rico, Hispaniola, and Cuba. These mountain peaks that are the Virgin Islands create some very interesting driving situations as you will find out the first time you rent a car on Tortola, or on St. John and St. Thomas in the USVI. Driving in the Virgin Islands is an experience that is not to be missed.

A Brief History

Columbus claimed these islands for Spain who cared little for the territory, preferring instead to concentrate on the richer islands of Puerto Rico and Hispaniola. Even the British passed the islands by for half a century, considering them too dangerous for navigation. However, for the very reasons the Spanish and British shunned the islands, another group found them quite adequate for their needs. The pirates were happy with the hiding places the islands offered just off the shipping routes and many islands in the archipelago bear piratical names.

Little Thatch Island got its name from Blackbeard, Edward Teach, and Norman Island was also the namesake of a buccaneer who is said to have buried Spanish gold on the island. Jost Van Dyke and Bellamy Cay are also both named after pirate figures (although it is also said that Jost Van Dyke was named after a planter).

By the mid-1600s, the British realized the importance of the Virgin Islands who used the waters to stage attacks on nearby Puerto Rico. In 1595, Sir Francis Drake, who had first stopped in the islands in 1585, stopped at *North Sound* on Virgin Gorda to prepare for his unsuccessful attack on the Spanish fleet at San Juan. Gradually the Spanish lost control of the islands and the British made their first claim to the Virgin Islands in 1628, when some of the islands were given to the Earl of Carlisle. The first European settlers arrived around 1640 when a group of Dutch colonists/pirates set up a colony at West End on Tortola.

The pirates were soon followed by other Dutch settlers who built a small fort for self-defense and began growing sugar cane. The colony thrived for almost three decades until most were driven away by British pirates in 1666. In 1672, at the outbreak of the Third Dutch War, Colonel William Stapleton captured Tortola, demolished the fort, moved the remaining Dutch settlers to St. Kitt's, and annexed the Virgin Islands to the government of the British Leeward Islands. With the Crown firmly in control, Virgin Gorda became the capital of the British Virgin Islands (Road Town became the capital in 1742) and British settlers arrive from Anguilla...a year later the first boatload of African slaves arrived. By 1680, Virgin Gorda and Anegada had been settled and the colonists in the British Virgin Islands created huge cotton and sugar cane plantations as well as several rum distilleries to process the molasses produced by the plantations, all powered by slave labor imported from Africa. In fact, some of the rum produced here was traded for slaves who in turn would produce more rum.

Several notable planters during this period were Quakers, a pacifist religious group known as the *Society of Friends*, members of whom were also abolitionists in an area dependent upon slave labor. The first Quaker to settle in the BVI was John Pickering who arrived in 1741 and eventually became Governor. But the best known of the Quakers was William Thornton who was born on Tortola in 1761.

The view from *Foxy's Taboo*, Jost Van Dyke — Photo by Todd Duff

Thornton learned medicine in England and eventually returned to Tortola to practice and run the family plantation. Thornton sailed to America to enter a design competition for the capital building in Washington D.C. and won. He remained in the U.S. and became head of the first *U. S. Patent Office*. The Quakers did not remain in the Virgins long due to their unpopular views of the wars and slavery issues and by 1786 only a handful were left in the islands.

The 1700s and the 1800s found wars abounding and several different countries vying for control of the Virgin Islands; the British, the French, the Dutch, the Danes, the Spanish, and even the *Knights of Malta* had a stake in the islands at one point or another. The Crown set up a series of forts on the islands including *Fort Charlotte* and its substantial armaments above Road Town, and *Fort George* and *Fort Burt* above Road Harbour. *Fort Recovery* and *Fort Purcell* guarded the western shores of Tortola while *Fort Hodge* protected the eastern access.

While all this was going on the first slave code was enacted on Tortola in 1783, wherein slaves were considered property and their owners were protected against damage to their "property." The hardships the slaves endured resulted in unsuccessful slave riots in 1790, 1823, and 1830. The slaves' conditions were improved ever so slightly by a law enacted in 1798, but their gain was minute. Slowly the abolitionist movement gained strength aided by an event in 1811 when one of planter Arthur Hodge's slaves was fined for eating one of the plantation's mangoes. The slave, unable to come up with the money to pay the fine, was flogged and eventually died. This act of cruelty enraged the populace and Arthur Hodge was tried and executed. In 1834, on the first Monday in August, the *Emancipation Proclamation* was read in Road Town and the 5,000 slaves throughout the islands became free men. Today this event is celebrated by the week-long *Emancipation Festival*.

Freed slaves could now earn 12 cents a day working in the fields they once toiled in for nothing, but the plantation era was rapidly drawing to an end as the cheap (free) labor force was forever gone. A hurricane in 1850, a drought, and a riot over a cattle tax, which left one man dead and much of Road Town and many of the great estate houses burned to their foundations, hastened the end of this era. The *Unencumbered Estates Act* of 1865 simplified the sale of the debt-ridden former plantations, but only former slaves and their descendants remained to purchase the properties so the lands went into local ownership. The majority of the people took to farming and fishing, raising cattle and goats, trading with St. Thomas, and even a bit of smuggling to survive and prosper.

The government of the British Virgin Islands, by now part of Britain's *Federation of the Leeward Islands*, later to be known as Britain's *Federation of the West Indies,* was ineffectual in fostering growth and often enraged the citizens by their actions. A rather unique incident occurred in 1890 when British *Customs* officials seized a local fishing boat enraging the local populace. Led by Christopher Fleming, the islanders stood up to the government forcing the Governor to flee to St. Thomas to seek aid. In his absence Fleming, although unable to read and write, sat at the Governor's desk and cleared boats through *Customs* with no duties charged.

The government continued in its ways for many years until 1901 when the Legislative Council dissolved and the BVI were administered to solely by the officials of the Leeward Islands with the Virgin Islanders having little or no say in their own affairs. This came to a head in 1949 in an open demonstration in front of the Governor of the Leeward Islands. A year later the British Virgin Islands again had their own Legislative Council and the islanders were progressing once again, slowly but surely. In 1956, the *Virgin Islands National Park* was created and thanks to contributors such as Laurance Rockefeller and his *Rock Resort Foundation*, much of the land and waters of the British Virgin Islands was protected forever.

In 1966, a new constitution was adopted which granted the territory, no longer referred to as a colony, a much greater measure of self-government. The entire decade of the 1960s was a coming of age for the British Virgin Islands as the islands entered the mainstream tourism industry with the construction of the first luxury hotel at *Little Dix Bay* on Virgin Gorda in 1964. By the end of the decade many charter boats were operating in the waters of the BVI and by the end of the 1970s the BVI was recognized as a major yachting center and the bareboat charter capital of the world. The prosperity brought about by the tourism industry was a terrific boost for British Virgin Islanders who soon entered the financial services industry with the passing of the *International Business Companies Ordinance (IBC)*. This act exempted offshore companies from BVI income tax making the BVI's one of the world's major registers of offshore companies with over 20,000 registered corporations.

Today the British Virgin Islands are a Crown Colony and the government of the islands is headed by the Queen's personal representative, the Governor, who is responsible for all internal and external affairs and is the head of the *Executive Council*, which is comprised of a chief minister, attorney general, and other ministers of government. The governor's term of office is set by the British government, while all other elected officials serve 5-year terms.

Tire swing, *Cane Garden Bay*, Tortola   Photo by Author

Tortola

Tortola, the principal island in the British Virgin Islands, is the commercial, cultural, and governmental center of the BVI. At almost 21 square miles in area Tortola is home to over 22,000 people, about 75-80% of the BVI's population. Columbus named the island *Tortola*, *turtle dove* in Spanish, in November of 1493. To the east of Tortola the *Sir Francis Drake Channel* separates the islands of Virgin Gorda and Anegada from their sister islands of Tortola and Jost Van Dyke, effectively splitting the British Virgin Islands in two.

Road Town

Important Lights:
Scotch Bank: Fl R 8s
Lark Bank: Fl G 3s
Wickham's breakwater: Fl R 3s
Cruise Ship Dock: Fl W 3s
Harbour Spit: Fl R 2s
Connall Shoal: Fl R 6s

Waypoints:
Road Harbour - ¾ nm SSE of entrance
18° 24.00' N, 64° 36.00' W

The British Virgin Island's only true city, Road Town is built almost entirely on land reclaimed from the sea and most of the buildings that you see were reconstructed after the devastating hurricane of 1924. Road Town is a very protected harbour and several charter companies are based here. As far as marine services, there's nothing you can't find in Road Town. The tides in *Road Harbour* are chiefly diurnal, and the range is small, usually only about 1'. In normal trade wind conditions *Road Harbour* can be choppy and the holding isn't the best. In strong southerly winds the harbour is downright untenable.

Navigational Information

A waypoint at 18° 24.00' N, 64° 36.00' W, will place you approximately ¾ mile south/southeast of the buoyed entrance channel leading into *Road Harbour* as shown on Chart BVI-1. If you're approaching from the west, from Nanny Cay or *Soper's Hole*, good landmarks are the fuel tanks located at *Fish Bay* (see Chart BVI-1).

From the waypoint you can head northwest (towards the cruise ship dock) passing between the markers that sit on *Lark Bank* to port and *Scotch Bank* to starboard. If you need to clear you must head for the *Customs* office at the ferry dock, southwest of the cruise ship dock as shown on Chart BVI-1. You must clear first before heading to a marina or another anchorage. Once clear of the marker at *Lark Bank*, head towards the red marker at the southeastern tip of *Harbour Spit* keeping it to starboard as you head

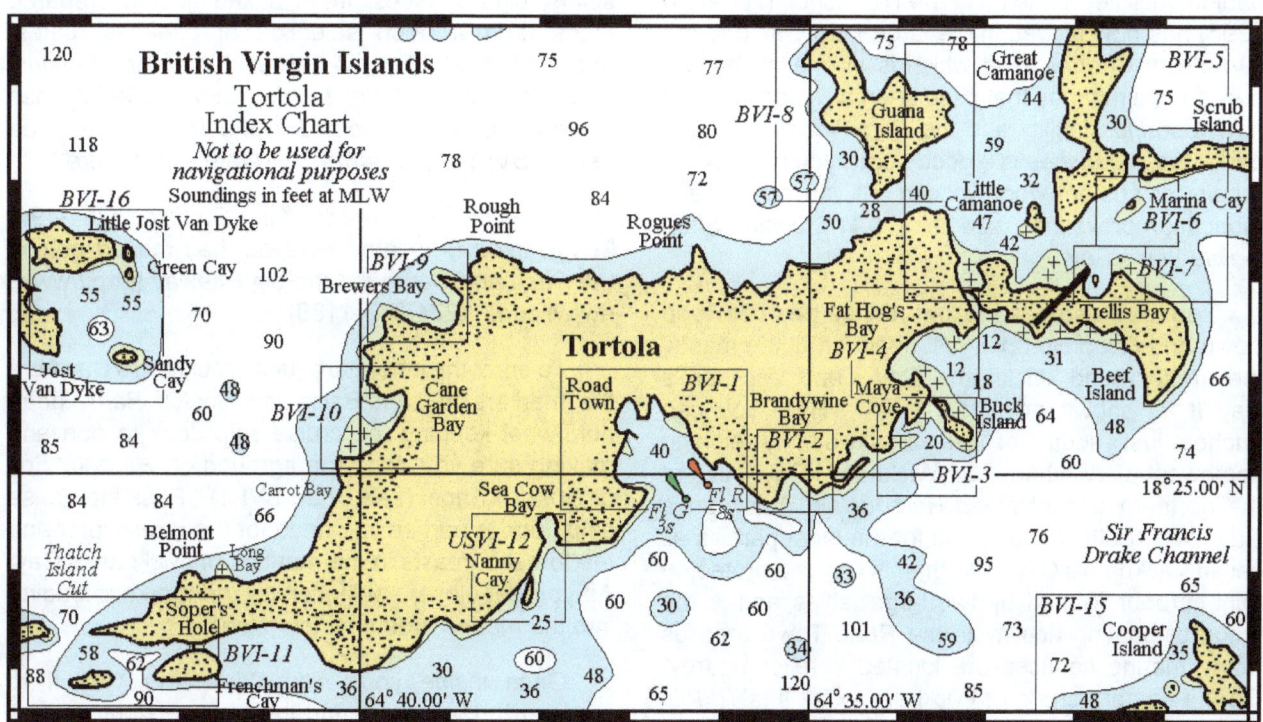

toward the dock at the *Customs* office. There is a lit range here to lead you in; if you are approaching from the east, from *Brandywine Bay* perhaps, this range will actually guide you from the red marker south of Hog's Valley Point (see Chart BVI-1 and Chart BVI-2). Anchor off the town dock and dinghy in (don't try to come alongside as the surge is usually quite strong here) and clear with *Customs* and *Immigration* before proceeding to your chosen marina or anchorage. Be sure to anchor well clear of the ferry lane as the ferries come and go quite often.

Across from the ferry dock is *Pussers Restaurant* and a great little French Restaurant called *Le Cabanon* (The Frog). There are a number of other places to eat in the immediate vicinity as well as one of the most poplar night spots called *Castaways*. Taxis are easy to find here, there's a taxi stand right off the ferry dock, and nearby is the *BVI Tourist Department* if you'd like to pick up some informative literature about the islands you have now entered.

As shown on the chart you can anchor on the eastern side of *Road Harbour*, directly across from *Harbour Spit* in *Baugher's Bay* (pronounced *Bogger's Bay*), just south of the *Peter Island Ferry Dock*. There are no longer any moorings for rent in the area and *The Moorings* has no services in this area, but there is a small marine railway that may be used for a haulout if you wish and it is less expensive than the other haulout facilities in the BVI. *The Woodshop* (284-494-2393) has now moved into a large facility next to the *BVI Yacht Charter* base which is in one of the two new private marinas that have been built between the new *Moorings* facility and the *Port Purcell* industrial park. *The Woodshop* is a good spot if you need wood repairs or custom woodworking. If you need metal fabrication or welding, see the *T & W Machine Shop* in *Baugher's Bay*.

You may also head in towards the heart of Road Town and *Road Harbour,* just head for all the masts, the area around Wickham's Cay I and Wickham's Cay II as shown on Chart BVI-1. Here you can anchor just south of the breakwater stretching southwest of Wickham's II. Wickham's Cay II lies at the northern end of *Road Harbour* and Wickham's Cay I lies southwest of it and for the most part it's all called Wickham's Cay. Wickham's Cay is a protected mini-harbour formed by two large jetties and is the focus of boating activity in the Road Town area as many marine services are located here or nearby. On the eastern shore of Wickham's Cay II is *Tortola Yacht Services* just across from *Port Purcell*. TYS is a full-service boatyard with a 37-ton and a 70-ton *Travelift* that can accommodate vessels with beams of up to 20'. The yard has trained specialists that can repair all manner of fiberglass problems, rigging repairs, electronic repairs, outboard and diesel sales and service. There is an on-site machine shop, a woodshop, and the well-stocked *Golden Hind Chandlery*. There is a rumor going around that TYS may move to *Fat Hog's Bay* in the near future. *Delta Petroleum* (284-494-3291)*,* is just .2 mile east of *TYS*.

At the north end of the cove at *Port Purcell* as shown on Chart BVI-1, is *Joma Marina*, home of *BVI Yacht Charters* (http://www.bviyachtcharters.com/).

Nearby are *Nautool Machine Shop* (284-494-3187), *Cay Electronics* (284-494-2400), *Doyle Caribbean Sails* (284-494-2569), *Omega Caribbean Woodworkers* (284-494-2943), *Wickham's Cay II Rigging, Marine Power Service* (*Johnson* and *Mercruiser*), *Tradewinds Yachting Services* (inflatables, batteries, Yamaha sales and service; http://www.tradewindsbvi.com/), and *Al's Marine*. *Al's Marine* (284-494-3883) sells and services electric motors, batteries, starters, and alternators as well as carrying some marine supplies and a propane refill service. Nearby is *Tico Liquors* (284-494-2211), and *Deli Tico*, just a short walk from *TYS* or any marina at Wickham's Cay. *Deli Tico* offers select wines and spirits, cigars, juices, fresh baked goods, prepared foods, and a good selection of cheeses, pates, and cold cuts. *Parts & Power* dealers for *Perkins*, *Yamaha*, and *Northern Lights;* (284-494-2830), has moved and is now located in the *Port Purcell* area behind *BVI Yacht Charters* and *Sim's Hardware*.

Clarence Thomas Plumbing Supplies (284-494-2959), used to located here but has moved behind the *Cash and Carry* and the big *Riteway* (http://www.rtwbvi.com/) (284-347-1188).

To enter the inner harbour at Wickham's Cay from the markers at *Lark Bank* and *Scotch Bank*, head northwest keeping the cruise ship dock to port and making sure you don't run aground on *Harbour Spit* or *Connall Shoal* (see Chart BVI-1). Pass the cruise ship dock to port as you head for the breakwater and the forest of masts in the marinas of Wickham's Cay. As you get closer you'll pick up the markers leading into the marina area past the jetties.

Once inside you'll find Wickham's Cay II to starboard. Here you'll find the *Moorings/Mariner Inn* complex; Since the consolidation of *Moorings* and *Sunsail*, all of these bases have been combined into one, creating the single largest charter yacht base in the world. There is no transient dockage available here, and the amount of activity in this area is simply phenomenal with boats coming and going all the time. If you want to shop in the immediate area it is best to either take a slip at *Village Cay*, or anchor outside of the seawall area and dinghy in.

To port when entering the inner harbour at Wickham's Cay you'll find *Village Cay Marina* and the *Inner Harbour Marina*, home of the *North South Vacation Company*. *Inner Harbour Marina* offers slips with full electric and water, ice, showers, fuel, ice, car rentals, and monitors VHF ch. 16. Also on site is *Cantik* gift shop and the *Ample Hamper Too* f (284-494-2494) for deli and provisioning items .

What You Will Find Ashore

Village Cay Marina (http://villagecaybvi.com/) has undergone an expansion of its facilities (aimed at the higher end yachting set) including a new office location, rewiring of the docks, and expanded phone service. The marina offers 106 slips for vessels up to 200 in length and with drafts to 11', full electric and water, cable TV, garbage and waste oil disposal, and just about anything a cruiser could want or need including a dinghy dock to make Road Town shopping available. *Village Cay Restaurant* offers a popular lunch buffet on Tuesdays and Thursdays featuring hot and cold West Indian Cuisine, a *Sushi Night* on Fridays, and their very popular *Sunday Brunch*. Village Cay Marina can be reached at (494-2771, or info@villagecaybvi.com).

Next to *Village Cay Marina* is the *Mill Mall* where you'll find the *Best of British* offering all manner of food and spirits from Britain, including magazines and newspapers, it's a bit of Britain in the British Virgin Islands. There is also a small but excellent marine store called *The Marine Depot* that is part of *BVI Marine Management* (located at Nanny Cay). There is also a mail service called *Rush It* that does mail deliveries each day to their office in St Thomas and is great for sending items to the states, saving weeks sometimes over the local mail system! *Richardson's Rigging* (284-494-2739), a *Harken* dealer and well-known local rigging company that can handle almost any rigging problem you may have, is located across from the main downtown ferry docks, about 200 yards west of *Pusser's Restaurant*. Also at the mall is the *Sole Day Spa* (284-494-5999).

Mega Services Marina offers fuel, showers, ice, water, full electric, a restaurant on site (*Spaghetti Junction*), and a haul-out yard. The marina can handle vessels to 150' LOA with drafts to 15'. Nearby is the *Chillin Cafe*.

There is so much shopping in Road Town, I cannot possibly list everything there is to see and do here, so I will just highlight the best of the best. And you'll find that exploration is fun in itself and then you can email me and tell me what to add in this section. Businesses come and go so quickly in the islands, by the time this is written I will wager at least one of the facilities I mention here is no longer in existence.

There are two main shopping areas in Road Town, *Main Street* and *Wickham's Cay I*. *Main Street* is exactly what its name implies, it is the principal thoroughfare in Road Town, the heart of its commercial district, and it dates back to the 1700s. *Main Street* is laid out like a reverse "L" with *Main Street* on the left and *Road Harbour* on the right. The narrow one-way street is home to many charming and colorful boutiques and gift shops and several historical buildings such as the *Post Office*. Located at the southern end of *Main Street* across from *Sir Olva Georges Plaza* (near the ferry docks, a wonderful place to sit and relax amid the hustle and bustle of nearby government offices including *Customs*), the *Post Office* was built in 1865 and was originally a government administration building. Located in the same building is the *Philatelic Bureau* if you'd care to pick up some BVI stamps. Next door is *Radical Designs* selling unique fashions crafted in Trinidad. Here too you'll find *J.R. O'Neal Ltd.*, a pharmacy that can handle your prescription needs.

Nearby you'll find the *Virgin Islands Folk Museum* depicting the history of the islands from pre-Columbian times to the present. Here you can view the Amerindian artifacts found at Belmont on Tortola's western end as well as artifacts from the well-known *Royal Mail Ship Rhone* which sank off Salt Island during a hurricane in 1867. Nearby is the *Sunrise Baker* if you'd like to munch on some fresh baked goodies as you stroll around. About midway on *Main Street* is *St. George's Anglican Church*, once *Her Majesty's Prison*. Along the waterfront is the bustling *Crafts Alive* market where you can choose from numerous stalls selling locally made handicrafts as well as T-shirts, clothing, and other items perfect for bringing back home as gifts.

Also located on *Main Street* is the *Pusser's Company Store* and *Esme's*, THE place to go for the latest magazines and newspapers. *Ooh La La* may be small but they are well stocked carrying all sorts of odd items. For nautical flavored gifts to bring home to friends and family visit the *Buccaneer's Bounty*, which also has a very good selection of greeting cards. Around the corner from *Main Street* wine lovers will want to visit *Fort Wine Gourmet* for fine wines and gourmet specialty items. *J.R. O'Neal* carries many imported items from Spain, Italy and India while the *Heritage Book Shop* specializes in Caribbean books. For exotic spices for the galley visit the *Sunny Caribbee Herb and Spice Company* and the *Sunny Caribbee Gallery* (http://sunnycaribbee.com/) for locally produced works of art. On the main square the *Sunrise Bakery* offers fine baked goodies, assorted sweets, and cold drinks, stop in and sample their wares.

Besides the *Main Street* area, *Wickham's Cay I* offers numerous shopping opportunities if you have money that is burning a hole in your pocket. If you're bored (how could you be in the Virgin Islands?) head for the *Learn & Fun Shop* to pick up a board game for onboard amusement. Also on *Wickham's Cay I* is the *Collector's Corner* for those who need a jewelry fix, and the *Sea Urchin* located in the *Old Mill*, which handles resort wear and books, and for designer lingerie visit *Violet's*. *Roy's Deli and Discount Liquors* is a good spot for deli goods and spirits, but for real provisioning the best spot is *Bobby's* (284-494-2189) near the roundabout while *Bolo's*, which is located next to *Bobby's*, handles everything from batteries to cosmetics, all manner of sundry goods and household items as well as office supplies. *Bobby's* also has an outlet in *Cane Garden Bay*.

Another provisioning option is *K-Mark's Food Market* (284-494-4649).The Port Purcell Market near the deep-water dock at Port Purcell burned down and is not being rebuilt. Another good spot for provisions, *Riteway Supermarket* (284-347-1188), is located between *Main Street* and the roundabout at *Pasea Estate* and nearby is another market, *SupaValu*. Diners who seek to eat healthy will want to sample the fare at *Healthy Choices* located near the roundabout. Located at Wickham's Cay 2 between *Tico* and *Burke's Garage* upstairs from *Compton Marine* is *Ms Penguin* (284-494-3690) where you can purchase gourmet meals carefully prepared and frozen for your convenience, you simply heat in a shallow pan of hot water and serve.

The *Government House* is located on a knoll above *Road Harbour* west of town on the waterfront road. Constructed in 1924, the Victorian style building is surrounded by beautiful, extensive gardens that are well worth spending some time viewing. The *Drake's Channel Museum* is a lovely garden dedicated to the memory of its namesake, Sir Francis Drake. The museum houses exhibits, memorabilia, and artifacts from centuries of old sailing ships.

Almost in the middle of Road Town are the peaceful *J.R. O'Neal Botanic Gardens*. At the heart of the gardens is a graceful fountain surrounded by wooden benches amid an extensive collection of tropical flowers, herbs, and indigenous plants from hybrid hibiscus to orchids and a wide variety of ferns. There's even a medicinal herb garden featuring a fascinating display of local flora that are used for their curative powers. If you like flowers, you will love the *Botanic Gardens Annual Flower Show*.

Near the ferry landing on *Waterfront Road* is a very popular hangout, *Pusser's Outpost* (https://www.pussers.com/t-outposts.aspx), brought to you by *Pusser's Rum*. The elegant two-story building is full of nautical memorabilia, paintings, model ships, and mementos of many sea voyages. The restaurant, *Pusser's Pub*, serves a mixture of classic British and Caribbean entrees and exotic tropical drinks all made with *Pusser's Rum*, which for over 300 years was the exclusive rum served on all Royal Navy ships and which only became available to the public after World War II. *Waterfront Road* is also home to many good restaurants such as Spanish flavored *Cafesito*, and the Italian flavored *Capriccio di Mare*. For ice cream visit *La Dolce Vita*, specializing in homemade Italian ice cream.

The stunning drive to *Skyworld* begins at the *Pusser's Outpost* in Road Town and takes you upwards to over 1,300 feet in only ten minutes. From *Pusser's* head east from the waterfront until you come to a roundabout where you will take your first left and follow this road to a "T" intersection. Turn right at the "T" and then take your first left leading uphill toward Cane Garden Bay on *Joe's Hill Road*. You will climb steeply as you maneuver through a series of switchbacks until you come to a short level stretch of road. Here you will see a white, two-story building on your left, take the first right after the building and you will come to a scenic overlook of Tortola's neighboring islands. Keep an eye out for the sign to *Skyworld* and the sharp right turn that will lead you uphill once

The British Virgin Islands - Tortola

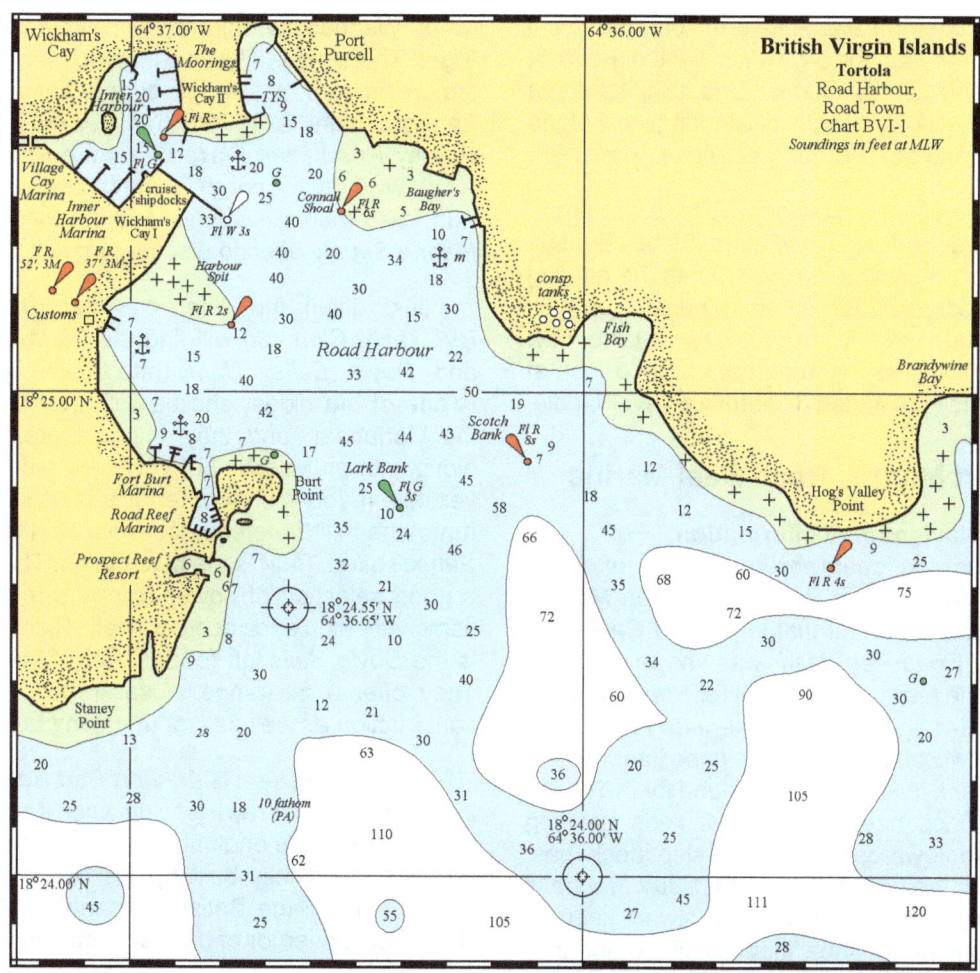

Road Town and *Road Harbour* Photo by Todd Duff

again. You'll pass an elementary school and you'll soon come to the sign for *Skyworld*. If the sign is not there don't panic, it's the first left and it will take you up the hill to a parking lot with its inspiring view of the Virgin Islands and the *Sir Francis Drake Channel*.

If you're hungry you can get a bite to eat at the *Skyworld Restaurant* and climb up to the observation tower for an even better view (360°) than the parking lot. On a good day you can see Anegada and St. Croix, which lies some 40 miles away. By the way, when you're dining at *Skyworld* take a good look at the napkins, they are folded differently on every table.

Fort Burt Marina, Road Reef Marina

Navigational Information

Located in the southwestern corner of *Road Harbour*, just west of Burt Point, is *Fort Burt Marina*, and the entrance channel that leads into *Careening Cove* and the *Road Reef Marina* as shown on Chart BVI-1. From the entrance waypoint for *Road Harbour*, 18° 24.00' N, 64° 36.00' W, steer generally northwest between the two buoys that mark *Lark Bank* to port and *Scotch Bank* to starboard and head for the cruise ship dock. Once past these banks keep heading northwestward towards the cruise ship dock past Burt Point until the northern tip of *Fort Burt Marina* is abeam. At this point you can steer westward keeping a sharp eye out for the shoal that lies off the northern tip of Burt Point. Don't try to cut this route short as the shoal off Burt Point is notorious for snagging unwary, careless skippers. You can anchor northwest of Burt Point and north of the *Fort Burt Marina* docks in about 7'-10' of water, but don't stray out of this area as the water shoals rapidly.

What You Will Find Ashore

Fort Burt Marina offers slips with full electric and water, fuel, ice, showers, telephone and cable TV hookups; call the marina on VHF ch. 12 before your arrival to secure a slip assignment. The *Fort Burt Marina* complex is the home of *Conch Charters* (284-494-4868), *Crandall's Pastry Plus Island Marine Supply*, and *Tradewinds* outboard repair shop (a Yamaha dealer). *The Pub* is a very popular boaters' hangout right on the water with their own dinghy dock and here you can dump your garbage off in the bins behind *The Pub* (check at the bar first as this policy may have changed). *The Pub* has happy hours Monday through Saturday from 1700-1900 with live entertainment on Fridays and Saturdays. Tuesday night at *The Pub* is *All You Can Eat Pasta Night*, Wednesday night is *All You Can Eat Mussels Night*, Thursday is *The Pub's* prime rib night, Friday's feature is free hot wings during happy hour, and Saturday night is *All You Can Eat BBQ Ribs Night!* Nearby *Road Reef Plaza* offers the *Riteway Market* (http://www.rtwbvi.com/), a fine place for provisioning with fresh meats, seafood, and produce, and *Island Marine Supply* offering discount marine supplies.

Just down the side road towards the *Royal BVI Yacht Club* you will find the *TMM* charter base and *Doyle Sails*. *TMM* (http://www.sailtmm.com/) is one of the oldest and best charter companies in the Caribbean and they enjoy a great reputation along with an eclectic but very new range of charter vessels. If you wish to charter a boat that is not the run of the mill *Beneteau* or *Jeanneau* that *Moorings/Sunsail* offer, *TMM* is the place to go. They also have a good selection of power cats and monohulls and some very high end yachts as well. Right above *TMM* is the *Doyle Sails* loft for this part of the Caribbean. They offer a full range of sail repairs or new sail construction as well as first rate canvas work.

Across the street is the *Fort Burt Hotel* (284-494-2587), once known as *Fort Burt* when it guarded *Road Harbour* (only the original foundations and magazine remain). Originally built by the Dutch the fort was later rebuilt by the British and named after William Burt, then Governor of the Leeward Islands.

Navigational Information

The *Road Reef Marina* lies inside *Careening Cove* south of *Fort Burt Marina* as shown on Chart BVI-1. The marina has a privately maintained marked entrance channel leading into *Careening Cove* that can accommodate a draft of 7'. The marina monitors VHF ch. 12 (*Tortola Marine Management* or *TMM*) and it's best to give them a hail on the radio for instructions on entering their channel.

What You Will Find Ashore

Road Reef Marina has no fuel service at this time, but does offer slips with full electric and water, ice, showers, and garbage disposal. The facilities here are the same as those I just mentioned at *Fort Burt Marina* with the exception of *Doyle Sailmakers* and *Island Care Electronics*, which are located in the *Road Reef Marina* complex. Also in the marina complex is the *BVI Marine Police* base and the headquarters for *VISAR*, *Virgin Islands Search and Rescue*.

Also located at the *Road Reef Marina* is the headquarters of the *Royal British Virgin Islands Yacht*

Club. Established in 1973 at the hotel, the yacht club *Royal BVI Yacht Club* (284-494-3286) (restaurant 284-494-8140) moved to its own clubhouse in 1975 when the membership climbed to over 100, but a hurricane destroyed the clubhouse forcing the yacht club to move back to the hotel until 1993 when the government of the BVI granted the club a lease on some land at *Road Reef Marina*. The *RBVIYC* was instrumental in putting together a team to represent the BVI in the *Summer Olympics* in Los Angeles in 1984, making the BVI the smallest nation to ever compete in the *Olympic Games*. Today the *RBVIYC* membership is over 500 and the club organizes racing events year round including the famous *BVI Spring Regatta* (http://www.bvispringregatta.org/).

Prospect Reef Resort

Waypoints:
Prospect Reef Resort - ¼ nm SE of
18° 24.55' N, 64° 36.65' W

Navigational Information
On the western side of *Road Harbour*, just south of Burt Point, is the entrance channel that leads into what was once known as the *Prospect Reef Resort Marina*. The *Prospect Reef Marina*, partially owned by the government, is only now becoming open to visiting cruisers offering slips, water, and fuel once again. It is currently the charter base for *North South Yachting Vacations*.

Prospect Reef is home to a very nice, though small, health club, and *Fresh Mango Technologies* (284-340-0466, a great place for computer repair as they are an authorized *Dell* repair facility.

To enter the *Prospect Reef* facility start at the entrance waypoint for *Road Harbour*, 18° 24.00' N, 64° 36.00' W, From this position, head for a waypoint at 18° 24.55' N, 64° 36.65' W. This waypoint will place you approximately ¼ mile southeast of the entrance into the marina as shown on Chart BVI-1. The entrance channel can be tricky, there is a reef to the north and south of it as well as a curving breakwater to the north of the channel. From the waypoint head to the southern tip of the breakwater keeping it to starboard as you pass between the breakwater and the reef to the south. Never attempt this channel at night or in periods of poor visibility unless you are familiar with the entrance. Once past the breakwater make a dogleg to starboard to pass along the inside of the breakwater to enter the marina area called *Lake Harbour*.

Brandywine Bay

Waypoints:
Brandywine Bay - ¼ nm SSE of ent.
18° 24.50' N, 64° 35.05' W

Navigational Information
Lovely *Brandywine Bay* lies about a mile east of Road Town just past Hog's Valley Point as shown on Chart BVI-1 (never attempt to enter *Brandywine Bay* at night or in poor visibility). When leaving *Road Harbour* head out the channel past the markers at *Lark Bank* and *Scotch Bank* that define the mouth of the entrance channel into the harbour. From the markers head a bit south of east keeping the red buoy off Hog's Valley Point to port and work your way to a waypoint at 18° 24.50' N, 64° 35.05' W, as shown on Chart BVI-2. At this point you are approximately ¼ mile south/southeast of the entrance to *Brandywine Bay*. From the waypoint you can head just a bit west of north as you angle into the bay staying in the center between the two reefs as shown on the chart. You can anchor here or use one of four moorings in the center of the bay maintained by the *Brandywine Bay Restaurant* (free for dinner guests of the restaurant; the restaurant monitors VHF, ch. 16). The other moorings you see in front of the conspicuous condos on the eastern shore are private, do not pick them up. You can anchor in about 10' of water in the center of the bay if the moorings are taken, but don't go too far north as the bay shoals.

What You Will Find Ashore
On the shore of *Brandywine Bay* can be found the best restaurant on Tortola if not the entire British Virgin Islands, the *Brandywine Bay Restaurant* (284-495-2301). The chef chooses the freshest fish, flies in ingredients from all over the world, and even makes his own mozzarella. This elegant restaurant is open for dinner only and guests have an extensive choice of fine Italian and Australian wines. You can phone the restaurant at anytime of day at 284-495-2301, or hail them on VHF ch. 16 after 1400 to request a dinner reservation and mooring instructions. There is a dinghy dock about 150' south of the condos where you can tie your dink while dining at the restaurant. From the dock follow the path to the left of the dock towards the road and the restaurant is a short walk up the hill.

About three miles east of Road Town, between *Fish Bay* and *Brandywine Bay*, in Kingstown, are the remains of the old *Anglican Church*, which was

A Cruising Guide to the Virgin Islands

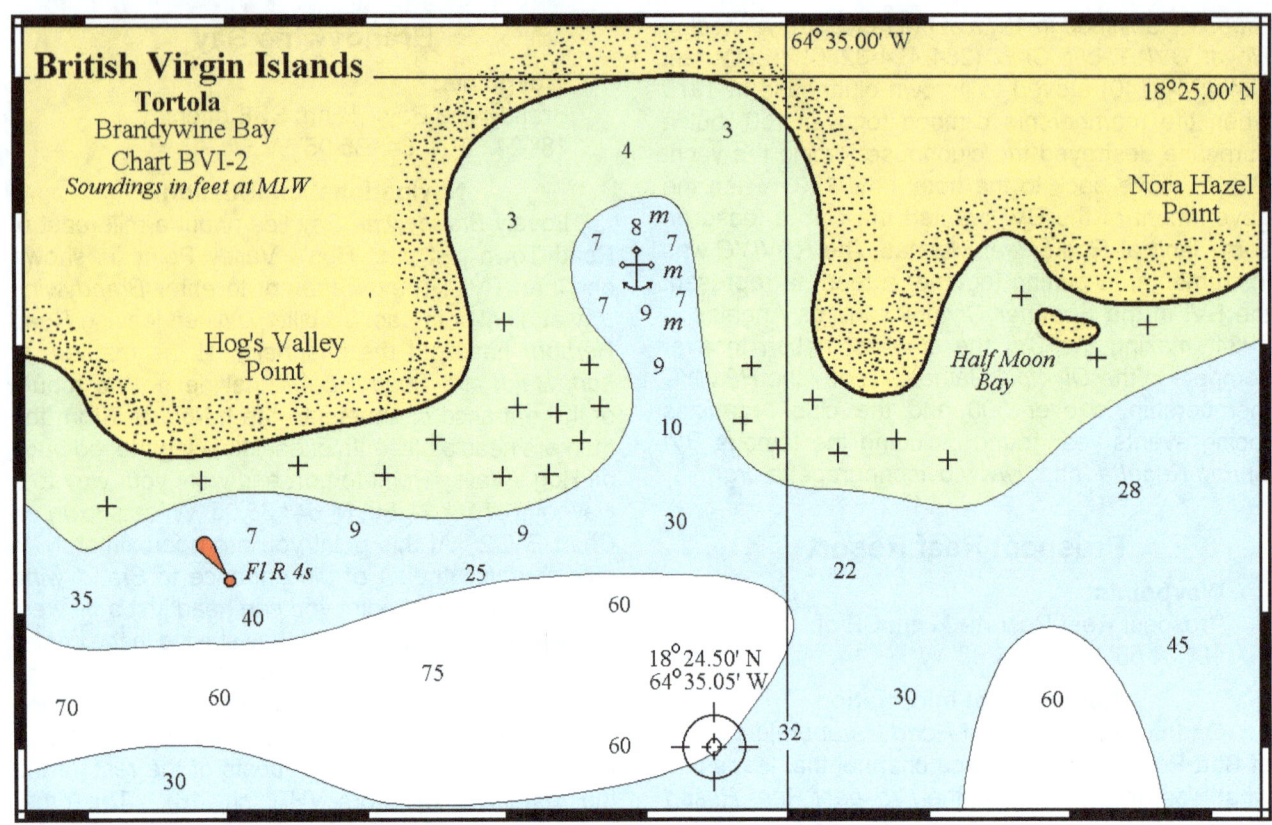

Brandywine Bay, Tortola

Photo by Todd Duff

part of a larger *Anglican Mission*. The church was constructed in 1833 by members of a group of 600 freed slaves who had been granted the land at Kingstown for a settlement. The 600 were part of a larger group of 1,000 who were aboard slave trading vessels and who were liberated in 1807. Some of the freed slaves were sent into military service while others were sent to Tortola to apprentice under local planters and who eventually settled at a place called *African Settlement* in Kingstown.

Maya Cove, Buck Island

Waypoints:
Maya Cove - ½ nm S of Buck Island
18° 24.80' N, 64° 33.40' W

Navigational Information

Leaving *Road Harbour* and *Brandywine Bay* behind and heading northeastward along Tortola's eastern shore the next anchorages with marine facilities are located at Buck Island and at *Maya Cove* as shown on Chart BVI-3. From *Road Harbour* or *Brandywine Bay* you can parallel the shoreline of Tortola staying at least ¼-½ mile off to avoid inshore shallows as you work your way past Whelk Point and the reef that stretches northeast from it towards Buck Island. If you are approaching from the east or from Beef Island or *Fat Hogs Bay*, you must pass south of Buck Island and make your way to a waypoint at 18° 24.80' N, 64° 33.40' W, ½ mile south of Buck Island.

From the waypoint you may head generally north/northwest towards the marked entrance channel into *Maya Cove*, or you may head up into the lee of Buck Island to anchor off its western shore just south of *Bar Bay*. Watch out for shoals here and never attempt to take your vessel between Buck Island and the mainland of Tortola. The anchorage here is very good though at times it can get a bit rolly from the surge.

If you do not wish to anchor at Buck Island and instead decide to avail yourself of the facilities in *Maya Cove* proceed towards the outer markers at the mouth of the entrance channel (8' at low water) and pass between them, remember, red, right, returning. Once past the second set of markers (there were two sets at the time of this writing and of course this may change) you will need to turn to port as the channel doglegs towards the southwest and you parallel the reef to port as you enter *Maya Cove*. Never attempt to enter *Maya Cove* by passing between the green outer marker and Whelk Point, this whole area is a shallow reef. In the harbor itself there are several moorings that you may pick up, they're maintained by *Tropic Island Yacht Management*, or you may anchor out of the channel in the southwestern section of the bay as shown on Chart BVI-3.

What You Will Find Ashore

On the west side of *Maya Cove* is *Hodges Creek Marina*, usually just called *Hodges Creek* (actually the northeastern corner of the bay is known as *Hodges Creek*), with all the amenities the cruiser needs as well as some studio apartments for rent. The marina offers dockage, water, ice, laundry, showers, and monitors VHF ch. 12. The restaurant, *Calamaya*, is right on the dock and serves breakfast, lunch, and dinner featuring Mediterranean and Caribbean cuisine including tapas with happy hour.

After *Sunsail* moved away, *Hodges Creek* became a bit of a ghost town and all of the major businesses, save the restaurant, closed down. *Sail Caribbean* (284-499-1759) runs a small operation out of here now and offers diving and sailing and the hotel is still in operation. *Admiral Marine Management* (284-394-3445) moved here and offers managed boat slips; there are also a number of transient slips available. The marina is now managed out of the hotel lobby, and may not respond to VHF radio.

The place to eat in *Maya Cove* is the new *Pusser's Restaurant* located where *Fat Hog Bob's* used to be, just a short walk from *Hodges Creek Marina*. Here you can relax and enjoy the beautiful view while seated in comfortable chairs on their 100' porch while dining on any of your *Pusser's* favorites like steak, burgers, ribs, and seafood. You can watch their 62" TV, browse their gift shop, try your skill in one of their two horseshoe pits, take a shower, or surf the net.

Navigational Information

Just to the west of *Maya Cove* is *Paraquita Bay* (see Chart BVI-3). This is often used as a hurricane hole by local boats and it's not unusual to see boats tied up here during the entire hurricane season. The mangrove-encircled bay was recently dredged and will allow slightly over 6' at high tide with 8' to 10' depths inside.

After the BVI boating community witnessed the devastation of some of the other nearby islands in recent hurricanes, the charter companies got together with the government and arranged for the Royal Navy to blast the channel. Then some 800 moorings were placed inside the two bays. The entire bay is full of

A Cruising Guide to the Virgin Islands

Maya Cove, Fat Hogs Bay in background — Photo by Todd Duff

Buck Island anchorage — Photo by Todd Duff

Western *Paraquita Bay*, a good hurricane hole — Photo by Todd Duff

Fat Hog's Bay — Photo by Todd Duff

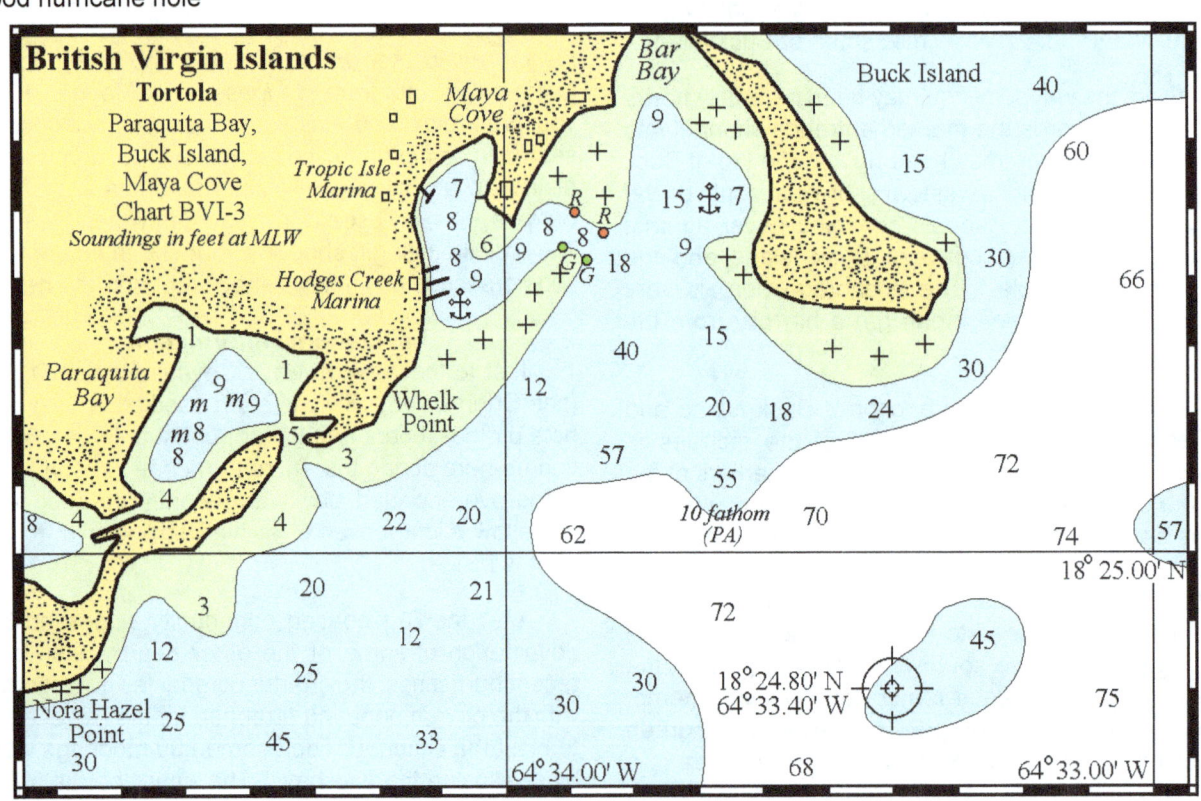

hurricane moorings and each and every charter boat in the BVI has a designated spot, so should a storm approach be sure to get in early and there are still some places to anchor in behind (north) of the mooring field and also to the east and southeast. Bear in mind that the locals will bring in their boats too, so don't plan to be alone. You will be sharing this harbor with up to a thousand other boats, all in giant rafts, tied bow and stern. In any case, if you should choose to enter *Paraquita Bay*, it would be wise to go in first by dinghy before entering with the big boat.

Fat Hog's Bay

Important Lights:
Fat Hog's Bay: Fl (2) W 5s

Waypoints:
Fat Hogs Bay - ¾ nm E of
18° 26.00' N, 64° 32.65' W

Navigational Information

Fat Hog's Bay lies just north of *Maya Cove* and Buck Island, and southwest of Beef Island as shown on Chart BVI-4. If you're arriving from *Maya Cove*, you just need to pass well south of Buck Island, rounding its eastern tip, and then working your way northwest paralleling the shoreline ¼ mile off as you work your way towards the marked entrance channel leading into *Fat Hog's Bay*. If you are approaching from Virgin Gorda or the northern shore of Tortola you must clear Beef Island, passing south of it, before heading to a waypoint at 18° 26.00' N, 64° 32.65' W, which will place you approximately ¾ mile east of *Fat Hogs Bay* as shown on Chart BVI-4. If you are approaching from Peter Island, or Cooper Island you may head to the same waypoint. From the waypoint you can head west and pass between the red light on Red Rock and the green buoy that marks the shoal lying off the northwestern tip of Buck Island as shown on the chart. Once inside *Fat Hog's Bay* you can turn to the north to tie up in a slip at *Harbourview Marina*, or *Penn's Landing Marina* (sometimes shown as H.R. Penn Marina) which has its own privately maintained buoyed channel (unlit and 6' at low water). There are several moorings available (maintained by *Penn's Landing*) east of the channel and boaters are requested not to anchor in the mooring field or in the channel.

What You Will Find Ashore

The old *Seabreeze Marina* is no longer in operation, its docks destroyed along with the old hotel but there is a rumor of the hotel being rebuilt. *Tradewinds Yacht Charters*, has also closed down. *Pro Valor Yacht Charters* (284-495-1931 runs a nice small charter operation out of the *James Young Marina* on the dock between what used to be *Seabreeze Marina* and where *Penn's Landing Marina* is located. This is a wonderful little 'family' type operation and Jim and Cecilia will do whatever they can to help you get sorted. They have slips at both the *James Young Marina* dock and the new *Harborview* dock and know the lay of the land out in East End. Also at the marina is the *Rite Breeze* grocery store, a *Riteway* convenience outlet, and nearby is the *Parham Town General Store*, the *Parham Food Market*, and the *Bistro Restaurant* which is open for lunch and dinner.

Penn's Landing Marina (http://www.pennslandingbvi.com/) is a full-service marina offering slips with full electric and water, moorings, showers, propane refills, and ice. *Marine Management Services* is also located here.

For dining try the *Emile's*, a Mexican restaurant, or the *Red Rock Restaurant and Bar* (284-495-1646). The *Sailors Ketch Seafood Market* offers the best fresh, locally caught seafood. Just past *Penn's Landing* is *Alphonso's Garage* where small boats and dinghies can get gasoline.

Ed Wheatley's *Harbour View Marina* is the home of *Trade Winds Yachts* and has slips with full electric, water, fuel, showers, diesel, and ice. Moorings are also available. Here you'll find the *UBS* dive shop and a very nice Thai restaurant, *Kong Ming Asian Terrace*, that is open for lunch and dinner. Within walking distance is *Emile's Mexican Restaurant*, the *Marine Depot* (a chandlery), and an ATM at *Barclays Bank*.

Marina Cay

Waypoints:
Scrub Island - ½ nm NNE of Scrub Island Cut
18° 28.75' N, 64° 31.25' W

Scrub Island - ¾ nm E of Marina Cay
18° 27.50' N, 64° 30.50' W

In 1937, Robb and Rodie White purchased the 6-acre Marina Cay for $60, then just a small, lonely bit of land called Diddledoe Island. Robb was a writer who, with his lovely wife Rodie, ran off to the tropics to find peace and inspiration. The Whites built a cottage atop the hill and left in 1940, Robb to fight in the war and Rodie to recover from an attack of appendicitis and during their absence they lost title to the island and never returned. But the Whites were not yet through with Marina Cay, Robb wrote a book about their 3 years on the island entitled *Two On The Isle* that later became a movie, starring Sydney Poitier and John Cassavettes. The movie was filmed on and around Marina Cay and was released in 1958. Today the masonry cottage built by Robb and Rodie when they came to live on the cay in 1936 is now a lending library and the peaceful *Fritz Seyfarth Reading Room* and Marina Cay boasts a 12-room inn and a great beach-front restaurant run by *Pusser's*.

Navigational Information

Marina Cay lies by itself just north of *Trellis Bay* on Tortola, southeast of Great Camanoe, and southwest of Scrub Island. If you are approaching from the east, say from Virgin Gorda, you can head for a waypoint at 18° 27.50' N, 64° 30.50' W, which will place you approximately ¾ mile east of Marina Cay and south of Scrub Island as shown on Chart BVI-5. From the waypoint you can head west passing either south or north of Marina Cay to anchor or moor off its western shore as shown in greater detail on Chart BVI-6. When passing north of Marina Cay stay approximately in mid-channel between Scrub Island and Marina Cay to avoid the reefs of each one. If you are passing south of Marina Cay, give the reefs south of the island a wide berth. Pass the red marker, which may or may not be there, well to the south to avoid the reef that stretches southwest of Marina Cay.

If you are approaching from the northeast, say from Anegada, you can access Marina Cay via *Scrub Island Cut* lying between Scrub Island and Great Camanoe as shown on Chart BVI-5. A waypoint at 18° 28.75' N, 64° 31.25' W, will place you approximately ½ mile north/northeast of *Scrub Island Cut*, and from this waypoint you can pass between the two islands staying approximately mid-channel to avoid the shoals off each one as shown on Chart BVI-5, and in greater detail on Chart BVI-6. Once clear of *Scrub Island Cut* you may head to the western shore of Marina Cay to anchor or pick up a mooring.

If you are approaching Marina Cay from the west, you'll have to thread your way between Tortola's northern shore and Guana Island. Once clear of that passage you must then pass between the shoals off Little Camanoe and Great Camanoe and the marked reefs off *Long Bay* and *Conch Bay* on the northern shore of Tortola just west of Trellis Bay as shown on Chart BVI-5. Never attempt this passage at night or in periods of poor visibility, and don't forget that there is a strong tidal current in this area.

What You Will Find Ashore

Pusser's Marina Cay offers 30 overnight moorings for vessels to 75' LOA, a full-service fuel dock, ice, water, a Laundromat, trash facilities, *Wi-Fi*, and some very nice showers. You can also drop off your garbage here at *Pusser's* for only $2 per bag, if you think that is high perhaps you should remember that *Pusser's* must do something with your garbage and it costs them to remove it to Tortola. There's a free ferry service from *Pusser's Marina Cay* dock on Beef Island to their restaurant for guests of the restaurant. *Pusser's Company Store* is built out over the water and features *Pusser's* line of clothing, books, nautical memorabilia, swimwear, and much, much more. *Pusser's Porch Grill* features fresh fish, barbecue ribs, steak, and daily Chef's specials.

The original building of the *Sunset Bar*, the *Ferngully* is the name of an original Marina Cay drink named after a Jamaican rainforest. And speaking of drinks let me just say that here you can get truly wonderful piña coladas. They dip the rim in *Coco Lopez* crème of coconut and then, just like a margarita, the rim is dipped and twisted in raw grated coconut, this alone should draw you here.

You can enjoy good snorkeling on the reef lying south and east of Marina Cay, and *Lee Bay* on Great Camanoe offers good snorkeling along the reef at its southern edge. *Lee Bay* is deep and should be considered only as a temporary anchorage in calm weather while diving. *Diamond Reef* is a good snorkeling and dive site for beginners as well as experts just off Great Camanoe well west of Marina Cay. The reef offers a shallow wall that drops from 10'-35'. It is said that the site was named after a huge diamond ring that was said to have been found here years ago. For more diving information, check with *Dive BVI* (http://www.divebvi.com/) at Marina Cay.

There is a free ferry to Marina Cay from the *Conch Shell Point Restaurant* on Conch Shell Point dock in the northwest part of *Trellis Bay*.

Scrub Island

As shown on Chart BVI-5 and Chart BVI-6, the western end of Scrub Island is home to the posh *Scrub Island Marina* (http://www.scrubisland.com/). The marina offers 55 slips including five slips for yachts

The British Virgin Islands - Tortola

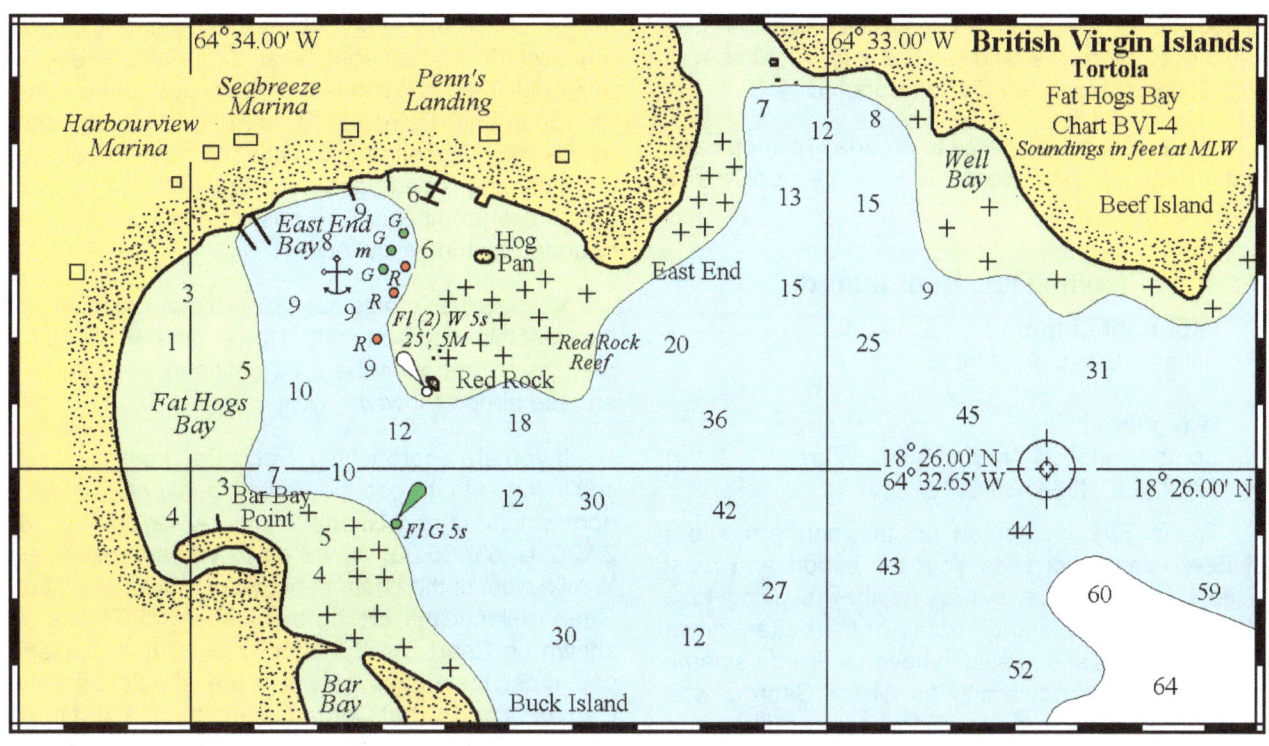

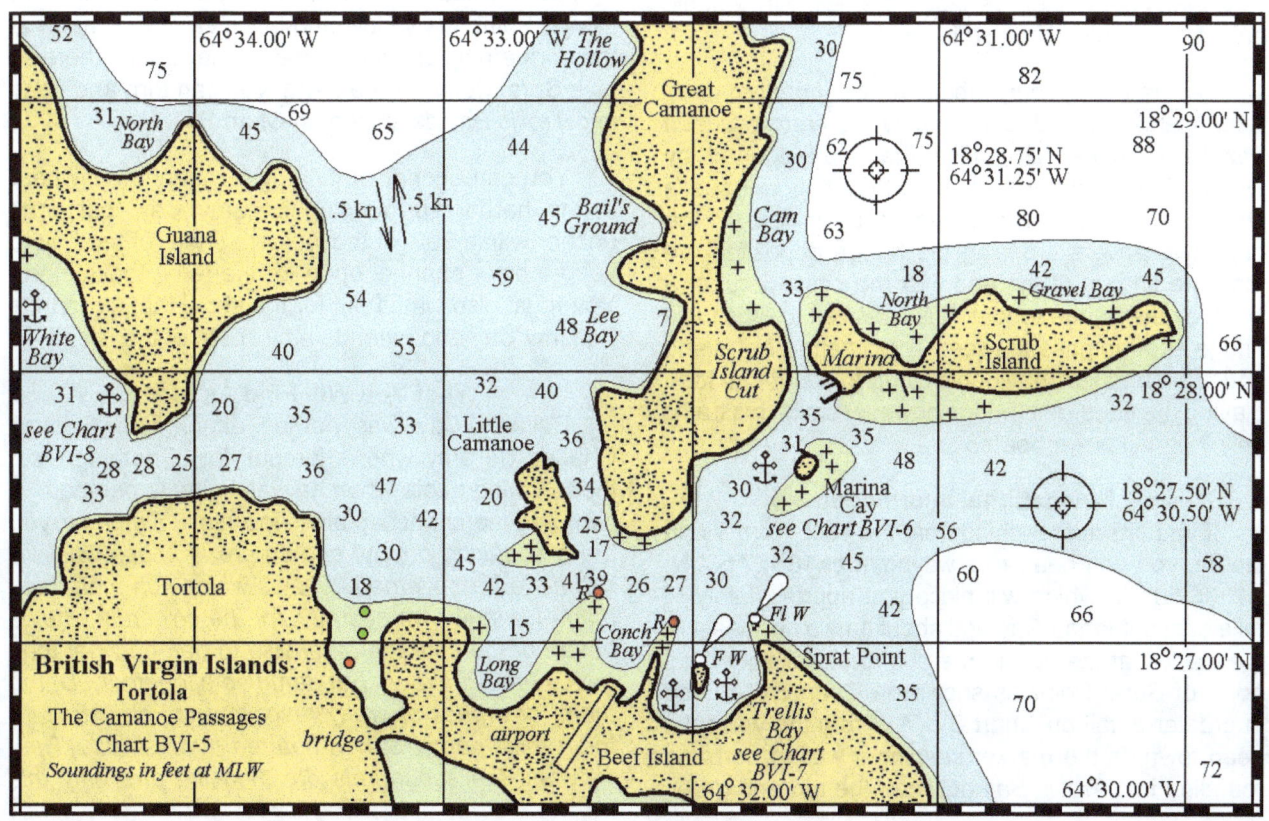

to 160' LOA. The marina boasts full electric, water, a fuel dock, showers, and is a focus for all manner of water sports, especially diving through *Dive BVI*.

The resort is also home to an array of shops and restaurants, a fitness center, a sailing school, and a gourmet market.

Trellis Bay, Beef Island

Important Lights:
Bellamy Cay Light: Fxd W

Waypoints:
Scrub Island - ¾ nm E of Marina Cay
18° 27.50' N, 64° 30.50' W

Trellis Bay is located on the northern shore of Beef Island, home to Tortola's airport and most visitors to the BVI wonder why they're flying to a place called Beef Island instead of the better known Tortola. The island is said to have received its name from a woman, known only as Widow George, who kept cattle on the island. Widow George lived in a plantation house atop the hill overlooking *Trellis Bay* and was plagued by passing pirates who preyed upon her cattle. Finally deciding to do something about it, Widow George invited 14 of the pirates to "tea." It is said that Widow George laced the tea with arsenic and thereby solved her problem.

Separated by only about a few hundred feet, Beef Island is linked to Tortola by the narrow *Queen Elizabeth Bridge* toll bridge that was opened by Queen Elizabeth II herself in 1966. You will see a small bridge tender's office and unused gate. In the old days, drivers crossing the bridge deposited the fare in a tin cup at the end of a rod passed out of a kiosk by the bridge tender. It is now free to cross this bridge and the pass between Tortola and Beef island under the bridge is navigable by up to about four feet, playing the tides. The bridge however limits this traffic only to small powerboats.

Navigational Information

If you are approaching from the east, from Virgin Gorda, you can head to a waypoint at 18° 27.50' N, 64° 30.50' W, which will place you approximately ¾ mile east of Marina Cay and about 1 mile northeast of the marker at the northern end of the reef and rocks north of Sprat Point as shown on Chart BVI-5, and in greater detail on Chart BVI-7. From the waypoint head towards the marker keeping it well to port and rounding into *Trellis Bay* between the red and green buoys. If you are approaching from Marina Cay you must avoid the reefs southwest of Marina Cay as you approach *Trellis Bay* and then keep clear of the reefs off Conch Shell Point and Sprat Point. Avoid the area off the end of the airstrip, it is marked by yellow buoys, no anchoring is permitted here and vessels over 8' in height are prohibited from passing through the area bounded by the yellow buoys.

Vessels with masts over 30' (10 meters) must call the Beef Island airport control tower on VHF ch. 10 for permission to transit the area between Bellamy Cay and the airport runway.

If you are approaching *Trellis Bay* from the west, you'll have to thread your way between Tortola's northern shore and Guana Island. A waypoint at 18° 27.70' N, 65° 35.00' W, will place you approximately ½ mile west of the channel between Monkey Point on Guana Island and the northern shore of Tortola as shown on Chart BVI-8. Once clear of that passage you must then pass between the shoals off Little Camanoe and Great Camanoe and the marked reefs off *Long Bay* and *Conch Bay* on the northern shore of Tortola just west of *Trellis Bay* as shown on Chart BVI-5. Never attempt this passage at night or in periods of poor visibility, and don't forget that there is a strong tidal current in this area. Once clear of Conch Point, the yellow and black cardinal marker at the northern tip of the reef may or may not be there so give Sprat Point a wide berth, you can turn and head into *Trellis Bay* as shown on Chart BVI-7.

You can anchor or pick up a mooring anywhere in the harbor surrounding Bellamy Cay, but don't anchor within 200' of the western shore of the bay to keep a clear channel open for the ferry docks there. You must also watch out for the shoal that surrounds Bellamy Cay and extends a bit south of the island.

What You Will Find Ashore

Bellamy Cay was named after pirate Captain Charles Bellamy who is famous for, if nothing else, the following quote when he was trying to persuade a captured merchant captain to join him. *"Damn ye, you are a sneaking puppy, and so are all those who will submit to be governed by laws which rich men have made for their own security, for the cowardly whelps have not the courage otherwise to defend what they get by their knavery. But damn ye altogether. Damn them for a pack of crafty rascals, and you, who sire them for a parcel of hen-hearted numbskulls. They vilify us, the scoundrels do; then there is only this*

The British Virgin Islands - Tortola

Anchorage at Marina Cay — Photo by Todd Duff

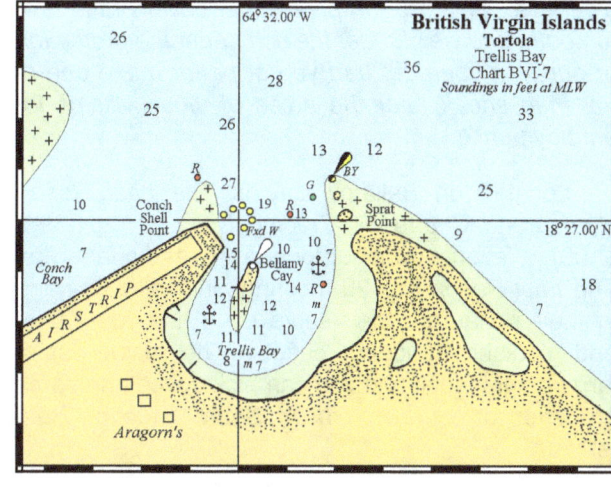

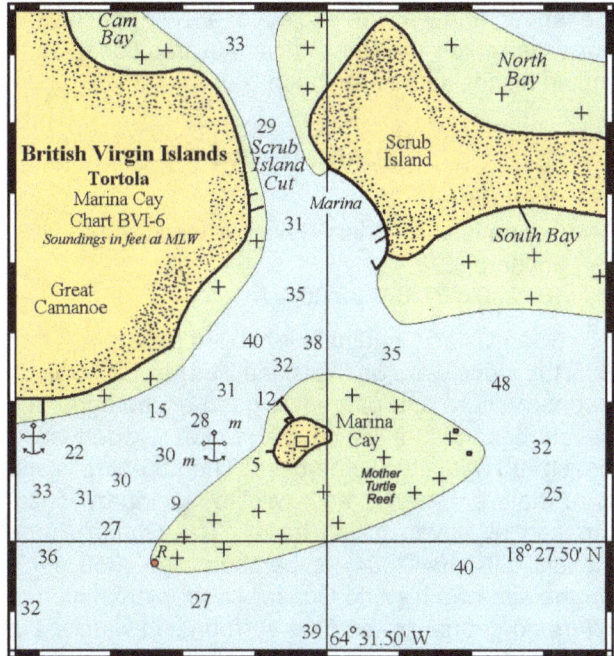

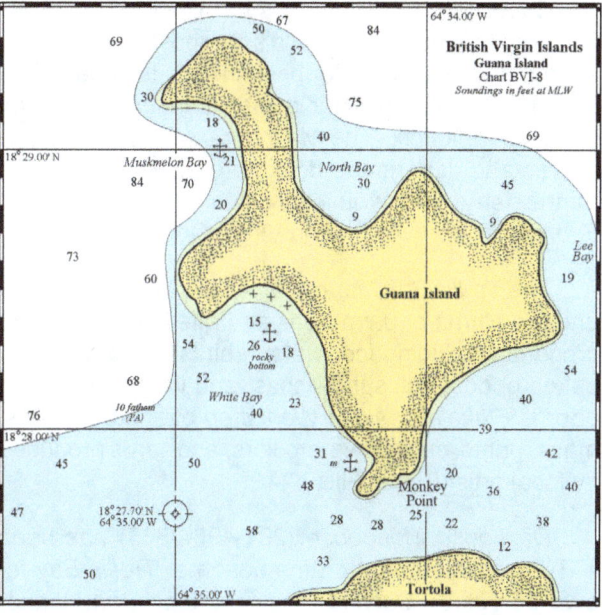

Trellis Bay anchorage, Bellamy Cay in the center — Photo by Todd Duff

131

difference, they rob the poor under cover of the law, forsooth, and we plunder the rich under the protection of our own courage; had ye not better make one of us, than sneak after the arses of those villains for employment?"

Located on Bellamy Cay is *The Last Resort Restaurant, Charter, & Trading Co. Ltd.* (284-394-0100), a favorite hangout for cruisers and charterers. *The Last Resort* has 29 moorings in *Trellis Bay* and in their restaurant they serve up a fine roast beef and Yorkshire pudding buffet. The resort has a large dinghy dock and you can pick up ice and some groceries at the *Last Resort Shore Base* on Beef Island.

Overlooking *Trellis Bay* is the *Conch Shell Point Restaurant* where the island's freshest seafood can be found. Their Euro-Caribbean menu is unbeatable, but they're only open for dinner, imagine what they could do for lunch. The *Marina Cay Ferry* is free and arrives and departs the dock here by the restaurant. At the ferry dock you can catch the *North Sound Express* to *North Sound* on Virgin Gorda.

The *Trellis Bay Market* lies opposite the ferry dock under a clump of palm trees and offers all manner of groceries including ice, water, spirits, fresh produce, baked goods, deli sandwiches, and ice cream. Next door is *Fluke's Designs Workshop* offering coasters, maps, prints, original watercolors, and cards produced by local artist Roger Ellis.

De Loose Mongoose (284-495-2303) has been a BVI institution right on the beach at *Trellis Bay* for over 25 years. Serving breakfast, lunch, and dinner (and a *Sunday BBQ*) with daily happy hours from 1700-1830, the food and ambiance is unbeatable. If you're too tired to head back to the boat, don't, take one of their guest rooms for the night. The owners are former cruisers and the current manager John lives aboard in the bay. Thursday nights are horseshoe tournament nights so tie up to the dinghy dock, forget your shoes and shirt, and step right up to the bar for an unforgettable time.

At the far eastern end of Tortola is the *Trellis Bay Cyber Cafe*. You can drop off your garbage in the bins near the concrete dock in Trellis Bay. South of Bellamy Cay on the shoreline of Beef Island is the *BVI Windsurfing School* and *Jeremy's Kitchen* (284-343-3075) which has several computers, high speed wireless links and great food. Be sure to try one of the owner Jeremy's *Awesome Sandwiches* and his fantastic fresh tropical fruit smoothies. Right next door is *Aragorn's Studio* (284-495-1849) offering fine example's of this Tortola-born artist's work in ceramics, copper, woodcuts, and silkscreen.

Aragorn also comes by the anchored boats in the morning offering fresh bread and fruits, crafts, and T-shirts. In the evening Anouk will pass by offering her handmade jewelry. *Aragorn's* is also home to the *Gli Gli*, a Carib Indian canoe that's available for charter. Aragorn orchestrated the construction of this amazing vessel in the wilds of Dominica with the help of Carib Indians from Dominica who crafted this 35' long canoe in the same manner that their ancestors did over 500 years ago. *Gli Gli* is the largest in the Caribbean and was the subject of a *CNN* special and is available for chartered trips with traditional Carib Indian dishes served for lunch.

Guana Island

Waypoints:
Guana Island - ½ nm SW of White Bay anchorage
18° 27.70' N, 64° 35.00' W

Guana Island, originally inhabited by Quakers that built the stone walls on the island, lies just off Tortola's northern shore and offers two good anchorages and seven beaches of which the white powdery-sand beach at *White Bay* is the best. The 850-acre island is a nature reserve and wildlife sanctuary criss-crossed by seven hiking trails. The *Guana Island Resort* (284-494-2354) is perched high atop a hill on the site of a historic Quaker sugar plantation that offers gorgeous views of the surrounding waters, but is a private resort whose dining room is only open for guests of the resort. Guests can rent the entire island or just a cottage for an overnight stay that includes three meals a day.

Navigational Information

If approaching from the east, from Marina Cay or *Trellis Bay*, you will have to negotiate the passage between the reefs off the northern shore of Tortola at *Long Bay* and *Conch Bay*, and the shoals off Little Camanoe and Great Camanoe as shown on Chart BVI-5. Never attempt this passage at night or in periods of poor visibility, and don't forget that there is a strong tidal current in this area.

If you are approaching from the west, from Jost Van Dyke perhaps, a waypoint at 18° 27.70' N,

The British Virgin Islands - Tortola

Brewer's Bay, Tortola — Photo by Todd Duff

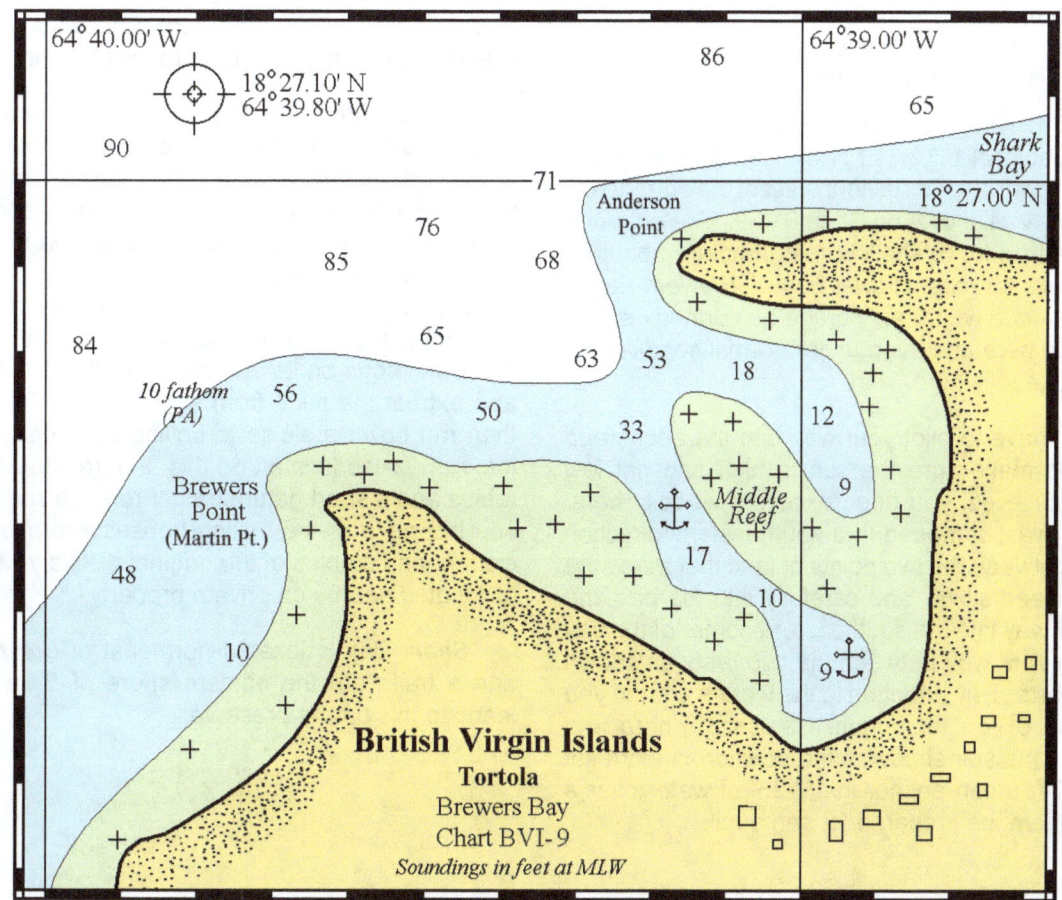

64° 35.00' W, will place you approximately ½ mile southwest of *White Bay* on Guana Island and about the same distance west of the channel between Tortola and Monkey Point on Guana Island as shown on Chart BVI-8.

You can anchor in the small cove in the lee of Monkey Point, this spot gets very rolly at times but it allows you easy access to the good snorkeling off Monkey Point. You can pick up a mooring here or anchor in about 15'-20' of water. A better anchorage is to the north at *White Bay*, but not much better. Not as rolly as the anchorage at Monkey Point perhaps, but *White Bay* shallows rapidly near shore and you'll have to anchor in water that is 20'-30' deep with scattered rocks waiting to foul your anchor. There are several coral heads near shore that you'll want to avoid when swimming or taking the dinghy to the beach. To the north of *White Bay* is *Muskmelon Bay* where you can anchor in calm weather and no swell. The anchorages at Guana Island should not be considered during periods of northerly swells.

Brewers Bay

Waypoints:
Brewers Bay - ½ nm NW of entrance
18° 27.10' N, 64° 39.80' W

Navigational Information

A waypoint at 18° 27.10' N, 64° 39.80' W, will place you approximately ½ mile northwest of the entrance to *Brewers Bay* as shown on Chart BVI-9. The entrance is tricky with a lot of shallow reef structure about so it is off limits for most charter boats. *Brewers Bay* is also not a good winter anchorage as northerly swells play havoc here and even under normal conditions it can be quite rolly here.

You'll have to pilot your way into the anchorage by eye so make sure the sun is high and not low and in your eyes, you need excellent visibility here. From the waypoint head in a southeasterly direction keeping between the two points of land that frame the bay. Proceed slowly and carefully into the bay and work your way into the southeastern corner of the bay threading your way between the two reefs as shown on the charts. Pay attention to the waters around you and in front of you, the bottom rises sharply here, and if you can, put somebody on the bow for an extra set of eyes. You can anchor in 15'-25' of water over a sandy bottom, be prepared for some roll.

What You Will Find Ashore

Brewers Bay takes its name from an old rum distillery that was located here, not far from the local sugar plantations, that was in operation until 1956. Some of the ruins of the distillery can still be found in the brush along the road just off the beach. On the former site of the distillery you'll find the *Brewer's Bay Campground* and the *Bamboo Beach Bar & Restaurant* serving breakfast, lunch, and dinner with a Sunday night BBQ. Here you'll find the remains of an old wooden boat that was originally built on the island in the traditional way, with ribs of white cedar and planks of pitch pine. The campground also boasts a store, picnic tables with grills, and camping areas. Nearby, *Nicole's Beach Bar* is open for lunch only and boasts palm and almond trees growing right up through the bar's deck. At the other end of the beach is the *Coconut Branch Beach Bar*.

Divers will want to check out the *Brewers Bay Pinnacles*, submerged towers of rock that rise hundreds of feet to within 30' of the surface off the westernmost tip of *Brewer's Bay*. The *Pinnacles* are one of those rare dive sites that are available from the shore, but divers will need to exercise extreme caution as the area is rife with currents, especially when northerly swells are running, it is best to visit the site by boat.

Just a short walk to the northeast of *Brewers Bay*, atop a grassy knoll above the bay, is *The Windmill* at the *Mount Healthy National Park*. Dating to the 1700s, the mill is constructed of local rock, coral, and ballast bricks from merchant vessels that called at Tortola, and is the only surviving mill of its kind in the British Virgin Islands. Once belonging to wealthy landowner Bezaliel Hodge, the mill used "sails" to turn a large shaft with cogs on its end that turned rollers to crush and extract the juice from sugar cane. The extract then ran down a sluice to boiling vats for distillation into rum. Also located on this .9 acre site are picnic tables and a short nature trail. From the site you can see the ruins of the boiling houses, storage rooms, cistern, and stables of the original distillery which are all located nearby on private property.

Shark Bay is located northeast of *Brewers Bay* and a trail from the eastern shore of *Brewers Bay* leads to this nature preserve.

The British Virgin Islands - Tortola

Cane Garden Bay, Tortola
Photo by Todd Duff

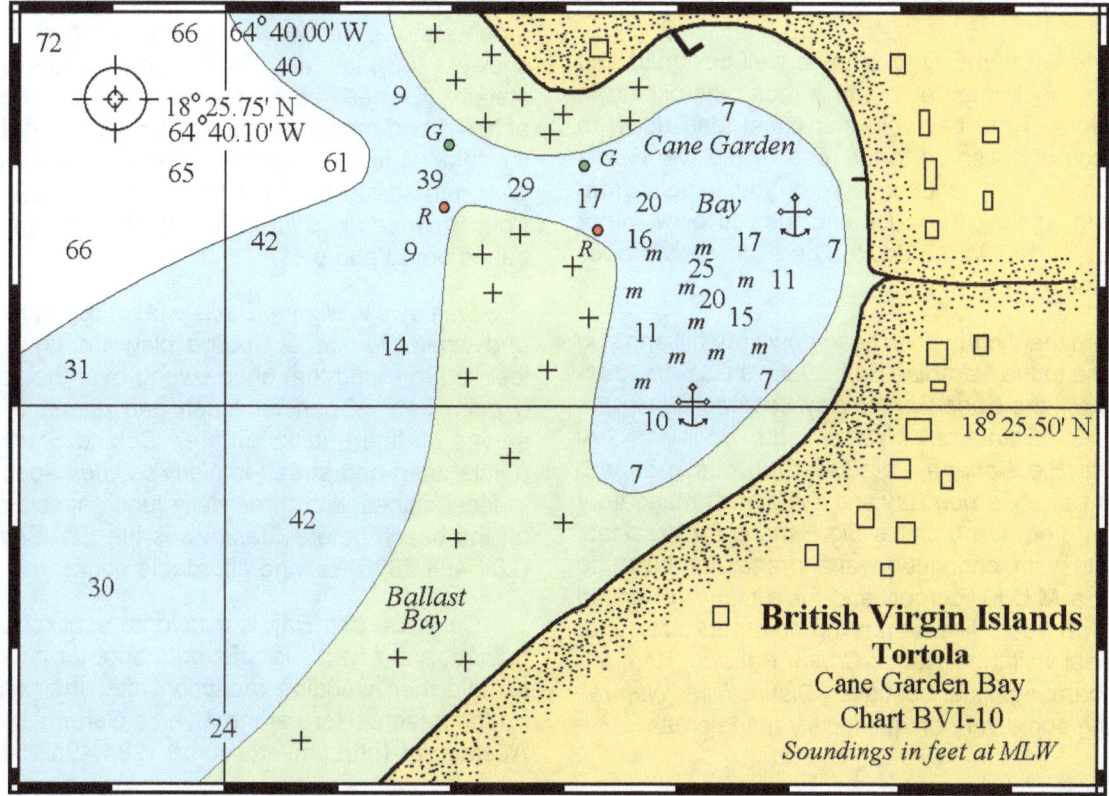

Cane Garden Bay

Waypoints:
Cane Garden Bay - ¼ nm WNW of entrance
18° 25.75' N, 64° 40.10' W

Navigational Information

Cane Garden Bay is one of the prettiest and est known of the BVI anchorages, no doubt due to Jimmy Buffet's songs, *Mañana* and *Tire Swing*. A waypoint at 18° 25.75' N, 64° 40.10' W, will place you approximately ¼ mile west/northwest of the entrance to Cane Garden Bay as shown on Chart BVI-10. From the waypoint you should head generally east/southeast entering the well-marked channel into the bay. Sometimes the marks are missing so don't panic if they are not there. Once inside the bay you can anchor wherever your draft allows or pick up a mooring, the best spot to anchor is in the northeastern part of the bay, but not too close to the marked swimming area, and give yourself plenty of swinging room as the wind tends to dance around here. Never try to anchor or moor here if northerly swells are running or predicted.

What You Will Find Ashore

On the eastern side of the bay is a public dock where you can tie up to top off your water and fuel tanks. Bear in mind that you cannot tie up here overnight.

Cane Garden Bay also has a well-designed and lit dinghy dock integrated into a rock outcropping in the middle of the bay with steps that lead down to the beach and also up to the road by the *Ole Works Inn*. Use a stern anchor to keep your dinghy from pounding against the dock and also to allow other dinghies access to the dock. There's usually a dock attendant on duty at night.

From the dinghy dock head down the hill and you will come to the *Paradise Club*, *Quito's Gazebo* (284-495-4837), the *Cane Garden Bay Seafood Superette*, *Rhymer's*, *Stanley's*, *Myett's*, and *Bobby's*. Al Henley's *Big Banana Paradise Club* has a superb view of *Cane Garden Bay* and it is almost mandatory that you dine at the club's *Big Banana* for breakfast complete with coconut/banana bread, for lunch to sample a M.O.M. burger, and for a dinner of grilled lobster. If you'd like something cold and tasty after your meal visit the *A&S Ice Cream Parlour*. Here too is a charming little boutique, *Distinctively Natural*, featuring some very unique locally made crafts.

Just down from the dinghy dock and *Paradise Club*, *Quito's Gazebo* is the location where the singer/owner Quito Rymer performs. Quito Rymer is a self-taught musician who was born and raised in *Cane Garden Bay*. Quito taught himself to play guitar using a large sardine can with fishing line for strings. Quito spent some time as a bartender in Jackson Hole, Wyoming, before returning to *Cane Garden Bay* in 1983 where he began his recording career in 1987. Besides his five albums, his song *Mix Up World* was part of the TV show *Paradise Beach*. Quito performs solo on Tuesday and Thursdays and on the weekends he plays with his band, *The Edge*. *Jan's Pot Pourri and Art Gallery* is located here and sells art by Quito Rymer as well as jewelry and handicrafts.

If you would like to purchase some fresh seafood, visit the *Cane Garden Bay Seafood Superette* for the freshest in locally caught seafood as well as groceries, freshly baked bread, and spirituous beverages.

Rhymer's Beach Hotel is a focus of activity here as well as a good spot to get a taxi (across the street is *Del's Jeep Rentals* if you would rather drive yourself around). *Rhymer's* has several moorings in front of their beach and their *Beach Bar and Restaurant* is open for breakfast, lunch, and dinner with a Tuesday and Saturday night buffet and a Thursday night lobster feast with live music. The resort also has a grocery store, gift shop, Laundromat, beauty salon, showers ($3), ice, and *Cane Garden Bay's* only gas station. Owner Patsy Rhymer hails from the island of Nevis and many say she reminds them of Nefertiti, the famous former Queen of Egypt. You may dump your garbage in the bins behind *Rhymer's*. Across from *Rhymer's* is *Cline's Bakery*, THE spot for fresh baked bread and pies.

Stanley's Welcome Bar is a favorite local hangout and when *Hurricane George* blew through the bar lost its tire swing that once swung over the bay from a palm tree. Open for lunch and dinner *Stanley's* serves up fine traditional fare. Behind *Stanley's* on a little dead-end street, is *Netty's Diner*, specializing in local dishes with three daily lunch specials. Just off the beach before *Stanley's* is the *Elm Beach Bar* (284-494-2888) serving affordable drinks.

Cane Garden Bay is a favorite spot for couples to wed, and *Myett's* is a favorite spot for newlyweds to hold their wedding reception after their marriage on the beach. Here at the *Myett's Garden and Grille Restaurant* (http://myetts.com/) (284-495-9649) you can pick your own lobster, chicken, or other entrée for grilling. *Myett's* was originally a two-story circular restaurant and bar, but has since added a separate bar and grill pavilions. *Myett's* peas and rice is well-known, the dish won 1st place in the *Festival Village* competition. You can access the Internet in *Myett's* office and you can check here for the latest weather reports. If you follow the road past the cemetery you'll come to the small *Columbus Sunset Store and Bar*, a good spot to stop and have a cold one.

Continuing south along the road on your left you will find the entrance to the *Callwood Rum Distillery*. *Cane Garden Bay* gets its name from the sugar cane that still is grown nearby to make rum, and for over two hundred years the *Callwood Rum Distillery* in *Cane Garden Bay* has been making that rum. Housed in its original stone plantation-era building, the distillery has been producing excellent rum from its copper and iron boiling kettles. Still in the hands of the same family, the distillery uses the same crushing machinery and still that it did when production first began two centuries ago. The product, *Arundel Rum*, is stored inside oak barrels after being distilled.

Just past the entrance to the distillery is *Da Wedding*, a friendly little beach front bar at the southern end of *Cane Garden Bay* and is owned by Poui, a local fisherman who supplies his own fresh seafood. Poui offers a fish fry on Wednesdays with live entertainment and is open daily for lunch and dinner.

West End

(Soper's Hole)

Important Lights:
Soper's Hole Light: Fl R

Waypoints:
Thatch Island Cut North - ¼ nm N of
18° 23.65' N, 64° 43.22' W

Little Thatch Island Cut - ¼ nm S of
18° 22.65' N, 64° 42.53' W

Colorful and picturesque, West End lies at the western end of Tortola. Most visitors here think the entire area is named *Soper's Hole*, but only the bay is called *Soper's Hole*. The entire area is known as West End, which is really just the area by the ferry docks while the cay to the south, which is connected to the mainland of Tortola by a small bridge, is called Frenchman's Cay and is the focus of most of the marine related activity in West End. Here you'll find excellent haul-out yards that can handle even the most delicate wooden boat projects. *Soper's Hole* was named after Cuthbert Soper, a prominent English landowner of the 1700s.

Navigational Information

If approaching from Jost Van Dyke head for a waypoint at 18° 23.65' N, 64° 43.22' W, which will place you approximately ¼ mile north of *Thatch Island Cut*, the passage between Great Thatch Island and the western tip of Tortola as shown on Chart BVI-11. From the waypoint head south passing mid-channel between Great Thatch Island and the western tip of Tortola and when clear of the cut you can turn east, keeping mid-channel between Tortola to your north and Little Thatch Island to your south, and head toward the marked channel leading into *Soper's Hole*. The areas of approach to Soper's Hole, *Thatch Island Cut* and *Little Thatch Island Cut* are rife with currents that can set as much as 3 knots at times. It's best to head south in *Thatch Island Cut* WITH the current instead of against you as it can be very strong.

Thatch Island is said to be named after the pirate Blackbeard, whose real name was Teach and which was sometimes written as Thatch...now why would that be? Along the southern shore of Thatch Island a point juts southward, this is Callwood Point and it lies about ½ mile west of *Thatch Island Cut*. You can anchor in the lee of the point, off its western shore in settled weather, but use caution as a wreck has been reported in the center of the anchorage. Little Thatch Island, said to have been purchases because the owner could have an unspoiled view, is a private resort where 1-4 guests can rent the entire island for approximately $8,000 a day, while 5-10 guests can rent it for approximately $10,000 a day. Around the eastern end of Frenchman's Cay is a small anchorage for vessels of 6' draft and less, but it is only recommended for daytime use in calm weather, if the trades build from the east or southeast you will be on a lee shore.

If approaching from the east, from Road Town or Nanny Cay, or from the eastern end of St. John or *Leinster Bay*, head for a waypoint at 18° 22.65'N, 64° 42.53' W, which will place you approximately ¼ mile south of *Little Thatch Island Cut*, the passage between Little Thatch Island and Frenchman's Cay as shown on Chart BVI-11. From the waypoint head northward keeping approximately mid-channel between the two points of land. Once clear of the tip of Frenchman's Cay you can turn to the east to enter *Soper's Hole*.

Vessels approaching from St. Thomas, or the northwestern tip of St. John, may pass through *The Narrows* to pass north of Little Thatch Island, or you may pass north of Great Thatch Island avoiding *The Narrows* to enter via *Thatch Island Cut* as described above. Bear in mind that *The Narrows* has a strong tidal current of 2-4 knots at times.

The typical cruising boat does not have to stay in the marked channel, *Soper's Hole* is very deep and the only shallows are toward the eastern end and off Frenchman's Cay where you'll find the only places to anchor with a reasonable depth. I suggest that you take a mooring here unless you can tuck in fairly close along the eastern shore or along the southern shore off Frenchman's Cay. There are many moorings in the harbor, the ones toward the eastern end belong to *Soper's Hole Wharf Marina*, while those further down along the Frenchman's Cay shoreline belong to the *Soper's Hole Yacht Services*.

What You Will Find Ashore

If you need to clear *Customs* and *Immigration*, their offices are located on the ferry dock at the northwestern end of *Soper's Hole* (their hours are 0830-1630, M-F). *Customs* requests that private vessels refrain from tying up to the ferry dock and suggest that you take a slip or mooring and mosey over to clear by foot or dinghy. From this spot ferries come and go from Jost Van Dyke, St. Thomas, and St. John. Here you'll find *Zelma's Variety Store* and the *Rocky Willow Snack Bar*, a popular spot for ferry passengers and locals.

On Frenchman's Cay you'll see the colorful buildings that make up the *Soper's Hole Marina* complex at the southeastern end of Soper's Hole, a site that screams Caribbean and is as picture postcard perfect as it gets. *Soper's Hole Marina* (http://www.sopersholemarina.com/port/default.aspx) is a full-service marina with moorings in the harbour, 50 slips with full electric and water that can accommodate a vessel up to 170' in length with a maximum draft of 36', showers, phone, fax, and internet services, fuel, ice, 24-hour security, and facilities for your garbage at the fuel dock.

Just west of *Soper's Hole Marina* is *Voyage Yacht Charters* (http://www.voyagecharters.com/) where you can perhaps get a slip if they have any available,

most are in use by their charter fleet. If *Soper's Hole Marina* is full you can contact *Voyage* on VHF ch. 12 to see if they have a slip available.

And just west of *Voyage Yacht Charters* is *Soper's Hole Shipyard and Marina*, a full-service facility that can accommodate vessels up to 150' in length with full power and electric (including 200-amp service), fuel, moorings, showers, a laundry service, a 200-ton *Travelift*, a 40-ton hoist, do-it-yourself facilities, a welding and fabrication service, a painting staff that are fantastic with Awlgrip, and if that's not enough, they have shipwrights on hand that specialize in wooden boats and multihulls. This operation just underwent a huge renovation and is owned by *Voyage Yachts* and is the primary storage facility for their fleet of cats during the off season. It is occasionally possible to get a space for the summer in amongst these cats, but don't wait too long to reserve your space! If you want to do a quick haulout and have a beamy cat, this is a great facility as they have an amazing radio controlled lift system that slides into the water under your boat and pulls it clear of the water, placing it in the yard all by remote control. Pretty incredible to watch actually! Sharn, the yard manager is from South Africa and is very knowledgeable and helpful so do not hesitate to contact them if you have a major project or emergency haulout that needs doing. Voyage Yacht Charters can be reached at (443-569-7007, or info@voyagecharters.com).

The new kid on the block is *Lighthouse Marina*, they are able to accommodate yachts up to 160 feet in length with a draft of up to 22 feet. Service includes gas & diesel, 30, 50, 100, & 125 amp service and 110/120 electricity, fresh water, ice, Wi-Fi, garbage and oil disposal. where you can also get internet access. *Lighthouse Marina* can be reached at (284-340-1715, or info@admiralbvi.com).

Shopping is good at West End, not as good as at Road Town perhaps, but you probably won't complain as *Soper's Hole Wharf* is the spot for groceries, produce, cheeses, and liquor, while the *Caribbean Corner Spice House* can sell you the spices you need to liven up the goodies you purchased at the *Ample Hamper*. *Island Treasures* carries a large selection of books as well as model ships and Caribbean art, and if you need a haircut, visit *Waves*. Internet access can be had at *Caribbean Jeweler's* at *Soper's Hole Wharf* behind the *Perfume Shoppe*. Here too you'll find a *Barclays' Bank ATM*, *Latitude 18°*, and of course, the obligatory *Pusser's Landing*. The

The British Virgin Islands - Tortola

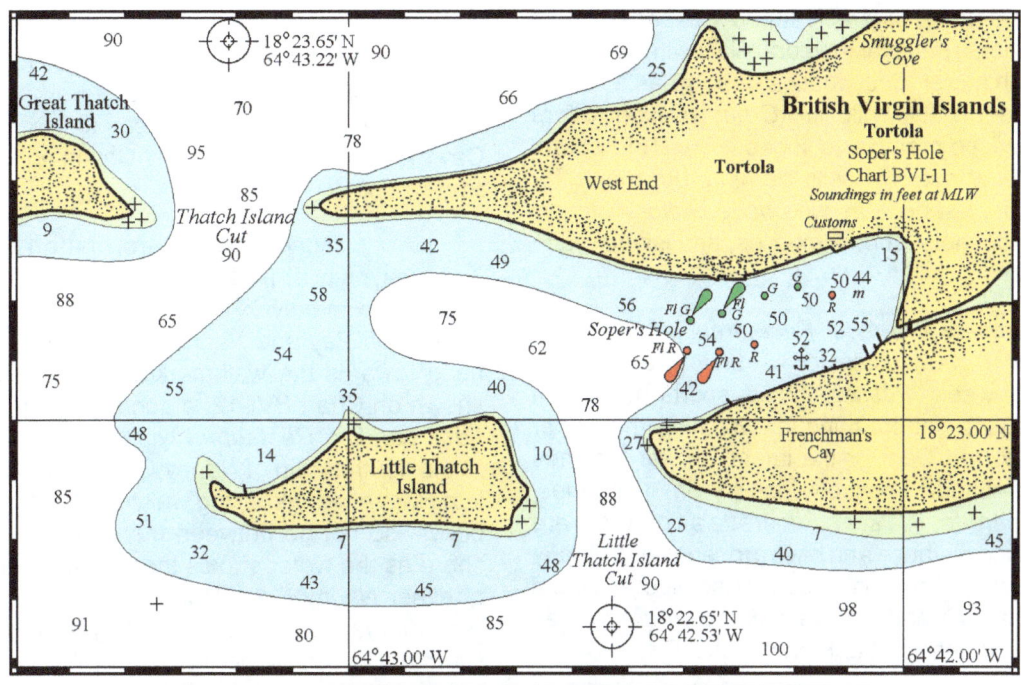

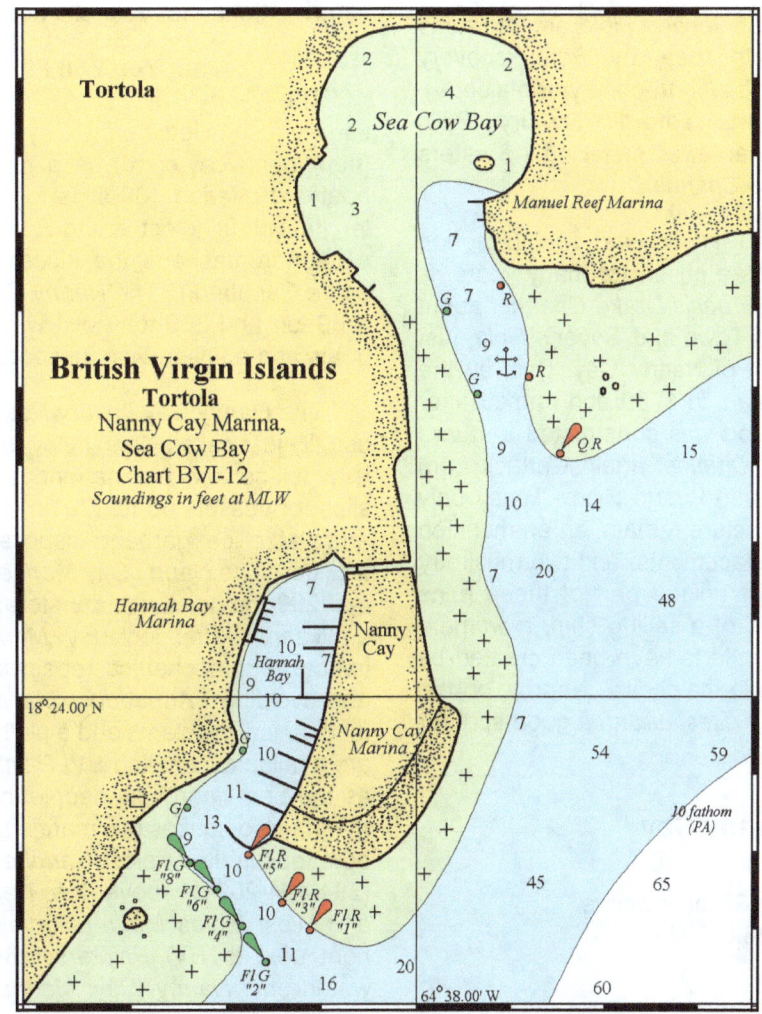

Pusser's Company Store features *Pusser's* line of clothing, books, nautical memorabilia, swimwear, and much, much more. *Buccaneer's Bounty* has a variety of hand-made gifts while *Ice Cream Delight* offers hand-dipped ice cream and sodas. The *BVI Apparel Factory Outlet* not only sells clothing, but they offer an embroidery service as well while *Culture Classic* sells sarongs, hats, shoes, mobiles, and island made charms.

The elegant *Terrace Restaurant* at *Pusser's Landing* is a great place for a sundowner, what a view to the west! *Pusser's* has a sports bar with a 15' screen, the perfect thing for watching the *Super Bowl*, the *World Cup*, or the latest *Cricket* matches from down-island. For provisions try *Bay Groceries*, *Kelly's Superette*, *Walker's Superette* all of which are within walking distance and have groceries and dinghy docks as well. There is a laundry service available from the marinas and the *West End Laundromat* lies ¾ mile east of the road to Frenchman's Cay.

A few miles east of *Soper's Hole* are the ruins of *Fort Recovery* located near the *Fort Recovery Estate Villas Resort* (http://fortrecoverytortola.com/). Here the un-restored remains of a 17th century (1660) Dutch fort, a large circular tower, sit facing the waters of the *Sir Francis Drake Channel*.

Fort Purcell, also known as *The Dungeon* because it was used as a prison for many years, is located just off the *Sir Francis Drake Channel* about halfway between Road Town and *Soper's Hole*, just a couple of miles west of Nanny Cay. Built by the *Royal Corps of Engineers* in 1750 and named after Governor Purcell, the fort was constructed to guard the *Sir Francis Drake Channel* against attack from St. Thomas, St Croix, and Puerto Rico. Today only parts of the original structure remain, an ammunition magazine, six gun emplacements, and two musketry platforms, but the most unique part of these ruins are the crude drawings of a sailing ship, a woman, and a soldier that are said to have been created by prisoners passing time in their cells. Nearby, on the *Purcell Estate*, is the *CF Restaurant*, a good spot for seafood (dinner only).

Nanny Cay

Waypoints:
Nanny Cay - ¼ nm SE of entrance
18° 23.60' N, 64° 38.00' W

Nanny Cay lies on the southern shore of Tortola a bit less than halfway between *Soper's Hole* and *Road Harbour* (about 3 miles from *Road Harbour*). The bay itself is *Hannah Bay* and the cay to its east is Nanny Cay. Please note that Nanny Cay is no longer a BVI *Port of Entry*.

Navigational Information

A waypoint at 18° 23.60' N, 64° 38.00' W, will place you approximately ¼ mile southeast of the entrance to *Hannah Bay* and Nanny Cay. From the waypoint head towards the well-marked entrance channel as shown on Chart BVI-12, a good landmark is the *Peg Legs Landing Restaurant* lying just east of the jetty at the southern tip of Nanny Cay. Follow the markers into Hannah Bay keeping well to the east of the green buoys, do not go between the green buoys and the shore as the water shoals there. You can take a slip at either *Nanny Cay Marina* to starboard or *Hannah Bay Marina* to port, but anchoring is not permitted in *Hannah Bay*. Call the marinas on VHF ch. 12 or 16 before entering for your slip assignment.

What You Will Find Ashore

The *Nanny Cay Luxury Resort Hotel and Marina*, usually just called Nanny Cay, or *Nanny Cay Marina* (http://nannycay.com/), is a full-service marina and boatyard offering 180 slips for vessels up to 170' in length with full electric and R.O. water, showers, ice, a Laundromat, and the nicest shower block in the entire Caribbean. The *Nanny Cay Marine Centre* has a 50-ton and 200-ton hoist with dry storage for 150 boats and a full-service fuel dock.

The *Nanny Cay Luxury Resort Hotel and Marina*, usually just called Nanny Cay, or *Nanny Cay Marina*, is a full-service marina and boatyard offering 180 slips for vessels up to 170' in length with full electric and water, ice, garbage disposal, and luxury shower facilities. *The Nanny Cay Marine Centre* has a 50-ton and 200-ton hoist with dry storage for 150 boats and a full service fuel dock. *BVI Marine Management* can handle your mechanical repairs including refrigeration and welding. *Auquadoc Marine* can handle any mechanical problems and a plethora of other services are available including *BVI Painters*, world renowned as the best fiberglass people in the Caribbean. The marina also houses two marine surveying companies, both tops in their fields; *Caribbean Marine Surveyors* (284-494-2091) above the *Nanny Cay Chandlery* and *West Indies Marine Surveyors* (284-494-0772), right next to *BVI Painters* (284-494-4365), on the waterfront. *Nanny Cay Marina* monitors VHF ch.

Nanny Cay, *Sea Cow Bay* on right   Photo by Todd Duff

Sea Cow Bay as seen from the south   Photo by Todd Duff

16, and can also be reached at (284-394-2512, or marina@nannycay.com).

The *Nanny Cay Chandlery* is a full-service store and is the best stocked chandlery in the BVI. They get all of their products through *Budget Marine* and are actually a part of that chain, so anything you wish can be shipped to them through the store. If they do not have what you want in stock, it can usually be ordered and be in stock within a few days.

Nanny Cay Marina also has the largest yacht brokerage in the Caribbean located in the building right at the end of B dock. *BVI Yacht Sales* (284-494-3260) is a first class full-service yacht brokerage offering sellers and buyers its extensive services. Contact Chris Simpson, Brian Duff, or Clive Allen who can help you sell or buy a boat anywhere in the Caribbean basin.

Blue Water Divers (284-494-2847) is a long established dive company with a nice retail outlet too. This is a great place to arrange for a trip to one of the famous dive spots or to pick up some great snorkel or diving gear to replace what has been lost or worn out on your way to the BVI.

Hannah Bay Marina, just across the little bay from Nanny Cay has slips for vessels with drafts to 9½' with full electric and water, showers, ice, telephone, a swimming pool, a Laundromat, and cable TV service at the dock.

For provisions try the small but well stocked *Bobby's Supermarket* (http://www.bobbyssupermarket.com/) at *Nanny Cay Marina*. For dining the best spot is *Peg Legs Landing* on the point,

it's a lively bar with a great view that is popular with locals as well as cruisers. The *Genaker Café* is an open-air dining establishment featuring Caribbean fare including a great breakfast menu and *Struggling Man's Place* is a nice waterfront spot a short walk outside the marina to sample local fare.

The most popular bar these days is *Captain Mulligans* (http://www.captainmulligans.com/) which is right at the entrance to Nanny Cay. They have a fabulous Friday afternoon happy hour and serve free ribs and chicken which is well attended by many of the local ex-pats that run and work in the businesses in and around Nanny Cay. They also offer a driving range with floating golf balls that you hit into the sea and have a big screen TV for sports events. This is a nice place to meet up with other cruisers and almost any evening there is a nice crowd in attendance.

Sea Cow Bay

Just north of Nanny Cay is *Sea Cow Bay* as shown on Chart BVI-12. The majority of this bay is very shallow, but a good portion has been dredged and is now the home of the *Manuel Reef Marina* and the *BVI Watersports Centre*. There is also a new restaurant above the sailing school.

Manuel Reef Marina is run by Jim Woods and he has transient and long term dockage available as well as showers and a nice clubhouse. The *Barecat Charter* (http://barecat.com/) operation is based in this marina as is *Husky Salvage*, the largest salvage operation in this part of the Caribbean. You can anchor just inside the entrance in the lee of the reef as shown or take one of the moorings that Jim Woods will assign you. *Manuel Reef Marina* monitors VHF ch. 16, and can also be reached at (284-494-0445, or dean@manuelreefmarina@yahoo.com).

Manuel Reef Marina offers all sorts of amenities to the cruising or charter yachtsman. With 40 slips available, the marina can handle vessels to 150' LOA with drafts to 6.5'. The marina boasts full electric, showers, water, ice, cable, yacht maintenance, and Wi-Fi. *Struggling Man's Place*, a short walk from the marina, serves up excellent local fare. *Wood's Marine Services* (284-495-206) offers fuel tank cleaning.

Driving Around Tortola

If you intend to drive on the island of Tortola, you must first decide whether you are prone to vertigo as some roads can be very steep with stunning vistas of nearby peaks and valleys, there are few flat roads. If you think you may not enjoy driving in these conditions, by all means hire a taxi or a tour guide. If you do decide to drive, you'll need a temporary driver's license ($10) which you can pick up at almost any rental car agency, and don't forget, you must drive on the left in the BVI.

The island of Tortola is not one huge mountain, rather it is an island composed of many hills and peaks with incredible views from one hairpin turn to the next. In contrast, the flat road on Tortola's southern shore that runs from Road Town to West End is fairly new, it was built in 1966 from land reclaimed from the sea. Prior to 1966 it was an all day trip by donkey from West End to Road Town, unless of course you had a boat. The *Sir Francis Drake Channel Coastal Road* runs along Tortola's southern and eastern shore from the *Beef Island Airport* to *Soper's Hole* at West End with Road Town located about midway. From the airport on Beef Island the road is known as *Blackburn's Highway* and passes *Fat Hog's Bay* and *Maya Cove* before coming into Road Town.

It's a lovely drive from Road Town to West End along the shore of the *Sir Francis Drake Channel* and from here you can venture northward along the western shore of Tortola towards *Cane Garden Bay*. Just past Nanny Cay are the remains of the old *William Thornton Plantation*, if you don't know who William Thornton was, read the section entitled *Norman Island*.

Heading north from West End you'll come to *Long Bay*, a mile-long stretch of pristine beach, perfect for sunbathing or long walks. In the winter the northerly swells make this a popular spot for surfers while the elegant *Garden Restaurant* is a popular spot for those who like fine dining. *Long Bay* was the site of a pre-Columbian Amerindian settlement just behind *Long Bay Beach*. Several hundred Arawaks were said to have lived here and the nearby triangular shaped Belmont mound, sometimes called *Sugar Loaf* for its resemblance to the peak of the same name in Rio de Janeiro, Brazil, was worshipped as being the home to a deity called a *zemi*. Recently found artifacts from this area are on display at the *Virgin Island Folk Museum* in Road Town. The Belmont mound is actually the core of an ancient volcano, all that remained after the erosion of the less resistant surrounding plain. The *Long Bay Beach Resort* (http://www.longbay.com/) is a popular spot with the tourists and is built within the walls of an old plantation building.

Near Belmont on Tortola's extreme western end is *Smuggler's Cove*, a lovely beach backed by equally lovely coconut palms and seagrape trees. This is one of Tortola's most beautiful and unique beaches. At the center of the beach is a most unusual beach bar with a cannon at the entrance and an old *Lincoln Continental* placed amid the tables and chairs scattered about the bar. The old *Lincoln* actually carried Queen Elizabeth around Tortola when she visited in 1977, the 25th anniversary of her coronation. This is a serve yourself honor bar with a handwritten sign containing the menu and price list. There is a small box for the money and everything is in multiples of fifty cents so change usually is not a problem. You can buy a beer, a pack of *Oreos*, or even rent a beach chair all on the honor system, tipping, as the sign says, is not necessary. If you need the assistance of the owner, "Uncle Bob" Denniston, he's not hard to find, he's usually the one in the pith helmet. Here too you can view a collection of memorabilia from the movie *The Old Man And The Sea* starring Anthony Quinn; parts of it were shot here at the beach bar. Just down the beach from *Uncle Bob's* is *Bazz's* drink stand. Here you can sample some of Bazz's delightful fruity libations created in his blender which is hooked up to his van at the edge of the beach.

Heading back northeastward past *Long Bay* you'll come to charming *Apple Bay* just west of *Long Bay*, actually *Apple Bay* is three bays in one. *Sebastian's on the Beach* (284-495-4212) sits above the beach at the western end of *Apple Bay* and is a great place to have breakfast and start your day. With a dining terrace overlooking the sea, *Sebastian's* offers live music on Sunday evenings courtesy of the *Spark Plugs*. At *Capoons Bay* you'll find yourself at a popular spot for surfers from all over the world during the winter who like to hang out at *Bomba's Surfside Shack* where owner Bomba serves up great rum libations late into the night. His all time specialty, and my personal favorite, is his *Mushroom Tea*, usually served at midnight...a drink not for the faint of spirit. Also, Bomba's monthly *Full Moon Party* is not to be missed, nor is the morning after fish fry, while Wednesdays and Sundays at Bomba's are packed with visitors treated to live entertainment.

At *Little Apple Bay* is the elegant *Sugar Mill Restaurant* set in the remains of a 365-year old sugar mill (284-495-4255). Nearby, *The Apple* serves up a fine mix of European and Creole dishes in *Little Apple Bay* while across the street is *The Fish Fry*. The *Fish Fry* is not a restaurant as you might think, it's entirely outdoors, but on Friday and Saturday nights the locals have a fish fry and this is an excellent spot to pick up some freshly fired local seafood, extremely casual.

Northeast of *Apple Bay* is *Great Carrot Bay*, once a picturesque fishing village, today *Great Carrot Bay* is a center of island life with some of the best dining establishments on Tortola. Here you can visit the *North Shore Shell Museum Restaurant* containing an eclectic array of seashells and odd memorabilia such as fish traps, driftwood, and old wooden boats. Located in owner Egbert Donovan's home, the restaurant features delicious West Indian and International dishes. The nearby restaurants offer excellent choices for dining and the village here is typical Caribbean in flavor as well as architecture. Here you'll find *Mrs. Scatliffe's*, the Queen of BVI cooks. *Mrs. Scatliffe's* is open for lunch and dinner (reservations requested) from Monday through Friday. Mrs. Scatliffe worked as a chef at several resorts including *Caneel Bay* before opening her own family style restaurant. The *Palm's Delight Snack Bar* is located just past *Mrs. Scatliffe's*, right on the seawall. The *Just Limin' Bar and Restaurant* offers lunch and dinner with spectacular views. Located on *Windy Hill* high above *Carrot Bay*, the *BVI Steak Chop and Pasta House* offers cliffside dining with a breathtaking view and a fresh water swimming pool. Heading northward again you'll come to *Cane Garden Bay* and the terminus of the *Ridge Road* and the *Cane Garden Bay Road*. Just north of *Cane Garden Bay* is the *Brewer's Bay* turnoff on the *Ridge Road* and here you'll find the *Cool Breeze Bar*, a good spot to stop and enjoy a cold soda, beer, or other libation.

The *Ridge Road* winds through Tortola's mountainous spine and offers breathtaking views of the island's bays, villages, and terraced valleys. It runs from *Sage Mountain National Park* on Tortola's western end to the *Josiah's Bay Road* at the eastern end of Tortola. The *Sage Mountain National Park* is home to *Sage Mountain*, the highest point on Tortola at 1,716'. Here, too, is the last of the rainforest that once covered much of Tortola. The *Mahogany Forest Trail* leads to the top of *Sage Mountain* while the *Rainforest Trail* and the *Henry Adam's Loop* lead into the densest and most primeval part of this 92-acre protected preserve. The land for this preserve, approximately 100 acres, was donated by Laurance Rockefeller in 1964 for the creation of the *Sage Mountain National Park*.

If you're hungry, stop in at the *Mountain View* located on the *Ridge Road* at the foot of *Sage Mountain*. Here you can have lunch from 1100-1500 and dinner from 1830-2200 sampling a variety of continental and local dishes.

On Tortola's northeastern shore are two very nice restaurants. Coming down from the *Ridge Road* you will first see the *Tamarind Club* (http://tamarindclub.com/) on your left. This is a very popular place for their well-known Sunday brunch and also their great Friday night English style quiz night. There is a small hotel and a beautiful pool with a swim-up bar. The food is excellent and the people who run it are superb.

Next down the road towards the beach is the *Josiah's Bay Plantation*, a former rum distillery that dates back to the 18th century. Here you'll find a gallery, the *Josiah's Bay Plantation Art Gallery*, a display of the boiling vats and cane crusher, a small boutique, and a restaurant. In the gallery you'll find Indonesian and African sculptures of all sizes including Zulu masks set on a background of wall paintings on beautiful stonework, while the *Secret Garden Café* restaurant offers elegant open-air dining among the ruins of the original plantation and features gourmet food in an unusual and enticing atmosphere.

Surfer's love *Josiah's Bay*, because it is an easy and safe sand break, a great place to learn how to surf. However, swimmers here must exercise caution and be wary of a strong undertow. On the beach you can dine at *Naomi's Grapetree Beach Bar* serving breakfast, lunch, and dinner featuring local and international dishes. *Naomi's* chef, Grant MacFarlane, has appeared in the pages of *Gourmet Magazine* and is known for his Caribbean "*Fusion*" cuisine. The nearby *Escape Restaurant* is open for lunch and dinner and features fresh local seafood. The salt pond at *Josiah's Bay* provides a habitat for many varieties of avian life such as white-cheeked pintail ducks and black necked stilts, also called *funeral birds* because of their black and white coloring.

Just east of *Josiah's Bay* is the secluded *Elizabeth Bay*, sometimes called *Lambert Bay*, a popular spot for locals as well as visitors. The *Rock Sculpture* is a rock outcropping that resembles a giant conch shell. Here the *Elizabeth Bay Resort* sits on the sparkling sands of this pristine beach where guests are assured of solitude and peace.

Jost Van Dyke

Jost Van Dyke, the *Barefoot Island* as it's sometimes called, is said to be named after a Dutch pirate who haunted these waters centuries ago, but a stronger, and less romantic rumor, has it being named after a Dutch planter who inhabited the island long, long ago. Jost Van Dyke, pronounced "Yost" (the J is pronounced like a Y), is known as the birthplace of the Quaker John Lettsome, the famous physician who founded the *Medical Society of London* and the *Royal Humane Society*. But tiny 4 mile-long Jost Van Dyke is much better known for one thing, or actually for one man, Foxy Callwood, owner of the *Foxy's Tamarind Bar* ((284-495-9258) in Great Harbour, an extraordinary entrepreneur and the founder and namesake of *Foxy's Wooden Boat Regatta* held annually in late May. It seems that the names Foxy and Jost Van Dyke are synonymous and wherever you go people who find out that you've been to Jost Van Dyke will often ask you "How is Foxy?"

Jost Van Dyke is home to approximately 175 people on a 3 square mile island with only one main road. You can take a ferry to Jost Van Dyke from West End on Tortola if you wish to visit without bringing your boat over. The ferry ride takes about a half-hour on the *Nubian Princess* or *When*, so named because it leaves whenever it is ready, if its cargo is loaded (note that I said cargo and not passengers), it's time to go, whether late or early.

To the west of Jost Van Dyke is Great Tobago, a nesting site for the magnificent frigate bird, while just south is Little Tobago, another bird sanctuary. A settled weather anchorage can be found on the western shore of Great Tobago; only overnight here if the weather is expected to remain calm.

Little Jost Van Dyke

Waypoints:
Green Cay - 1 nm ESE of Green Cay
18° 26.55' N, 64° 41.50' W

Sandy Cay - ½ nm SSW Sandy Cay
18° 25.75' N, 64° 43.00' W

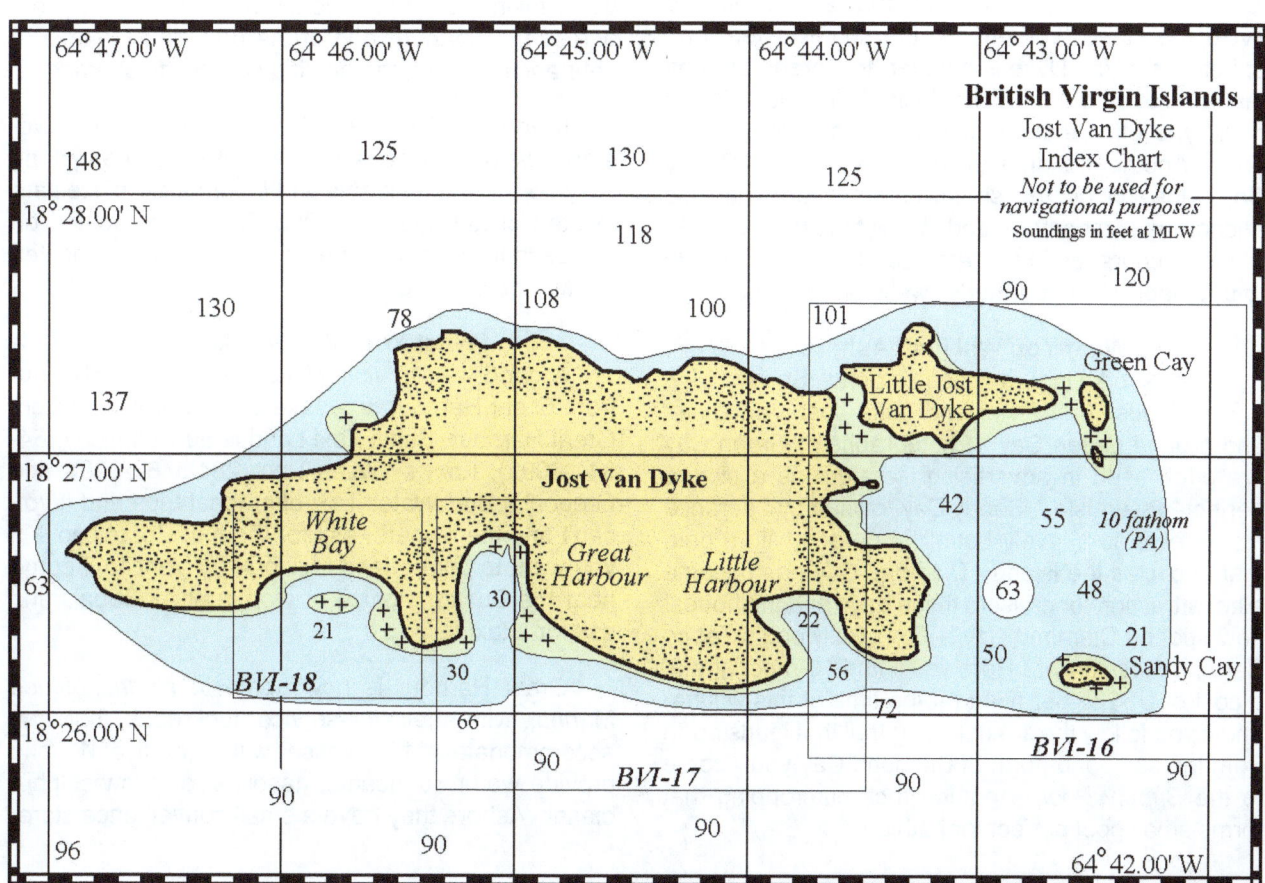

A Cruising Guide to the Virgin Islands

Navigational Information

Cruisers arriving from the east often stop and anchor off the eastern end of Jost Van Dyke south of Little Jost Van Dyke and in the lee of Green Cay. If you are approaching Jost Van Dyke from the east a waypoint at 18° 26.55' N, 64° 41.50' W, will place you approximately 1 mile east/southeast of Green Cay as shown on Chart BVI-16. From the waypoint head west passing between Sandy Cay to the south and Green Cay to the north. Once clear of the shoals south of Green Cay you can turn to starboard to anchor in the lee of Green Cay or at the far western end of Little Jost Van Dyke.

If you are approaching from the west, from *Great Harbour* perhaps, or from the south, say Soper's Hole, a waypoint at 18° 25.75' N, 64° 43.00' W, will place you approximately ½ mile south/southwest of Sandy Cay. From the waypoint head north in the center of the passage between Sandy Cay and Jost Van Dyke as shown on Chart BVI-16.

The best anchorage here is in the lee of Green Cay just west of the conspicuous sandbar where the water is anywhere from 12'-30' deep. It's best to anchor as close to the sandbar as possible to avoid the steep drop-off. At the southwestern end of Little Jost Van Dyke is another anchorage area off the ruins of an old concrete dock. Here, close to the dock, you'll find a sandy bottom in which to set your hook. Another option is to anchor in the lee of Sandy Cay, close in on the southwestern shore, but this anchorage is recommended for daytime use only. All of the anchorages in this area can be uncomfortable to untenable when northerly swells are running.

What You Will Find Ashore

The snorkeling is good around Sandy Cay, between Jost Van Dyke and Little Jost Van Dyke, and around Green Cay. Photographs of Green Cay are often used in advertising literature as a picture perfect "desert isle." Sandy Cay, owned by Laurance Rockefeller, is a lovely botanical garden with a path that encircles the island. Diamond Cay has become a hot attraction for cruisers these days and the hottest new spot on Diamond Cay is Foxy Callwood's *Taboo Bar and Restaurant*. Here you'll find 10 moorings at a cost of US$25 per night (at the time of this writing) and if you follow the 1/4 mile long trail that leads north from the salt pond north of Diamond Cay you'll come to the *Bubbly Pool*, a natural rock outcropping that forms small pool perfect for bathing.

Great Harbour

Waypoints:
Great Harbour - ½ nm S of
18° 25.90' N, 64° 45.05' W

Without a doubt, *Great Harbour* is the focus of boating activity on Jost Van Dyke. Not only because it has a ferry dock and a *Customs* office, but because of places such as *Foxy's Tamarind Bar*, an institution that is known worldwide, and soon you'll know all about *Great Harbour*, the *Tamarind Bar*, and its owner, Foxy Callwood.

Navigational Information

A waypoint at 18° 25.90' N, 64° 45.05' W, will place you approximately ½ mile south of *Great Harbour* as shown on Chart BVI-17. By looking at the chart you'll notice a string of red buoys leading into the harbour, this is the marked entrance channel (12') that is frequented by the ferries. A private yacht can actually take the red buoys to port, but care must be exercised as there's a reef that works its way westward towards the outer red buoy. It's simple enough to use the marked channel, and it won't take you any longer. Anchor to the east of the line of buoys in 15'-35' of water taking care not to go too far in as there's a reef across the northern end of the bay, and make sure your anchor is set, the holding can be iffy at times.

If you need to clear *Customs*, the white, two-story *Customs* office is located just to the west of the ferry dock. The *Customs* and *Immigration* offices are located on the first floor, the *Police* are located on the second floor, and public restrooms are located behind the building.

What You Will Find Ashore

A good way to visit White Bay or Little Harbour from Great Harbour is to take a water taxi over from Great Harbour. Bun's Taxi Land & Sea Service (284-341-6092), Foxy's Water Taxi (284-546-1905), and Gregory's Brat Water Taxi offer local trips and if you can't find the owners, ask for them in CocoLoco's. If you want to take a land taxi look up Vancito George near the Customs office or stop in at Ali Baba's and ask for a taxi.

Great Harbour is now home to *North Latitude Marina*, with their full-service fuel dock that can accommodate a 100' vessel with a draft of 12 and provide water, lubricants, gasoline, and low-sulphur diesel. Ashore they have a small convenience store.

The British Virgin Islands - Jost Van Dyke

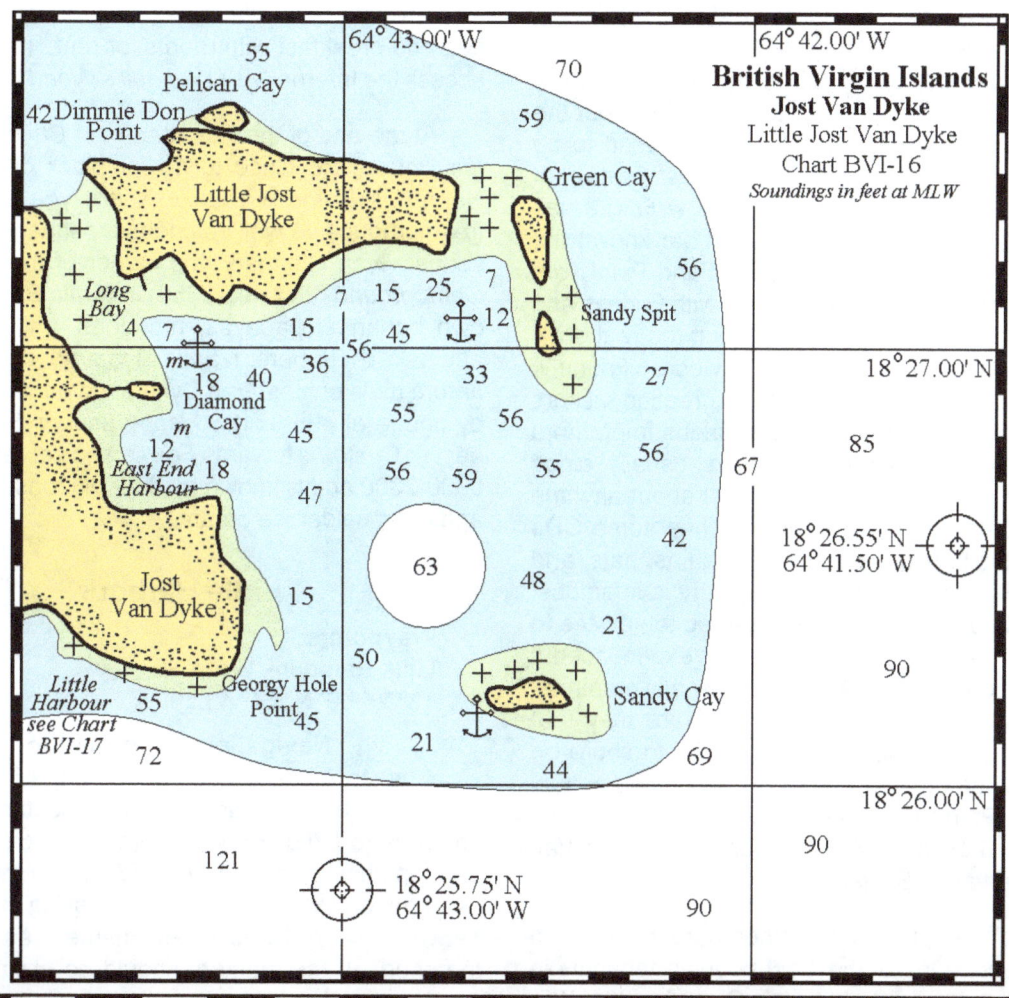

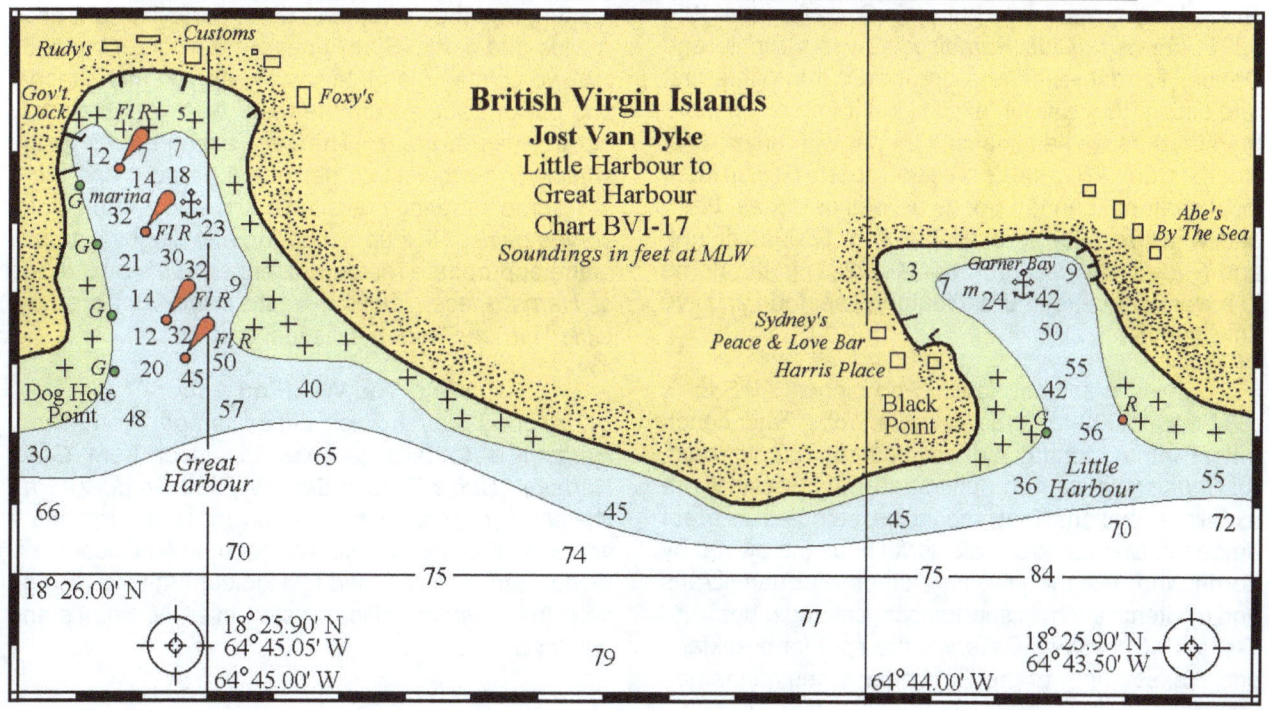

Okay, since everybody loves to hear about *Foxy's*, let me tell you a bit about the place. *Foxy's Tamarind Bar* (http://foxysbar.com/) sits at the eastern end of beach at *Great Harbour* and was originally about the size of a lemonade stand and was supposed to be open for only one day during the *Harvest Festival* of 1967. Well, things snowballed and now *Foxy's* has evolved into the quintessential beach bar known the world over. *Foxy's* serves good food and *Painkillers* and features a live band on Sundays with Fridays and Saturdays being barbecue nights. But the real draw here is the man himself, Foxy Callwood. Friendly, convivial Foxy is the ultimate host, greeting visitors as old friends and often singing hilarious impromptu calypso ballads about them. Foxy usually sings during lunch and happy hour and just about anytime you can coerce him into it, and he has some CDs for sale in his boutique as well as T-shirts, hats, and clothing. *Foxy's New Year's Eve Party* is infamous, in fact, it's been hailed as one of the top ten places to spend *New Year's*, and if you've ever experienced it you would agree. *Great Harbour* is usually crammed full of boats on New Year's, so thick are they that you can practically walk from your boat to shore on the decks of other vessels. Foxy also has an annual *Halloween Party*, his famous annual *Wooden Boat Regatta*, and Foxy is the founder of the *Jost Van Dyke Preservation Society*.

Now let's explore what other attractions lie in *Great Harbour*. One of the most popular hangouts in *Great Harbour* is the bright pink *Corsairs* (284-495-9294), formerly *Club Paradise*. Owners Vinnie and Debbie Terranova have a great spot that offers first rate dining (they call it Mexican, but it's so much more than that) as well as libations on par with anybody's. Nearby *Rudy's Superette* is a good spot to pick up fresh local seafood, canned goods as well as sodas, beer, and whatever else is available from 0800-midnight, and *Rudy's Mariner Inn* (284-340-9282) is the home to a wonderful a restaurant featuring seafood and live entertainment.

Serving breakfast, lunch, and dinner, *Ali Baba's* (284-945-9280) features burgers, rotis, and conch fritters with a Monday night all you can eat pig roast. *Ali Baba's* special rum punch and *Bushwacker's* are excellent libations that should be sampled in great amounts. *CocoLoco's* is a colorful boutique owned by Lorrin who designs jewelry, clothes and handicrafts and gift items such as sundresses, painted mugs, and T-shirts. *Christine's Bakery* is the spot for breakfast, she makes some of the Caribbean's best cinnamon rolls. Upstairs is *Christine's Guest House*, a small bed and breakfast with rooms for rent. If you need to access the Internet visit *Wendell's World Watersports*.

At the end of the little road past *Christine's* is the *Ice House*, the place to go for block or cubed ice. Nearby is *Nature's Basket* where you can pick up fresh produce as well as cheese, canned goods, and sodas. Ivan Chinnery, the owner of the *White Bay Campground* (284-495-9358) in *White Bay*, grows his own bananas, papayas, mangoes, and pineapples and sells them here. Ivan is also a good guide to the nature trails on Jost Van Dyke and you can reach him by phone at 495-9312. *Happy Laury's Snack Bar* is east of *Customs* towards *Foxy's* and serves food from 0800-2300 and is known for their pig roasts, cold beer and even colder ice cream.

Little Harbour

Waypoints:
Little Harbour - ¼ nm SE of
18° 25.90' N, 64° 43.50' W

Navigational Information

A waypoint at 18° 25.90' N, 64° 43.50' W, will place you approximately ¼ mile southeast of the entrance to *Little Harbour*, sometimes called *Garner Bay*, as shown on Chart BVI-17. From the waypoint head generally north/northwest passing in the center between the red and green markers as shown on the chart. If the markers should be missing for any reason, and they often are, don't panic, the entrance is wide and deep. Simply pass in the center between the two points of land, this will keep you mid-channel and out of trouble from the reefs that work their way out from each point. The best anchorage is in the shallower northwest corner of the harbour and there are some moorings available on a first-come first-served basis. Pick up a mooring and dinghy in to pay at the appropriate restaurant, either *Abe's by the Sea* or *Harris' Place*. On the western shore of the bay, *Little Harbour Marina* sells fuel and ice.

What You Will Find Ashore

A good way to visit *Little Harbour* from *Great Harbour* is to take a water taxi over from *Great Harbour*. *Bun's Tequila Sea Taxi* and *Gregory's Brat Water Taxi* costs $5 per person for local trips and if you can't find the owners, ask for them in *Cocoloco's*. If you want to take a land taxi look up Vancito George near the *Customs* office or stop in at *Ali Baba's* and ask for a taxi.

The British Virgin Islands - Jost Van Dyke

Sandy Cay with Green Cay in the background — Photo by Todd Duff

The anchorage off *Foxy's Taboo* — Photo by Todd Duff

Great Harbour, Jost Van Dyke — Photo by Todd Duff

Little Harbour, Jost Van Dyke — Photo by Todd Duff

White Bay, Jost Van Dyke — Photo by Todd Duff

A Cruising Guide to the Virgin Islands

Little Harbour refuses to take second seat to *Great Harbour* in anything, especially in attracting visitors, and *Little Harbour* boasts a fine selection of choices if you want to go out and have a good time. To begin with there's *Sydney's Peace and Love Bar*, what a great place! In his 28th year of operation, Sydney serves breakfast, lunch, and dinner from 0900, has live music several nights a week, and pig roasts on Mondays and Saturdays with Sydney's own special barbecue on Sundays. Sidney has been known to catch the lobster he serves and he cooks it according to an old family recipe on an open fire. Sidney's daughter Rena, the *hostess with the mostess*, describes her dad's lobster as "finger lickin good."

Not to be outdone, *Harris' Place* serves breakfast, lunch, and dinner with a Monday night all-you-can-eat lobster feast featuring Ruben Chinnery who plays guitar and sings. Harris' Place, near the western side of the harbour, also has mooring for rent in the harbour as well as some grocery items for sale in the store and a spot on their T-head dock when available. See Cynthia!

Abe's by the Sea (Abe also drives a taxi) has a pig roast every Wednesday night, a pool table, and moorings for rent on the eastern side of the harbour. *Tee's and Tings* sells T-shirts and several kinds of jewelry in their shop as well as boat to boat as *Nippy's Traveling Salesman*.

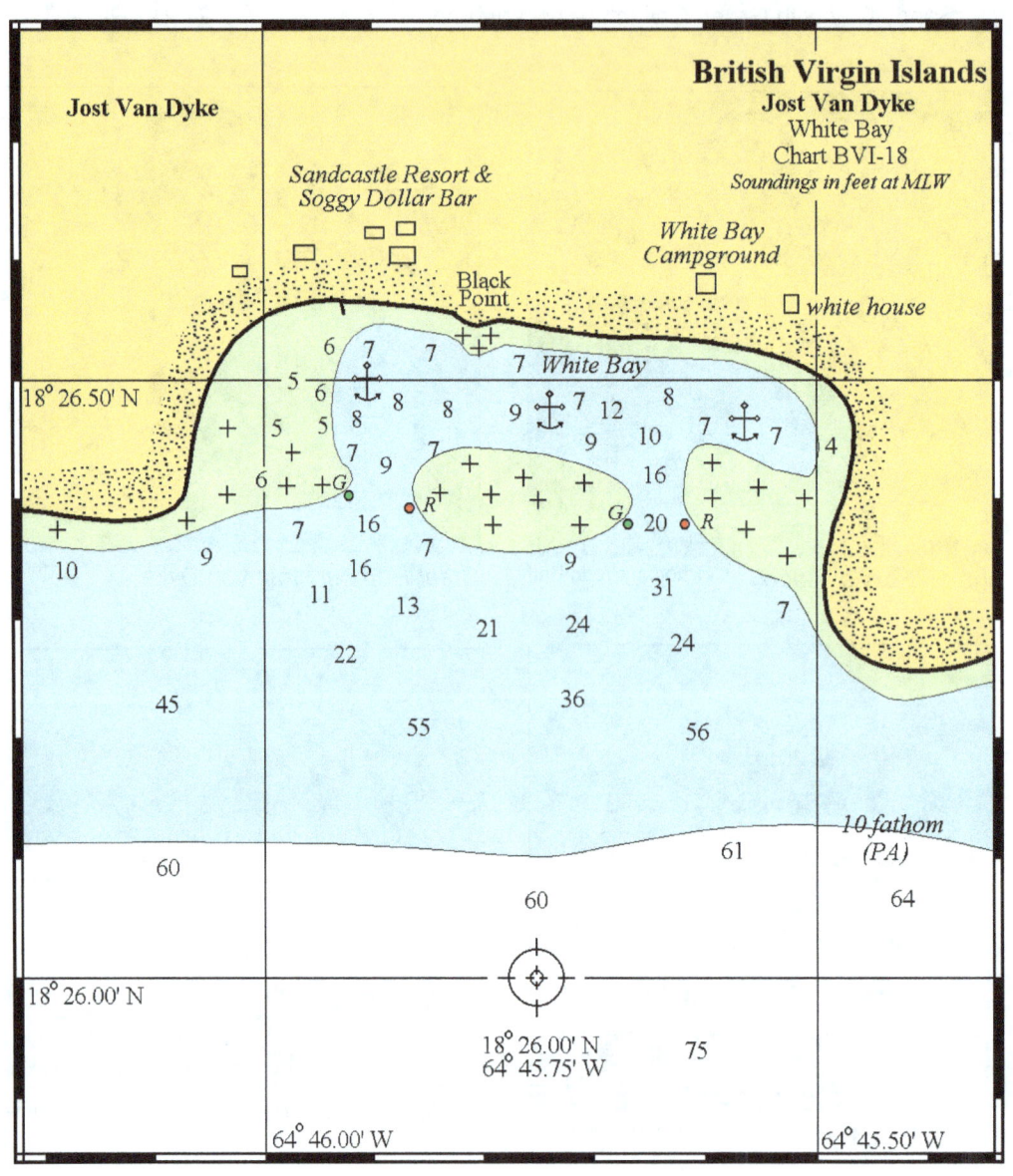

150

White Bay

Waypoints:
White Bay - ½ nm S of
18° 26.00' N, 64° 45.75' W

White Bay is probably named after the long white beach on the north side of the harbour and in most conditions is an excellent anchorage but the bay is fairly full of rental moorings. There is room for a few additional anchored boats in less than ideal parts of the bay. That having been said, this is one of the prettiest anchorages in the BVI and so if you wish to find a spot here, arrive by around 1100 and if no mooring is available, anchor just outside and wait. Day charter boats come over from the USVI throughout the day and many people leave here in the early afternoon, no doubt reluctant to move on from such a beautiful spot. When they do, up your anchor and pounce!

White Bay is susceptible to ground swells, especially in the winter months Check your weather forecast and anchor accordingly.

Navigational Information

A waypoint at 18° 26.00' N, 64° 45.75' W, will place you approximately ½ mile south of the entrance to *White Bay* as shown on Chart BVI-18. As shown on the chart a reef runs across the mouth of the harbour broken by two marked channels, and a third (far western) channel that is shallow and unmarked. The most popular entrance is via the center channel, the westernmost of the two marked channels. Once inside the reef turn to port or starboard and anchor wherever your draft allows without blocking either entrance channel or pick up a mooring (more on where to pay later). Make sure you have enough swinging room and make sure your anchor is set well. Watch out for the reef off Black Point, it's easily recognized by the conspicuous black rocks on shore.

What You Will Find Ashore

A good way to visit White Bay without having to anchor there is to take a water taxi from *Bun's Taxi Land & Sea Service* (284-341-6092), *Foxy's Water Taxi* (284-546-1905), and *Gregory's Brat Water Taxi* offer local trips and if you can't find the owners, ask for them in Coco Locos. If you want to take a land taxi look up Vancito George near the *Customs* office or stop in at *Ali Baba's* and ask for a taxi.

You can hike to *White Bay* from *Great Bay*; it's a good 30-45 minute walk over a very tough hill that only worsens in the afternoon sun. But have faith weary trekkers, as you approach the eastern end of the beach at *White Bay* you can stop in at Ivan Chinnery's *White Bay Campground* for a cold one at the *Local Flavor Beach Bar*, also called the *Stress Free Bar*. *Local Flavor* serves breakfast, lunch, and dinner and has a Sunday night barbecue. If you have an instrument aboard bring it along and play during their Saturday night jam session. Ivan runs this as the last "Honor Bar" still operating in the BVI. Once he has looked you in the eye, you can just make your own drinks and write them in the book, and at the end of your visit, drop the money in the jar.

Almost north of the center entrance channel is the *White Bay Sandcastle Resort* and the famous *Soggy Dollar Bar* (http://www.soggydollar.com/) where swimming ashore is part of the initiation. The *Soggy Dollar Bar* got its name from the soggy condition of the dollar bills from sailors whom swam ashore. The *Soggy Dollar Bar* claims to be the originator of the *Painkiller*, and theirs certainly live up to the name. The *Sandcastle Resort* offers breakfast, lunch, and four course candlelight dinners as well (reservations by 1600 please). And to relax after a meal simply slip into one of their hammocks. Ruben Chinnery, who often plays on two islands on the same day, sings and plays guitar here every Sunday afternoon. Next to the *Sandcastle* is *Gertrude's Beach Bar and Boutique* for sodas, beer, and mixed drinks as well as hair braiding and bungalow rentals.

Just to the west is *Wendall's World*, *One Love Bar and Grill*, and the *White Bay Superette*. *Jewel's Snack Shop* sells light snacks all afternoon from 1100-1600 including burgers, dogs, fries, and even ice cream. At the east end of the bay is Ivan Chinnery's *Stress Free Bar and Restaurant* (http://www.ivanscampground.com/), the place you go to pay for your mooring. For ATV rentals visit *Sea and Land Adventure Centre*. Also check out Ivan's *Stress Free Guesthouse* (http://www.ivansstressfreeguesthouse.com/).

A Cruising Guide to the Virgin Islands

Norman Island to Virgin Gorda

Norman Island

Norman Island has quite a rep going for it. Said to be named after a pirate who is believed to have buried Spanish gold on the island (in the Caves at the northwestern point), Norman Island is also alleged to be the island upon which Robert Louis Stevenson based his masterpiece *Treasure Island*. However, at the risk of bursting somebody's bubble, if you read *Treasure Island* in some depth you will see that Treasure Island could not have been Norman Island, Treasure Island had two rivers and was not part of an archipelago as is Norman Island. But who knows what lurked in the mind of Stevenson when he wrote that epic of all pirate stories?

Norman Island is the traditional first day easy sail for charters as it lies just across the *Sir Francis Drake Channel* from Tortola. About 700 acres and mostly undeveloped, Norman Island was purchased by its new owner in 1999 and it was estimated that the island had a population of one goat per acre. Local authorities aided the owner by putting radio transmitters on certain goats to assist in locating the herd. Today, the loss of the herd has brought back a lot of greenery to Norman Island, something that has been missing since the goats had been eating it all for some time.

A few years ago, the BVI approved a plan for a new resort and marina to be built at Norman Island. Plans include a small marina with guest houses, an RO plant, and condos scattered about the island at scenic points with roads kept to a minimum. The owner intends to create a BVI museum that will also trace the history of piracy throughout the Caribbean.

Although no significant construction has begun as of the spring of 2011, narrow access roads have been created that now allow access to most of the island and a new jetty was built, unfortunately, right smack dab in the middle of the nice little beach that used to be so special in *Money Bay*. On the bright side however, the roads make great trails and the hiking on Norman Island is arguably the best of any island in the BVI. Be sure to hike up the road which begins right behind *Pirates Restaurant* in the Bight for the short ten minute walk up to the helipad for fantastic views of The Bight and the windward side.

Also, be sure to hike the trail down to the bay behind the helipad for some of the best and most unspoiled snorkeling you will find anywhere short in the BVI.

Navigational Information

If approaching from Peter Island, pass to the east of Pelican Island and The Indians (and do not pass between the Indians and Pelican Island). If approaching from the southern shore of St. John be

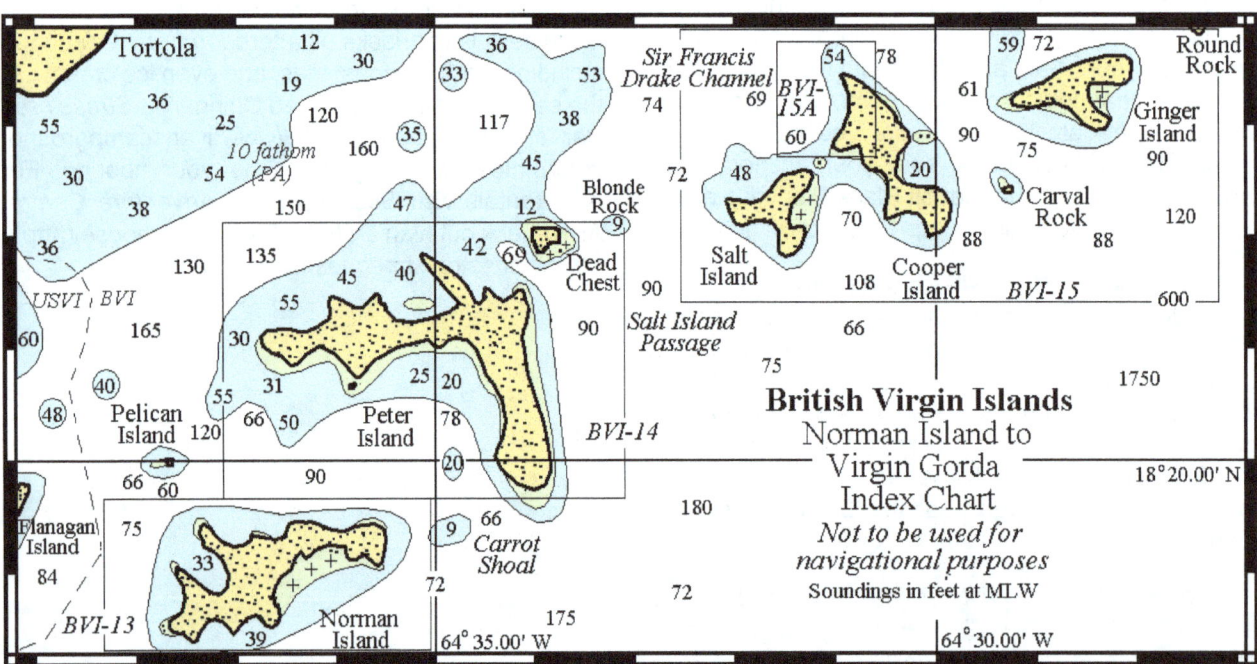

The British Virgin Islands - Norman Island to Virgin Gorda

sure to pass south of Flanagan Island as you work your way eastward to The Bight. If approaching from St. Croix beware of the Santa Monica Rocks lying southwest of Norman Island, they have less than 6' of water over them. Santa Monica Rocks has a mooring available if you care to dive here, the rock itself is a pinnacle that rises from about 90' to within a few feet of the surface.

Benures Bay

Waypoints:
Benures Bay - ½ nm N of
18° 19.80' N, 64° 36.55' W

Navigational Information

If you are approaching from the north a waypoint at 18° 19.80' N, 64° 36.55' W, will place you approximately ½ mile north of the anchorage area in *Benures Bay*. *Benures Bay* is a good anchorage, an alternative to the usually crowded Bight, especially when the wind is southerly. The best spot to anchor is off the beach in the northeastern portion of the bay in about 20' of water.

What You Will Find Ashore

Nearby *Spy Glass Hill* offers a 360° panoramic view of the *Sir Francis Drake Channel* and the surrounding islands. It was once used by pirates and privateers as a lookout for Spanish ships back in the days when the *Sir Francis Drake Channel* was known as the *Freebooters Gangway*. *Spyglass Wall* is a nice dive just NNE of *Benures Bay*; here a vertical face over 1/3 of a mile long drops down from 20'-60'.

The Bight

Waypoints:
The Bight - ¾ nm NW of
18° 19.40' N, 64° 38.00' W

Navigational Information

The most popular anchorage at Norman Island is located on the northwestern shore of the island and is known as The Bight. A waypoint at 18° 19.40' N, 64° 38.00' W, will place you approximately ¾ mile northwest of The Bight as shown on Chart BVI-13. From the waypoint head southeast into the harbor and anchor in the northeast corner in 15'-30' of water on a shelf by *Billy Bones Bar & Grill*, there are also moorings for rent in The Bight ($5 per night-somebody

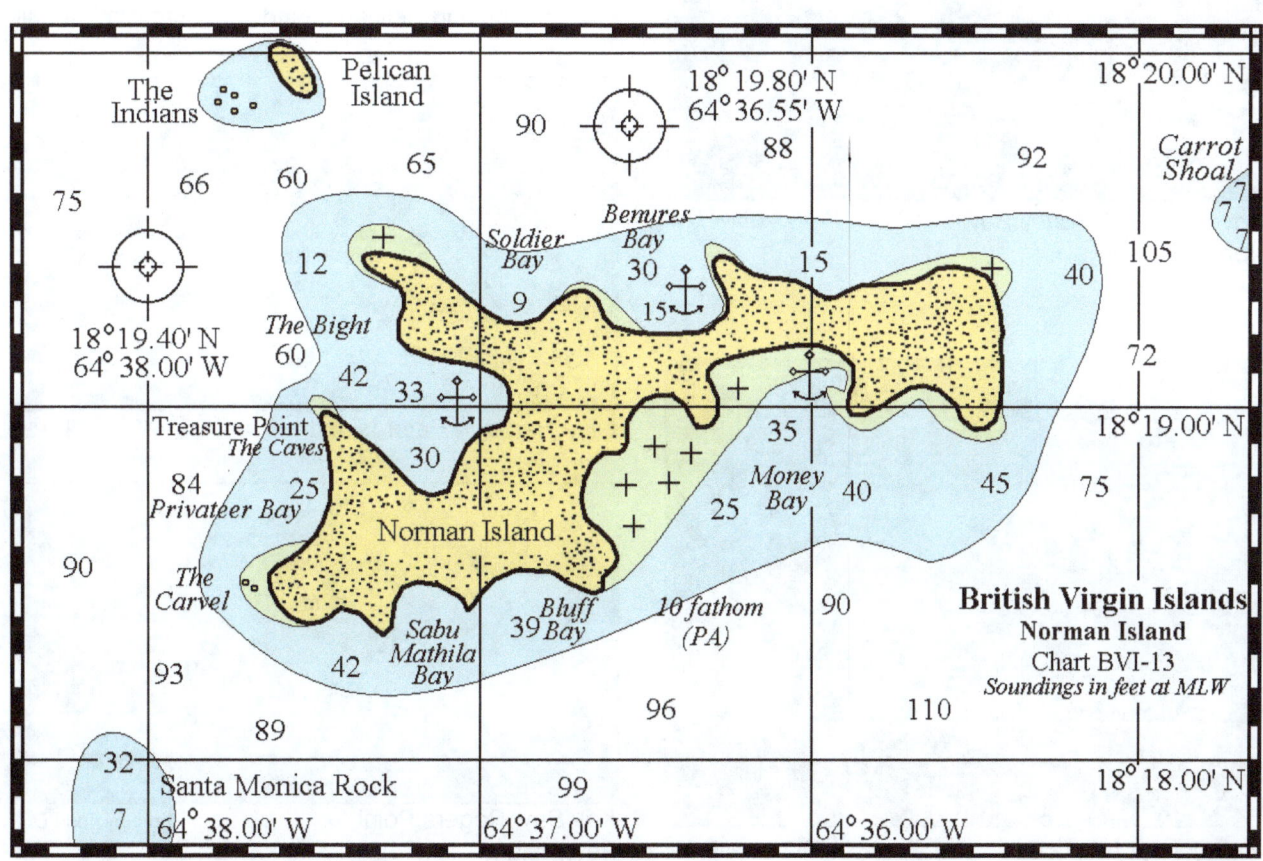

British Virgin Islands
Norman Island
Chart BVI-13
Soundings in feet at MLW

153

A Cruising Guide to the Virgin Islands

The Caves, The Bight, and *Privateer Bay*, Norman Island — Photo by Todd Duff

The *Willy-T*, Norman Island — Photo by Todd Duff

Coves west of *Money Bay*, Norman Island — Photo by Todd Duff

The Indians and Pelican Island — Photo by Todd Duff

Little Harbour, Peter Island — Photo by Todd Duff

Money Bay, Norman Island — Photo by Todd Duff

Key Bay, Rogers Point, Peter Island — Photo by Todd Duff

will be by to collect before sundown). The wind here tends to funnel so bear that in mind when you are planning to leave as it may give you the mistaken impression that the waters outside The Bight are far rougher than they may truly be.

What You Will Find Ashore

Pirates Beach Bar & Grill is open for lunch and dinner from 1000-midnight and serves grilled dishes with an emphasis on seafood and ribs. Their daily happy hour is from 1700-1800 and their supply boat brings patrons from Nanny Cay leaving at 1100 and at 1630 and returning to Nanny Cay somewhere between 1530-1600 and 2030-2230. *Pirates* also has a gift shop, a family museum, and an online picture gallery where you might see photos of yourself having a good time in the BVI.

If you need to get rid of your garbage while here, *Deliverance* can handle that task for you. *Deliverance* is a small supply boat that comes around about dusk and offers its wares and takes your garbage. *Deliverance* can be reached on VHF ch. 16 and can deliver ice, block or cubed, fresh baked breads and pastries, fresh produce, all manner of beverages, and can even handle special orders "From birthday cakes to Cuban cigars" as their ad boasts.

Now for the big draw in The Bight, the infamous *Willy-T*. The *Willy-T* (284-340-8603) is a replica of a 93' topsail schooner that has been converted into a bar/restaurant and is permanently anchored in The Bight. Actually named the *William Thornton II*, it was named for a native of the BVI. During the plantation era several notable planters were Quakers, a pacifist religious group known as the *Society of Friends*, members of whom were also abolitionists in an area dependent upon slave labor. The first Quaker to settle in the BVI was John Pickering who arrived in 1741 and eventually became Governor. But the best known of the Quakers was William Thornton who was born on Tortola in 1761. Thornton learned medicine in England and eventually returned to Tortola to practice and run the family plantation. Thornton sailed to America to enter a design competition for the capital building in Washington D.C., and won. Although Thornton's design was submitted after the 1792 competition had closed, President Washington approved it and Thornton won a $500 prize and a city lot in the District of Columbia. Thornton remained in the U.S. and became the head of the first *U.S. Patent Office*.

The *Willy-T* is now a BVI tradition and the original *Williy-T*, the *William Thornton*, is now a dive site located off nearby Peter Island. Unlike anything closely resembling its Quaker namesake of 2½ centuries ago, the *Willy-T* is wild and woolly place where a *body shot,* a shot slurped out of a young lady's naval, a run around the deck, and a leap off the boat is normal behavior. This is not a place to come if you have any inhibitions, but it is certainly the place to come if you want to have fun. The annual *William Thornton Virgins Cup Race* is a regatta that must not be missed. Usually held in October, one rule is that a woman must be at the helm of all competing vessels, although she does not have to be a virgin.

Just south of the northwestern tip of Norman Island, Treasure Point, are *The Caves*, an excellent snorkeling adventure that is not to be missed. You can anchor in The Bight and dinghy over and tie up to one of the *National Park* moorings, or bring the big boat over to tie up or anchor in 30'-40' of water (please anchor in the sand, not in coral). *The Caves* are allegedly where pirate treasure was buried and many stories still surface of treasure finds inside. Only 4' deep, *The Caves* drop off to 40' near the entrance and the northernmost cave stretches back 70' into the island at the end of which is a small room. The next cave is deeply indented into the rock face while still another cave lies just above the waterline.

The southernmost cave, the one that has been rumored to be a treasure cave, has a rounded rock bottom on which you can stand underneath a natural skylight. This is a good photo op so don't forget your camera, and also watch out for the surge when diving here, be careful.

To the east of The Bight, is a small anchorage that's suitable only for a lunch stop. Just to the west of Water Point, the northernmost point of Norman Island, and north of The Bight, is a small cove called *Water Bay* where you can tuck into the northwestern corner in 25'-35' of water. You'll be backwinded here so bear that in mind. There is good snorkeling along the northern section of this bay.

On the southern shore of Norman Island is *Money Bay*, a day anchorage sometimes shown as *Soldier Bay*. To the west are two unnamed coves where a very tricky reef entrance offers a bit of protection inside the reef (not recommended for inexperienced reef navigators and off limits for charter boats-see photo).

Pelican Island and The Indians

Although this area is only for daytime use in settled weather, the snorkeling here is great. Approach from the north and pick up a *National Park* mooring or anchor between The Indians and Pelican Island, but don't try to pass south between the two. One of the best shallow dives in the BVI, The Indians, said to be named because they resemble Indian teepees, are rock pinnacles that rise from a sandy bottom at 50' to a height of about 50' above sea level and offer walls, coral gardens, and some nice shallow pools for exploration. Pelican Island offers a combination of coral gardens and terraces with a maximum depth of about 60'-75'.

Peter Island

Peter Island's 1,800 acres lie about 5 miles south of Tortola, directly across the *Sir Francis Drake Channel*, and about 1½ miles north/northeast of Norman Island. If you are approaching Peter Island from Tortola there are no dangers, but if you are approaching from the east, from Salt Island, it's best to pass north of Dead Chest Island as you approach the northern shore of Peter Island. If approaching from Norman Island you must avoid Pelican Island and The Indians just north of the Bight, and Carrot Rock and *Carrot Shoal* east of Norman Island and just off the southeastern tip of Peter Island. *Carrot Shoal* lies almost ½ mile west of Carrot Rock. Here a shallow ridge rises from 70' to within a few feet of the surface. *Carrot Shoal* is named after Carrot Rock, which is so named because it looks like a carrot.

If you need to get rid of your garbage while here at Peter Island, *Deliverance* can handle that task for you. *Deliverance* is a small supply boat that comes around in the late afternoon and offers its wares and takes your garbage. *Deliverance* can be reached on VHF ch. 16 and can deliver ice, block or cubed, fresh baked breads and pastries, fresh produce, all manner of beverages, and can even handle special orders "From birthday cakes to Cuban cigars" as their ad boasts.

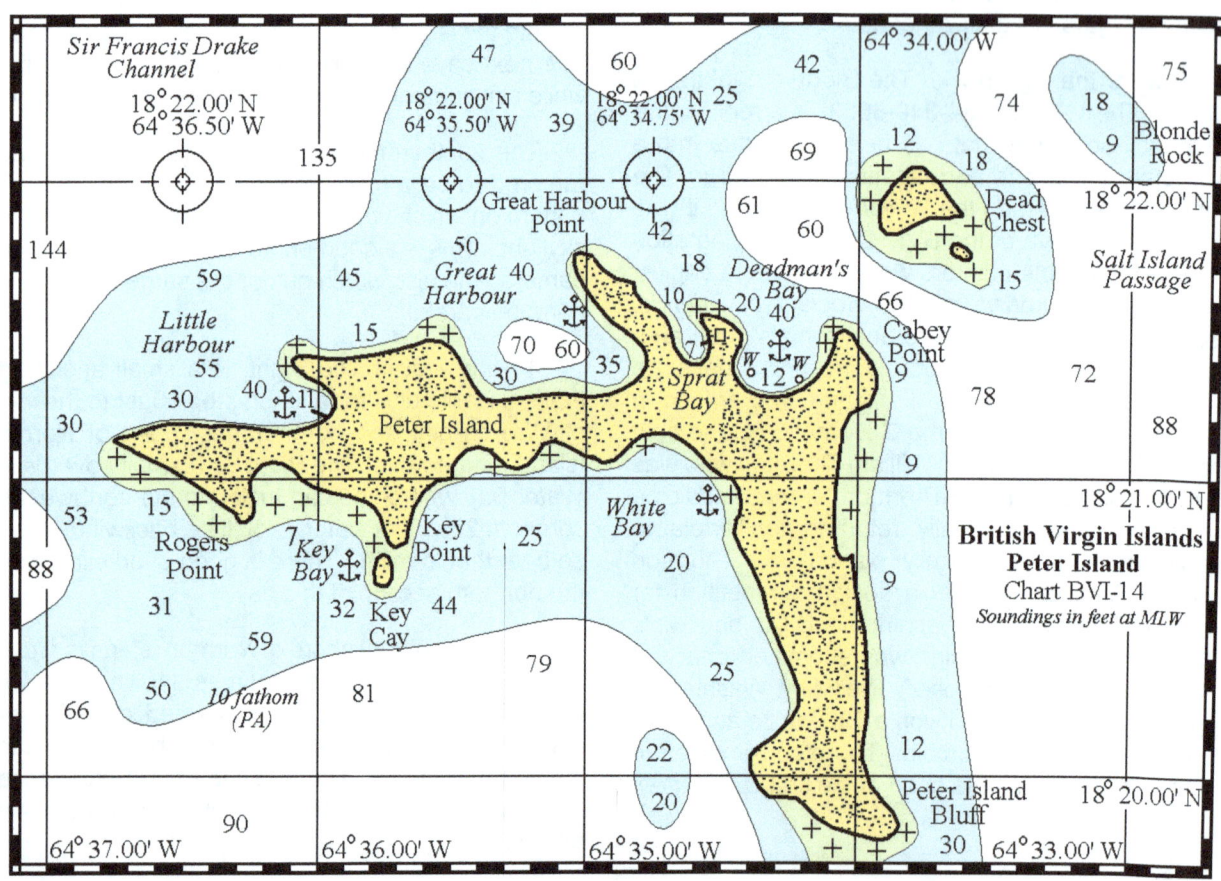

Little Harbour

Waypoints:
Little Harbour - ¾ nm NNW of
18° 22.00' N, 64° 36.50' W

Navigational Information

Little Harbour is a well-protected anchorage and a waypoint at 18° 22.00' N, 64° 36.50' W, will place you approximately ¾ mile north/northwest of the harbour as shown on Chart BVI-14. The best spot to anchor is in the eastern or southeastern end of the bay in 15'-30' of water over a hard sand bottom, make sure your anchor is well set.

Great Harbour

Waypoints:
Great Harbour - ½ nm NW of
18° 22.00' N, 64° 35.50' W

Navigational Information

Although quite deep, anchorage can be found here in *Great Harbour*. A waypoint at 18° 22.00' N, 64° 35.50' W, will place you approximately ½ mile northwest of *Great Harbour* as shown on Chart BVI-14. From the waypoint head generally southeast keeping well clear of the shoals off both points as you enter the harbour and anchor in about 20' on the south side of the bay midway along the beach. Unfortunately, if the local fishermen are working their nets you'll have to wait to anchor until after they're done. Of course there's another spot you can anchor with about 20' of water, it lies along the northeastern shore of the harbour, about 1/3 of the distance in from Great Harbour Point.

Just north of *Great Harbour* divers can visit 65' deep *Bank Reef*, the site of the 3,000 lb. anchor, 300' of chain, and other debris from the *RMS Rhone*, left here before she fled and sank off Salt Island. Along the western shore of *Great Harbour* is a nice snorkeling reef in about 10'-20' of water. The small beach is home to the ruins of the coaling station used by the *RMS Rhone*.

Sprat Bay

Waypoints:
Sprat Bay - ½ nm NNW of entrance
18° 22.20' N, 64° 34.75' W

Navigational Information

Sprat Bay is the most popular stop on Peter Island and the focus of all shoreside activity. If approaching from Great Harbour just round *Great Harbour* Point and parallel the shoreline into *Sprat Bay*. If approaching from offshore a waypoint at 18° 22.20' N, 64° 34.75' W, will place you approximately ½ mile north/northwest of the entrance to *Sprat Bay*. From the waypoint head south/southeast to enter the bay on a heading of approximately 165°, the heading is not that important here, what IS important is that you keep in the center of the channel avoiding the reefs that work their way north and northwest from the resort, favor the western shore. You are not permitted to anchor in *Sprat Bay,* but you can tie up to the *Peter Island Yacht Harbour* dock (calling first for a reservation would be a very good idea, 284-494-2591) or pick up one of some thirty moorings at the southern end of the bay. If you pick up a mooring be advised that the owners of the resort ask that no generators be run after 2100, that halyard noise be kept to a minimum, and that your head not be pumped out into *Sprat Bay*, you are welcome to use the resorts bathroom facilities ashore.

What You Will Find Ashore

By far one of the prettiest island getaways, the *Peter Island Resort* was built by Norwegian Pieter Smedvig who enlarged the harbor when he constructed the 50-room resort (which won an award for being one of the top ten hotels in the Caribbean). 284-495-2000 The *Peter Island Resort* (284-495-2000) offers a free launch from Road Town for those with dinner reservations. If you don't wish to have dinner here, the cost of the ferry trip is $14 per person one way.

The very exclusive *Peter Island Resort* can accommodate up to 50 guests and their *Tradewinds Restaurant* requests that gentlemen wear a jacket and tie for dinner. This elegant restaurant features German china, French silverware, Italian crystal, and the cuisine of Chef Willo Stout, a member of the award winning *BVI Culinary Team*. The restaurant serves up an impressive breakfast buffet as well as an even more impressive Saturday night *Grand Buffet*. Weekly wine tastings are followed by a progressive "fusion" dinner while at other times there may be a Cuban cigar tasting or a Caribbean rum tasting. *Drake's Channel Lounge* offers a killer *Mango Smoothie* blended with ice cream, rum, and coconut cream.

A Cruising Guide to the Virgin Islands

Deadman's Bay, Peter Island — Photo by Todd Duff

Monte Bay, Sand Pierre Bay, Peter Island — Photo by Todd Duff

Salt Island as seen from the West — Photo by Todd Duff

Manchioneel Bay, Cooper Island — Photo by Todd Duff

Markoe Bay, Cooper Island — Photo by Todd Duff

Reef passage, south shore of Ginger Island — Photo by Todd Duff

The British Virgin Islands - Norman Island to Virgin Gorda

Deadman's Bay

Navigational Information

Deadman's Bay is a good daytime stop as it can be a bit surgy, but it's a good spot to launch a dinghy on calm days for the ½ mile run over to the diving at Dead Chest Island. The best spot to anchor is in the extreme southeastern part of *Deadman's Bay*, but the bottom is grassy and it's hard to get an anchor to hold here in the seagrass beds.

What You Will Find Ashore

The beach here, one of 5 beaches on Peter Island, is one of the prettiest in the Caribbean. The *Deadman's Bay Bar & Grill* is right on the beach and is open for lunch and on Sunday's features a *West Indian Brunch* with live music. The villas and restaurant here are part of the *Peter Island Resort* complex centered in *Sprat Bay*.

White Bay, on the southern shore of Peter Island, is rarely visited and there's a trail leading there from *Deadman's Bay*, it's only a short hike. You can anchor in the extreme northeastern part of *White Bay*, but only on the calmest of days with little or no sea running. It is not my job to discourage you from anchoring anywhere, but I must warn you that you will be backwinded here so set out two anchors, and lest I forget, the holding isn't the greatest here either, but the lovely beach may make up for all of that.

Key Bay

Navigational Information

On the southern shore of Peter Island is Key Point, Key Cay, and *Key Bay*. It's best to approach this anchorage from the western tip of Peter Island passing well south of Roger's Point to approach the anchorage at *Key Bay* on a northeast or east/northeast heading. If you are approaching from the east, from *White Bay* perhaps, pass well south of Key Cay to round up into *Key Bay*. You can anchor in *Key Bay* just west of Key Point to enjoy the snorkeling here, but I don't recommend it as an overnight anchorage, it can be very rolly when the trades are up.

Dead Chest Island

Dead Chest Island lies off the northeastern tip of Peter Island and is allegedly where the infamous pirate Blackbeard marooned 15 of his errant crew with naught but their sea chests and a bottle of rum, hence the line from the old song "Fifteen men on a dead man's chest, yo ho ho and a bottle of rum."

While this may have once been Dead Chest Island, today it is a *National Park* with four excellent dive sites, *Coral Gardens*, *Dead Chest West*, *Blonde Rock*, and *Painted Walls*, best reached by dinghy from *Deadman's Bay* when there is little or no surge present. The *Painted Walls* lie just south of Dead Chest Island and are an underwater series of canyons that reach from an average depth of 35' to just below the surface and at the end of the third canyon are two arches covered in multi-colored sponges. This is a difficult dive when seas are running. *Blonde Rock* lies just a bit over ½ mile east/northeast of Dead Chest Island and is a pinnacle reaching from 60' deep to within 7' of the surface, and this site too can only be dove on calm days with little or no sea running. There are dive moorings available at both Blonde Rock and Dead Chest Island.

Salt Island

Important Lights:
Salt Island Light: Fl W 10s

Waypoints:
Salt Island - ½ nm NNW of
18° 23.00' N, 64° 32.00' W

Salt Island was once a vital port for the provisioning of salt on sailing ships and several salt ponds are still to be found here. Once the residents made their living from the salt ponds, but today the last resident has moved away and so nobody is farming the salt except about once a year when a former resident or two will come over from Tortola, scrape up a single bag of salt to be sent to the Queen via the Governor each year as rent for the island.

Salt Island is forever bound to the wreck of the RMS *Rhone,* a 310' long *Royal Mail Ship* that sank here during a hurricane in 1867. When the *Rhone* tried to escape to open sea, she was overtaken by the eyewall of the hurricane and she foundered on the rocks. It is said that the *Rhone* is haunted by the souls of the 124 people that died aboard her, some of whom were strapped to their bunks, only 23 of the ship's complement survived. Experienced *Rhone* divers will tell you tales of hearing ghostly noises and other paranormal activity when diving on the wreck.

When the *Rhone* went down, the local villagers spent many hours and managed to save a number of the ship's company, but at the personal expense of a number of their own villagers who were drowned in the rough waters. In gratitude for this act of heroism, the Queen granted the island to the villagers in perpetuity for the annual rent of one bag of salt per year.

There are two anchorages here and both can be rolly at times and should not be considered for overnight stays except in settled conditions with no significant swell.

Salt Island Bay

Navigational Information
A waypoint at 18° 23.00' N, 64° 32.00' W, will place you approximately ½ mile north/northwest of *Salt Island Bay* as shown on Chart BVI-15. From the waypoint head south/southeast to anchor off the town in 10'-30' of water. If you walk into the now abandoned village you can find the trail to take you to the salt ponds and you can even scrape up your own bag of island salt.

What You Will Find Ashore
There are a few trails on the island and those with a good sense for finding buried treasure are urged to scout the island for a treasure chest. This 'chest' is small and hidden well, but not actually buried, so leave your shovels on the boat. Started by a cruising family back in the 80s, the rule is that IF you find the treasure, you can take any of the loot you find inside, but you must sign the register book with your boat's name and date and a few well-chosen words and then leave an equal amount of booty to what you have taken for the next group of treasure seekers to find. I have visited this site several times over the years and it appears that the 'chest' is only found about once or twice a year. Good fun!

Lee Bay

Navigational Information
Lee Bay lies on the western shore of the island and is not a good anchorage at all, its main attraction is that it is a good spot to stop and visit the *Wreck of the Rhone Marine Park*. There are several moorings here that will accommodate a vessel of 50' in length.

The Wreck of The Rhone Marine Park is the location of the RMS *Rhone*. The ruins of the ship, which was dashed to pieces off the southwest coast of Salt Island, lie on a reef in 20'-80' of water just off Black Point Rock and are quite extensive. This is a fascinating dive (and/or snorkel) that is alive with all manner of sea life including an octopus. The underwater sequences for the movie *The Deep* were filmed here. Moorings are available and anchoring is not permitted at the site (it IS a *National Park*). If no moorings are available, anchor at nearby *Lee Bay* and take the dinghy over and tie up to one of the park's dinghy moorings. The 800-acre national park also includes part of Dead Chest Island and part of Peter Island. The *Rhone* had originally been anchored at Peter Island to take on water, but steamed toward Salt Island seeking sea room to escape the oncoming hurricane and unfortunately ended up on the rocks where she sank taking most of her crew and 313 passengers with her. The ship's anchor lies in about 65' of water near Peter Island. The same hurricane sank 75 ships and killed over 500 people.

Another good dive site is Vanish Rock, about ¼ mile northeast of the northeast tip of Salt Island where a series of rock pinnacles, running roughly north to south, rise from about 45' to just below the surface.

Cooper Island

Important Lights:
Ginger Island Light: Fl W 5s

Waypoints:
Manchioneel Bay - ¼ nm NNW of 18° 23.40' N, 64° 31.20' W

Navigational Information
Cooper Island lies east/northeast of Salt Island and a waypoint at 18° 23.40' N, 64° 31.20' W, will place you approximately ¼ mile north/northwest of *Manchioneel Bay* as shown on Chart BVI-15. From the waypoint head southeast to anchor in the northern part of the bay (see Chart BVI-15A) where the holding is iffy in sand and grass and you can expect to be back-winded. *Manchioneel Bay* is home to the *Cooper Island Beach Club* and they have 20 moorings for rent for $20 per night. You'll see two small docks ashore, the northern dock is for dinghies while the southern dock is for powerboats such as *Underwater Safaris* dive boats.

What You Will Find Ashore
The *Cooper Island Restaurant* (284-495-9084) is a nice little open-air place looking out over the bay, a casual barefoot type of place serving West Indian and International cuisine from 1130-1420 for lunch, and from 1830-2100 for dinner. Also on site is the *Underwater Safaris Dive Shop and Boutique* (get

The British Virgin Islands - Norman Island to Virgin Gorda

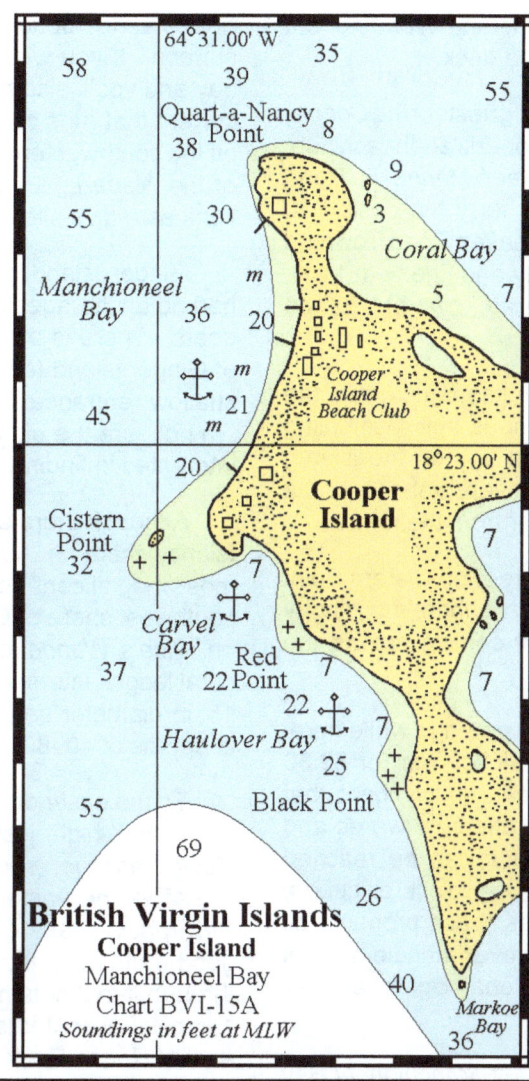

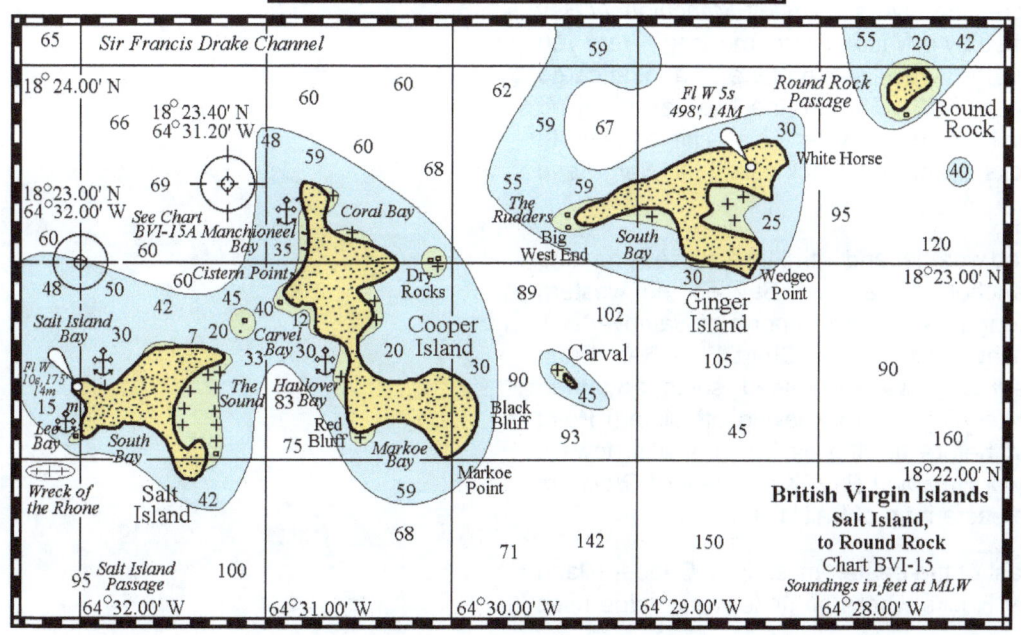

your tanks filled here), and the *Island Wonders Gift Shop*, which is located next to the dock.

There is a free ferry service for guests of the *Cooper Island Beach Club* (http://cooperislandbeachclub.com/) to and from *Prospect Reef Marina* in Road Town, if you're not a guest the ferry trip costs $10 per person one way. The ferry leaves Road Town on Monday at 1400 and Wednesday and Friday at 1100, and leaves Cooper Island for Road Town at 0700 on the same days.

Manchioneel Bay received its name from the Manchioneel tree with its poisonous fruit resembling small, green apples. If you see any on the island, do not touch them, and don't even stand under a Manchioneel tree seeking shelter from the rain.

For great snorkeling try the reef off Cistern Point at the south end of the bay where there's a dinghy mooring. Watch out for current coming around the point.

If you need to get rid of your garbage while here, *Deliverance* can handle that task for you for $2.50 per bag. *Deliverance* is a small supply boat that comes around about dusk and offers its wares and takes your garbage. *Deliverance* can be reached on VHF ch. 16 and can deliver ice, block or cubed, fresh baked breads and pastries, fresh produce, all manner of beverages, and can even handle special orders "From birthday cakes to Cuban cigars" as their ad boasts.

An interesting dive site lies off *Manchioneel Bay* and is marked by a *National Park* mooring. Here you can dive on the wreck of the *Marie L*, a local cargo boat, and the *Pat*, a 75' tug, the two vessels lying side by side in 45'-90' of water. Just a bit to the north of the wrecks is another wreck called the *Barge and Grill*.

In settled weather and with little or no seas running you can anchor in *Haulover Bay* on the western shore of Cooper Island or just north of *Haulover Bay* at *Carvel Bay* as shown on Chart BVI-15A. From *Manchioneel Bay* waypoint head south and then southwest keeping the rock laying off Cistern Point well to port before turning back to the east toward *Carvel Bay* or *Haulover Bay*. Keep clear of *Groupers Nest* at the eastern tip of Salt Island.

Just east of the easternmost tip of Cooper Island are the Dry Rocks where an underwater ridge rises from a sandy bottom at 55' to just above the water's surface. If you wish to dive here you'll need a calm day and you'll also have to be aware of a subsurface current that runs counter to the surface current. Just off the southwestern tip of Cooper's Island is the wreck of the *Marie L*, a 90' freighter that was intentionally sunk as a dive site in 85' of water.

Ginger Island, just to the east of Cooper Island had no anchorages and is only inhabited by a herd of goats. There is a small cove on the southern shore of Ginger Island (see photo page 155) with a narrow, shallow, entrance. I haven't tried this passage yet, I'm not sure the big boat could get through it, but I'm interested in finding out if anybody else has tried it.

Although there are no true anchorages at Ginger Island, there is however, what may well be the most magnificent coral reef in the BVI lying off the southwest shore of Ginger Island. Here you can dive on *Alice's Wonderland* where you'll find a series of coral ledges interspersed with massive brain corals of 15' in diameter separated by sandy floored canyons in depths of 40'-80'.

To the east/northeast of Ginger Island lies Round Rock, 220' high, just across the ¾-mile wide *Round Rock Passage* (see Chart BVI-15). *Round Rock Passage*, the easternmost passage leading into the *Sir Francis Drake Channel* from the south, is a very good route even though it has a tidal current running through it that sets northwest and southeast at about 1 knot. Fallen Jerusalem lies about 1¼ miles to the east of Round Rock

Virgin Gorda

Important Lights:
Pajaros Point Light: Fl (3) W 15s
Cow's Mouth Light: Fl (2) Y 10s

Virgin Gorda, the *Fat Virgin*, was named by Columbus because her profile appeared to the Admiral to be that of a Reubenesque figure reclining on her back. The 10-mile long island is a flurry of boat activity concentrated in North Sound and at the *Virgin Gorda Yacht Harbour*, and The Baths is one of the most popular cruising destinations in all of the Virgin Islands. British settlers flocked to Virgin Gorda between 1680 and 1743, when Road Town took over as the capital of the British Virgin Islands. Today, Virgin Gorda is the 2nd most populous island in the BVI with a population of about 3,000. Virgin Gorda has been described as "unpretentious" and I agree. Although the island is geared for the boating visitor, especially *North Sound*, the people are as open, warm, and friendly as anybody anywhere. Virgin Gorda is usually one of the high points of everybody's Virgin Islands cruise.

Approaching from St. Martin across the *Anegada Passage*, many cruisers leave Sint Maarten's *Simpson Baai* at the afternoon bridge opening, cross the *Anegada Passage*, and arrive at *North Sound* early the next day where they find a wonderful anchorage in which to rest and recuperate. Virgin Gorda is also the staging grounds for voyages across the *Anegada Passage* to St. Martin/Sint Maarten as well. Speaking only for myself, depending on the wind I'll either stage at *North Sound* or The Baths and head to Sint Maarten's *Simpson Baai* in the mid-afternoon hours to arrive at Sint Maarten for the morning bridge

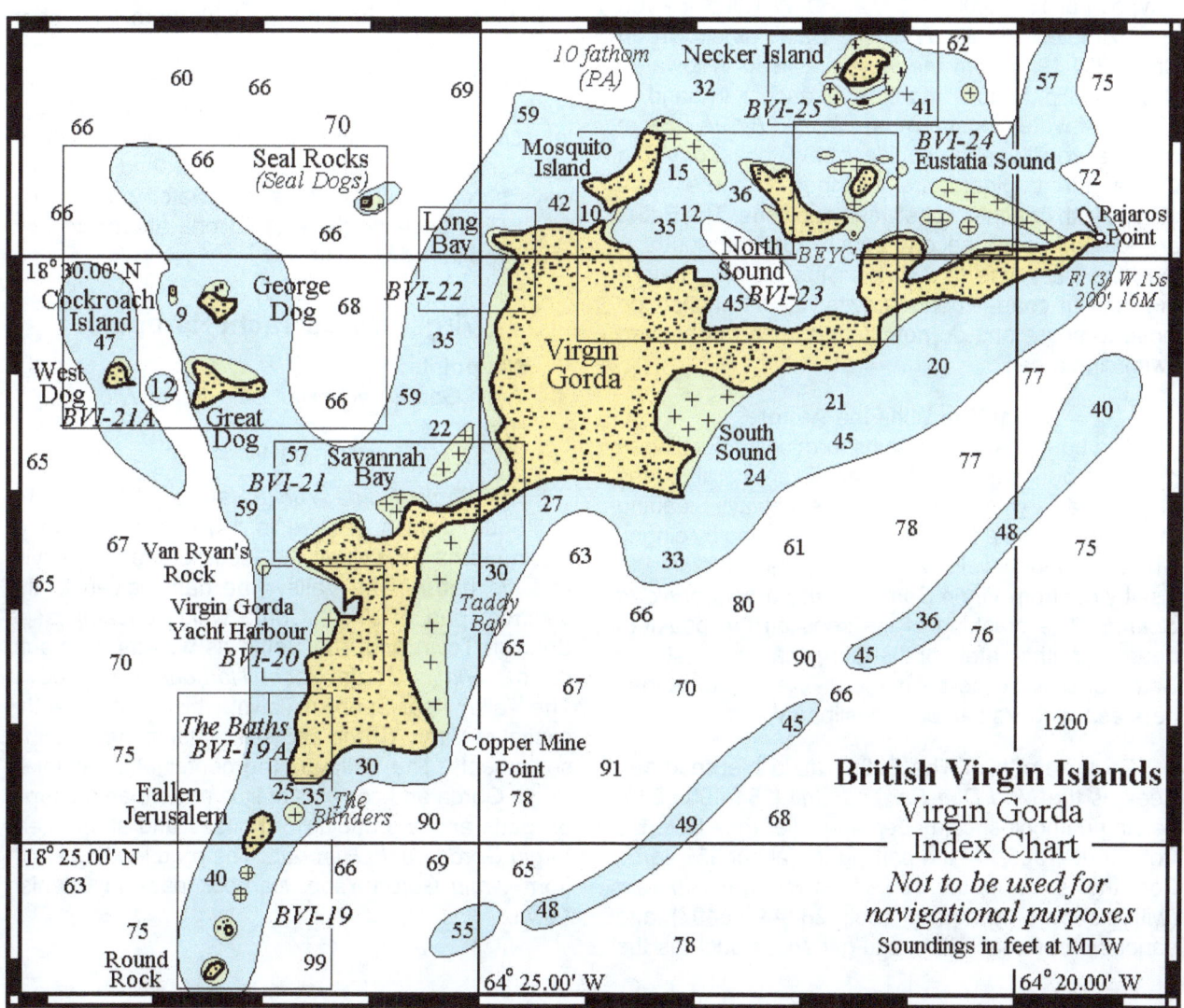

A Cruising Guide to the Virgin Islands

opening. If I leave from The Baths I'll pass south of Virgin Gorda, between Virgin Gorda and Fallen Jerusalem keeping a sharp eye out for *The Blinders*, the rocky shoal in the middle of that passage (see Chart BVI-19).

The Baths

Waypoints:
The Baths - ¾ nm WNW of
18° 26.00' N, 64° 27.50' W

Ask anybody to tell you about Virgin Gorda and usually the first words spoken will describe to you The Baths. Jost Van Dyke has Foxy, Virgin Gorda has The Baths (514-839-9673), a truly magical place that once visited will never be forgotten.

Navigational Information

Access to The Baths could not be easier. A waypoint at 18° 26.00' N, 64° 27.50' W, will place you approximately ¾ mile W of The Baths as shown on Chart BVI-19. From the waypoint head in towards shore and pick up a mooring or anchor in sand in 20'-40' of water as shown on Chart BVI-19A. From the west you'll see the boulder strewn coast of Virgin Gorda, the boulders are arranged in three large groups with beaches in between each one, The Baths are located at the second beach from the south. A hint, the best time to visit is in the morning before the rush of charter boats arrives. Don't anchor too close to shore and do not infringe upon the buoyed swimming areas.

What You Will Find Ashore

The boulders at The Baths form delightful hidden rooms lit by shafts of light, magnificent coral ledges and caves, with intricate passageways leading throughout. The area is not safe for landing by dinghy when northerly swells are running, that's the time to visit by car from *Virgin Gorda Yacht Harbour* or *North Sound*. The crashing of the seas on the boulders heard from the safety of the roomy caverns that The Baths offer is not to be missed. Wear good shoes here as the rocks can be very slippery.

To the north of The Baths, amid the seagrape trees, is the *Mad Dog Bar and Grill* (284-495-5830) serving munchies, cold beer, and killer Pina Coladas from 1000-1900. At the parking lot (about 350 yards from the Baths) is the *Top of the Baths Restaurant* (with its own swimming pool; 284-495-5497) and various other snack bars and gift shops such as the *Caribbean Flavor Gift Shop*, *Easy Bargains*, *Tropical Gift Collections*, and *Nauti Virgin Beachwear*.

Just south of The Baths is the *Devil's Bay National Park* were you'll find the *Poor Man's Bar* selling burgers, dogs, sandwiches, and cold drinks. The powdery sand beach at *Devil's Bay* is one of the BVI's finest. *Devil's Bay* is usually less crowded than The Baths and can be reached by an interesting trail from The Baths. To the north of The Baths are the lovely beaches of *Spring Bay* and *The Crawl*.

To the south/southwest of The Baths is Fallen Jerusalem where small beaches hide amid huge boulders similar to those found at The Baths and in the Virgin Gorda Valley. The island is also a seabird nesting ground. It is said to have received its name because the boulder-strewn island resembles the fallen walls of Jerusalem.

There is one mooring available here for a short visit, but this is only recommended in flat calm conditions as landing on the tiny beach ashore can be quite hazardous in a swell. For those lucky enough to visit when the time is right, Fallen Jerusalem offers rock scrambling at its best and in many ways surpasses The Baths, but watch out and BE CAREFUL because there is no one around to help you if you fall or get lost!

Virgin Gorda Yacht Harbour

Waypoints:
Virgin Gorda Yacht Harbour - ½ nm W of entrance
18° 27.25' N, 64° 26.00' W

The *Virgin Gorda Yacht Harbour*, VGYH (284-495-5500), which opened in 1971, is the heart of Virgin Gorda as well as the focus of marine activity and the hub of The Valley, the name given to the southern part of Virgin Gorda which encompasses Spanish Town and The Baths as well as the yacht basin. *Virgin Gorda Yacht Harbour* is located in The Valley near Spanish Town, which was once the capital of Virgin Gorda and still remains the principal settlement. The Valley is the center and capital of Virgin Gorda and consists of little more than a couple of roads and a grouping of houses and shops near *Virgin Gorda Yacht Harbour*. The road leading south from *Virgin Gorda Yacht Harbour* leads to Spanish Town.

The British Virgin Islands - Virgin Gorda

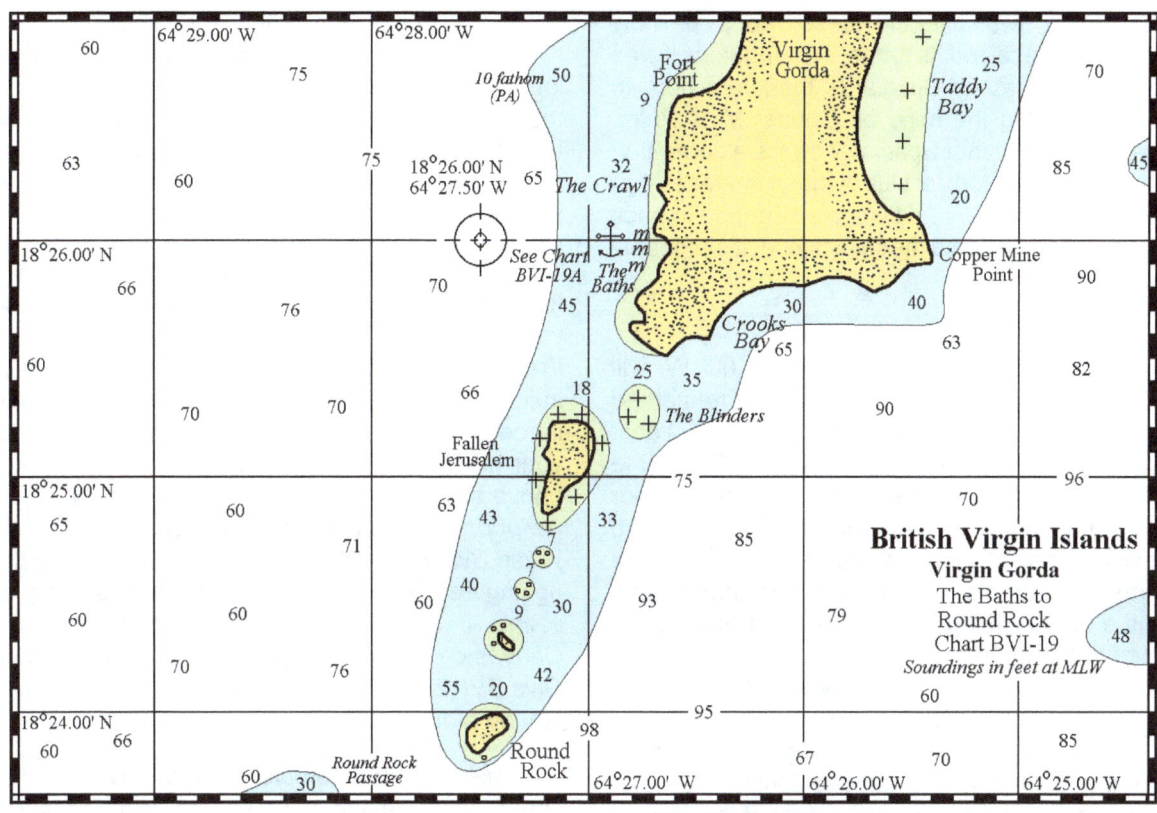
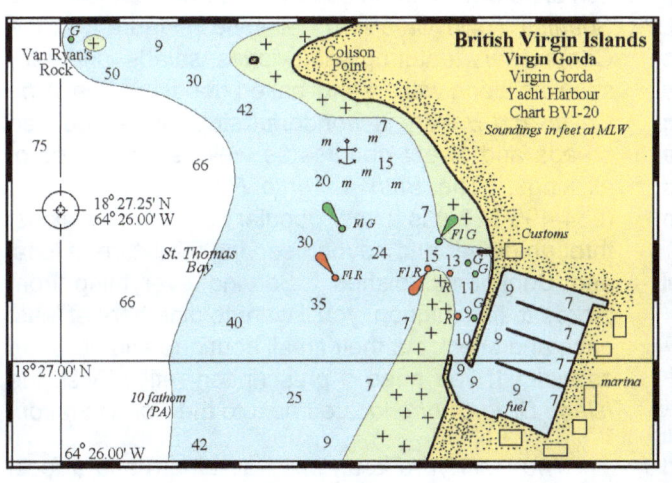
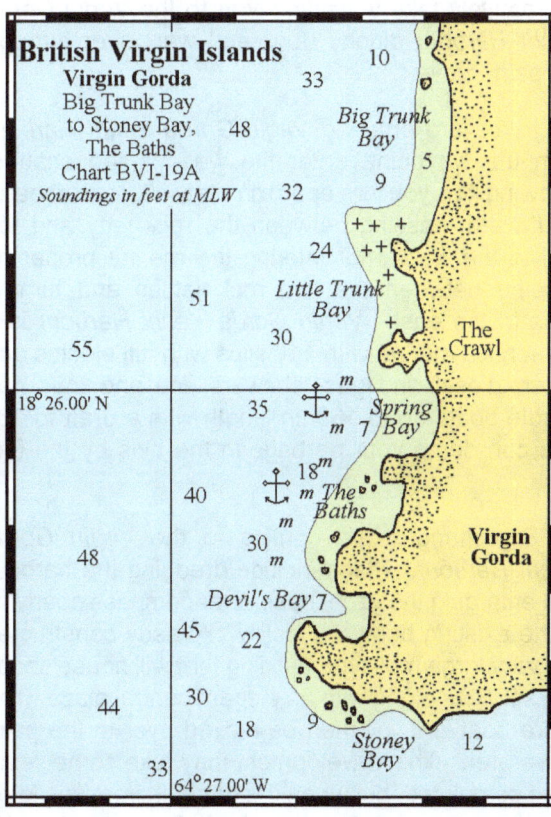

I've heard two different descriptions of how Spanish Town received its name, one suggests it was named after the many Spaniards that were here in the 1600s working the mine on Copper Mine Point. Another story has it that Spanish Town is a corruption of the word *penniston*, a blue woolen material that was worn by slaves. I could find no evidence to back up either one of these claims so pick one, it's probably as good as the other.

Navigational Information

A waypoint at 18° 27.25' N, 64° 26.00' W, will place you approximately ½ mile west of the marked entrance channel leading in to *Virgin Gorda Yacht Harbour* as shown on Chart BVI-20. From the waypoint you can head east where you may anchor or pick up a mooring just south of Colison Point, especially handy if you just need to run into the *Customs* office to clear. *Customs* and *Immigration* are in the blue building at the ferry dock outside the entrance to *Virgin Gorda Yacht Harbour* as shown on the chart. Walk to the rear of the building and the door on your right is *Customs* and *Immigration*. Do not block the ferry dock with your dinghy, ferries from Tortola arrive here with great regularity. You can however land on the beach to the east of the pier, or alternatively take your dinghy in to the *Virgin Gorda Yacht Harbour* dinghy dock and walk over through the palm grove.

If you are entering *Virgin Gorda Yacht Harbour* from the waypoint, enter the well-marked channel following it as you turn approximately 90° to starboard, southward, passing between the rock jetty and the reef to the west and entering the marina proper by passing between the two rock jetties and turning back to the east. *Virgin Gorda Yacht Harbour* is a full-service marina with 110 slips with full electric and water, diesel and gas, showers, ice and they can handle boats up to 160' in length with a draft to 10'. You can dump your garbage in the bins by the fuel dock.

Big changes are coming to the *Virgin Gorda Yacht Harbour*. Plans include dredging the harbour and enlarging the yacht basin to encompass nearly all of the existing boatyard facility. Already constructed is a very large mall type building that will house shops and services along with an elegant central plaza. The entire boatyard will then be moved over to the palm grove area. This development may take some years to be completed, but when it is done, it promises to be the premier marina facility in the BVI.

What You Will Find Ashore

You can find a taxi at the taxi stand in the parking lot south of the yacht basin or by the ferry dock. In the middle of the parking lot check out the bulletin board where you can learn about what's happening and where as well as previewing some of the local restaurant's menus.

On the southern side of the harbour near the fuel dock is the *Virgin Gorda Yacht Services* haul-out yard and dry-storage facility. The yard has a 70-ton *Travelift* and can haul and store multihulls up to 40' in length with their *Conolift* trailer. In 2017, the yard introduced their new 350-ton lift. The yard can repair your hull, treat it for osmosis, and paint your vessel above and below the waterline and can even handle *Awlgrip*. The *Workbench* specializes in woodworking, *West System* repairs, fabrication, mechanical and rigging repairs, and the general refurbishing of all yachts including multihulls. *Next Wave Sail and Canvas* can handle all your sail and canvas repairs. *Dive BVI* (284-495-5513) can fill your air tanks or take you on a dive tour.

The marina complex offers two banks, a supermarket, along with several pubs, boutiques, restaurants, bakeries, and car rental companies. Buck's Food Market has closed. However there are plans for a new Gourmet Market to be opening soon. *The Commissary and Ship Store* is owned by the *Little Dix Resort* and carries groceries, gourmet items, as well as fresh sandwiches and pastries. The *Spanish Town Café* is a deli-style restaurant at the *Commissary* featuring sandwiches, salads, and daily specials along with freshly baked goodies. *The Wine Cellar and Bakery* is wonderful stop for fresh baked breads and sweet goodies as well as beverages of all kinds. The *Bath & Turtle Restaurant and Pub* (284-495-5239) is a very popular spot from breakfast through dinner and beyond serving a mixture of local and Continental dishes. Serving everything from pizzas to filet mignon, you'll want to dine here at least once and check out their small boutique and gift shop as well. If you need a prescription refilled visit the *Island Drug Centre* located next to the *Police Station*.

The Courtyard is an open-air atrium and a focal point for shopping, dining, and nightlife while *The Wine Cellar and Bakery* is run by Ziggi and Melody and offers tasty pastries, sandwiches, hot dogs, sodas, wine, and spirits. The *Virgin Gorda Craft Shop* features locally made crafts as does *Margo's Jewelry Boutique* (along with *Margo's* own line of jewelry).

The British Virgin Islands - Virgin Gorda

VGYH to The Baths (foreground), Virgin Gorda — Photo by Todd Duff

The Baths, Virgin Gorda — Photo by Todd Duff

Fallen Jerusalem with Round Rock in the background — Photo by Todd Duff

The Baths, Virgin Gorda — Photo by Todd Duff

Anchorage at the BEYC, Virgin Gorda — Photo by Todd Duff

The Baths, Virgin Gorda — Photo by Todd Duff

Across the parking lot is *Flamboyance* with watches, and name brand perfumes and colognes, *Dior*, *Cartier*, and *Calvin Klein*. Also here is the *Artistic Gallery* an intimate shop selling jewelry, gems, nautical prints and wooden sculptures. *Stevens Laundry* has coin operated machines or they'll do your laundry for you. *Kaunda's Kysy Tropix* carries Caribbean and local music such as Reggae and Calypso and can also develop your film for you while *RTW*, *Riteway's* wholesale outlet, offers cash and carry bulk provisions for serious provisioning.

Near the yacht basin is *Chez Bamboo* (http://www.chezbamboo.com/) (284-495-5752), formerly the *Big Bamboo* and *Chez Michelle*, serving dinner only and featuring a blend of French and Caribbean dishes. A short walk to the right across a fenced-in park takes you to several eateries as well as the BVI *Tourist Board* where you can pick up a wealth of information on the islands. *Fischer's Cove Restaurant* (http://www.fischerscove.com/) (284-495-5252) is only a few minutes away from the yacht basin by foot and features great local fare on their lovely verandah overlooking the water. The *Rock Café & Sports Bar* (284-495-548) is open for dinner only and features Italian/Caribbean cooking and live music. The *Lobster Pot* at *Andy's Chateau* has great lobster and the *Crab Hole* offers economical West Indian fare, they're located near the *Rock Café* off a dirt driveway. For take-out and delivery in The Valley try *Anything Goes*, a West Indian restaurant serving authentic local dishes from 1100-2000.

If you head straight out the road from the ferry dock you'll come to the *Virgin Gorda Village* (http://www.virgingordavillage.com/) on the left. Located on a lovely 4-acre compound, the *Village* boasts one of the best restaurants on the island (*The Village Café & Restaurant*; open for lunch, dinner, and weekend breakfast), a truly romantic tropical setting with live music on Mondays and Fridays, and a gym to work off those romantic, tropical calories.

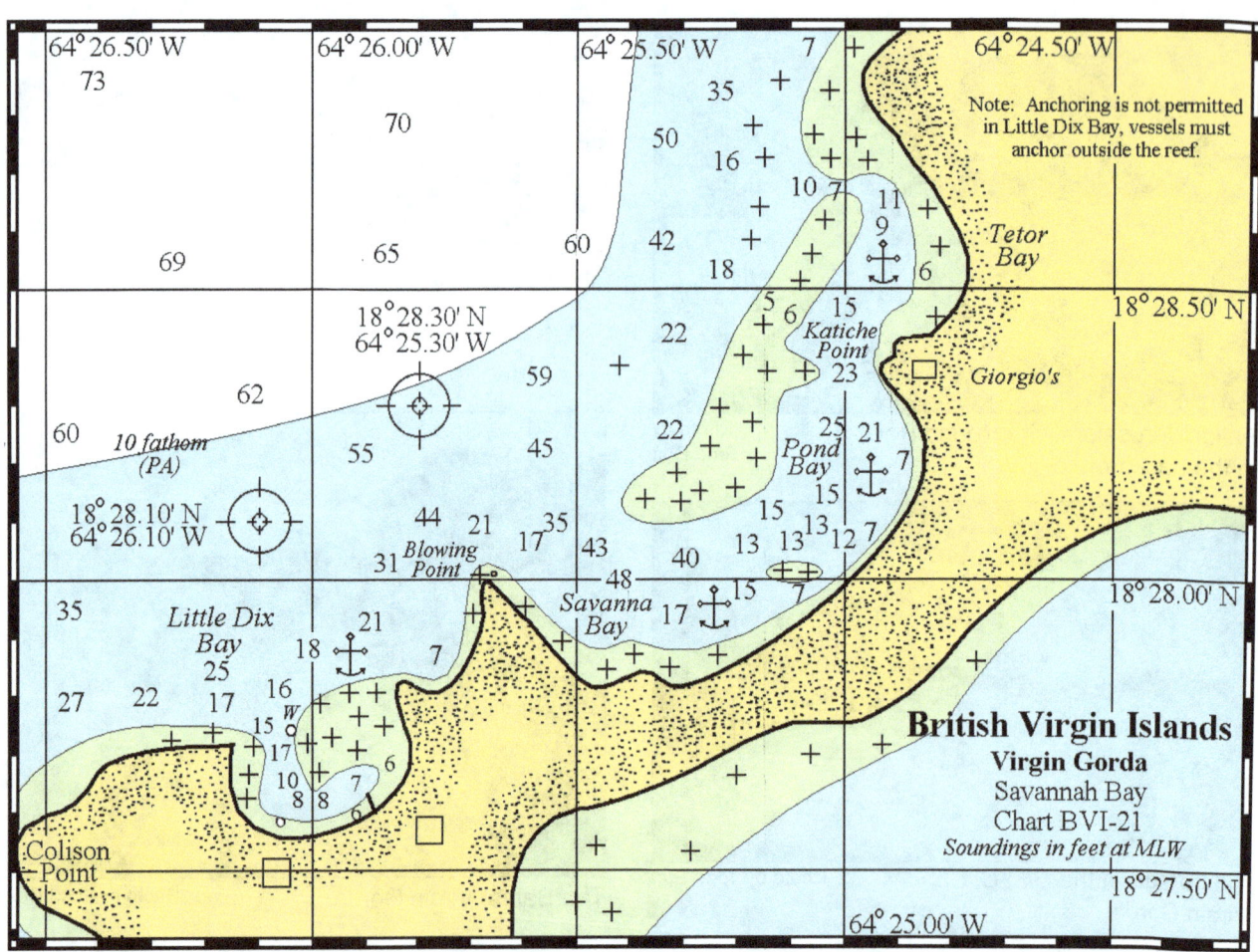

The British Virgin Islands - Virgin Gorda

Little Dix Bay

Waypoints:
Little Dix Bay - ¼ nm N of entrance
18° 28.10' N, 64° 26.10' W

Navigational Information

Little Dix Bay is the home of the first luxury hotel to be built in the BVI in 1964. *Little Dix Bay* is beautiful but private, no anchoring is permitted by order of the government of the British Virgin Islands, although you may anchor outside *Little Dix Bay* just north of the reef in the lee of the eastern headland.

A waypoint at 18° 28.10' N, 64° 26.10' W, will place you approximately ¼ mile north of the entrance into *Little Dix Bay* as shown on Chart BVI-21. When arriving from *Virgin Gorda Yacht Harbour* head west until you can turn to the north to avoid the shoals off Colison Point and work your way to the waypoint as shown. From the waypoint head southeast to anchor wherever your draft allows and you feel comfortable and protected. This anchorage is to be considered for daytime use only and not during periods of northerly swells.

What You Will Find Ashore

Laurance Rockefeller built the *Little Dix Bay Resort* for $8 million in 1964 and pampered is what you are when you're here with 3 staff for every guest being the norm. The resort is known as *The Rosewood Little Dix Bay* (212 758 1735, littledixbay@rosewoodhotels.com) offers three restaurants, the *Sugarmill*, the *Beach Grill*, and the resort's main dining room, *The Pavilion*, an open-air pavilion with a great view. Monday night at the *Pavilion* you'll find candlelight dining featuring a grand buffet being served (breakfast and lunch here are always buffets), while the *Sugar Mill* offers fine Italian cuisine in a romantic setting. If you intend to dine at the resort, the management requests that boaters do not dinghy in to their beach, instead they suggest you arrive by taxi from *Virgin Gorda Yacht Harbour*. Reservations are required for dinner at the *Pavilion*, and shorts are not permitted after 1800. Along the entry road to *Little Dix Bay* is *Thelma's* for good local food and darts.

A specialty only to be found in *Little Dix Bay* is *Mistress Bliden*. This potent libation, made from prickly pear cactus, is only served during the winter holidays.

Savannah Bay

Waypoints:
Savannah Bay - ¼ nm NW of entrance
18° 28.30' N, 64° 25.30' W

Just to the east of *Little Dix Bay* is a series of three small but lovely bays, *Savannah Bay*, *Pond Bay*, and *Tetor Bay*. Here you'll find a quiet place to get away from it all with lovely beaches and good snorkeling. The main entrance and the tricky reef entrances at the northern end all require excellent visibility for navigation, and the anchorages in these three bays are never to be considered if northerly swells are running, and some would argue that they should only be used for daytime stops.

Navigational Information

A waypoint at 18° 28.30' N, 64° 25.30' W, will place you approximately ¼ mile northwest of the entrance to *Savannah Bay* as shown on Chart BVI-21. From the waypoint head southeasterly passing between the southern end of the reef on your port side and the shoals off Blowing Point to your starboard. Never attempt entry here at night or during periods of poor visibility. As you enter *Savannah Bay* you must also avoid the shoals off the shore and a small reef lying to the east. You can anchor off the shore southwest of that reef for daytime use, but the better anchorages are in *Pond Bay* and *Tetor Bay*. Following the chart work your way past the small reef I just mentioned and you'll be in *Pond Bay* where you can anchor north of the small reef, or you can proceed northward passing between the outer reef and Katitche Point at the northern end of *Pond Bay* to enter *Tetor Bay* where you can anchor a bit off the shore to avoid the shoals close in. The entrance through the reef at the northern end of *Tetor Bay* is difficult to discern and is best avoided.

What You Will Find Ashore

Located atop the point between *Pond Bay* and *Tetor Bay* is *Giorgio's Table* (http://www.giorgiobvi.net/), open for breakfast, lunch, and dinner from May to October 6 every day except Sunday. *Giorgio's* has a 5,000-gallon lobster tank and offers 100% Italian food with all the regions of Italy represented, they even make their own pasta and have a dinghy dock for your convenience.

The Dogs

West Dog is a 24-acre bird sanctuary just to the north of Virgin Gorda. Nearby West Dog, George

A Cruising Guide to the Virgin Islands

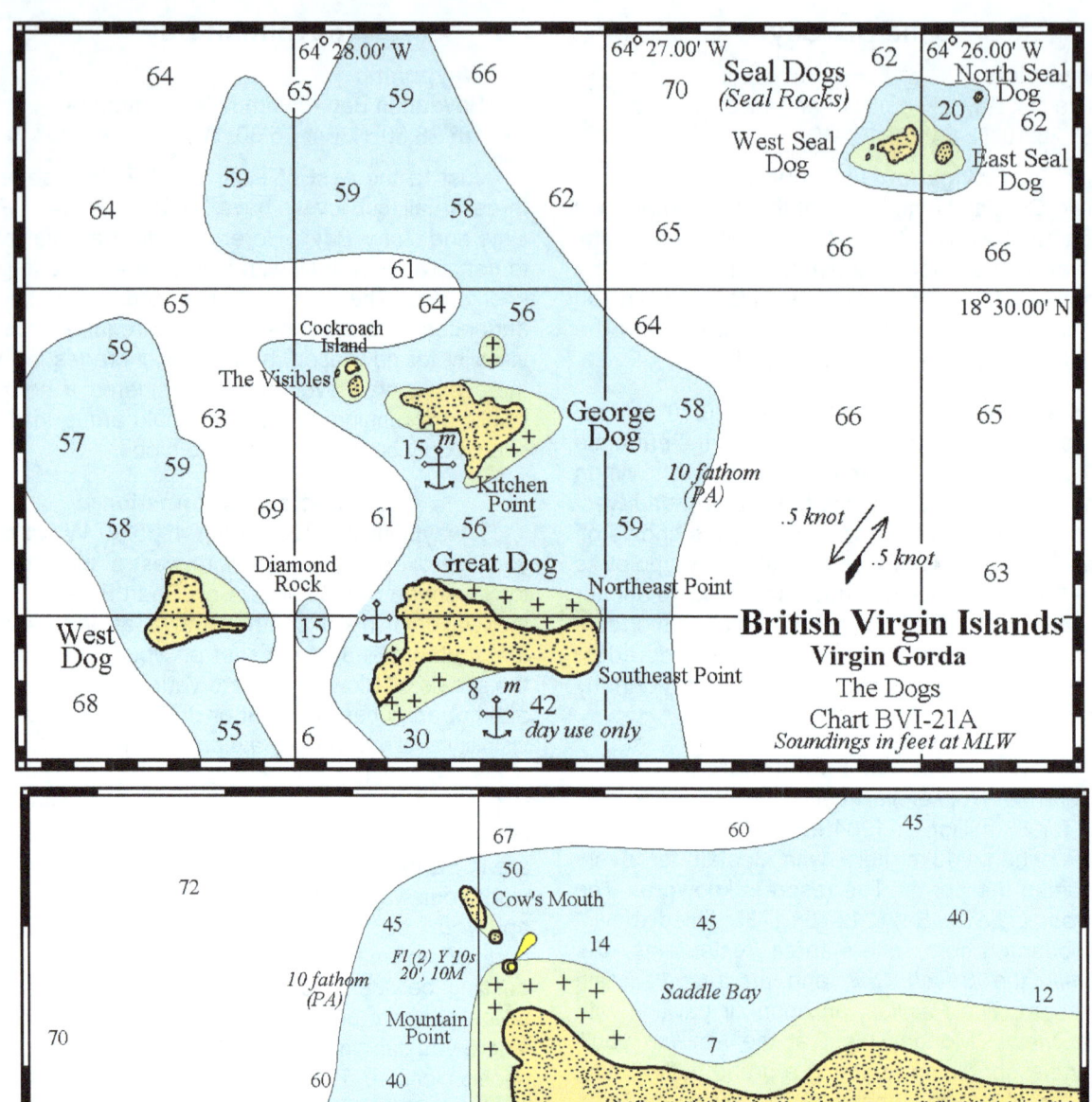

170

Dog, and Seal Dog offer good snorkeling and are shown on Chart BVI-21A. A nice dive site named *The Chimney* lies just west of Great Dog. The site got its name for its resemblance to a rock climbing slot called a *chimney*. At this site a narrow crack between two large boulders rises from a depth of 25' to the surface with a backdrop of two beautiful canyons and a massive arch. The bay to the east of *The Chimney* has a nice rock tunnel and tidal pool. There's good snorkeling on the southern side of Great Dog and at the extreme east and west ends of George Dog. You can anchor of the southwest coast of George Dog in the lee of Kitchen Point in calm weather, or off the southern shore of Great Dog (rocky bottom), of off the northwestern coast of Great Dog of the small beach. These anchorages are for daytime use only, they are subject to backwinding, and last but not least, do not try to anchor at any of the Dog Rocks if northerly swells are running or predicted.

Long Bay

Waypoints:
Long Bay - ½ nm W of anchorage
18° 30.00' N, 64° 25.30' W

Navigational Information

At the northwestern tip of Virgin Gorda there is a nice lee-side anchorage located at *Long Bay* as shown on Chart BVI-22. A waypoint at 18° 30.00' N, 64° 25.30' W, will place you approximately ½ mile west of the anchorage area in *Long Bay* as shown on the chart. From the waypoint head east and anchor wherever you like in about 15'-30' of water, but don't go too far in as the bay shoals rapidly. This is a pleasant enough anchorage for an overnight stay as long as northerly swells, or any type of ground swell for that matter, are not running.

North Sound

(Gorda Sound)

Waypoints:
North Sound - ¼ nm NW of entrance
18° 31.05' N, 64° 22.90' W

North Sound - ½ nm W of Anguilla Point entrance
18° 30.45' N, 64° 24.35' W

What a fantastic spot! Well-protected in all conditions, shelter can be found here from any wind direction. Inside the sound are several resorts and marinas and you'll even see a cruise ship in here every so often. *North Sound*, often shown as *Gorda Sound* on some charts, has a rich history, it was here that Sir Francis Drake and Sir John Hawkins took a respite to arrange their forces before heading into battle at San Juan in 1595 where Hawkins died and Drake tasted defeat.

Navigational Information

The tide in *North Sound* is primarily diurnal, meaning one high and one low per day. The tidal currents at the entrance are rarely over ½ knot, but the inward current sets toward Prickly Pear Island. Between Mosquito Island and Anguilla Point the eastward flowing tidal current can attain a velocity of 1-1½ knots.

There are two viable entrances into *North Sound*, the best entrance is via the well-marked channel at the northern side of *North Sound* between *Cactus Reef*, lying west of the northwestern tip of Prickly Pear Island, and *Colquhoun Reef* lying west of the northern portion of Mosquito Island.

If you are approaching from the east, from the Anegada Passage or St. Martin and you've never been in here before, use caution in Virgin Sound.

If you have a GPS you can follow latitude 18° 31.00' N to pass between Necker Island reefs and Prickly Pear Island until abeam of the lit channel. If you don't have a GPS you can eyeball your way between Necker Island and the northern tip of Virgin Gorda staying in mid-channel. If you're approaching from Anegada it's a straight shot, just watch out for the reefs west of Necker Island. If you're approaching from the west, from Tortola or Jost Van Dyke, you will need to pass north of Mosquito Island giving Mosquito Rock a wide berth.

A waypoint at 18° 31.05' N, 64° 22.90' W, will place you approximately ¼ mile northwest of the entrance channel as shown on Chart BVI-23. Although the channel is well-marked, strong northerly swells can damage or destroy the buoys so bear that in mind if you're approaching the channel and the buoys don't agree with what's on the chart. From the waypoint head generally southeast, passing between the marked reefs until you are inside *North Sound* and can take up a course to your favorite cove or marina.

There is another entrance to *North Sound*, the Anguilla Point entrance, is on the Virgin Gorda side of Mosquito Island at the western end of *North Sound* and is used routinely by ferries, small powerboats, and catamarans. Charterers are not advised to use this entrance especially when the seas are up and in fact it may be off limits so check with your charter company.

A waypoint at 18° 30.45' N, 64° 24.35' W, will place you approximately ½ mile west of the Anguilla Point entrance as shown on Chart BVI-23. Approaching from the waypoint line up in the middle of the channel, approximately halfway between Anguilla Point and the southern tip of Mosquito Island. Steer approximately 100° magnetic and you can take 5' through the pass, and if you dogleg south inside the entrance, you can take 6' through. Once inside *North Sound* you can take up your course to your next destination.

Drake's Anchorage

Navigational Information

If you are headed to Drake's Anchorage from the northern entrance to *North Sound*, once you clear the last markers at the south end of the entrance channel, you will have to pass two more red markers that define the southeastern and southern tips of *Colquhoun Reef* before rounding up to enter Drake's Anchorage as shown on Chart BVI-23. If you are approaching from the Anguilla Point entrance you can head north/northeast to Drake's Anchorage after you are abeam of the docks and shoreside facilities at the northwestern end of Drake's Anchorage to avoid the shallows off the eastern shore of Mosquito Island. You can anchor here or pick up one of ten moorings for $15 per night as of this writing (pay at the resorts restaurant). Drake's Anchorage is usually calm in most conditions, but in a strong easterly I suggest moving.

What You Will Find Ashore

Drake's Anchorage was built in 1963 by Bert Killbride, the patriarch of BVI diving. Bert moved an anchor from the wreck of the *Rhone* and a cannon to the shallow waters of Drake's Anchorage from their initial resting site off Black Rock. From here Bert moved the relics to the museum located on nearby Saba Rock.

Drake's Anchorage and Resort serves lunch and dinner on the water's edge and if you intend to dine here, *Drake's* will pick you up and return you to *Leverick Bay*, *Gun Creek*, the *Bitter End Yacht Club*, and *Biras Creek* for free. You must call in the morning to make a reservation for dinner and to arrange transportation.

Mosquito Island has been purchased by Sir Richard Branson (who also owns nearby Necker Island) and he is turning it in to a completely sustainable "green" (and very exclusive) resort. Although this island always had a great reputation for its beautiful hiking trails and pretty little beaches, you must check with the resort for permission to visit Mosquito Island. Mosquito Island is home to several secluded beaches such as *Skinny Dipping Beach*, *Honeymoon Beach*, and *Rocky Beach*, a good snorkeling spot. *Long Beach* lies directly opposite Anguilla Point and offers great snorkeling on its reef and good snorkeling can also be found at *Colquhoun Reef*. The latest news has Sir Richard Branson bringing 30 ring-tailed lemurs to the island to create a colony for preservation.

Prickly Pear Island

My favorite anchorage in *North Sound* is in the lee of Prickly Pear Island, calm, shallow, protected, and you're surrounded by beautiful water. Prickly Pear Island is a nature refuge earning its name by being a habitat of the prickly pear cactus.

Navigational Information

From the northern entrance to *North Sound* you can head over to the western shore of Prickly Pear Island to anchor off Vixen Point at the southern tip of Prickly Pear Island, or behind the small reef on the western shore of the island.

What You Will Find Ashore

Vixen Point is the location of a beautiful beach, the best one in *North Sound*, as well as the *Sand Box Seafood Grill & Bar* (284-495-9122), a true barefoot beach front bar that is open for lunch and dinner. The *Sand Box* offers complementary boat pickup from *Gun Creek* and *Leverick Bay* upon request. Moorings, ice, and showers are available here as well as beach volleyball and a gift shop. There are daily happy hours from 1600-1800 Monday night is *Ladies Night* while Wednesday night is *Lobster Night*. When the cruise ships are in the *Sand Box* will be full of people enjoying *North Sound* with skiers and banana-boat riders everywhere, that's when I head for the shelter on the western shore of Prickly Pear Island!

The British Virgin Islands - Virgin Gorda

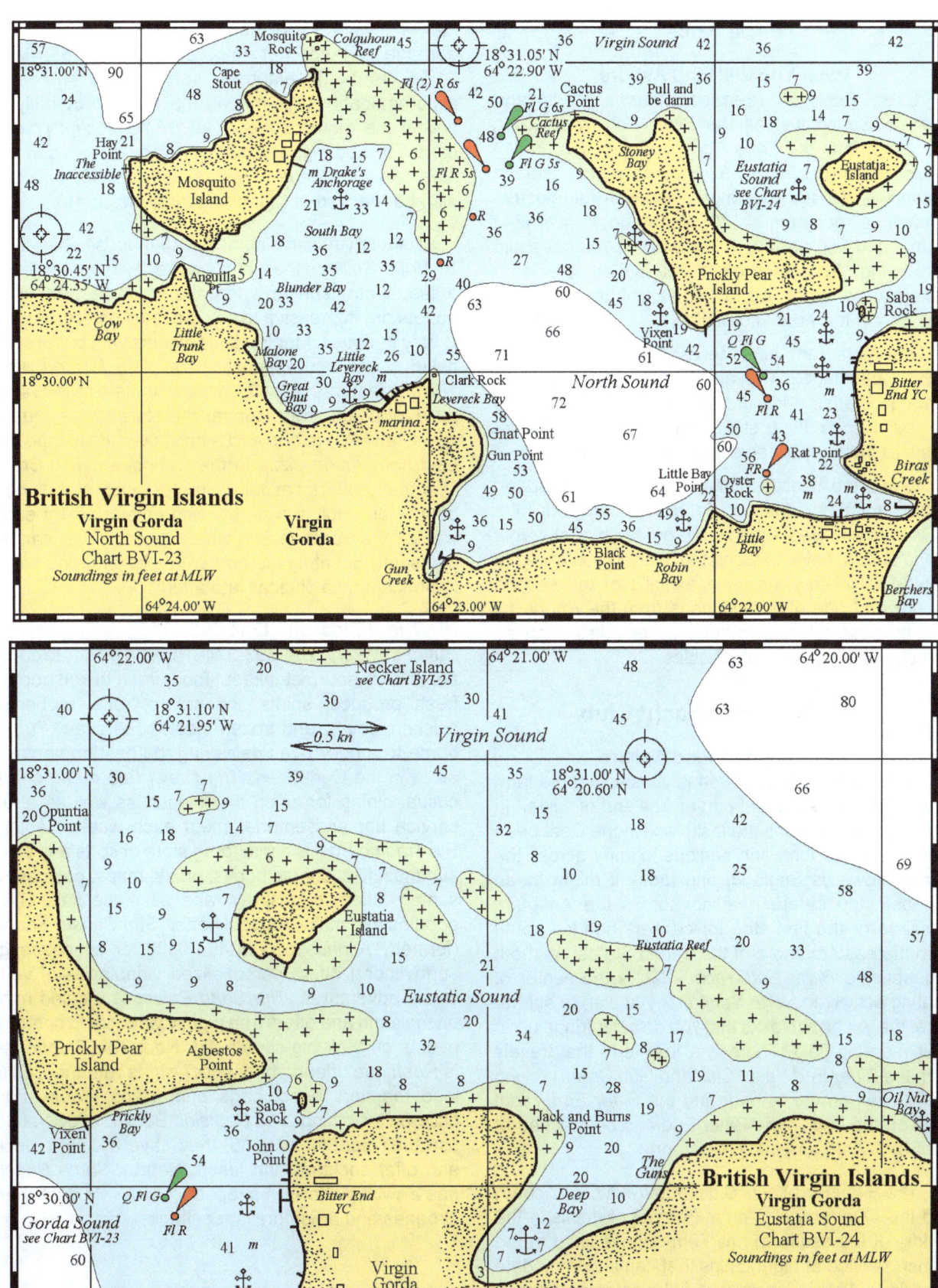

A Cruising Guide to the Virgin Islands

Saba Rock

What You Will Find Ashore

Saba Rock lies between *North Sound* and *Eustatia Sound* just off the *Bitter End Yacht Club* and is home to the *Saba Rock Island Resort* (info@sabarock.com) (284-495-9966). The resort offers a restaurant, 2 bars, moorings, slips with full electric, a maritime museum, a 130' dinghy dock, overnight rooms, and 250 gallons of free water if you get a slip or mooring. The resort offers free launch service for pickup anywhere in *North Sound*, call the resort on VHF ch. 16 for more information.

The restaurant here serves up an unbeatable nightly buffet for $25 with a constantly changing menu although there's a leg of lamb and prime rib waiting for you at the cutting station where head chef Chef Shelford Tucker will carve your meat for you.

One of the most popular attractions in *North Sound* is the maritime museum on Saba Rock. Owners John McManus and Bert Kilbride, the patriarch of all *Virgin Island divers*, have collaborated to bring you a wealth of nautical history including exhibits of the second anchor and one of two cannons from the *Rhone* as well as a selection of other smaller relics such as porcelain plates, jugs, and bottles.

The Bitter End Yacht Club

What You Will Find Ashore

If you're a sailor you probably know that the term *bitter end* means the last part or free end of a line. In *North Sound* it means the last place in the Caribbean before facing a long and perilous journey across the Atlantic towards England, and today it might mean the last stop before heading across the *Anegada Passage* or the first stop for cruisers headed south from the eastern shore of the United States. Without a doubt, the *Bitter End Yacht Club* is the center of boating activity in *North Sound*. If you plan to anchor here, the yacht club asks that you do not infringe upon their mooring field. There is a free ferry that travels from the *Bitter End Yacht Club* and *Gun Creek* leaving Gun Creek on the ½ hour and the *Bitter End Yacht Club* on the hour. The Bitter End can be reached at (284-393-2745, or binfo@beyc.com).

The *Bitter End Yacht Club* (http://www.beyc.com/) and the *Quarterdeck Marina* (the set of docks in the middle of the seafront) has 70 moorings (with a free launch service at night), slips that can accommodate vessels to 100' in length with full electric and water, fuel, showers ($3 for non-guests), ice, provisioning, garbage pickup (for moored vessels as well-$1.50 per bag), telephone service, and shoreside accommodations. A marina rep will stop by daily to collect the mooring fee. The *BEYC* accepts credit cards for mooring fees but only when paying ashore. *Quarterdeck Marina* monitors VHF ch. 16, and can also be reached at (qdmanager@beyc.com).

Ashore you can dine at *The Clubhouse Steak and Seafood Grille* on the water's edge. Here you will find a casual atmosphere where the breakfast and lunch buffets are impressive to say the least, the restaurant is truly famous for their nightly dinners with buffet style salad, pasta, and appetizer bars. The *Almond Walk Terrace* features lavish Caribbean buffets at THE spot for a late night dance under the stars to live music. *The Crawl Pub* is home to a brick oven delivering the best homemade pizza in the Caribbean. *The Crawl Pub* menu offers casual dining for lunch and dinner, as well as a full service bar and entertainment each week. *The Poolside Bar*, where an entire day can be pleasantly spent by the pool with a light curried salad for lunch, and a cocktail late afternoon.

The Emporium (284-393-2745), and *Winston Butler's Bakery* (284-393-2745) are the places to go for provisions, gourmet takeout food, fresh baked goods, fresh produce, spirits, ice cream, rotis, barbecue chicken, spirits, and frozen meats. *The Crawl Pub* is home to a brick oven delivering the best homemade pizza in the Caribbean. *The Crawl Pub* menu offers casual dining for lunch and dinner, as well as a full service bar and entertainment each week. *Captain B's Trading Post* is a mini-drug store of sorts and sells sundries, film, charts, books, prints, maps, postcards, suntan lotion, bug spray, and all those little OTC goodies that make you feel better. *Sun Chaser Scuba* (formerly *Kilbride's*) (284-495-9638, or sunchaser@surfbvi.com) offers personalized videotapes of your diving adventures. *The Sand Palace* is located right on the sand and offers free nightly videos and sporting events on their big-screen TV. Near *The Clubhouse* is *Reeftique* offering hats and T-shirts with the *BEYC* logo, toe rings, beach bags, print wraps, jewelry, and children's clothing. *The Poolside Bar* will allow you to use their pool for only $5, they have a dinghy dock and offer cocktails and lunch. Nearby *South Beach* has a swim platform in a roped off area with dual chair cabanas and an umbrella for shade.

Biras Creek

Navigational Information
Biras Creek is located in the extreme southeastern tip of *North Sound*. As you approach *Biras Creek* keep a sharp eye out for Oyster Rock as shown on Chart BVI-23, it only has 2' of water over it at low tide.

You can anchor or pick up a mooring in *Biras Creek* (sometimes shown as *Deep Bay*), if any are available since the marina closed in 2015.

What You Will Find Ashore
The old *Biras Creek Marina* was closed, and been replaced by the *Yacht Club Costa Smerelda & Marina*. Customs clearance is available at the club. The *Yacht Club* has 38 berths (both alongside and stern to) for a maximum length of 300' and a draft of 30'. Other amenities include diesel, gas, pump out, water, trash removal, free *Wi-Fi*, ice, laundry service, on-board special event catering, and provisioning services. There are two dining options available at the Yacht Club. The clubhouse's elegant *Azzurra* restaurant offers a fine dining experience featuring international cuisine with Caribbean accents. The restaurant is open for lunch and dinner, offering outdoor or indoor tables with the best views in the BVI. The informal waterside restaurant *Bar Aqua* specializes in light, tasty and healthy craft food. *Yacht Club Costa Smerelda & Marina* monitors VHF ch. 08, and can also be reached a (284-393-2000, or info@yccs.vg).

The dinghy dock is located at the *Fat Virgin's Café*, a small terraced dockside dining area that is open for breakfast, lunch, and dinner with an espresso bar serving gourmet coffees.

The trail from the *Bitter End Yacht Club* to *Biras Creek* is not difficult. It begins in *Biras Creek*, not far from the main dock at the plant nursery, taking about 45 minutes to an hour of easy, mostly level walking.

Gun Creek

Gun Creek is now a **Port of Entry** for the BVI.

Gun Creek lies at the extreme southwestern tip of *North Sound*, west of *Biras Creek*, almost due south of the northern entrance to *North Sound*, and just "around the corner" from *Leverick Bay*. You can anchor here and enjoy the shoreside delights here and in Creek Village, the local community.

The *Gun Creek* dock usually has small local powerboats tied up there. There is a free ferry that travels from the *Bitter End Yacht Club* to *Gun Creek* and back leaving *Gun Creek* on the ½ hour and the *Bitter End Yacht Club* on the hour. A short walk from the *Gun Creek* dock is *Captain Poncho's*, a popular local eatery with your typical West Indian fare as well as burgers and such (dinner by reservation only); here too is the *Last Stop Bar*, a good spot for a cold one right by the ferry dock.

Up the hill, at the *Leverick Bay* turnoff, at the area called the *Top of Gun Creek*, there is an interesting assortment of snack and other bars. *The Butterfly* is pink with a white porch and is a popular spot for those that love to play dominos, *The Twin House* is open for lunch and dinner, while *Gunny's Cool Corner* features island style fast food and *Angie's* caters and has a nice barbecue on Fridays. The *Gun Creek Convenience Center* is the place to go for provisions, ice cream, spirits, fresh produce, and sandwiches. They're open Monday through Friday from 0700-2100, Saturday from 0800-2000, and on Sunday from 0900-1900. The *North Sound Superette* has groceries and pharmaceuticals, but no alcohol or tobacco.

Leverick Bay

Navigational Information
Leverick Bay lies a bit east of south from Drake's Anchorage just across *South Bay* and *Blunder Bay* as shown on Chart BVI-23.

What You Will Find Ashore
Leverick Bay Marina is your host here and they offer 36 moorings, 15 slips with full electric and water, free showers, laundry facilities, a dive shop *Dive BVI* (284-495-7328), market, a fresh-water swimming pool, craft shops, car rentals, Internet access, and villa rentals. *Pusser's Leverick Bay Marina* monitors VHF ch. 16, and can also be reached at (284-495-7421, or leverick@surfbvi.com).

Buck's Supermarket carries fresh groceries, fresh produce, and spirits. The *Pusser's Company Store* features *Pusser's Beach Bar* for breakfast, lunch, and dinner, and *Pusser's Terrace Restaurant* located on the 2nd floor serving dinner only (check out the observation tower for great views). *Pusser's* offers a Wednesday night barbecue with live music and Saturday's are *Mexican Night*.

A Cruising Guide to the Virgin Islands

The *Jumbies Beach Bar* (284-495-7421) at Leverick Bay is open daily for lunch and dinner with a daily happy hour from 1700-1900 with 2 for 1 Painkillers and delicious chicken wings. You can even use their fresh water pool, two beaches, showers, and TV before or after dining. If you need to rent a car, Leverick Bay is reachable by road, *Speedy's Car and Jeep Rental* (284-495-5235) is located here, and if you need to access the Internet visit *Digital Jamming*. SPA is a woman's body salon and the *Palm Tree Gallery* carries 14k gold jewelry featuring nautical and marine life themes, Caribbean made handicrafts, and even Africa raku pottery.

Eustatia Sound

Waypoints:
Eustatia Sound - ¼ nm N of
18° 31.10' N, 64° 21.95' W

Eustatia Sound - ½ nm NE of pass through reef
18° 31.00' N, 64° 20.60' W

Before I begin this section let me say that yes, you can enter *North Sound* from *Eustatia Sound*. Why then did I not mention that fact when I discussed the two routes into *North Sound*? For the simple fact that I believe it is far easier and safer for the average cruiser and charter to enter *North Sound* by the aforementioned routes. *Eustatia Sound* is full of reefs and coral heads that pose a true threat to you and your vessels safety and that must be negotiated in good visibility by a skipper that is used to piloting by eye through reef-strewn waters with little or no margin of error. Besides, the sound is off limits for some charter boats, so check with your charter company.

Navigational Information

Eustatia Sound lies northeast of Saba Rock and offers a quick, though not easy passage into and out of *North Sound*. The sound is thick with reefs and heads and excellent visibility is necessary to venture in these waters. Never attempt to pass through *Eustatia Sound* during periods of poor visibility, such as a squall, and never attempt it at night. There are two good entrances to *Eustatia Sound*, the first is through *Eustatia Reef* and is a bit more difficult, the second lies to the east of Opuntia Point at the northern tip of Prickly Pear Island, between the point and Eustatia Island. Never attempt to enter *Eustatia Sound* from the north when northerly swells are running.

A waypoint at 18° 31.00' N, 64° 20.60' W, will place you approximately ½ mile northeast of the pass through *Eustatia Reef* as shown on Chart BVI-24. From this position you will have to eyeball your way through the maze of reefs, never attempt to enter *Eustatia Sound* from the waypoint with a sun that is low in the west, conversely, never attempt to exit *North Sound* via *Eustatia Sound* with the sun low in the west.

From the waypoint you'll be steering in a general southwesterly direction passing through a large and deep (18') gap in *Eustatia Reef*. Once through the reef you can work your way southwest towards Saba Rock passing on the southern side of Saba Rock to enter *North Sound*. You can round Jack and Burns Point to anchor in *Deep Bay*, or head westward passing between the southern shore of Eustatia Island and Asbestos Point to anchor in the lee of Eustatia Island. Please note that Eustatia Island is private and visits ashore must be by invitation only.

A waypoint at 18° 31.10' N, 64° 21.95' W, will place you approximately ¼ mile north of the entrance between Opuntia Point and Eustatia Island. From the waypoint pass southward between Prickly Pear Island and Eustatia Island keeping an eye out for the shoals along the shore of Prickly Pear Island and the reef that works its way westward from the northern shore of Eustatia Island. You can round up to the east and anchor off Eustatia Island or continue on passing between Eustatia Island and the reefs off Asbestos Point. Once clear of the reefs off Asbestos Point you can turn to back to the southwest to pass south of Saba Rock and enter *North Sound*, or you can continue south of east passing Jack and Burns Point to anchor in *Deep Bay*.

There is plenty of good snorkeling in *Eustatia Sound* as you might well imagine from all the reef structure that you had to bypass to enter. It's best to explore the sound by dinghy from *North Sound* or from one of the anchorages such as *Eustatia Island* or *Deep Bay*. Never anchor in *Deep Bay* with northerly swells running or forecast.

All the way at the end of *Eustatia Sound* is *Oil Nut Bay*. This bay has to be entered by passing between Saba Rock and Virgin Gorda and then carefully threading your way through the numerous coral heads dotting the passage between the outer reef and the shoreline. Most have at least 6' over them and the depths in between the heads are 10-12'. Still a few coral heads have less than 5' so a good lookout and good light are essential to a safe arrival and *Oil Nut Bay*.

Why go there? Once you have your hook down there is an incredible white sand shoal area that you could call the world's biggest swimming pool. This is a great a place to spend the afternoon with kids or friends in waist deep water, bobbing and snorkeling around the few scattered shallow heads in the area. The beach surrounding the bay is mostly sand and then gradually turns to very tough broken coral as it reaches out towards the SE point of Virgin Gorda. Truly a spectacular place!

Unfortunately, *Oil Nut Bay* has been discovered and building lots are being sold now which promises to turn this formerly untouched place into an exclusive resort area, but the water and coral is still fantastic and if you have the skills to navigate in here, by all means stop there! I do not recommend this as an overnight anchorage however, so try to arrive by 1100 and leave by 1400 or 1500 at the latest. Good light is essential. If you don't feel like braving all that coral with your mothership, just take a mooring at Saba Rock or anchor behind Prickly Pear Island and take your dinghy. It's only about a mile away from *North Sound*.

South Sound

The last, and the most remote anchorage on Virgin Gorda, is *South Sound*. To get there you can pass between the *Blinders* and Fallen Jerusalem and then proceed north east along the Caribbean side of Virgin Gorda. An alternative route is to round Virgin Gorda's southeastern tip and proceed to a point just off the entrance clearly shown on the charts.

There is a small reef smack dab in the middle of the entrance with less than 4' over it, but 6-7' can safely be carried either side of it and up into the sound. Once past the small reef, it is all eyeball navigation to round the inner tip of the barrier reef and proceed in as far as you wish. This whole sound is a marine sanctuary and has fine white sand bottom with conch grass in patches and a few scattered houses on the shore.

There is a small cove that some locals use as a hurricane hole in the far corner that carries 5-6' with mangroves all around. If you wanted to use this one, be sure to get there early as the locals also know about it and there are in fact a couple of 'hurricane moorings' in place within the bay. Personally I would use this as a last resort since the entire sound is very open to a violent storm surge.

Since *South Sound* is off limits to all charter vessels you will likely have this beautiful spot all to yourself although a local fisherman or two may come by to offer you lobster or conch. The snorkeling on the reef is spectacular and in anything short of a stiff southeasterly breeze the anchorage will be flat calm.

Driving Around Virgin Gorda

Let's begin our tour of Virgin Gorda at the *Virgin Gorda Yacht Harbour* by leaving the ferry dock and taking a right, to head south down the coast on *Lee Road* toward The Valley (please don't complain about the roads on Virgin Gorda, until the 1960s there were no cars on the island). The Valley stretches out in a square with extensions to the north and south, both of which lead to some very interesting places. Just south of *Virgin Gorda Yacht Harbour* and Spanish Town is the *Little Fort National Park*, a 37-acre wildlife sanctuary that was once the site of a Spanish fort, little remains today save for the old *Powder House*. A bit further south you will come to the "T," a small roundabout where if you turn to the east you'll arrive at The Baths. Continuing south you'll come to *Millionaire Road* on the other side of *The Valley Square* and at the next roundabout take a right and then a left on *Coppermine Road* to go to the ruins at Coppermine Point.

Located at the southwestern tip of Virgin Gorda is the *Coppermine*, a *National Park* and a protected area located between Coppermine Point, *Coppermine Bay*, and *Mine Hill*. The mine was said to have first been used by Amerindians who Columbus stated wore "gold" jewelry when he passed this way in 1493, while in later years Cornish miners removed ore from the mine from 1838-1842 and later, from 1860-1867. It is said that Spanish miners may have worked the same mine as far back as 3 centuries earlier. Nearby Mine Point and Coppermine Point are home to several small buildings believed to be the miner's cottages. Use caution when exploring here, there are at least seven underground shafts from 15'-200' deep and although the *National Trust* is attempting to stabilize the area, you must exercise caution when strolling here.

On the left just before the pavement ends as you approach Coppermine Point is *The Mine Shaft Café*

Bitter End anchorage (background), *Biras Creek* in the foreground
Photo by Todd Duff

Eustatia Sound, Gorda Sound in background, Virgin Gorda
Photo by Todd Duff

Oil Nut Bay, Eustatia Sound, Virgin Gorda
Photo by Todd Duff

South Sound, Virgin Gorda
Photo by Todd Duff

(284-495-5260, or mineshaftcafe@hotmail.com) with their daily sunset happy hour. Here too you can go a round on their mini-golf course and you must try one of their full moon parties.

On the return from Coppermine Point head up the far side of The Valley Square past a picturesque church where you can turn right at the *Police Station* to reach the airport. Take a few minutes and stop for a drink at the *Flying Iguana* (284-495-5277) at the airport. Featuring eclectic gourmet cuisine and fresh seafood in an open-air pavilion overlooking the sea you can enjoy their *Tuesday Prime Rib Nights* or their *West Indian Night* on Wednesdays complete with live entertainment.

Returning from the airport take a right at the entrance road by the *Police Station* and then a left at the next roundabout to head to *Little Dix Bay*.

To visit the northern part of Virgin Gorda from the *Virgin Gorda Yacht Harbour* leave the ferry dock behind heading straight out the road past *Virgin Gorda Village* (hours vary depending on the day of the week) on the left. The *Village*, (284-495-5350) (hours vary depending on the day of the week) is located on a lovely 4-acre compound boasts one of the best restaurants on the island (open for breakfast and dinner only), a truly romantic tropical setting with live music on Mondays and Fridays, and a gym to work off those romantic, tropical calories. Also here is the *Sip and Dip Grill*, an outdoor poolside grill featuring Italian dishes and ice cream. Continuing along the road you'll cross a ridge with a wonderful view of both the *Sir Francis Drake Channel* and the *Caribbean Sea*. This road wasn't completed until 1969 and was not paved until 1980 and soon you'll find yourself climbing *Gorda Peak*, the highest point on Virgin Gorda. The *Gorda Peak Trail* starts at 1,000' and continues to an observation tower with a stunning view at the highest point at 1,359' (the focus of the 247-acre *Gorda Peak National Park*). The trail showcases a variety of indigenous plants and offers a spectacular view of the BVIs from the observation tower.

The road continues north towards *Biras Creek* and *North Sound* and steeply descends to the *Top of Gun Creek* village where you can stop and have a bite to eat or a cold beverage. Stunning views of *North Sound* are the norm here, so don't forget your camera. Heading down you'll come to the turnoff to *Leverick Bay* on the left taking you down a series of ridges before terminating in the parking lot at the resort. If you ignore the turnoff to *Leverick Bay* and continue down you'll come to the mouth of *Gun Creek* with its ferry dock where you can take a ferry to the *Bitter End Yacht Club* or the launch to *Biras Creek*.

Necker Island

Waypoints:
Necker Island - ¼ nm SW of entrance to anch
18° 31.10' N, 64° 21.90' W

Necker is an exclusive, private island and visits ashore must be by invitation only. The infrastructure on Necker Island was constructed in 1985 as a Bali-esque home for its wealthy owner, Sir Richard Branson, the owner of *Virgin Records* and *Virgin Airlines*. Designed by British architect John Osman, who has an office on Tortola, 72-acre Necker Island was designed to be Sir Richard's personal kingdom and was built from rock quarried from the very hill upon which the buildings stand.

Today, Necker Island is rebuilding. Once an exquisite all-inclusive resort with a gym, whirlpool, tennis courts, a 300-year old Hindu meditation hut, carefully hidden hammocks, a 10-bedroom villa that can accommodate 24 guests, two private Balinese-style cottages, an elaborate dining room with a 22' long table made of Brazilian hardwood as its centerpiece, superb chefs, a staff of 22 to cater to your every whim, it rented for only $54,000 a day. However, a lightning strike during the passing of *Hurricane Irene* on August 22, 2011, burned the Great House to the ground. By the way, if you wondering, Necker Island received its name from the Necker Berries found on the island.

Navigational Information

Bear in mind that the waters around Necker Island are off limits to most charter boats so if you chartering, check with your company. A waypoint at 18° 31.10' N, 64° 21.90' W, will place you in *Virgin Sound* approximately ¼ mile southwest of the entrance to the anchorage at Necker Island as shown on Chart BVI-25. Don't forget that *Virgin Sound* has a tidal current flowing approximately east and west at about ½ knot. If approaching from St. Martin, you may enter *Virgin Sound* (only during daylight unless you're familiar with these waters) and head for the waypoint. If you are approaching from *North Sound* you may exit the sound via the marked entrance channel west of the northwestern tip of Prickly Pear Island and once clear of all obstructions head directly for the waypoint. In approaching from Anegada make sure that you clear the reefs west of Necker Island before turning to the east towards the waypoint.

From the waypoint head generally in a northeasterly direction to pass between two reefs as shown on the charts. Necker Island is almost completely surrounded by a reef and the entrance off the southern tip of the island is the best entrance. You'll have to eyeball your way in here, there are no markers to guide you. As you pass abeam of the eastern reef and the small cay that lies southeast of Necker Island you may turn northward towards the conspicuous dock and work your way up the western shore of Necker Island to the anchorage area in *Devil Hill Bay*. Do not block the dock or go ashore without permission.

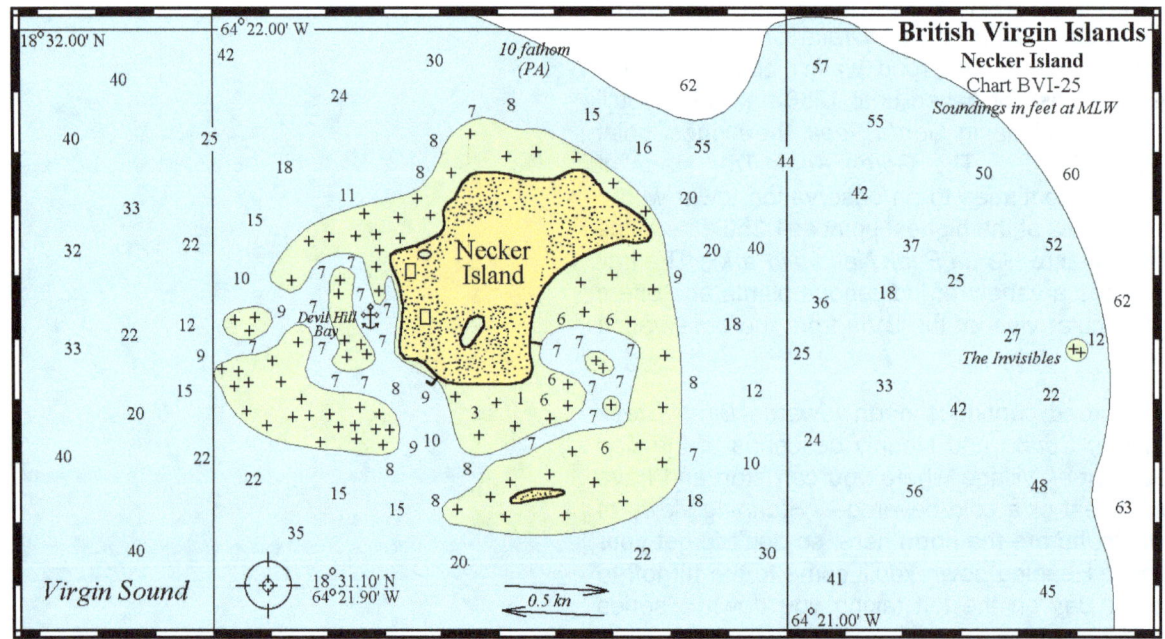

Anegada

Important Lights:
Anegada Light: Fl W 10s
Anegada Passage
Sombrero Light: Fl W 10s

Waypoints:
Anchorage - 1 nm SW of entrance channel
18° 42.50' N, 64° 25.00' W

Columbus named this most northern island of the British Virgins, *Anegada*, meaning place of drowning, which is why it's often called the *drowned island*. Anegada, unlike her sister islands of the BVI, is coral in formation and quite flat, its highest point being only about 28' above sea level. Anegada is some 11 miles long and lies about 15 miles north of the northern tip of Virgin Gorda at *Gorda Sound* and about 20 miles northeast of Tortola. Vessels wishing to go to Anegada should consider sailing for the island from Gorda Sound on the northern tip of Virgin Gorda unless you like beating to windward from Tortola or Jost Van Dyke. Anegada is off limits for several bareboats so check with your charter company if you wish to head to Anegada, they might suggest that you take along one of their experienced captains.

Navigational Information

Leaving *Gorda Sound* you can head for a waypoint at 18° 42.50' N, 64° 25.00' W, which will place you approximately 1 mile southwest of the marked entrance channel leading to the anchorage at Anegada as shown on Chart BVI-26. The marks here make entering the anchorage at Anegada very easy in good light and if you can read the water you should not have a problem, except if you're trying to enter the anchorage at the same time as a half-dozen other boats. Never attempt to enter here at night or in periods of poor visibility such as a squall.

From the waypoint you can turn to the east/northeast past the outer red and green markers and continue on past the next red marker when you will be approximately south of the entrance channel that leads northwest of Setting Point. If you draw more than 7' you should anchor off the town dock south of Setting Point. If you draw less than 7' you can continue northward into the first of two anchorage/mooring areas west of Setting Point (see photo). Heading west from Setting Point the channel is well-marked and the reef south of *Neptune's Treasure* can be easily avoided. You can anchor wherever your draft allows or pick up a mooring off *Neptune's Treasure* or the *Anegada Reef Hotel*. If you have any trouble entering, or if the markers are not there and you're confused, call the *Anegada Reef Hotel* or *Neptune's Treasure* on VHF ch. 16 and they'll do what they can to talk you in.

If you don't wish to enter the anchorage area west of Setting Point, you can continue north past the waypoint given to anchor in the small cove north of Pomato Point as shown on Chart BVI-26.

What You Will Find Ashore

Just up from the anchorage the *Pomato Point Restaurant* has a small museum with many items recovered from *Horseshoe Reef* wrecks. Here you'll find a map showing the location of over 200 wrecks as well as exhibits of cannon and musket balls, copper rivets, jars, bottles, ink pots, a silver teapot, and coins of many nations. The restaurant serves local dishes with a great view of the waters in the lee of Anegada.

For touring the island you can rent a car, jeep, or ATV from places like *ABC Car Rentals*, *DW Jeep Rentals*, *Egbert Wheatley Car Rentals*, and *Lil Bit Cash and Carry*.

There are many good places to dine on Anegada, in fact, there are over 20 beach bars and they all monitor VHF ch. 16. The *Anegada Reef Hotel* (284-495-9362, or info@anegadareef.com), owned by Lowell and Sue Wheatley, has taxis, car rentals, bike rentals, bait and tackle, deep-sea and bonefishing guides, air fills, and a self-service honor bar for guests. The hotel's restaurant serves breakfast, lunch, and dinner and they ask that cruisers make their dinner reservations by 1600. For a good read, pick up a copy of *Tales of Billygoat Charlie of Anegada* (by Sue Wheatley) at the hotel. Sue also owns *Sea Tour*, a sea kayaking business and when you finish your trip you can help yourself to a delicious cold rum smoothie back at the hotel. Just outside the hotel by the town dock is *Kenneth's Gas Station* if you need to jerry-jug some gasoline to your boat. Next door to the hotel is *Lowell's Soap Factory* if you want to pick up some locally made soaps and lotions.

A bit west of the hotel is *Neptune's Treasure* (284-495-9439, or neptunestreasures@surfbvi.com) where you can get breakfast, lunch, and dinner featuring seafood caught by the owners, the Soares family who cook their lobster using an old family recipe. If you want the scoop on local fishing talk to Mark Soares, he's the largest supplier of deep-sea fish to the BVI's dining tables. Here too is *Pam's*

A Cruising Guide to the Virgin Islands

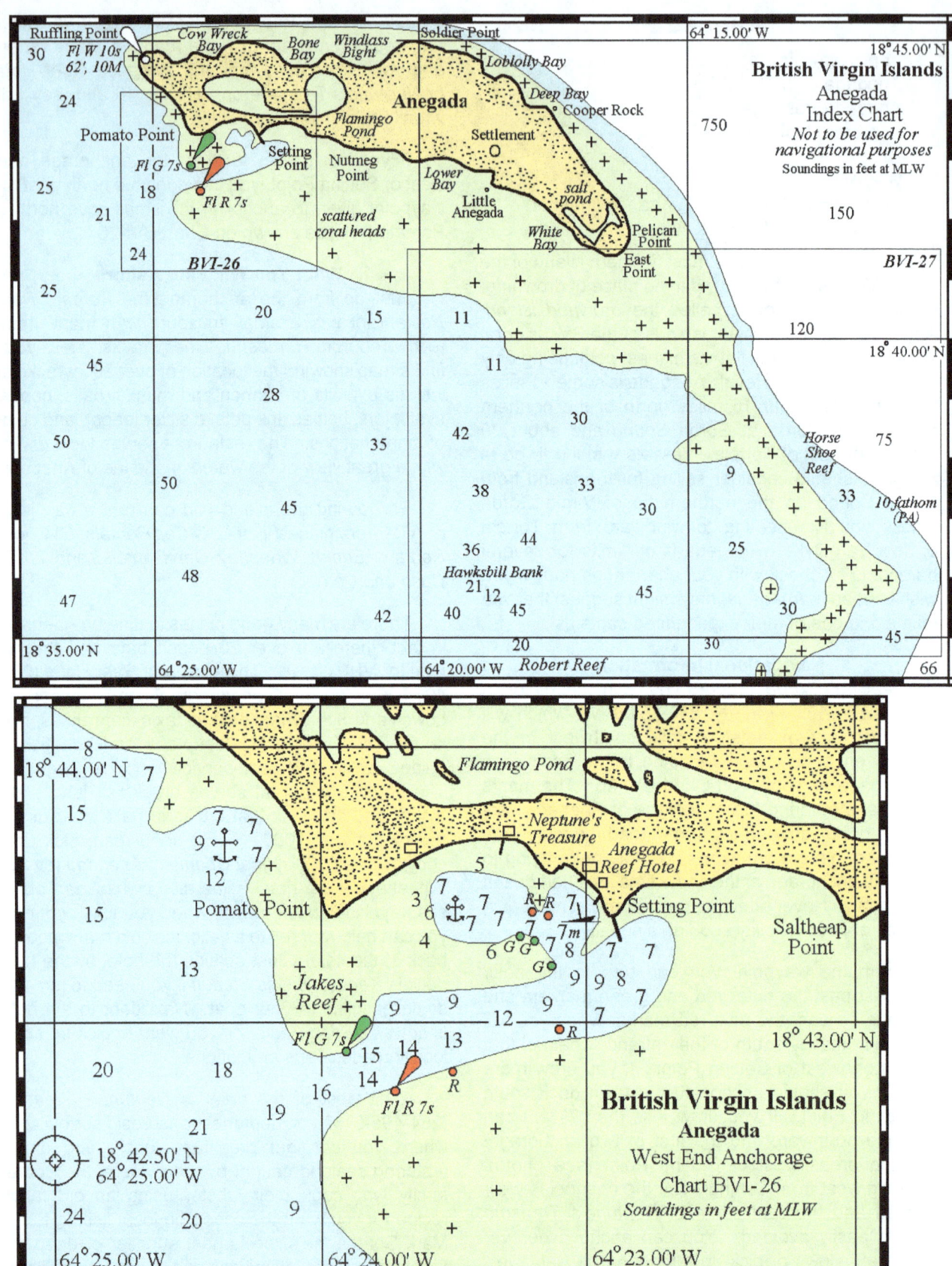

Kitchen, open from 0800-1700. You don't even have to leave your boat to get some locally made treats. Around sunset a small boat comes out from *Pam's Kitchen* to sell delicious baked goodies such as muffins, cookies, and breads. Also west of Setting Point is the new *Whistling Pines Restaurant*, named for the sound of the wind in the trees. The restaurant has live music on Wednesdays and Fridays as of this writing. Nearby is the *Anegada Beach Club* (284-340-4455, or info@anegadabeachclub.com) where you dine and/or rent a car or jeep. The restaurant is open from 0900-1800 and if there are not enough people for dinner, they'll take those that are there over to Pomato Point for dinner.

There's a lot to see on Anegada that is far from the anchorage. You can't help but notice nature all around you on Anegada. Anegada is home to the highly endangered *Anegada Rock Iguana* that can grow to 6' long. Harmless and very rare, the iguanas can sometimes be seen at Bones Bight with its new nature trail. The iguanas are in danger from the feral cats on Anegada and a program of neutering the cats is underway.

The ocean side of Anegada is an important nesting site for green sea turtles while the beaches and sea grass beds from Pomato Point to *Cow Wreck Bay* are important to the hawksbill turtle. Even the Anegada "Outback," an area of scrubland to many, has interest, if you but take a moment to notice it; bromeliads and termite mounds in the trees, the fascinating wild frangipani tree, and even Anegada's own exotic caterpillar with bold yellow and black stripes. The small concrete pads near Nutmeg Point are a good spot to try to catch a glimpse of the pink flamingos that frequent the nearby salt pans. Once thousands of these birds inhabited the islands, but often their young were rounded up and loaded into boats to be sold for food.

East of the anchorage off Setting Point is the only town on Anegada, a small settlement that is rarely visited and named appropriately enough, The Settlement. Once called *The Village*, The Settlement has a population of about 250 with about 120 residences, a post office, police station, a bar, two restaurants, the *Ocean Range Hotel*, a bakery, two grocery stores, and two general stores. Everywhere in The Settlement you'll see *The Walls*, remains of stone wall enclosures where fields of bananas, corn, sweet potatoes and other crops were planted when agriculture was the big ticket here. The goats and cattle you see wandering around are trained not to climb over the low 4' walls and they still return to their pens at night.

In the Settlement stop in the "village square" to visit *Pal's General Store* and *Faulkner's General Store*, actually the square is *Pal's* parking lot. Just down the side road from the square is *Dotsy's Bakery & Sandwich Shop* where you can pick up fresh baked goodies or have lunch or dinner made to order. There are a lot of businesses in town and walking around to discover them is half the fun, you'll find *Sue's Gift Shop*, *Pam's Kitchen*, *Pat's Pottery*, and *V&J's Souvenir & Gift Shop*. *Sue's Gift Shop* has an interesting display of items from island dresses to Indonesian batik sarongs, hats, and even children's wear. *Sue's* also carries music, books, Haitian art, postcards, and locally made spices and relishes and soaps and lotions from *Lowell's Soap Factory*. *Pat's Pottery and Art* offers locally made artwork and pottery and *Pam's Kitchen and Bakery* is a good stop for delicious baked goodies as was well as sauces, salsas and homemade jams and moisturizing lotions.

North of The Settlement is the airport. Anegada has one of the Virgins smallest airport terminal buildings with one of the smallest snack bars, *Lil's*, which is open only when flights are arriving and offers two tables on a shaded porch with sodas, beer, mixed drinks, sandwiches, and a small collection of gift items for sale.

There are some nine miles of beaches on Anegada with *Loblolly Bay* on the northeastern coast being one of the finest. At *Loblolly Bay* you can have lunch or dinner at the *Big Bamboo* (284-495-8129, or bigbamboovillas@gmail.com), a nice beachfront open-air bar and restaurant that sits behind a grove of sea grape trees hung with huge hammocks. The lobster at the *Big Bamboo* is simply fantastic, and lots of cruisers will tell you that Diane, the cook here, is the best lobster cook anywhere and that's saying something! The *Flash of Beauty* is a simple little beach bar on Loblolly Bay and serves all day from 1000-2100.

Cow Wreck Bay is named for cow bones that are said to have washed ashore from a shipwreck. The bones were being shipped to a processor to turn into fertilizer. The *Cow Wreck Beach Bar* (284-495-8047, or cowwreckbeachbvi@gmail.com) serves lunch and dinner upon request so make your reservations early and they'll be happy to send a free shuttle to pick

A Cruising Guide to the Virgin Islands

Setting Point anchorage, Anegada
Photo by Todd Duff

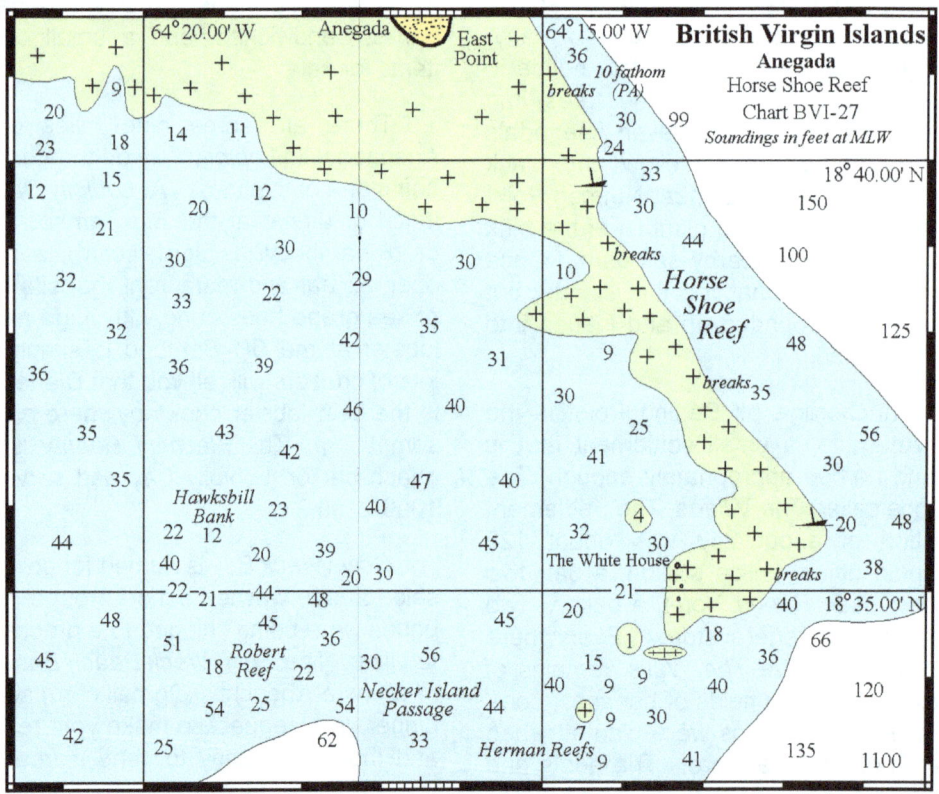

you up and return you to the anchorage. They also have a shower and changing area here if you wish to snorkel before or after your meal.

Stretching southeast from Anegada, *Horse Shoe Reef* (see Chart BVI-27) is off limits for charter boats, fishing, and anchoring to replenish both the reef and the creatures that live on it. At the eastern end of Anegada are large piles of conch shells, some of which date back centuries.

There are 250-300 wrecks said to be on the reefs surrounding Anegada. The most famous is the *Paramatta*, a paddle steamer that sank over 100 years ago on her maiden voyage, and the *Astrea*, a British frigate of 32 guns that sank in 1808. The *Rocus* is known as the bone ship, she was carrying a cargo of cattle bones destined to be made into fertilizer when she sank in 1929. One famous wreck that is earnestly being searched for is the Spanish galleon, *San Ignacio*. Wrecked on Anegada's reefs in 1742, she was en route to Cartagena with a cargo of gold and silver, pay for the Spanish troops stationed there.

One of the more notable shipwrecks, the 32-gun, 689-ton British frigate, the *HMS Astrea*, saw action in the American Revolution and gained fame by capturing the large French frigate *Glorie* in 1795 in a classic sea battle. In 1808 she was escorting a mail packet past Caribbean privateers to Puerto Rico when her skipper mistook Anegada for Puerto Rico and wrecked on the reef losing all but 4 of her crew. In a later court martial it was declared that she came upon the reef due to an "extraordinary weather current." The *Astrea* has been honored on a BVI stamp. The wreck has been found and some items have been salvaged but not the cannons.

Dining in the Spanish Virgin Islands

In the Spanish Virgin Islands you will find Puerto Rican cuisine, *comida criolla*, which is a unique blend of Spanish, Taino, and African influences. There are several dishes that you'll find in most restaurants that are unique to Puerto Rico and the Spanish Virgin Islands and we shall touch on them briefly here.

For the newcomer, dining in the Spanish Virgins may take some getting used to, if for no other reason than the language barrier alone. So, let's tuck a napkin under our chins and begin with some of the basics.

Sofrito is a staple of Puerto Rican cuisine and serves as a base in stews, soups, casseroles, and beans and rice. It is a mixture of peppers, onions, garlic, coriander, and other ingredients. In lieu of saffron to color the food, crushed annatto seeds, *Achiote,* is used, while *adobo* (a blending of several spices) is rubbed on meat prior to cooking.

Let's talk staples! Rice and beans is a staple at almost every meal, along with *tostones*, fried slices of plantain, *amarillos* (ripe plantains served boiled or fried), *pan de agua* (a "light" bread), and *arroz con gandures* (seasoned rice with pigeon peas).

A particular favorite at most meals is *mofongo*, smashed plantain or yucca with garlic and other seasonings. Now if you prefer meat with your *mofongo*, try the *mofongo relleno*, which is usually seafood or chicken inside a *mofongo* crust. The well known black bean soup, *frijoles negros*, should not be missed and is a great way to start a meal.

For the main course, you can sample any of several dishes such as *asopao*, a rich stew made with rice and either fish, shellfish, or chicken. Another stew, *sancocho*, is a combination of pork, beef, and various vegetables. *Lechon* is roasted pork and is usually sold at roadside stands along with roasted chicken almost everywhere on the island.

Empanadillas are meat-filled pastries as are *pasteles*, a meaty treat inside a *mofongo* paste wrapped in green banana leaves and boiled. *Surullitos* are fried cornmeal "fingers", *bacalaitos* are deep-fried codfish fritters, and *alcapurrias* are meat or fish in a deep-fried casing of finely grated plantains and taro.

For dessert you might try *flan*, a custard dish, or candied fruit such as *dulce de papaya*, or *tembleque*, a coconut pudding.

For a beverage you might have *parcha* (a drink made from passion fruit), or *tamarindo* (a drink made from the tamarind). Also popular is *mavi*, a fermentation made from tree bark, and my personal favorite, *aqua de coco*, the juice of an unripe coconut served chilled in the shell.

Whatever you choose to dine upon, I doubt you'll regret it. Dig in and enjoy! Now let's look at a recipe for sofrito.

Sofrito

Sofrito is a staple of Puerto Rican cuisine and serves as a base in stews, soups, casseroles, and beans and rice. It is a mixture of peppers, onions, garlic, coriander, and other ingredients. The following recipe for sofrito is written by my good friend, Dr. Juan M. "Van" Vicens, who is as good a cook as can be found anywhere on the island. Doc, you can cook on my boat anytime!

Basic Ingredients:
- Fatback and salt pork
- Olive oil
- Onions (minced)
- Garlic (minced or crushed)
- Peppers (cubanelle or mixed green and red bell peppers-minced)
- Salt & pepper
- Oregano
- Olives
- Capers
- Parsley
- Tomatoes
- Tomato sauce
- Chicken stock (broth), may substitute cubes
- White wine & vinegar

Cooking

Heat 2 tbsp. of olive oil in a hot pot and crisp the fatback and salt pork. Add the minced onions, peppers, and garlic. After onions blanch, add the tomatoes and/or tomato sauce, olives capers, oregano, parsley, and add salt and pepper to taste. Deglaze with a capful of vinegar and ½ cup white wine. Add 1 cup chicken stock and simmer until mixture thickens. Congratulations, you have the basic *Sofrito* recipe...now it gets interesting!

French/Catalan Version
(Marseilles Bouillabaisse)

Same as above, plus add minced fennel (the bulb not the seeds; looks like a fat celery and tastes like anisette). Add saffron to color.

Italian Picatta

Same as the Spanish version, but you add basil, fresh or dried, to the mix.

Mexican

Add cumin to the mix, plus chipotle, serrano and jalapeno peppers to the cubanelle and bell peppers. If you are making Mole, add 1-2 tbsp. unsweetened cocoa to the mix.

Puerto Rican and Cuban Variations

Add annatto-colored oil instead of saffron, deeper red...an Arawak/Taino recipe.

Jamaican and Bahamian Variations

Add 1 scotch bonnet pepper (the fresh kind, once dried they are called *habanero*, very hot!) and allspice, whole to the peppers.

Creole Variation

Add andouille sausage to the fatback and salt pork. Add chopped celery to the onions, and add Louisiana hot sauce and *Tabasco* to taste. If you must, add the burned flour laughingly called a *roux* (a true *roux* in the French tradition is a beef or veal stock reduced to thick jelly consistency).

Final Notes

If you make enough of this, you will be rewarded with a thick, chunky, red tasty base for all your Creole, Caribbean, and Mediterranean dishes. You can freeze it in trays and separate the cubes afterwards. Use a couple of cubes to initiate your stews and add to whatever you are cooking: lobster, beef, chicken, shrimp, or any type of bean dish. Stir fry for a few minutes then add water and rice. If you keep it at approximately 1½ cups of liquid for each cup of rice, let it boil almost dry at high heat, turn it over, cover, and let finish cooking at low heat and you have a dry rice dish (e.g.; *arroz con pollo*).

If you use 2 cups of chicken stock, and add fresh seafood such as clams, mussels, lobster, shrimp, or prawns, as well as chicken parts, using the Spanish variation you will have *paella*.

If you use 2 cups of white wine, or a can of beer and the Creole variation, add shrimp, chicken, crawfish, and smoked sausage, with white rice on the side and you have *jambalaya*. For the Creole variation with crawfish, cover with 1 cup white wine and one can of beer, plus as much hot sauce as you can stand.

Fait les bon temps roule!

Enjoy!

Fresh SVI lobster — Photo by Author

Dining in the U.S. and British Virgin Islands

One thing travelers everywhere have in common is eating, and a good knowledge of what's cooking is handy to have when presented with a menu you don't understand. The following is small list of foods that you might encounter while dining in the U.S. and British Virgin Islands.

Most entrees will generally be stewed, fried, or boiled, and several starchy side dishes may accompany each meal. Many restaurants serve American style food, but don't expect too much as the cooking style is different in the Virgin Islands and supplies are limited, almost all produce has to be shipped in from Puerto Rico, the U.S., or other Caribbean islands and shortages are not a rarity.

You will find that many restaurants listed in this guide feature fresh seafood, of course, what else would they feature, it's not likely they'll be serving up walrus, camel, or kangaroo steaks, these are the islands and seafood abounds. And don't think a restaurant is not popular just because it has few patrons, you must remember that there are far fewer people here than where you may be from.

Don't expect fast service, this is the Virgin Islands, relax and enjoy life. And don't expect water to be served with every meal, it is scarce and is usually served only when requested.

Breadfruit: Brought to the West Indies by Captain Bligh (of *Mutiny on the Bounty* fame) in 1793, *breadfruit* is usually baked or boiled.

Bullfoot Stew: Basically this is tripe and dumplings.

Callaloo: A green leafy vegetable very similar to spinach, it is most frequently served as a soup.

Cassava: A root vegetable that is used as an addition to soups and meat dishes. In the BVI, *cassava* flour is often used in a flat bread cooked on a large griddle. Besides modern day cooks, the pre-Columbian Amerindians made good use of *cassava*.

Dasheen: *Dasheen*, sometimes called *tannia*, is a tuber whose flesh is boiled and cut into cubes for soups or served as a side dish

Dumb Bread: *Dumb Bread* is a dense, crusty, yeast-free bread that derives its name from *Dum*, an old Amerindian way of baking bread.

Fungi: This dish is made from okra and cornmeal and most resembles mashed potatoes; it is similar to the Italian *polenta*. Sometimes shown as *funchi* or *fungee, fung* is also called *coo coo* in Barbados and *tum-tum* in Haiti.

Ginnep: A plum-like fruit with a large seed.

Goat Water: Besides stewed or curried goat you might find this goat soup on the menu.

Johnny Cake: *Johnny Cake* is a fried dough that is usually served with a meal instead of bread. It had its origins in British Journey Cake hence the name.

Mauby: Sometimes shown as *Maubi* and pronounced *moby*, this drink is made from the bark of the *Mauby* tree. It is said to be helpful for pregnant women and men who need stamina. *Mauby* is definitely an acquired taste.

Paté (or Pattie): This is usually a meat-filled pastry that may contain salt fish, tuna, spiced beef, or curried chicken. The pastry may be made from white or whole wheat dough and may be either fried or baked.

Plantains: *Plantains* are members of the banana family, but larger than the traditional yellow banana and not as sweet. They are sliced and deep-fried making for a very tasty side dish, in the SVI they are called *tostones*.

Roti: This is an import from Trinidad that has become popular in the Virgin Islands. A *roti* consists of thin Indian bread filled with curried chicken or beef, and sometimes conch and whelk.

Run Down (Run Dun): A coconut cream usually used on fish; it may also be a coconut cream stew.

Salt Fish: Dried, salted fish, usually cod, but sometimes haddock or pollock, it is often used as a filling, but may be served cooked in a sauce of tomato, onion, and herbs. Before cooking the fish is usually soaked overnight in cold water to remove the salt.

Souse: A stew that can be made from chicken, sheep's tongue, or the head, tail, and feet of a pig.

References

A Cruising Guide to the Caribbean and the Bahamas; Jerrems C. Hart & William T. Stone, Dodd, Mead & Co., New York, 1982
The Abaco Guide; Stephen J. Pavlidis, Seaworthy Publications, Cocoa Beach, FL 2000
American Practical Navigator; Nathaniel Bowditch, LL.D., DMA Hydrographic Center, 1977
A Short History of Puerto Rico; Morton J. Golding, American Library, NY, 1973
Best Dives of the Caribbean; Joyce and Jon Huber, Hunter Publishing, Edison, NJ 1998
Caribbean; James A. Michener, Random House, NY, 1989
Caribbean Cooking; Judy Bastyra, Exeter Books, NY, 1987
Caribbean Ways, A Cultural Guide; Chelle K. Walton, Westwood, Riverdale, CA, 1993
The Concise Guide to Caribbean Weather; David Jones, 1996
Diving and Snorkeling Guide to the Virgin Islands; Linda Sorenson, Pisces Books, 1992
Don't Stop the Carnival; Herman Wouk, Doubleday, NY, 1965
Easy in the Islands; Bob Shacochis, Viking, NY, 1985
The Exuma Guide, 3rd Edition; Stephen J. Pavlidis, Seaworthy Publications, Cocoa Beach, FL 2011
The Islands; Stan Steiner, Harper & Row, NY, 1974
Isles of the Caribbees; Laddie McIntyre, National Geographic Soc., Washington DC, USA, 1966
La Vida; Oscar Lewis, Irvington, NY, 1982
The Ocean Almanac; Robert Hendrickson, Doubleday, New York, 1984.
The Other Puerto Rico; Kathyrn Robinson, Permanent Press Inc., Santurce, Puerto Rico, 1984
Passages South; Bruce Van Sant, Cruising Guide Publications, Dunedin, FL, 2000
The Pirates Own Book; published by A. & C. B. Edwards, New York, and Thomas, Cowperthwait, & Co., Philadelphia, 1842
Portrait of Puerto Rico; Louise C. Samoiloff, A.S. Barnes, San Diego, 1979
The Puerto Rican's Spirit; Theresa Maria Babin, Collier Books, NY, 1971
Puerto Rico and the Puerto Ricans; Clifford A. Hanberg, Hipocrene, NY, 1975
The Puerto Rico Guide, 2nd Edition; Stephen J. Pavlidis, Seaworthy Pub., Cocoa Beach, FL 2011
Puerto Rico, Island Between Two Worlds; Lila Perl, William Morrow & Co., NY, 1979
Penguin Book of Caribbean Verse; Paula Burnett, editor, Viking Penguin Books, NY, 1986
Sailing Directions for the Caribbean Sea; Pub. #147, Defense Mapping Agency, #SDPUB147
Snorkeling Guide to Marine Life; Paul Humann, 1995
The Spanish Virgin Islands; Bruce Van Sant, Cruising Guide Publications, Dunedin, FL., 1998
St. Croix Under Seven Flags; Florence Lewisohn, Dukane Press, Hollywood, Fla., 1970
Street's Cruising Guide to the Eastern Caribbean; Donald M. Street Jr., W.W. Norton, New York, 1985
Tales from La Isla del Encanto; Haydée Reichard de Cancio, Vantage Press, NY, 2000
Tales of Billygoat Charlie of Anegada; Sue Wheatley
Tales of the Caribbean; Fritz Seyfarth, Spanish Main Press, St. Thomas, USVI, 1978
The Ocean Almanac; Robert Hendrickson, Doubleday, New York, 1984
Where the Trade Winds Blow; Bill Robinson, Charles Scribner's Sons, New York, 1963

Appendices

Appendix A: Navigational Lights

Navigational lights in the Virgin Islands are generally very reliable, but as with any light anywhere, never doubt that it could be not functioning when you need it most. The following characteristics may differ from those published and are subject to change without notice. Listing of lights reads from north to south and west to east. Range is in nautical miles.

Puerto Rico

LIGHT	LOCATION	CHARACTERISTICS	HT.	RANGE
Eastern Coast (S to N)				
Light #1 (priv.)	Palmas del Mar	Fl G 6 sec	12'	3 M
Light #2 (priv.)	Palmas del Mar	Q W/R	16'	3 M
Light #3 (priv.)	Palmas del Mar	Q G	6'	
Light #4 (priv.)	Palmas del Mar	Q R	6'	
Channel lighted buoy #1	Roosevelt Roads	Fl G 6 sec		4 M
Channel lighted buoy #2	Roosevelt Roads	Fl R 6 sec		4 M
Channel lighted buoy #3	Roosevelt Roads	Fl G 4 sec		4 M
Channel lighted buoy #6	Roosevelt Roads	Fl R 2.5 sec		3 M
Channel light #7	Roosevelt Roads	Fl G 4 sec	16'	4 M
Range-front	Roosevelt Roads	Q W	36'	
Range-rear (315°)	Roosevelt Roads	ISO W 6 sec	66'	
Isla Cabras	Roosevelt Roads	Q W	70'	9 M
Punta Puerca	Punta Puerca	ISO W 6 sec	142'	
Cabeza de Perro #7	Cabeza de Perro	Fl G 6 sec		4 M
Bajos Chinchorro del Sur	Bajos Chinchorro del Sur	Fl W 4 sec	25'	8 M
Isla Cabeza de Perro light*	Isla Cabeza de Perro	Fl W 6 sec	80'	8 M
Bajos Largo #3	Bajos Largo	Fl G 2.5 sec		3 M
North channel light #4	Puerto del Rey	Fl R 5 sec	10'	
North channel light #5	Puerto del Rey	Fl G 5 sec	28'	
South channel light #4	Puerto del Rey	Fl R 4 sec	28'	
South channel light #5	Puerto del Rey	Fl G 4 sec	6'	
Cayo Largo #1A	Cayo Largo	Fl G 4 sec		4 M
Isla Palominos #2	Isla Palominos	Fl R 4 sec		3 M
Lighted buoy #1	Fajardo	Fl G 2.5 sec		4 M
Puerto Chico Mar.	Fajardo	Fl R	13'	
Cayo Obispo Pier A	Fajardo	Q W	12'	
Cayo Obispo Pier B	Fajardo	F G	12'	
Cayo Obispo Pier C	Fajardo	F G	12'	
Cayo Obispo Pier D	Fajardo	F G	12'	

Spanish Virgin Islands

LIGHT	LOCATION	CHARACTERISTICS	HT.	RANGE
Puerto Rico to Culebra				
Isla Palominos #2	Isla Palominos	Fl R 4 sec		3 M
Cayo Lobito light	Cayo Lobito	Fl W 6 sec	110'	8 M
Punta Melones light	Culebra	Fl W 6 sec	45'	6 M
Punta del Solado light	Culebra	Fl W 2.5 sec	65'	5 M
Bajo Amarillo #2	Culebra	Fl R 4 sec		3 M
Cabezas Crespas #3	Culebra	Fl G 4 sec		4 M
Bajo Snapper #8	Culebra	Q R		3 M
Punta Colorada #9	Culebra	Fl G 4 sec		4 M

LIGHT	LOCATION	CHARACTERISTICS	HT.	RANGE
Isla Culebrita	Isla Culebrita	Fl W 10 sec	305'	13 M
Bajos Grampus #2	Bajos Grampus	Fl R 4 sec		3 M

Puerto Rico to Vieques

LIGHT	LOCATION	CHARACTERISTICS	HT.	RANGE
Range-front	Isla Cabras	Q W	70'	
Range-rear (025.4°)	Isla Cabras	ISO W 6 sec	142'	
Lighted Buoy #2	Pasaje de Vieques	Fl R 2.5 sec		4 M
Lighted Buoy #3	Pasaje de Vieques	Fl G 2.5 sec		4 M
Lighted Buoy #6	Pasaje de Vieques	Fl R 2.5 sec		3 M
Lighted Buoy #11	Radas Roosevelt Passage	Fl G 4 sec		4 M
Lighted Buoy #10	Radas Roosevelt Passage	Fl R 4 sec		3 M
Lighted Buoy #9	Radas Roosevelt Passage	Fl G 4 sec		4 M
Lighted Buoy #8	Radas Roosevelt Passage	Fl R 2.5 sec		3 M
Lighted Buoy #7	Radas Roosevelt Passage	Fl G 6 sec		4 M
Lighted Buoy #6	Radas Roosevelt Passage	Q R		3 M
Lighted Buoy #5	Radas Roosevelt Passage	Q G		3 M
Lighted Buoy #3	Radas Roosevelt Passage	Fl G 2.5 sec		3 M
Lighted Buoy #2	Radas Roosevelt Passage	Fl R 4 sec		3 M
Lighted Buoy #1	Radas Roosevelt Passage	Fl G 6 sec		4 M
Naval Pier lights (2)	Isla de Vieques	F R	15'	
Naval breakwater light	Isla de Vieques	Q R	10'	
Punta Mulas light	Isla de Vieques	Oc R 4 sec	68'	7 M
Punta Este light	Isla de Vieques	Fl W 6 sec	43'	7 M
Punta Conejo	Isla de Vieques	Fl W 6 sec	58'	7 M
Puerto Ferro	Isla de Vieques	Fl W 4 sec	56'	7 M

Spanish Virgin Islands to St. Thomas

LIGHT	LOCATION	CHARACTERISTICS	HT.	RANGE
Sail Rock #1	Sail Rock	Fl G 6s		4 M
Savana Island Light	Savana Island	Fl W 4s	300'	7 M

* W-8 M, R-6 M, R 021°-031° and 066°-161°, obscured 031°-066°

United States Virgin Islands

Approaches to St. Thomas

LIGHT	LOCATION	CHARACTERISTICS	HT.	RANGE
Sail Rock #1	Sail Rock	Fl G 6s		4 M
Savana Island Light	Savana Island	Fl W 4s	300'	7 M

St. Thomas/Charlotte Amalie

LIGHT	LOCATION	CHARACTERISTICS	HT.	RANGE
#2 W. Gregerie Channel	St. Thomas	Fl R 4s		3 M
#4 W. Gregerie Channel	St. Thomas	Fl R 2.5s		3 M
#5 W. Gregerie Channel	St. Thomas	Fl G 4s		4 M
#6 W. Gregerie Channel	St. Thomas	Fl R 4s	16'	4 M
WR1 W. Gregerie Channel	St. Thomas	Q G		3 M
#2 E. Gregerie Channel	St. Thomas	Fl R 2.5s		3 M
#3 E. Gregerie Channel	St. Thomas	Fl G 4s		4 M
#2 St. Thomas	St. Thomas	Fl R 6s		4 M
#3 St. Thomas	St. Thomas	Fl G 4a		4 M
#6 St. Thomas	St. Thomas	Fl R 4s		3 M
Berg Hill Range F.	St. Thomas	Q G	197'	
Berg Hill Range R.	St. Thomas	Oc G 4s	302'	

Southeastern St. Thomas

LIGHT	LOCATION	CHARACTERISTICS	HT.	RANGE
Buck Island	St. Thomas	Fl W 4s	125'	8 M
#1 (Priv)	Benner Bay	Fl G 2s		
#2 (Priv.)	Benner Bay	Fl R 2s		
Current Rock Light	Current Rock	Fl W 6s	20'	6 M

A Cruising Guide to the Virgin Islands

LIGHT	LOCATION	CHARACTERISTICS	HT.	RANGE
Pillsbury Sound and St. John				
Two Brothers Light	Two Brothers	Fl W 6s	23'	5 M
Stevens Cay Light	Stevens Cay	Fl W 4s	14'	5 M
Mingo Rock	Mingo Rock	Fl R 4s		4 M
Cruz Bay Sea Buoy	Cruz Bay	Fl W 4s	12'	5 M
Johnson Reef #1JR	Johnson Reef	Fl G 4s		4 M
"B" (NPS)	Johnson Reef	Fl Y 4s		
"D" (NPS)	Johnson Reef	Fl Y 4s		
St. Croix-Christiansted and Approaches				
Ham's Bluff Light	Ham's Bluff	Fl (2) W 30s	394'	16 M
St. Croix FAD "A" (Priv.)	St. Croix	Fl Y 4s		
St. Croix FAD "B" (Priv.)	St. Croix	Fl Y 4s		
#1	Christiansted	Fl G 2.5s		4 M
Entrance Channel range-F	Christiansted	Q W	45'	
Entrance Channel range-R	Christiansted	ISO W 6s	93'	
#3	Christiansted	Fl G 4s		
#6	Christiansted	Q R		3 M
#7	Christiansted	Fl G 4s	16'	4 M
Round Reef Light	Christiansted	Fl (2+1) G 6s		3 M
#9	Christiansted	Fl G 2.5s	16'	5 M
#10	Christiansted	Fl R 2.5s	17'	3 M
#11	Christiansted	Q G	10'	2 M
#12	Christiansted	Fl R 4s		3 M
#13	Christiansted	Fl G 4s	16'	4 M
#14	Christiansted	Fl R 6s		4 M
#5	Schooner Channel	Q G		
#6	Schooner Channel	Q R		
#7	Schooner Channel	Q G		
#8	Schooner Channel	Q R		
#9	Schooner Channel	Fl G 4s		
#10	Schooner Channel	Fl R 4s		
#11	Schooner Channel	Fl G 4s		
Wharf lights (2-Priv.)	Christiansted	Fxd W	12'	
St. Croix-North Coast				
Coakley Bay Light	Coakley Bay	Fl G 4s	16'	3 M
Buck Island Light	Buck Island	Fl W 4s	344'	6 M
St. Croix-South Coast				
Lime Tree Bay Range F.	Lime Tree Bay	Fxd G	165'	
Lime Tree Bay Range R.	Lime Tree Bay	Fxd G	195'	
Ch. East Aux. Range F.	Lime Tree Bay	Fxd R	55'	
Ch. East Aux. Range R.	Lime Tree Bay	Fxd R	70'	
#1	Lime Tree Bay	Q G		
#2	Lime Tree Bay	Q R		
#3	Lime Tree Bay	Fl G 5s		
#4	Lime Tree Bay	Fl R 5s		
#5 (Priv.)	Lime Tree Bay	Fl G 4s	14'	
#6 (Priv.)	Lime Tree Bay	Fl R 4s		
#7 (Priv.)	Lime Tree Bay	Fl G 2.5s	14'	
#8 (Priv.)	Lime Tree Bay	Fl R 2.5s	14'	
#9 (Priv.)	Lime Tree Bay	Fl G 2.5s	14'	
#11 (Priv.)	Lime Tree Bay	Fl G 2.5s	14'	

LIGHT	LOCATION	CHARACTERISTICS	HT.	RANGE
Channel Junction Light	Lime Tree Bay	Fl (2+1) G 6s	14'	
Basin #13 (Priv.)	Lime Tree Bay	Fl G 5s	14'	
Basin #15 (Priv.)	Lime Tree Bay	Fl G 4s	14'	
Basin #17 (Priv.)	Lime Tree Bay	Fl G 2.5s	14'	
#1 (Priv.)	Krause Lagoon	Fl G 4s		
#2 (Priv.)	Krause Lagoon	Fl R 6s		
#3 (Priv.)	Krause Lagoon	Fl G 4s		
#4 (Priv.)	Krause Lagoon	Fl R 4s	18'	
#4A (Priv.)	Krause Lagoon	Q R		
#5 (Priv.)	Krause Lagoon	Q G	14'	
#6 (Priv.)	Krause Lagoon	Q R	14'	
#7 (Priv.)	Krause Lagoon	Fl G 4s	15'	
#8 (Priv.)	Krause Lagoon	Fl R2.5s	15'	
#9 (Priv.)	Krause Lagoon	Fl G 4s	16'	
#10 (Priv.)	Krause Lagoon	Fl R2.5s	16'	
#11 (Priv.)	Krause Lagoon	Fl G4s	16'	
#12 (Priv.)	Krause Lagoon	Fl R 2.5s	16'	
#13 (Priv.)	Krause Lagoon	Fl G 4s	16'	
#14 (Priv.)	Krause Lagoon	Fl R 2.5s	16'	
#16 (Priv.)	Krause Lagoon	Fl R 2.5s	16'	
#17 (Priv.)	Krause Lagoon	Fl G 4s	16'	
E. Mooring (Priv.)	Krause Lagoon	Fl R 5s	12'	
W. Turning (Priv.)	Krause Lagoon	Fl W 5s	12'	
Cross Channel Range-f	Krause Lagoon	Q G	14'	
Cross Channel Range-r	Krause Lagoon	Oc G 4s	28'	
Cross Channel #1	Krause Lagoon	Fl G 4s		
Cross Channel #2	Krause Lagoon	Fl R 4s	14'	
Cross Channel #3	Krause Lagoon	Fl G 2.5s	14'	
Cross Channel #4	Krause Lagoon	Fl R 2.5s	14'	
Cross Channel #5	Krause Lagoon	Q G		
St. Croix-Frederiksted				
Southwest Cape Light	Frederiksted	Fl W 6s	45'	7 M
Mooring Light (Priv.)	Frederiksted	Fl W 4s	18'	
Harbor Light	Frederiksted	Fl W/R 4s	42'	8 M
Pier Lights (Priv.)	Frederiksted	Fl R 4s	12'	

British Virgin Islands

LIGHT	LOCATION	CHARACTERISTICS	HT.	RANGE
Tortola				
Soper's Hole Light	Soper's Hole	Fl R	16'	
Hog's Valley Point	Hog's Valley Point	Fl R 4s		
Scotch Bank	Road Harbour	Fl R 8s		
Lark Bank	Road Harbour	Fl G 3s		
Road Harbour Range F	Road Harbour	Fxd R	37'	3 M
Road Harbour Range R	Road Harbour	Fxd R	52'	3 M
Harbour Spit	Road Harbour	Fl R 2s		
Connall Shoal	Road Harbour	Fl R 6s		
Wickham's Breakwater	Road Harbour	Fl R 3s		
Cruise Ship Dock	Road Harbour	Fl W 3s		
Fat Hog's Bay	Fat Hog's Bay	Fl (2) W 5s	25'	5 M
Beef Island				
Bellamy Cay Light	Trellis Bay	Fxd W		

LIGHT	LOCATION	CHARACTERISTICS	HT.	RANGE
Salt Island				
Salt Island Light	Salt Island	Fl W 10s	175'	14 M
Ginger Island				
Ginger Island Light	Ginger Island	Fl W 5s	498'	14 M
Virgin Gorda				
Pajaros Point Light	Pajaros Point	Fl (3) W 15s	200'	16 M
Cow's Mouth Light	Cow's Mouth	Fl (2) Y 10s	20'	10 M
Anegada				
Anegada Light	Anegada	Fl W 10s	62'	10 M
Anegada Passage				
Sombrero Light	Sombrero	Fl W 10s	157'	20 M

Appendix B: Marinas

Some of the marinas listed below may be untenable in certain winds and dockside depths listed may not reflect entrance channel depths at low water. Always check with the Dockmaster prior to arrival. All the marinas can handle your garbage disposal problems however some may levy a charge per bag for those who are not guests at their docks. For cruisers seeking services *Nearby* may mean either a walk or short taxi ride away.

Puerto Rico - Eastern Coast

MARINA	LOCATION	FUEL	SLIPS	WEB SITE, EMAIL, PHONE
Puerto Rico				
Cangrejos Y.C.*	Carolina	D & G	110	http://www.cangrejosyachtclub.com/
Cayo Obispo Marina	Fajardo	D	239	787-643-2180
Club Náutico de San Juan	San Juan	D & G	Ltd.	http://www.nauticodesanjuan.com/
El Conquistador	Fajardo	D & G	18	http://www.elconresort.com/
Mar. del Conquistador**	Fajardo	Private	Private	
Puerto Chico Marina	Fajardo	D & G	276	http://www.marinapuertochico.com/
Puerto Real Marina***	Fajardo	None	None	863-2188
San Juan Bay Marina	San Juan	D & G	120	http://www.sjbaymarina.com/
Sea Lover's Marina	Fajardo	None	130	
Sun Bay Marina	Fajardo	D & G	282	http://www.sunbaymarina.com/
Villa Marina	Fajardo	D & G	400	http://villamarinapr.com/

* *Congrejos Yacht Club* is a private facility for members only. A bridge with 24' vertical clearance limits entry.
** *Marina del Conquistador* is a private facility for guests of the *El Conquistador* resort.
****Puerto Real Marina* is a dry-stack storage facility with no amenities or even a dock.

United States Virgin Islands

MARINA	LOCATION	FUEL	WEB SITE, EMAIL, PHONE
St. Croix			
Green Cay Marina	Christiansted	D & G	http://www.tamarindreefresort.com
Jones Maritime Co.	Christiansted	None	www.jonesmaritime.com
Salt River Marina	Salt River	24-hour advance notice for fuel	
Silver Bay Dock	Gallows Bay	None	
St. Croix Marine	Gallows Bay	D & G	www.stcroixmarine.com
St. Croix YC Marina	Teague Bay	None	http://www.stcroixyc.com/
St. John			
Caneel Bay Shipyard	Caneel Bay	D & G	340-693-8771
St. Thomas			
American Yacht Harbour	Red Hook	D & G	http://www.igy-americanyachtharbor.com/
Boater's Haven Marina	Charlotte Amalie	None	
Compass Point Marin	Benner Bay	None	

MARINA	LOCATION	FUEL	WEB SITE, EMAIL, PHONE
Crown Bay Marina	Crown Bay	D & G	http://www.crownbay.com/
Fish Hawk Marina*	Benner Bay	None	340-775-9058
Frenchtown Harbour	Charlotte Amalie	None	
Independent Boatyard	Benner Bay	None	http://ibyvi.com/
La Vida Marina	Benner Bay	None	
Oasis Cove Marina	Benner Bay	None	340-244-0442
Saga Haven	Benner Bay	None	http://www.sagahaven.com/
Sapphire Beach	Sapphire Beach	None	http://www.sapphirebeachmarina.com/
Tropical Marine	Benner Bay	None	
Vessup Point Marina	Red Hook	None	
Yacht Haven Grande	Charlotte Amalie	D & G	http://igy-yachthavengrande.com/

* *Fish Hawk Marina* is used primarily by shallow draft powerboats

British Virgin Islands

MARINA	LOCATION	FUEL	WEB SITE, EMAIL, PHONE
Jost Van Dyke			
Foxy's Taboo	Long Bay	None	http://foxysbar.com/
Little Harbour Marina	Little Harbour	None	
North Latitude Marina	Great Harbour	D & G	http://northlatitudemarina.com/
Peter Island			
Peter Island Yacht Harb.	Sprat Bay	D & G	http://peterisland.com/marina
Tortola			
Baugher's Bay Marina	Road Town	D & G	mcconsultants@surfbvi.com/
Fort Burt Marina	Road Harbour	D & G	fortburt@surfbvi.com
Hannah Bay Marina	Nanny Cay	D & G	marina.reservation@gmail.com
Harbour View Marina	Fat Hogs Bay	D & G	http://www.bviharbourview.com
Hodges Creek Marina	Maya Cove	D & G	284-494-5000
Village Cay Resort	Road Town	D & G	
Inner Harbour Marina	Road Town	D & G	
Joma Marina	West End	D & G	http://www.admiralbvi.com/
Manuel Reef Marina	Sea Cows Bay		http://www.manuel-reef-marina.com/
Mega Services Marina	Road Town	D & G	
Moorings Mariner Inn	Road Harbour	D & G	
Nanny Cay Marina	Nanny Cay	D & G	http://nannycay.com/
Penn's Landing Marina	Fat Hogs Bay	D & G	http://www.pennslandingbvi.com
Prospect Reef	Road Town	D & G	
Pusser's Marina Cay	Marina Cay	D & G	http://www.pussers.com/t-marina-cay.aspx
Road Reef Marina	Road Harbour	None	
Scrub Island Marina	Scrub Island	D & G	http://www.scrubisland.com/
Soper's Hole Marina	Frenchman's Cay	D & G	www.sopersholemarina.com/port/Home.aspx
Sunsail	Frenchman's Cay	D & G	
Tortola Yacht Services	Road Town		
Tropic Isle	Maya Cove	D & G	
Village Cay Marina	Road Town	D & G	http://villagecaybvi.com/
Virgin Gorda			
Bitter End Yacht Club	North Sound	D & G	http://www.beyc.com/
Pussers Leverick Bay	North Sound	D & G	https://www.pussers.com/t-leverick-bay.aspx
Saba Rock Island Marina	North Sound	None	http://www.sabarock.com/
Virgin Gorda Yacht Harb.	The Valley	D & G	http://www.virgingordayachtharbour.com/
YC Costa Smeralda	Biras Creek	D & G	http://marina.yccs.com/

Appendix C: Service Facilities

As with any place, businesses come and go, sometimes seemingly overnight. Certain entries on the following lists may no longer exist by the time this guide is published or may have changed their names or phone numbers.

When renting a car in the U.S. Virgin Islands and British Virgin Islands, you might wish to consider a four-wheel drive vehicle as some of the roads can be quite steep. If you wish to rent a car in the British Virgin Islands you will need your driver's license and you will also need to purchase a temporary driving permit available at any car rental agency. Don't forget, in the United States and British Virgin Islands you must drive on the left.

Appendix C1: Spanish Virgin Islands
(and Puerto Rico)

All telephone numbers in Puerto Rico and the Spanish Virgin Islands are area code 787,
1-787 must be dialed as a prefix before dialing all the numbers listed below when in Puerto Rico.

FACILITY	LOCATION	PHONE	WEB SITE OR EMAIL ADDRESS
AUTO RENTALS			
A Car Rental	Vieques	319-5739	
AAA	San Juan	791-1465	
Ambassador	San Juan	726-6982	
Allied	San Juan	725-5350	http://www.alliedcarrentalpr.com/
Avis	Mayaguez (Airport)	842-6154	www.avis.com
Avis	Ponce (Airport)	842-6154	www.avis.com
Avis	San Juan (Airport)	253-5926	www.avis.com
Blackbeards	Vieques	741-1892	http://www.blackbeardsports.com/
Budget	Aguadilla (Airport)	890-0110	www.budget.com
Budget	Ponce (Airport)	848-0907	www.budget.com
Budget	San Juan (Airport)	791-0600	www.budget.com
Cabrera	Fajardo	860-0880	
Carlos Jeep Rental	Culebra	742-3514	http://www.carlosjeeprental.com/
Charlies Car Rental	Aguadilla (Airport)	890-8929	http://www.charliecars.com/
Charlies Car Rental	San Juan (Airport)	728-2418	http://www.charliecars.com/
Charlies Car Rental	San Juan (Condado)	721-6525	http://www.charliecars.com/
Culebra UTV Rentals	Culebra	525-5456	culebrautvrental@yahoo.com
Coral Reef Car	Culebra	742-0055	
Culebra Car Rental	Culebra	742-3277	
Diaz Rental	Vieques	741-0135	
Dick and Cathy	Culebra	742-0062	
Dollar Renta A Car	San Juan (Airport)	791-5500	https://www.dollar.com
Dreda & Fonsin's	Vieques	741-8163	
Enterprise	Aguadilla (Airport)	890-3732	www.enterprise.com
Enterprise	Ponce (Airport)	844-4534	www.enterprise.com
Enterprise	San Juan (Airport)	253-3722	www.enterprise.com
Hertz	Aguadilla (Airport)	890-5650	www.hertz.com
Hertz	Mayaguez	851-3830	www.hertz.com
Hertz	Ponce (Airport)	843-1685	www.hertz.com
Hertz	San Juan (Airport)	791-0840	www.hertz.com
Island Car Rental	Vieques	741-1666	http://www.islandcarrentalpr.com/
Jerry's Jeeps	Culebra	742-0587	http://www.jerrysjeeprental.com/
Leaseway	Aguadilla	337-0828	leaseway@leasewaypr.com
Leaseway	Bayamón	337-0828	leaseway@leasewaypr.com

FACILITY	LOCATION	PHONE	WEB SITE OR EMAIL ADDRESS
Leaseway	Carolina (Airport)	337-0828	leaseway@leasewaypr.com
Maritza's Car	Vieques	741-0078	http://www.maritzascarrental.com/
National	Aguadilla (Airport)	877-222-9058	https://www.nationalcar.com/
National	San Juan (Airport)	977-222-9058	https://www.nationalcar.com/
Payless	San Juan (Airport)	625-8880	https://www.paylesscar.com/
Popular	Humacao	852-4848	https://www.popularautorentals.com/english/
Popular	Mayaguez	265-4848	https://www.popularautorentals.com/english/
Popular	Ponce	259-4848	https://www.popularautorentals.com/english/
Popular	San Juan	763-4848	https://www.popularautorentals.com/english/
Prestige	Culebra	742-3242	
Quality Car Rental	San Juan	791-3800	
R & W Jeep Rental	Culebra	742-0563	
Rancho Ruvy	Culebra	742-0237	
Scooters for Rent	Vieques	741-7722	http://www.scootersvieques.com/
Seaside Rentals	Culebra	742-3855	
Steve's Car Rentals	Vieques	741-8135	
Target	San Juan (Airport)	728-1447	http://www.targetrentacar.com/
Thrifty	Aguadilla (Airport)	890-4070	https://www.thrifty.com/
Thrifty	Fajardo	860-2030	https://www.thrifty.com/
Thrifty	Mayaguez	834-1590	https://www.thrifty.com/
Thrifty	Ponce	290-2525	https://www.thrifty.com/
Thrifty	San Juan (Airport)	256-2525	https://www.thrifty.com/
Vias Car Rental	Arecibo	879-1132	http://www.viascarrental.com/
Vias Car Rental	Humacao	223-3448	http://www.viascarrental.com/
Vias Car Rental	Palmas del Mar	852-1591	http://www.viascarrental.com/
Vieques Car Rental	Vieques	741-1037	http://viequescarrental.com/
Vieques Cars	Vieques	741-1212	
World Car Rental	Fajardo	863-9696	
DIESEL/GENERATOR REPAIR & PARTS			
Basic Marine	Fajardo	860-5151	
Basic Marine	Puerto Nuevo	793-6000	
Basic Marine	San Juan	780-5151	
Caribbean Marine	San Juan	765-7417	
Cayo Obispo Mar.	Cayo Obispo	863-0370	
Continental Marine	San Juan	765-7440	
Cummins Marine	Puerto Nuevo	793-0300	
Diesel Generator	Caguas	646-9023	
Industrial & Marine	Fajardo	725-5946	http://www.industrialmarinepr.com/
International Mar.	Guayanabo	782-1396	
International Mar.	Rio Pedras	782-1396	
Lumar Marine	San Juan	722-9414	
Luscar Marine	Cabo Rojo	851-4945	
Luscar Marine	La Parguera	851-4945	
Marina Costa Azul	La Parguera	899-1179	
Marine Center	Cabo Rojo	255-4480	
Marine Center	Fajardo	863-0680	
Marine Center	Puerto Chico Marina	860-5150	
Marine Center	Puerto Del Rey Mar.	863-3863	
Marine Center	San Juan	792-9666	
Marine Mechanical	Fajardo	655-3702	http://marinemechanicalservice.com/
Miguel Figueroa	Fajardo	863-5219	

FACILITY	LOCATION	PHONE	WEB SITE OR EMAIL ADDRESS
Monterey Marine	Fajardo	863-0680	
Motor Sport	Guaynado	790-4900	http://motorsport-pr.com/
Motor Sport	Puerto Del Rey Mar.	801-4521	http://motorsport-pr.com/
National Marine	San Juan	782-1396	
Performance Engine	Fajardo	860 2140	
Ponce Yacht	Ponce	842-9003	http://ponceyachtandfishingclub.com/
Ponce Yacht & F. C.	Ponce	842-9003	
Powerboat Marine	San Juan	771-6372	fernandokuan@gmail.com
Re-Power Marine	Fajardo	863-9786	
Rimco- *Caterpillar*	San Juan	792-4300	http://www.rimcocat.com/
San Juan Bay Mar.	San Juan	235-9633	http://www.sjbaymarina.com/
San Juan Towing	San Juan	370-1690	
Veradero Puerto V.	La Parguera	899-5588	
Villa Marina	Fajardo	863-5131	http://www.villamarinapr.com/
West India Mach. & Sup.	San Juan	721-7640	

DIVING

FACILITY	LOCATION	PHONE	WEB SITE OR EMAIL ADDRESS
Aqua Adventure	San Juan	636-8811	info@aquaadventurepr.com
Aquatica	Aguadilla	890-6071	info@aquaticapr.com
Blackbeards	Vieques	741-1892	info@blackbeardssports.com
Culebra Divers	Culebra	742-0803	contact@culebradivers.com
Culebra Island Adv.	Culebra	529-3536	Info@CulebraIslandAdventures.com
Culebra Snorkel & Dive	Culebra	435-3662	questions@culebrasnorkelingcenter.com
Dive Puerto Rico	Fajardo	863-3483	seaventures@divepuertorico.com
Paradise SCUBA	La Parguera	899-7611	paradisescubapr@gmail.com
Rincon Diving	Rincon	506-3483	rincondiving@gmail.com
San Juan Divers	San Juan	309-6556	info@sanjuandiver.com

ELECTRONICS - MARINE

FACILITY	LOCATION	PHONE	WEB SITE OR EMAIL ADDRESS
El Pescador	Fajardo	863-0350	
Industrial & Marine	Fajardo	725-5946	http://www.industrialmarinepr.com/
Lumar Marine	San Juan	235-9633	http://www.sjbaymarina.com/
Marine Center	Cabo Rojo	255-4480	
Marine Center	Fajardo	863-0680	
Marine Center	Puerto Chico Marina	860-5150	
Marine Center	Puerto Del Rey Marina	863-3863	
Marine Center	San Juan	792-6188	
Martinez Marine Serv.	Puerto Del Rey Marina	863-4646	info@martinezmarine.com
Motor Sport	Guaynado	790-4900	http://motorsport-pr.com/
Motor Sport	Puerto Del Rey Marina	801-4521	http://motorsport-pr.com/
Playa Marine	Salinas	824-5337	http://www.playamarine.com/
Professional Yacht	Puerto Del Rey Marina	860-8524	
San Juan Towing	San Juan	723-0011	
Schafer & Brown	Cabo Rojo	255-2351	
Skipper's Shop	Fajardo	863-2455	
West Marine	Fajardo	801-2700	http://www.westmarine.com/
West Marine	San Juan	998-1891	http://www.westmarine.com

FABRICATION

FACILITY	LOCATION	PHONE	WEB SITE OR EMAIL ADDRESS
Caraousel	Puerto Real	396-3650	
Grafton Machine	Mayaguez		
Island Marine	Cayo Obispo	382-3051	
Negron Arron Work	Salinas	487-7064	
Puerto Del Rey Marina	Ceiba	860-1000	http://www.puertodelrey.com/

FACILITY	LOCATION	PHONE	WEB SITE OR EMAIL ADDRESS
San Juan Propeller	San Juan	721-7403	octagonmarine@aol.com
San Juan Towing	San Juan	370-1690	
Vall-Llobera	Fajardo	860-8801	
Villa Marina	Fajardo	863-5131	http://www.villamarinapr.com/
Willco Welding	Ceiba	860-4471	

HAUL-OUT

FACILITY	LOCATION	PHONE	WEB SITE OR EMAIL ADDRESS
Cangrejos YC -24' brid.	Carolina	727-4150	cangrejosyachtclub@yahoo.com
Cayo Obispo Marina	Cayo Obispo	863-0370	
Island Marine	Cayo Obispo	382-3051	
Palmas Del Marina	Humacao	285-8454	http://www.palmasdelmar.com/
Ponce Yacht	Ponce	842-9003	http://ponceyachtandfishingclub.com/
Puerto Del Rey Mar.	Ceiba	860-1000	http://www.puertodelrey.com/
San Juan Bay Mar.	San Juan	235-9633	http://www.sjbaymarina.com/
Veradero Fajardo	Las Croabas	656-7300	
Veradero Puerto V.	La Parguera	899-5588	
Villa Marina	Fajardo	863-5131	http://www.villamarinapr.com/
Villa Pesquera	Puerto Real	458-4332	

HULL REPAIR/PAINTING

FACILITY	LOCATION	PHONE	WEB SITE OR EMAIL ADDRESS
Cayo Obispo Mar.	Cayo Obispo	863-0370	
Island Marine	Cayo Obispo	382-3051	
Los Españoles Repair	Ceiba	860-1000	info@losespanolesboatrepair.com
Marina Palmas del Mar	Humacao	285-8454	info@theyachtclubmarina.com
Mejia Marine Serv.	Salinas	824-4929	
Ponce Yacht	Ponce	842-9003	http://ponceyachtandfishingclub.com/
Professional Yacht	Puerto Del Rey Marina	860-8524	
Puerto Del Rey Marina	Ceiba	860-1000	http://www.puertodelrey.com/
San Juan Bay Marina	San Juan	235-9633	http://www.sjbaymarina.com/
Vall-Llobera	Fajardo	860-8801	
Veradero Puerto Viejo	La Parguera	899-5588	
Villa Marina	Fajardo	863-5131	http://www.villamarinapr.com/
Villa Pesquera	Puerto Real	458-4332	

INFLATABLES & LIFE RAFTS

FACILITY	LOCATION	PHONE	WEB SITE OR EMAIL ADDRESS
Captain's Warehouse	Fajardo	860-8591	
Life Rafts of PR	San Juan	723-3237	http://www.liferafts-inc.com/
Marine Inflatables	Fajardo	801-2018	
Monterey Marine	Fajardo	863-0680	
Playa Marine	Salinas	824-5337	http://www.playamarine.com/
PostNet	Ponce	840-8227	
Schafer & Brown	Cabo Rojo	255-2351	
Skipper's Shop	Fajardo	863-2455	
West Marine	Fajardo	801-2700	http://www.westmarine.com/
West Marine	San Juan	998-1891	http://www.westmarine.com

INTERNET ACCESS

FACILITY	LOCATION	PHONE	WEB SITE OR EMAIL ADDRESS
AWA Comouter	Salinas	824-3883	
Boqueron Travel	Boqueron	851-4751	
Caribbean Internet	San Juan	728-3992	
Excetera	Culebra	742-0844	
Ricky's Pizzeria	Fajardo	860-4215	
Sears (Plaza Caribe)	Ponce	259-6000	

MARINE SUPPLIES

FACILITY	LOCATION	PHONE	WEB SITE OR EMAIL ADDRESS
A.E. Marine	La Parguera	899-4075	

FACILITY	LOCATION	PHONE	WEB SITE OR EMAIL ADDRESS
Astro Industrial Sup.	San Juan	721-4046	
Basic Marine	Fajardo	860-5151	
Basic Marine	Puerto Del Rey Marina	801-2605	
CEA Industrial Sup.	San Juan	751-6570	http://www.ceaindustrialpr.net/
Costa Parguera	La Parguera	899-1933	
Industrial & Marine	Fajardo	725-5946	http://www.industrialmarinepr.com/
Lumar Marine	La Parguera	851-4945	
Lumar Marine	San Juan	722-9414	
Marine Center	Fajardo	863-0680	
Marine Center	Puerto Chico Marina	860-5150	
Marine Center	Puerto Del Rey Marina	863-3863	
Marine Mechanical Ser.	Fajardo	655-3702	marinemechanicalservices@gmail.com
Monterey Marine	Fajardo	863-0680	
Motor Sport	Guaynado	790-4900	http://motorsport-pr.com/
Motor Sport	Puerto Del Rey Marina	801-4521	http://motorsport-pr.com/
Playa Marine	Salinas	824-5337	http://www.playamarine.com/
Skipper's Shop	Fajardo	863-2455	
Villa Marina	Fajardo	863-5131	http://www.villamarinapr.com/
West Marine	Fajardo	801-2700	http://www.westmarine.com/
West Marine	San Juan	998-1891	http://www.westmarine.com

OUTBOARD REPAIR

FACILITY	LOCATION	PHONE	WEB SITE OR EMAIL ADDRESS
A.E. Marine	La Parguera	899-4075	
Basic Marine	Fajardo	860-5151	
Basic Marine	Puerto Del Rey Mar.	801-2605	
Basic Marine	Puerto Nuevo	793-6000	
Carib. Mar. Supply	San Juan	765-7417	
Costa Parguera	La Parguera	899-1933	
Lumar Marine	La Parguera	851-4945	
Lumar Marine	San Juan	722-9414	
Marine Center	Fajardo	863-0680	
Marine Center	Puerto Chico Mar.	860-5150	
Marine Center	Puerto Del Rey Mar.	863-3863	
Monterey Marine	Fajardo	863-0680	
Motor Sport	Guaynado	790-4900	http://motorsport-pr.com/
Motor Sport	Puerto Del Rey Mar.	801-4521	http://motorsport-pr.com/
Motor Sport- Yamaha	Puerto Del Rey Marina	801-4521	
Outboard Motor Center	Santurce	728-5395	
Skipper's Shop	Fajardo	863-2455	
Tropical Marine-OMC	San Juan	750-4125	
Veradero Puerto Viejo	La Parguera	899-5588	

PROPANE

FACILITY	LOCATION	PHONE	WEB SITE OR EMAIL ADDRESS
Empire Gas	Salinas	824-6204	Empire@prtc.net
Perez Gas	Culebra	598-7769	
Playa Marine	Salinas	824-5337	crew@playamarine.com
Puerto Del Rey Marina	Ceiba	860-1000	marina@puertodelrey.com

PROPELLERS

FACILITY	LOCATION	PHONE	WEB SITE OR EMAIL ADDRESS
FJ Propeller	Puerto Del Rey Marina	236-8812	Bob@fjprop.com
Performance Engine	Fajardo	860 2140	
San Juan Propeller	San Juan	721-7403	octagonmarine@aol.com

REFRIGERATION & AIR CONDITIONING

FACILITY	LOCATION	PHONE	WEB SITE OR EMAIL ADDRESS
Basic Marine	Fajardo	860-5151	

FACILITY	LOCATION	PHONE	WEB SITE OR EMAIL ADDRESS
Basic Marine	Puerto Nuevo	793-6000	
Basic Marine	San Juan	780-5151	
Best AC & Refrigeration	Villa Marina	462-1336	
Centro Cruisair	San Juan	727-3637	
Cool Tech	Fajardo	860-2615	
May Day Marine	Area Este	376-6967	
Ocean Marine	Rio Piedras	763-7285	
Professional Yacht	Puerto Del Rey Marina	860-8524	
San Juan Towing	San Juan	723-0011	
Simcox Ref. Supply	San Juan	724-0254	http://www.simcoxrefrigerationpr.com/
Twin Marine	Puerto Real		
Vall-Llobera	Fajardo	860-8801	
RIGGING			
Howie Rayber	Salinas	824-1611	
Rig Keepers	Puerto Del Rey	698-2026	
The Rigging Shop	Puerto Del Rey	860-1000	riggingshop@hotmail.com
Tradewinds	Salinas	824-1611	
Vall-Llobera	Fajardo	860-8801	
SAIL AND CANVAS REPAIR			
Armstrong Sails	San Juan	724-3336	
Atlantic Canvas	Puerto Del Rey Marina	860-1433	atcan@coqui.net
Caribbean Sails	Cayo Obispo Marina	463-7245	
Fajardo Canvas	Fajardo	863-3761	http://fajardocanvasandsa.wix.com/
Pomce Sailing Center	Ponce	378-5032	flugo@quantumsails.com
Rigging Works		313-9344	rigging.w@gmail.com
Tradewinds	Salinas	863-3761	

Appendix C2: U. S. Virgin Islands

The area code for the United States Virgin Islands is 340.

FACILITY	LOCATION	PHONE	WEB SITE OR EMAIL ADDRESS
AUTO RENTALS			
ABC Rentals	Havensight	776-1222	
Amalie Car Rentals	Charlotte Amalie	774-0688	https://www.amaliecar.com/
Atlas Leasing	Christiansted, S. C.	773-2886	
Avis	Frederiksted, S. C.	778-9365	https://www.avis.com/en/locations/cx
Avis	St. Thomas (Airport)	774-1468	https://www.avis.com/en/locations/cx
Avis	Christiansted	713-1347	https://www.avis.com/en/locations/cx
Best Rent-a-Car	St. John	693-8177	
Bougainvillea	St. John	776-6420	
Budget	Christiansted, S.C.	778-9636	https://budgetstcroix.com/
Budget	Frederiksted, S.C.	713-9289	asimmonds@budgetstcoix.com
Budget	Sapphire Bay	776-5744	asimmonds@budgetstcoix.com
C&C Car Rental	Cruz Bay	693-8164	http://www.cccarrental.com/
Caribbean Jeep	Christiansted, St. Croix	773-7227	
Centerline Rentals	Christiansted, S.C.	713-0550	http://www.stxrentalcar.com/
Centerline Rentals	St. Croix (Airport)	778-0441	airport@ccrvi.com
Conrad Sutton Car	Cruz Bay	776-6479	https://www.conradcars.com/
Cool Breezes Jeep	Cruz Bay	776-6588	http://www.coolbreezecarrental.com/
Courtesy Car Rental	Cruz Bay	776-6650	https://www.courtesycarrental.com/
Cowpet Auto Rental	Frenchtown	775-7213	
Delbert Hill Jeep	Cruz Bay	776-6637	

FACILITY	LOCATION	PHONE	WEB SITE OR EMAIL ADDRESS
Denzil Cline Car	Cruz Bay	776-6715	
Discount Car Rental	Charlotte Amalie	776-4858	http://www.discountcar.vi/
Go Around Car	Christiansted, St. Croix	778-8881	
Hertz (Airport)	Frederiksted, St. Croix	778-9744	
Hertz (Airport)	St. Thomas	774-1879	http://www.rentacarstcroix.com/
Jeeps VI	St. Thomas	774-5840	http://www.jeepsvi.com/
Judi of Croix	Christiansted, St. Croix	773-2123	info@judiofcroix.com
L&L Jeep Rental	St. John	776-1120	http://bookajeep.com/contact-us.html
L&L Jeep Rentals	St. Thomas	774-4889	http://bookajeep.com/contact-us.html
Lionel Jeep Rental	Cruz Bay	693-8764	lioneljeeprental@hotmail.com
Midwest Car Rental	Christiansted, St. Croix	772-0438	info@midwestautorental.com
National	Subbase	776-3616	http://www.subbasedrydock.com/
Olympic Rent A Car	Christiansted, St. Croix	773-2200	http://www.olympicstcroix.com/
Pais Car Rental	Cruz Bay	776-6173	
Paradise Car Rental	Charlotte Amalie	774-2203	
Penn's Jeep Rental	Cruz Bay	776-6530	
Rent A Motion	St. Thomas	774-5840	http://www.rentamotion.com/
Spencer's Jeep	Cruz Bay	693-8784	
St. Croix Car Rental	Christiansted, St. Croix	778-7444	
St. John Car Rental	Cruz Bay	776-6103	https://www.stjohncarrental.com/
St. Thomas Comm.	Crown Bay	776-4324	
Thrifty	Christiansted, St. Croix	773-7200	
Traveler's	Christiansted, St. Croix	778-6849	
Tri-Island Rent A Car	Havensight	776-2879	e.laborde@worldnet.att.net
Tri-Island Rent A Car	Red Hook	775-1200	e.laborde@worldnet.att.net
Varlack Ventures	St. John	776-6412	http://www.varlack-ventures.com/

CHARTER BOATS

FACILITY	LOCATION	PHONE	WEB SITE OR EMAIL ADDRESS
Adventure Cat	Charlotte Amalie	775-7245	
Adventure Centers	Charlotte Amalie	774-2992	adventurecenteroffice@gmail.com
Admiralty Yacht	Charlotte Amalie	800-544-0494	
Bajor Yacht Charters	Charlotte Amalie	800-524-8292	http://www.bajoryachts.com/
Bilinda Charters	St. Croix	514-2270	http://www.sailbilinda.com/
Caribbean Soul	St. Thomas	690-1121	www.caribbeansoulcharters.com
Charterboat Center	Red Hook	775-7990	
Cruzin Away	Cruz Bay	244-9633	http://www.cruzinaway.com/
Dancing Dolphin	Frenchtown	774-8899	
Daydreamer	Charlotte Amalie	775-2584	
Daysail Fantasy	Red Hook	513-3212	http://daysailfantasy.com
Diva to Buck Island	St. Croix	778-4675	
Fanfare Charters	Red Hook	775-1326	
Flagship	Charlotte Amalie	774-5630	http://www.flagshipvi.com/
Grand Nellie	Red Hook	513-4643	ellen@grandnellie.com
Heavenly Days Cats	Bolongo Bay	800-524-4746	http://www.bolongobay.com/
Iguana Sailing Ch.	Long Bay	513-2693	
Isle Okopa Charters	St. Thomas	227-2474	http://isleokopa.com/
Jester Sailing Ch.	Point Pleasant Resort	513-2459	http://www.sailjester.com/
Jones Maritime Co.	Christiansted, St. Croix	773-4709	www.jonesmaritime.com
Lady Lynsey Cat.	Charlotte Amalie	775-3333	
Latitude	Red Hook	779-2495	
Mile Mark Charters	Christiansted, St. Croix	773-2628	
Morningstar Charters	Point Pleasant Res.	775-1111	http://www.morningstarcharter.com/

FACILITY	LOCATION	PHONE	WEB SITE OR EMAIL ADDRESS
New Horizons	Sapphire Beach Res	775-1171	http://newhorizons.daysails.com/
Nightwind Charters	Sapphire Beach Mar.	775-4110	http://www.stjohndaysail.com/
Ocean Runner	Cruz Bay	693-8809	info@oceanrunnerusvi.com
Red Hook Boat Service	Red Hook	775-6501	
Reef Queen	Christiansted, St. Croix	773-3434	
Sadie Sea Charters	St. John	514-0778	http://www.sadiesea.com/
Sea Gypsy Charters	Cruz Bay	693-8020	
Simplicity Charters	Red Hook	774-9348	http://www.simplicitycharters.com/
Stand Up Paddleboards	Cruz Bay	514-5527	supstjohn@gmail.com
Stewart Yacht Charters	Red Hook	800-432-6118	http://www.stewartyachtcharters.com/
Sundance	Red Hook	779-1722	
Sunny Liston Tours	St. Thomas	777-3451	http://www.sunnylistontours.com/
The Cat	St Thomas	998-6789	http://thevicat.com/
Tropic Isle Charters	Cruz Bay	776-6863	
True Love	Sapphire Beach Mar.	779-1640	
VIP Yacht Charters	Charlotte Amalie	774-9224	http://www.vipyachts.com/
Waterplay	Charlotte Amalie	774-2584	
Watersports Safaris	Charlotte Amalie	776-1690	
Wayward Sailor	St. John	473-9705	waywardsailor@hotmail.com
Winifred	Red Hook	775-7898	
Yacht Vacations	Charlotte Amalie	776-5300	
DIESEL REPAIR/PARTS			
ABC Rentals	Havensight	776-1222	
Al's Marine	Christiansted, S.C.	773-5611	
Coral Bay Marine	Coral Harbor	776-6665	
Crown Bay Maritime	Subbase	774-5432	http://www.subbasedrydock.com/
DDS (Dave's Diesel)	Benner Bay	775-9912	davesdiesel@islands.vi
Diesel Power	St. Thomas	775-3855	
Gary's Marine Service	St. Thomas	779-2717	
Haulover Marine	Subbase	776-2078	http://www.subbasedrydock.com/
Independent Btyd.	Benner Bay	776-0466	http://ibyvi.com/
Island Marine	Gallows Bay, St. Croix	773-0289	
Island Marine	Crown Bay	714-0788	
Island Marine	Red Hook	775-6789	
Island Marine	Subbase	776-0753	http://www.subbasedrydock.com/
Island Yachts	Red Hook	775-6666	sailing@iyc.vi
Lighthouse Marine	Vitraco Park	774-4379	lighthouse@islands.vi
Marine Power Systems	Christiansted, S.C.	692-9900	
Marine Repairs	St. Thomas	775-7075	
Marine Warehouse	Subbase	774-2667	http://www.subbasedrydock.com/
Mike Mechanic	Christiansted, S.C.	773-3686	
Offshore Marine	Subbase	776-5432	info@offshorevi.com
Power & Data Systems	St. Thomas	779-1950	
Power Distributors	Crown Bay	774-6085	PDI@islands.vi
RPM Diesel Serv.	Benner Bay		
St. Croix Marine	Gallows Bay, St. Croix	773-0289	http://stcroixmarinecenter.com/
DIVING			
Admiralty Dive Center	St. Thomas	774-9802	http://www.admiraltydive.com/
Aqua Action Divers	Red Hook	775-6285	http://www.aadivers.com/
Blue Island divers	St. Thomas	774-2001	http://www.blueislanddivers.com/
Caribbean Sea Adv.	Cruz Bay	773-2628	http://www.caribbeanseaadventures.com/

FACILITY	LOCATION	PHONE	WEB SITE OR EMAIL ADDRESS
Dive Experience	Christiansted, S.C.	773-3307	http://divexp.com/
Low Key Water Sports	Cruz Bay	693-8999	http://www.divelowkey.com/index.htm
Patagon Dive Center	Caneel Bay	776-6111	http://www.patagondivecenter.com/
Red Hook Dive Center	St. Thomas	777-3483	http://www.redhookdivecenter.com/
St. Thomas Diving	Bolongo Bay	776-2381	http://www.stthomasdivingclub.com/

ELECTRONICS/ELECTRICAL

FACILITY	LOCATION	PHONE	WEB SITE OR EMAIL ADDRESS
A & J Power Sys.	Subbase	774-5590	
Al's Marine	Christiansted, S.C.	773-5611	
Bradford Air. & Marine	Subbase, St. Thomas	774-5811	
Caribbean Battery	Charlotte Amalie	776-3780	http://caribbeanbattery.angelfire.com/
Clines Marine	St. Thomas	775-4576	
Coral Bay Marine	Coral Harbor	776-6665	
Crown Bay Mar.	Subbase	774-5432	http://www.crownbay.com/
Electro Nautical Sys.	Benner Bay	775-4540	
Glentronics	Christiansted, St. Croix.	778-6505	
Independent Btyd.	Benner Bay	776-0466	http://ibyvi.com/
Kramer Electric	Christiansted, St. Croix	778-5888	
Lighthouse Marine	Vitraco Park	774-4379	lighthouse@islands.vi
Marine Warehouse	Subbase	774-2667	
Nautelect, Inc.	Benner Bay	775-1863	nautelect@viaccess.net
Quality Electric Supply	Christiansted, St Croix	773-4630	www.qualityelectricvi.com
St. Croix Marine	Gallows Bay, St. Croix	773-0289	http://stcroixmarinecenter.com/
TropiComm	Charlotte Amalie	775-4107	tropicomm1@yahoo.com
VI Yacht Systems	St. Thomas	774-5505	
TropiComm	Charlotte Amalie	775-4107	
VI Yacht Systems	St. Thomas	774-5505	

FABRICATION

FACILITY	LOCATION	PHONE	WEB SITE OR EMAIL ADDRESS
All Island Machine	Red Hook		
Bruce Merced	Benner Bay	775-7075	
Haulover Marine	Subbase	776-2078	http://www.subbasedrydock.com/
Independent Btyd.	Benner Bay	776-0466	http://ibyvi.com/
St. Croix Marine	Gallows Bay, St. Croix	773-0289	http://stcroixmarinecenter.com/
Subbase Drydock	Subbase - phone	776-2078	http://www.subbasedrydock.com/

HAUL OUT

FACILITY	LOCATION	PHONE	WEB SITE OR EMAIL ADDRESS
Avery's Boathouse	Charlotte Amalie	776-0113	
Caneel Bay Ship	Cruz Bay	693-8771	
Haulover Marine	Subbase	776-2078	
Independent Btyd.	Benner Bay	776-0466	http://ibyvi.com/
Salt River Marina	Salt River, St. Croix	778-9750	
St. Croix Marine	Gallows Bay, St. Croix	773-0289	http://stcroixmarinecenter.com/

HULL REPAIR/PAINTING

FACILITY	LOCATION	PHONE	WEB SITE OR EMAIL ADDRESS
Caneel Bay Ship	Cruz Bay	693-8771	
Haulover Marine	Subbase	776-2078	
Mike Sheen's	Benner Bay	776-0466	
Salt River Marina	Salt River, St. Croix	778-9750	
St. Croix Marine	Gallows Bay, St. Croix	773-0289	http://stcroixmarinecenter.com/
Subbase Drydock	Subbase - phone	776-2078	http://www.subbasedrydock.com/

INFLATABLES & LIFE RAFTS

FACILITY	LOCATION	PHONE	WEB SITE OR EMAIL ADDRESS
Caribbean Inflatable	St. Thomas	775-6159	http://www.caribbeaninflatable.com/
Island Marine	Crown Bay	714-0788	
Island Marine	Gallows Bay, St. Croix	773-0289	

FACILITY	LOCATION	PHONE	WEB SITE OR EMAIL ADDRESS
Island Marine	Red Hook	775-6789	
Island Marine	Subbase	776-0753	
Noah's Little Arks	Cruz Bay	693-9030	http://www.noahslittlearks.com/
Offshore Marine	Subbase	776-5432	info@offshorevi.com
St. Croix Marine	Gallows Bay, St. Croix	773-0289	http://stcroixmarinecenter.com/
INTERNET ACCESS			
A Better Copy	Christiansted, St. Croix	692-5303	
Caneel Bay Resort	Caneel Bay	776-6111	info@caneelbay.com
Connections	Cruz Bay	776-6922	stjohnconnections@gmail.comm
Connections East	Coral Bay	779-4994	connectionseast@gmail.com
East End Secretarial	Red Hook	775-5262	
Fill The Bill	Cruz Bay	693-8022	
Hemmingway's	Red Hook	775-2272	
Maho Bay Camps	Maho Bay	776-6226	
Stixx	Christiansted, St. Croix	773-5157	stixxstx@viaccess.net
Sunny Strand	Christiansted, St. Croix	719-6245	
Yacht Haven Grande	St. Thomas	774-9500	YHGST@igymarinas.com
MARINE SUPPLIES			
Al's Marine	Christiansted, St. Croix	773-5611	
Budget Marine	St. Thomas	779-2219	http://www.budgetmarine.com/
Clines Marine	St. Thomas	775-4576	
Coki of St. Thomas	Benner Bay	775-6560	
Colorama	Sunny Isle	778-6920	
Coral Bay Marine	Coral Harbor	776-6665	
Electro Nautical Sys.	St. Thomas	775-4540	
Gary's Marine	St. Thomas	779-2717	
Green Cay Marina	St. Croix	718-1453	GCMarina@tamarindreefresort.com
Haulover Marine	Subbase	776-2078	
Independent Btyd.	Benner Bay	776-0466	http://ibyvi.com/
Island Marine	Gallows Bay, St. Croix	773-0289	
Island Marine	Crown Bay	714-0788	
Island Marine	Red Hook	775-6789	
Lighthouse Marine	Vitraco Park	774-4379	lighthouse@islands.vi
M & S Marine	Cruz Bay	693-7200	
Marine Warehouse	Subbase	774-2667	
NAPA	Christiansted, St. Croix	772-0155	http://www.napaonline.com/vi/st-croix
Sailboat Supply	Christiansted, St. Croix	778-1992	
St. Croix Marine	Gallows Bay, St. Croix	773-0289	http://stcroixmarinecenter.com/
Salt River Marina	Salt River, St. Croix	778-0706	
OUTBOARD REPAIR			
Al's Marine	Christiansted, St. Croix	773-5611	
Budget Marine	St. Thomas	774-2667	
Crown Bay Marina	Subbase	774-5432	comments@crownbay.com
Gary's Marine	Benner Bay		
Independent Btyd.	Benner Bay	776-0466	http://ibyvi.com/
Island Marine	Gallows Bay, St. Croix	773-0289	
Island Marine	Crown Bay	714-0788	
Island Marine	Red Hook	775-6789	
Island Marine	Subbase	776-0753	
Lighthouse Marine	Vitraco Park	774-4379	lighthouse@islands.vi
Offshore Marine	Subbase	776-5432	info@offshorevi.com

FACILITY	LOCATION	PHONE	WEB SITE OR EMAIL ADDRESS
Outboards Only	Calquohoun, St. Croix	772-0300	
St. Croix Marine	Gallows Bay, St. Croix	773-0289	http://stcroixmarinecenter.com/
TJ's Outboard	Benner Bay	775-5505	
Tropical Marine	Benner Bay		

PROPANE

FACILITY	LOCATION	PHONE	WEB SITE OR EMAIL ADDRESS
Al's Marine	Christiansted, St. Croix	773-5611	
Antilles Gas Corp.	Subbase	776-9426	
Independent Btyd.	Benner Bay	776-0466	http://ibyvi.com/
Marine Warehouse	Subbase	774-2667	
St. Croix Gas	Christiansted, St. Croix	778-6500	
St. Thomas Gas	St. Thomas		

PROPELLERS

FACILITY	LOCATION	PHONE	WEB SITE OR EMAIL ADDRESS
Bruce Merced	Benner Bay	775-7075	
Proper Pitch	Charlotte Amalie	774-9965	
Ruan's Marine	St. Thomas	775-6345	

REFRIGERATION & AIR CONDITIONING

FACILITY	LOCATION	PHONE	WEB SITE OR EMAIL ADDRESS
Al's Marine	Christiansted, St. Croix	773-5611	
Caneel Bay Ship	Cruz Bay	693-8771	
Holiday Ref. & AC	Christiansted, St. Croix	773-4710	
Reefco	St. Thomas	776-0038	
R. Lee Kingery	St. Thomas	775-6822	
St. Croix Marine	Gallows Bay, St. Croix	773-0289	
Tropical Ref.	Benner Bay		
VI Yacht Systems	St. Thomas	774-5505	

RIGGING

FACILITY	LOCATION	PHONE	WEB SITE OR EMAIL ADDRESS
Clarke Rigging	Christiansted, St. Croix	773-6078	
Independent Btyd.	Benner Bay	776-0466	http://ibyvi.com/
Island Marine	Crown Bay	714-0788	
Island Marine	Gallows Bay, St. Croix	773-0289	
Island Marine	Red Hook	775-6789	
Island Marine	Subbase	776-0753	
Island Rigging	Subbase	774-6833	islrig@viaaccess.net
Lighthouse Marine	Vitraco Park	774-4379	lighthouse@islands.vi
Skip's Rigging	Benner Bay	779-1651	
St. Croix Marine	Gallows Bay, St. Croix	773-0289	http://stcroixmarinecenter.com/

SAIL AND CANVAS REPAIR

FACILITY	LOCATION	PHONE	WEB SITE OR EMAIL ADDRESS
Banks Sails	Subbase	779-2078	
Bayside Canvas	Crown Bay	775-4422	
Caneel Bay Ship	Cruz Bay	693-8771	
Canvas Loft	Christiansted, St. Croix	773-3044	
Clines Marine	St. Thomas	775-4576	
Coki of St. Thomas	Benner Bay	775-6560	
Compass Point Canvas	Benner Bay	774-5777	
Coral Bay Marine	Coral Harbor	776-6665	
Custom Canvas	St. Thomas	775-6511	
Leading Edge	Christiansted, St. Croix	773-7414	
Lighthouse Marine	Vitraco Park	774-4379	lighthouse@islands.vi
Manfred Dittrich	St. Thomas	774-4335	
Marine Tech	St. Thomas	774-4363	http://www.marinetechvi.com/
Quantum Sails	St. Thomas	777-5639	http://www.sails.vi/
Sail Loft	Red Hook	775-1712	sailloft@islands.vi

FACILITY	LOCATION	PHONE	WEB SITE OR EMAIL ADDRESS
Shadows Sails	St. Thomas	777-5638	shadowsvi@hotmail.com
Shipshape	Christiansted, St. Croix	778-5731	
Skip Thyberg	St. Thomas	779-1651	
UK Sail Loft	St. Thomas	775-7990	
Virgin Canvas	Cruz Bay	776-6223	
Virgin Islands Cnv.	St. Thomas	774-3229	
Wesco Marine Cnv.	Christiansted, St. Croix	778-9446	
WATER MAKERS			
Reefco	St. Thomas	340-776-0038	reefcoservices@gmail.com

Appendix C3: British Virgin Islands

The area code for the British Virgin Islands is 284

FACILITY	LOCATION	PHONE	WEB SITE OR EMAIL ADDRESS
AUTO RENTALS			
Aaron Rental's Ltd.	Road Town	494-8917	https://www.aaronrentalsbvi.com/
ABC Car Rentals	Anegada	495-9466	
Airway's Rent-a-Car	Nanny Cay	494-0075	
Alphonso Rentals	Road Town	494-8746	alphonso_ent@e-mail.com
Andy's Jeeps	Virgin Gorda	495-5252	fischers@candwbvi.net
Anegada Reef Hotel	Anegada	495-8002	http://www.anegadareef.com/
Avis	Road Town	494-3322	https://www.avis.com/en/home
Avis	West End	495-4973	https://www.avis.com/en/home
Budget	Road Town	494-2639	
Courtesy Car Rent.	Road Town	494-6443	courtesy.cars.bvi@gmail.com
D & D Car Rentals	Soper's Hole	495-4765	danddcarrental@surfbvi.com
Dede's Car Rental	East End, Tor.	495-2041	http://www.dedescarrentals.com/
Del's Jeep Rentals	Cane Garden Bay	495-9356	
Denzil Clyne	Soper's Hole	494-4900	www.denzilclynerentals.com
Dollar Rent a Car	Prospect Reef Resort	494-6093	dollar@surfbvi.com
DW's Jeep Rental	Settlement, Anegada	495-9677	
Hertz	Road Town	495-4405	hertzbvi@hotmail.com
Hertz	Tortola (Airport)	495-6600	hertzbvi@hotmail.com
Hertz	Virgin Gorda	495-5803	hertzbvi@hotmail.com
Intl. Car Rentals	Road Town	494-2516	www.internationalcarrentalsbvi.com
Island Style	Virgin Gorda	495-6300	http://www.islandstylebvi.com/
Itgo Car Rental	Road Town	494-5150	www.itgobvi.com
J & L Jeep	Settlement, Anegada	495-3138	j&l@surfbvi.com
Jerry's Car Rentals	Soper's Hole	495-4111	http://www.jerrysrental.com/
L & S Jeep Rentals	Virgin Gorda	495-5297	http://www.landsjeeprental.com/
Last Stop Sports	Road Town	494-1120	http://www.laststopsports.com/
Mahogany Rentals	Virgin Gorda	495-5469	mahoganycarrentals@surfbvi.com
National	Tortola	494-3197	http://www.nationalcarbvi.com/
Prospect Reef Mar.	Tortola	494-3311	reservations@prospectreef.com
SNK Amazing Rent.	Road Town	495-9296	http://www.snkamazingrentals.com
Speedy's Rentals	Virgin Gorda	495-5235	http://www.speedyscarrentals.com/
Tola Rentals	Road Town	494-8652	rent@tolarentals.com
Tony's Taxi	Anegada	495-8027	
CHARTER BOATS			
Aristocat	Soper's Hole	495-4087	http://aristocatcharters.com/
Barecat Charters	Fat Hogs Bay	800-296-5287	http://barecat.com/
Bitter End Y.C.	Virgin Gorda	800-872-2392	www.beyc.com

FACILITY	LOCATION	PHONE	WEB SITE OR EMAIL ADDRESS
Blue Ocean	Road Town	494-2872	http://www.blueoceanbooking.com/
BVI Yacht Charters	Road Town	494-4289	http://www.bviyachtcharters.com/
Cane Garden Boats	Cane Garden Bay	495-9660	
Catamaran Charters	Nanny Cay	800-262-0308	info@catamaranco.com
Charter Port BVI	Road Town	494-7955	http://www.charterportbvi.com/l
Charter Yacht Serv.	Nanny Cay	494-6017	cysofbvi@surfbvi.com
Chocolat Blanc	Fat Hogs Bay	495-1266	choblanc@surfbvi.com
Classic Charters	Road Town	494-5943	
Conch Charters	Road Town	494-4868	http://www.conchcharters.com/
Destination BVI	Road Town	494-8782	http://destinationbvi.com/
Double D Charters	Virgin Gorda	499-2479	http://www.doubledbvi.com/
Dual Bliss	Road Town	496-7149	dbliss@surfbvi.com
Endless Summer II	Nanny Cay	800-368-990	info@endlesssummer.com
Euphoric Cruises	Virgin Gorda	495-5542	
Goddess Athena	Nanny Cay	494-0000	athena@surfbvi.com
Golden Spirit	Fat Hog's Bay	495-1479	goldenspirit@surfbvi.com
Horizon Yacht Ch.	Nanny Cay	494-8787	http://horizonyachtcharters.com/
Jolly Mon Rentals	Maya Cove	495-9916	jollymon@surfbvi.com
King Charters	Nanny Cay	494-5820	http://www.kingcharters.com/
Kuralu Charters	Soper's Hole	495-4381	http://kuralu.com/kuralu.htm
Leverick Bay Wspts.	Virgin Gorda	495-7376	
M&M Powerboats	Road Town	495-9993	mljbvi@surfbvi.com
Moorings	Road Town	494-2333	www.moorings.com
North South Yacht	Road Town	800-387-4964	
Patouche II	Road Town	494-6300	patouche@surfbvi.com
Pro Valor Yacht	Fat Hog's Bay	495-1931	
Promenade Cruises	Road Town	496-0999	saildive@yachtpromenade.com
Regency Yacht	Road Town	495-1970	liz@regencyvacations.com
Sail Caribbean	Hodges Creek Mar.	495-1675	http://www.sailcaribbeandivers.com/
Silmaril Charters	Peter Island	342-6248	http://www.silmarilsailing.com/
Spice Charters	Virgin Gorda	496-6633	www.spicebvi.com
Spirit of Anegada	Virgin Gorda	340-7777	http://www.spiritofanegada.com/
Tamarin II & III	Road Town	495-9837	tamarin@surfbvi.com
The Ulti-Mate	Road Town	494-6977	rita@bvicharters.com
Tortola Marine Mgt.	Road Town	494-2751	http://www.sailtmm.com/
Trimarine/Cuan Law	Road Town	494-2490	http://www.bvisailing.com/
Tropic Islands Yacht	Maya Cove	494-2450	tropicis@candwbvi.net
Virgin Traders	Nanny Cay	495 2526	http://virginmotoryachts.com/
Voyage Charters	Soper's Hole	888-869-2436	http://www.voyagecharters.com/
Wanderlust Charters	Trellis Bay	800-724-5284	wanderer@surfbvi.com
White Squall II	Road Town	494-2564	http://www.whitesquall2.com/
Yacht Connections	Road Town	800-386-8185	yachting@surfbvi.com
DIESEL REPAIR/PARTS			
Al's Marine	Road Town	494-4529	alsmarine@surfbvi.com
BVI Diesel Sales	Road Town	494-2298	
BVI Marine Depot	Road Town	494-0098	
BVI Marine Mgt.	Nanny Cay	469-2938	www.bvimarinedepot.com/services.html
BVI Marine Services	Road Town	494-2393	
Island Marine	Fort Bay	494-2251	
Island Marine	Nanny Cay	494-0329	
Marine Power Serv.	Road Town	494-2738	

FACILITY	LOCATION	PHONE	WEB SITE OR EMAIL ADDRESS
The Moorings	Road Harbour	494-2332	
Nanny Cay Marina	Nanny Cay	494-2512	chandlery@nannycay.com
Parts & Power	Road Town	494-2830	http://www.partsandpower.com/
Soper's Hole	Soper's Hole	494 2983	http://www.sopersholemarina.com/
Tortola Yacht	Road Town	494-2124	tys@tysbvi.com
Tradewind Yacht	Road Town	394-2517	www.tradewindsbvi.com/Directions.htm
Virgin Gorda Yacht	Virgin Gorda	495-5500	
Workbench	Virgin Gorda	495-5310	workbenchbvi@gmail.com
DIVING			
Blue Water Divers	Nanny Cay	494-2847	http://www.bluewaterdiversbvi.com/
Blue Water Divers	Soper's Hole	495-2847	http://www.bluewaterdiversbvi.com/
BVI SCUBA	Long Bay Resort	495-0271	www.bviscubaco.com
BVI SCUBA	Road Town	443-2222	www.bviscubaco.com
Dive BVI	Little Dix Bay	495-5513	http://www.divebvi.com/
Jost Van Dyke Scuba	Jost Van Dyke	495-0271	http://www.jostvandykescuba.com/
Sail Caribbean Dive	Manchioneel Bay	495-1675	http://www.sailcaribbeandivers.com/
Sun Chaser Scuba	Virgin Gorda	495-9638	http://www.sunchaserscuba.com/
ELECTRONICS/ELECTRICAL			
Al's Marine	Road Town	494-4529	alsmarine@surfbvi.com
BVI Electronics	Road Town	494-2723	
BVI Marine Mgt.	Nanny Cay	469-2938	
Cay Electronics	Road Town	494-2400	http://cayelectronics.com/
Island Care	Nanny Cay	494-6183	
Island Car	Road Reef Mar.	494-3998	
Nanny Cay Marina	Nanny Cay	494-2512	chandlery@nannycay.com
Parts & Power	Road Town	494-2830	http://www.partsandpower.com/
Tortola Yacht	Road Town	494-2124	tys@tysbvi.com
Virgin Gorda Yacht	Virgin Gorda	495-5500	
Workbench	Virgin Gorda	495-5310	workbenchbvi@gmail.com
FABRICATION			
BVI Marine Mgt.	Nanny Cay	469-2938	www.bvimarinedepot.com/services.html
Nanny Cay Marina	Nanny Cay	494-2512	chandlery@nannycay.com
Nautool Machine	Road Town	494-3187	http://www.nautool.com/
Parts & Power	Road Town	494-2830	http://www.partsandpower.com/
Soper's Hole	Soper's Hole	494 2983	http://www.sopersholemarina.com/
T & W Machine	Road Town	494-3342	tandwmachineshop@surfbvi.com
Tortola Yacht	Road Town	494-2124	tys@tysbvi.com
Virgin Gorda Yacht	Virgin Gorda	495-5500	
Workbench	Virgin Gorda	495-5310	workbenchbvi@gmail.com
HAUL OUT			
Nanny Cay Marina	Nanny Cay	494-2512	chandlery@nannycay.com
Soper's Hole	Soper's Hole	494 2983	http://www.sopersholemarina.com/
Tony's Refinishing	Road Town	499-4189	
Tortola Yacht	Road Town	494-2124	tys@tysbvi.com
Virgin Gorda Yacht	Virgin Gorda	495-5500	
VI Shipwrights	Soper's Hole	495-4496	
Workbench	Virgin Gorda	495-5310	workbenchbvi@gmail.com
HULL REPAIR/PAINTING			
BVI Painters	Road Town	494-4365	picasso@surfbvi.com
CYR	Virgin Gorda	495-0051	kaya4u54@hotmail.com
Nanny Cay Marina	Nanny Cay	494-2512	nannycay@surfbvi.com

FACILITY	LOCATION	PHONE	WEB SITE OR EMAIL ADDRESS
Soper's Hole	Soper's Hole	494 2983	http://www.sopersholemarina.com/
Tony's Refinishing	Road Town	499-4189	
Tortola Yacht	Road Town	494-2124	tys@tysbvi.com
Virgin Gorda Yacht	Virgin Gorda	495-5500	
Workbench	Virgin Gorda	495-5310	workbenchbvi@gmail.com
INFLATABLES/LIFE RAFTS			
Island Marine	Fort Bay	494-2251	
Island Marine	Nanny Cay	494-0329	
Nanny Cay Marina	Nanny Cay	494-2512	chandlery@nannycay.com
Tradewind Yacht	Road Town	394-2517	www.tradewindsbvi.com/Directions.htm
INTERNET ACCESS			
Baugher's Bay Mar.	Road Town	494-2393	fkrouwel@surfbvi.com
Caribbean Jewelers	Soper's Hole	495-4137	samarkand@tortola.com
Click-Online	Wickham Cay		
Cyber Cafe	Trellis Bay	495-2447	
Digital Jamming	Leverick Bay	495-7013	
Elan E-Commerce	Road Town	494-7362	
Myett's Enterprises	Cane Garden Bay	495-9649	http://myetts.com/
Pusser's Restaurant	Maya Cove	495-1010	
Wendell's World	Jost Van Dyke	495-9259	
Virgin Gorda Yacht	Virgin Gorda	495-5500	
MARINE SUPPLIES			
Al's Marine	Road Town	494-4529	alsmarine@surfbvi.com
Cay Marine	Road Town	494-2992	
Clarence Thomas	Road Town	494-2359	http://ctlbvi.com/
Clarence Thomas	Virgin Gorda	495-5091	http://ctlbvi.com/
Soper's Hole	Frenchman's Cay	495-4353	
Golden Hind Chand.	Road Town	494-2756	ghc@surfbvi.com
Island Marine	Fort Bay	494-2251	
Island Marine	Nanny Cay	494-0329	
Marine Depot	Road Town	494-0098	http://www.bvimarinedepot.com/
Marine Power	Road Town	494-2738	
Nanny Cay Marina	Nanny Cay	494-2512	chandlery@nannycay.com
Parts & Power	Road Town	494-2830	http://www.partsandpower.com/
Richardson's Rig.	Road Town	494-2739	
Ship's Store	Virgin Gorda	495-5500	
Soper's Hole	Soper's Hole	494 2983	http://www.sopersholemarina.com/
Tortola Yacht	Road Town	494-2124	tys@tysbvi.com
Tradewind Yacht	Road Town	394-2517	www.tradewindsbvi.com/Directions.htm
Virgin Gorda Yacht	Virgin Gorda	495-5500	
Wickham's Cay II	Road Town	494-3979	
OUTBOARD REPAIR			
Al's Marine	Road Town	494-4529	alsmarine@surfbvi.com
Island Marine	Fort Bay	494-2251	
Island Marine	Nanny Cay	494-0329	
Marine Power	Road Town	494-2738	
Nanny Cay Marina	Nanny Cay	494-2512	chandlery@nannycay.com
Soper's Hole	Soper's Hole	494 2983	http://www.sopersholemarina.com/
Tortola Yacht	Road Town	494-2124	tys@tysbvi.com
Tradewind Yacht	Road Town	394-2517	www.tradewindsbvi.com/Directions.htm
Virgin Gorda Yacht	Virgin Gorda	495-5500	

FACILITY	LOCATION	PHONE	WEB SITE OR EMAIL ADDRESS
Workbench	Virgin Gorda	495-5310	workbenchbvi@gmail.com
PROPANE			
Al's Marine Services	Road Town	494-4529	
Launch Services	Soper's Hole	495-4571	
Penn's Landing Mar.	Fat Hog's Bay	495-1134	pennslandingmarina@gmail.com
PROVISIONING			
Bitter End Yacht Club	North Sound	393-2745	binfo@beyc.com
Shore Side Yacht Ser.	Road Town	494-5135	http://www.shoresideservices.com
Y. C. Costa Smeralda	north Sound	393-2000	info@yccs.vg
REFRIGERATION & AC			
Air Devices	Road Town	494-2314	
Al's Marine	Road Town	494-4529	alsmarine@surfbvi.com
BVI Marine Mgt.	Nanny Cay	469-2938	www.bvimarinedepot.com/services.html
Cay Electronics	Road Town	494-2400	
Nanny Cay Marina	Nanny Cay	494-2512	chandlery@nannycay.com
Parts & Power	Road Town	494-2830	http://www.partsandpower.com/
Soper's Hole	Soper's Hole	494 2983	http://www.sopersholemarina.com/
Village Cay Marina	Road Town	494-2771	info@villagecaybvi.com
Virgin Gorda Yacht	Virgin Gorda	495-5500	
RIGGING			
Golden Hind Chand.	Road Town	494-2756	ghc@surfbvi.com
High Tech	Road Town	494-3811	
Island Marine	Fort Bay	494-2251	
Island Marine	Nanny Cay	494-0329	
Richardson's Rig.	Road Town	494-2739	http://www.richardsonsrigging.com/
Tortola Yacht	Road Town	494-2124	tys@tysbvi.com
Village Cay Marina	Road Town	494-2771	info@villagecaybvi.com
Wickham's Cay Rig.	Road Town	494-3979	
Wood's Marine Serv.	Benner Bay	494-0002	http://woods-marine-services.com/
Workbench	Virgin Gorda	495-5310	workbenchbvi@gmail.com
SAIL AND CANVAS REPAIR			
Doyle Sailmakers	Road Reef Marina	494-2569	http://www.doylecaribbean.com
Next Wave Sail	Virgin Gorda Y.H.	495-5623	nextwavebvi@hotmail.com
Phillip's Sail	Road Town	494-4982	
Virgin Gorda Yacht	Virgin Gorda	495-5500	

Appendix D: Waypoints

Waypoints are NOT to be used for navigational purposes. The author and publisher take no responsibility for the misuse of the following waypoints. Latitude is "**North**" and longitude is "**West**." Datum used is WGS84.

Eastern Shore of Puerto Rico

Waypoint Description	Latitude	Longitude
Eastern Coast		
Las Croabas - ½ nm SE of entrance channel	18° 21.70'	65°37.28'
El Conquistador Marina - ½ nm SE of entrance	18° 21.30	65° 37.40'
Playa Sardinera - ½ nm ENE of entrance	18° 20.85'	65° 37.70'
Cayo Obispo - ½ mile east of entrance channel	18° 20.80'	65° 36.75'
Puerto del Rey Marina - ½ nm ENE of entrance to marina	18° 17.45'	65° 37.45'
Puerto Medio Mundo - ½ nm NE of entrance to Bahia	18° 16.50'	65° 36.55'
Pasaje de Medio Mundo (N waypoint) - ½ nm N of channel	18° 15.75'	65° 36.10'
Isla Cabeza de Perro - ½ nm E of	18° 15.00'	65° 34.30'

A Cruising Guide to the Virgin Islands

Waypoint Description	Latitude	Longitude
Pasaje de Medio Mundo (S waypoint) - 1 nm S of channel	18° 13.70'	65° 35.10'
Bahia de Puerca - ½ nm SE of entrance	18° 13.05'	65° 35.40'
Ensenada Honda (Roosevelt Roads) - ½ nm SE of and on range	18° 11.65'	65° 36.00'
Cayo Santiago - ¼ nm S of	18° 08.00'	65° 44.00'
Palmas del Mar - ½ nm SE of entrance	18° 04.45'	65° 47.45'
Puerto Yabacoa - 2 nm SE of entrance and on range	18° 01.75'	65° 46.90'

The Spanish Virgin Islands

Waypoint Description	Latitude	Longitude
Pasaje de San Juan - ½ nm NE of Cabo San Juan	18° 23.28'	65° 36.50'
Cayo Icacos - ½ nm SW of anchorage area	18° 23.10'	65° 35.85'
Cayo Lobos (La Cordillera) - ½ nm SW of anchorage area	18° 22.60'	65° 34.65'
Canal de Cayo Norte - 1 nm NW of	18° 21.00'	65° 17.35'
Isla Palominos - ½ nm W of anchorage area	18° 20.70'	65° 34.80'
Bahia Flamenco (Culebra) - ½ nm N of	18° 20.70'	65° 18.90'
Isla de Culebrita - ¾ nm N of anchorage on N shore	18° 19.90'	65° 13.95'
Cayo Lobo (near Culebra) - ½ nm SW of	18° 19.50'	65° 23.00'
Cayo de Luis Pena - ½ nm NNW of	18° 19.10'	65° 20.30'
Bahia Tamarindo (Culebra) - ¼ nm SW of	18° 19.00'	65° 19.35'
Bahia de Sardinas (Dewey, Culebra) - ½ nm SW of	18° 17.90'	65° 18.65'
Puerto del Manglar (Culebra) - ¼ nm SE of anchorage entrance	18° 18.05'	65° 14.50'
Cayo de Luis Pena - ½ nm S of	18° 17.50'	65° 19.75'
Ensenada Honda (Culebra) - 1 nm SE of marked entrance channel	18° 17.33'	65° 16.35'
Punta del Soldado (Culebra) - ¼ nm S of point	18° 16.30'	65° 17.30'
Ensenada Honda - ½ nm SE of RN "4"	18° 16.00'	65° 15.50'
Isabel Segunda (Vieques) - 1 nm NW of Bahia de Mulas	18° 09.80'	65° 27.50'
Bahia Icacos (Vieques) - ¾ nm N of Cayo Yallis	18° 09.50'	65° 18.55'
Bahia Icacos (Vieques) - ½ N of Punta Salinas	18° 09.33'	65° 17.40'
Bahia Salina del Sur (Vieques) - ½ nm S of entrance	18° 07.00'	65° 18.27
Punta Arenas (Vieques) - ½ nm W of anchorage area	18° 06.80'	65° 35.00'
Ensenada Honda (Vieques) - ½ nm S of entrance	18° 06.05'	65° 21.90'
Bahia de Chiva (Vieques) - ¼ nm S of entrance to western bay	18° 06.05'	65° 23.35'
Puerto Ferro (Vieques) - ½ nm SE of entrance	18° 05.40'	65° 24.70'
Puerto Mosquito (Vieques) - 1 nm S of entrance	18° 04.50'	65° 26.50'
Puerto Negro - ¼ nm S of entrance	18° 05.00'	65° 27.00'
Ensenada Sun Bay (Vieques) - ¼ nm S of entrance	18° 05.00'	65° 27.75'
Puerto Real, Esperanza (Vieques) - ¼ nm S of entrance	18° 05.00'	65° 28.28'
Punta Este (Vieques) - 1 nm E of	18° 08.10'	65° 14.90'
Punta Arenas (Vieques) - 1¼ nm NW of point	18° 07.80'	65° 35.70'

The United States Virgin Islands

Waypoint Description — Latitude — Longitude

St. Thomas

Waypoint Description	Latitude	Longitude
Sapphire Beach Marina - .1 nm ENE of entrance	18° 20.05'	64° 50.75'
Red Hook Bay - .1 nm NE of marked entrance channel	18° 19.77'	64° 50.50'
Druif Bay - ¼ nm W of	18° 19.02'	64° 57.75'
Current Cut - .1 nm NNE of	18° 19.00'	64° 49.97'
Current Cut - ¼ nm SSW of	18° 18.70'	64° 50.05'
Christmas Cove - .1 nm WNW of	18° 18.70'	64° 50.05'
Cas Cay Anchorage - .2 nm E of entrance channel	18° 18.68'	64° 52.00'
Jersey Bay - ¼ nm NE of Cas Cay	18° 18.65'	64° 51.50'

Waypoint Description	Latitude	Longitude
Charlotte Amalie - 1 nm SSE of entrance channel	18° 18.50'	64° 55.40'

St. John

Waypoint Description	Latitude	Longitude
Fungi Passage - ¼ nm N of	18° 22.40'	64° 45.25'
Leinster Bay - ¼ nm N of	18° 22.30'	64° 43.70'
Francis Bay - ¾ nm W of	18° 21.90'	64° 45.70'
Trunk Bay - .2 nm NW of marked entrance channel	18° 21.40'	64° 46.35'
Hawksnest Bay - ¼ nm N of entrance	18° 21.40'	64° 46.90'
Haulover Bay - ¼ nm N of anchorage area	18° 21.16'	64° 40.62'
Newfound Bay - ¼ nm NE of	18° 21.00'	64° 39.80'
Caneel Bay - ¼ nm W of entrance	18° 20.60'	64° 47.60'
Coral Harbor - ½ nm E of entrance	18° 20.30'	64° 42.15'
Cruz Bay - ½ nm W of marked entrance channel	18° 20.00'	64° 48.30'
Great Cruz Bay - ¼ nm SW of entrance	18° 19.07'	64° 47.80'
Coral Bay - 1 nm SE of	18° 19.00'	64° 40.00'
Great Lameshur Bay - ½ nm SSW of	18° 18.30'	64° 43.70'
Saltpond Bay - ½ nm S of	18° 17.85'	64° 42.50'

St. Croix

Waypoint Description	Latitude	Longitude
Salt River Bay - ½ nm N of entrance channel	17° 47.35'	64° 45.30'
Buck Island - ½ nm S of entrance through reef	17° 46.50'	64° 37.80'
Green Cay Marina - ¼ nm W of Green Cay, ¼ nm NW of marina	17° 45.95'	64° 40.25'
Christiansted - .1 nm NW of marked entrance channel	17° 45.80'	64° 41.90'
Frederiksted - ½ nm W of anchorage S of pier	17° 42.65'	64° 53.70'

The British Virgin Islands

Waypoint Description	Latitude	Longitude

Tortola

Waypoint Description	Latitude	Longitude
Scrub Island - ½ nm NNE of Scrub Island Cut	18° 28.75'	64° 31.25'
Guana Island - ½ nm SW of White Bay anchorage	18° 27.70'	64° 35.00'
Scrub Island - S of and ¾ nm E of Marina Cay	18° 27.50'	64° 30.50'
Prospect Reef Resort - ¼ nm SE of	18° 24.55'	64° 36.65'
Brandywine Bay - ¼ nm SSE of entrance	18° 24.50'	64° 35.05'
Road Harbour - ¾ nm SSE of buoyed entrance channel	18° 24.00'	64° 36.00'
Brewers Bay - ½ nm NW of entrance	18° 27.10'	64° 39.80'
Cane Garden Bay - ¼ nm WNW of entrance	18° 25.75'	64° 40.10'
Fat Hogs Bay - ¾ nm E of	18° 26.00'	64° 32.65'
Maya Cove, Paraquita Cove, Buck Island - ½ nm S of Buck Island	18° 24.80'	64° 33.40'
Nanny Cay - ¼ nm SE of entrance	18° 23.60'	64° 38.00'
Thatch Island Cut North - ¼ nm N of	18° 23.65'	64° 43.22'
Little Thatch Island Cut - ¼ nm S of	18° 22.65'	64° 42.53'

Norman Island

Waypoint Description	Latitude	Longitude
Benures Bay - ½ nm N of	18° 19.80'	64° 36.55'
The Bight - ¾ nm NW of	18° 19.40'	64° 38.00'

Peter Island

Waypoint Description	Latitude	Longitude
Sprat Bay - ½ nm NNW of entrance	18° 22.20'	64° 34.75'
Little Harbour - ¾ nm NNW of	18° 22.00'	64° 36.50'
Great Harbour - ½ nm NW of	18° 22.00'	64° 35.50'

Salt Island

Waypoint Description	Latitude	Longitude
Salt Island - ½ nm NNW of	18° 23.00'	64° 32.00'

Cooper Island

Waypoint Description	Latitude	Longitude
Manchioneel Bay - ¼ nm NNW of	18° 23.40'	64° 31.20'

Waypoint Description	Latitude	Longitude
Virgin Gorda		
Necker Island - ¼ nm SW of entrance to anchorage	18° 31.10'	64° 21.90'
Eustatia Sound - ¼ nm N of pass between Eustatia I. & Opuntia Pt.	18° 31.10'	64° 21.95'
North Sound - ¼ nm NW of entrance between Mosq. I & Pkly. Pear I.	18° 31.05'	64° 22.90'
Eustatia Sound - ½ nm NE of pass through Eustatia Reef	18° 31.00'	64° 20.60'
North Sound - ½ nm W of Anguilla Point entrance	18° 30.45'	64° 24.35'
Long Bay - ½ nm W of anchorage	18° 30.00'	64° 25.30'
Savannah Bay - ¼ nm NW of entrance	18° 28.30'	64° 25.30'
Little Dix Bay - ¼ nm N of entrance	18° 28.10'	64° 26.10'
Virgin Gorda Yacht Harbour - ½ nm W of marked entrance channel	18° 27.25'	64° 26.00'
The Baths - ¾ nm WNW of	18° 26.00'	64° 27.50'
Jost Van Dyke		
Green Cay - 1 nm ESE of Green Cay	18° 26.55'	64° 41.50'
White Bay - ½ nm S of	18° 26.00'	64° 45.75'
Little Harbour - ¼ nm SE of	18° 25.90'	64° 43.50'
Great Harbour - ½ nm S of	18° 25.90'	64° 45.05'
Sandy Cay - ½ nm SSW Sandy Cay	18° 25.75'	64° 43.00'
Anegada		
Anchorage - 1 nm SW of marked entrance channel	18° 42.50'	64° 25.00'

Appendix E: Metric Conversion

Visitors to the Virgin Islands will find the metric system in use and many grocery items and fuel measured in liters and kilograms. As a rule of thumb, a meter is just a little longer than a yard and a liter is very close to a quart. If in doubt, use the following table.

1 centimeter (cm) = 0.4 inch	1 inch = 2.54 centimeters
1 meter (m) = 3.28 feet	1 foot = 30.48 centimeters
1 meter = 0.55 fathoms	1 fathom = 1.83 meters
1 kilometer (km) = 0.62 miles	1 yard = 0.91 meters
1 kilometer = 0.54 nautical miles	1 nautical mile = 1.852 kilometers
1 liter (l) = 0.26 gallons	1 gallon = 3.79 liters
1 gram (g) = 0.035 ounces	1 ounce = 28.4 grams
1 metric ton = 1.1 tons	1 pound = 454 grams

Appendix F: A Little Spanish

(Just enough to get you into trouble!)

While command of the Spanish language is not a prerequisite for happy cruising in Puerto Rico and the Spanish Virgin Islands, knowing a little will certainly help you get by better and everybody will love you for at least trying.

Buenos Dias. Good morning.
Buenas tardes. Good afternoon.
Buenas noches. Good night.
¿Cómo está usted? How are you?
¿Muy bien gracias, y usted? I am fine thank you, and you?
¿Como se llama? What is your name?
Me llamo es . . . My name is. . .

¿Habla usted inglés? Do you speak English?
¿Habla usted Español? Do you speak Spanish?
¿Hay alquien aqui que hable ingles? Is there anybody here who speaks English?
No muy bien. Not very well.
Muy poco. Very little.
¿Cómo se dice. . . ? How do you say. . .?
*¿Como? Wh*at did you say?
No entiendo. I don't understand.
No se. I don't know.
Escríbamela, por favor. Please write it down for me.
¿Donde está e. . .? Where is . . .?
   anclaje-anchorage
   arrecife-reef
 bahia-bay
 bano- bathroom
 bajo-shoal
   banco-bank
   Capitán de Puerto-Harbormaster
   caleta-cove
   canal-channel
   desembarcadero-landing
   ducha-shower
   embarcadero-wharf, quay
   ferretería-hardware store
   Immigración-Immigration
   lavandería-laundry
   mecánico-mechanic
   médico-doctor
   pasaje-passage
   punta-point
   radas-roadstead
   supermercado-supermarket
   telefono-telephone
¿Donde puedo comprar . . .? Where can I buy . . .?
Necesito. . . I need. . .?
¿Tiene usted . . .? Do you have. . . ?
   agua-water
   agua potable-drinking water
   arroz- rice
   azúcar-sugar
   café-coffee
   camarones-shrimp
   carne-meat
   cebolla- onions
   cerveza-beer
   chillo- snapper
   cigarillos-cigarettes
   ensalada- salad
   fosforos-matches
   fuego-a light
   gasoil-diesel

gasolina-gasoline
helado- ice cream
hielo- ice
huevos-eggs
jamón-ham
jugo-juice
jugo de naranjas- orange juice
langosta- lobster
leche-milk
limones-limes
mantequilla-butter
mero- sea bass
narnaja- orange
pan-bread
patatas-potatoes
pavo- turkey
pina- pineapple
plátanos-bananas
pollo-chicken
propano-propane
queso-cheese
setas- mushrooms
sopa- soup
té- tea
tomate-tomato
vino-wine

Colors, Numbers, Directions, and Days:

blanco-white
negro-black azul-blue
rojo-red
verde-green
amarillo-yellow
aquí-here
allí-there
la derecha-right
la izquierda-left
uno-1
dos-2
tres-3
quatro-4
cinco-5
seis-6
seite-7
ocho-8
nueve-9
diez-10
once-11
doce-12
trece-13
catorce-14
quince-15
diéz y seis-16

diéz y seite-17
diéz y ocho-18
diéz y nuevo-19
veinte-20
veinte y uno-21
treinta-30
cuarenta-40 *cincuenta*-50
sesenta-60
setenta-70
ochenta-80 *noventa*-90
cien-100
ciento y uno-101
mil-1,000
mil uno-1,001
lunes-Monday
martes-Tuesday
miércoles-Wednesday
juevos-Thursday
viernos-Friday
sábado-Saturday
domingo-Sunday
ahora-now
manana- tomorrow
¿Quién? Who?
¿Qué? What?
¿Cuando? When?
¿Donde? Where?
¿Por qué? Why?
¿Cómo? How?
¿Qué lejos? How far is it?
   Está lejos. It's far.
   Está cerca. It's near.
¿Qué hora es? What time is it?
¿A qué hora? At what time?
Tengo hambre. I'm hungry.
Perdóneme. Excuse me.
¿Puede ayudarme? Can you help me?
¿Qué es eso? What is this (that)?
¿Cuánto cuesta? What does it cost?
Por favor. Please.
Quisiera... I would like...
Quiero... I want...
  comer to eat
  lo mejor the best
  un habitacion a room
Dame éste. Give me this one.
Dame eso. Give me that one.
No tengo dinero. I have no money.
¡No se mueva! Don't move!
¡Manos arriba! Put your hands up!
¡Buena suerte! Good luck!

Index

A

Alcarraza 49
Alice's Wonderland 162
Anegada 181
Anegada Passage 163, 171, 174, 181, 194
Anegada Rock Iguana 183
Anguilla Point 171, 172, 214
Annaberg Sugar Mill 96, 101
Apple Bay 143
Arrecife Barriles 39
Arrecife Culebrita 44, 46
Arrecife Hermanos 39
Asbestos Point 176
Astrea 185

B

Bahia Almodovar 46
Bahia de Fajardo 36
Bahia de la Chiva 56
Bahia de Sardinas 26, 39, 41, 46, 212
Bahia de Tortuga 47, 48
Bahia Icacos 54, 212
Bahia Salina del Sur 212
Bahia Salinas 54
Bahia Tamarindo 41, 212
Bajo Amarillo 41, 44, 190
Bajo Grouper 44
Bajos Grampus 41, 49, 63, 191
Bank Reef 157
Barrel of Beef 65
Baths, The 163–165, 167, 177, 214
Battery Point 86, 87
Baugher's Bay 118, 195, 210
Beef Island 16, 125, 127, 128, 130, 132, 143, 192
Bellamy Cay 60, 114, 130–132, 193
Belmont 119, 143
Benner Bay 20, 71–75, 191, 194, 195, 203–206, 211
Benures Bay 153, 213
Berg Hill 64, 191
BEYC 167, 174
Bight, The 153–155, 213
Biras Creek 172, 175, 178, 179
Bitter End 178
Bitter End Yacht Club 172, 174, 175, 179, 195
Black Point Rock 160
Blinders Rocks 92
Blonde Rock 159
Blowing Point 169

Bones Bight 183
Booby Rock 92
Bordeaux Mountain 84, 101
Botany Bay 82
Bovoni Cay 75
Brandywine Bay 118, 123–125, 213
Brewers Bay 134, 213
Brewers Bay Pinnacles 134
Buck Island 63, 68, 103, 106, 107, 125–127, 191, 192, 202, 213
Buck Island Channel 103
Buck Island Reef National Monument 106
Burt Point 122, 123

C

Cabeza del Pero 47
Cabo del Pasaje 49
Cabo San Juan 26, 34–39, 212
Cactus Reef 171
Callwood Point 137
Camelberg Peak 101
Canal de Cayo Norte 212
Canal de Culebrita 47
Canal del Sur 42, 46
Canal de Luis Pena 26, 41
Caneel Bay 16, 86, 87, 96, 99, 100, 144, 194, 204–206, 213
Cane Garden Bay 23, 116, 120, 135, 136, 137, 143, 144, 207, 208, 210, 213
Capoons Bay 143
Carbrita Point 77
Careening Cove 65, 122
Carlos Rosario 47, 49
Caroline Bay 72
Carrot Rock 156
Carrot Shoal 156
Carvel Bay 162
Cas Cay 71, 74, 75, 212
Cave Cove 82
Cayo Botella 47, 49
Cayo de Luis Pena 26, 37, 39, 212
Cayo de Tierra 56
Cayo del Agua 39
Cayo Diablo 38
Cayo Icacos 26, 37, 212
Cayo Lobito 37, 39, 190
Cayo Lobos 37, 38, 212
Cayo Norte 47, 212
Cayo Obispo 19, 35, 36, 190, 199, 201, 211
Cayo Pirata 44
Cayo Raton 39
Cayo Ratones 38

Index

Cayo Real 56
Cayos Geniqui 49
Cayo Tiburon 49
Cayo Yerba 39
Centerline Road 100, 112
Cerro Matias 51
Charlotte Amalie 15, 16, 20, 25, 59–62, 64–68, 70, 71, 74, 77, 83, 86, 191, 194, 195, 201–204, 206, 213
Chocolate Hole 88, 90
Christiansted 15, 20, 25, 59, 65, 102–104, 106–110, 112, 113, 192, 194, 201–207, 213
Christiansted Harbor 103, 107
Christmas Cove 75–77, 81, 212
Cinnamon Bay 96, 98
Cistern Point 162
Coakley Bay 108, 109, 192
Coakley Bay Cut 109
Cockroach Island 82
Coconut Bay 82
Colison Point 166, 169
Colquhoun Reef 172
Columbus Point 109
Conch Bay 128, 130, 132
Conch Point 130
Conch Shell Point 128, 130
Congo Cay 99, 100
Connall Shoal 117, 118, 193
Cooper Island 127, 158, 160, 162, 213
Coppermine Point 177, 179
Copper Mine Point 166
Coral Bay 60, 61, 86, 91–94, 96, 101, 203–206, 213
Coral Gardens 159
Coral Harbour 92
Cow and Calf 77
Cowpet Bay 77, 78
Cow Wreck Bay 183
Cramer's Park 113
Crown Bay 70, 72, 195, 202–206
Crown Mountain 83
Cruz Bay 15, 20, 59, 65, 79, 84–89, 92, 94, 98, 100, 101, 192, 201–213
Culebra 39, 41
Current Cut 75, 77, 78, 81, 86, 212

D

Dead Chest Island 156, 159, 160
Dead Chest West 159
Deadman's Bay 158, 159
Deep Bay 175, 176
Devil Hill Bay 180
Devil's Bay 164

Dewey 15, 39, 41, 43, 44, 46, 49, 212
Diamond Cay 146
Diamond Reef 128
Dog Island 63, 77
Drake's Anchorage 172, 175
Drake's Seat 83
Druif Bay 72, 74, 212
Druif Point 72
Dry Rocks 162
Durloe Cays 96, 100
Durloe Channel 100

E

Eagle Shoal 92
East End 74, 75, 113, 127
East Gregerie Channel 69, 70
Elephant Bay 72
Elizabeth Bay 144
Elk Bay 92
El Mono 39
Ensenada Dikity 44
Ensenada Fulladosa 44
Ensenada Honda 39, 41
Ensenada Malena 44
Ensenada Sun Bay 56, 57, 212
Escollo de Arenas 52
Esperanza 50–52, 56–58, 212
Eustatia Island 176
Eustatia Reef 176, 214
Eustatia Sound 174, 176, 178, 214

F

Fajardo 15, 16, 19, 26, 35, 36, 41, 44, 46, 51, 190, 194, 196–201
Fallen Jerusalem 162, 164, 167, 177
False Entrance 74
Fat Hogs Bay 125, 127, 195, 207, 208, 213
Fish Bay 90
Fish Cay 77
Flamenco Beach 49
Flamingo Bay 71–74
Flamingo Point 65
Flanagan Island 92, 94, 99, 153
Fort Berg 94
Fort Burt 115, 122, 195
Fort Christian 60, 65, 67
Fort Christiansvaern 106
Fort Conde de Mirasol 51, 54
Fort Frederik 110
Fort Louisa Augusta 103
Fort Purcell 115, 140
Fort Recovery 115, 140

Fort Sofia Frederika 104
Foxy Callwood 145, 146, 148
Francis Bay 84, 86, 96, 98, 99, 213
Frank Bay 88
Frederiksted 20, 25, 106, 110, 112, 193, 213
Frederiksted Beach 112
Frederiksted Pier 110
Freebooters Gangway 153
Frenchman Hill 64
Frenchtown 70, 72, 83, 201, 202

G

Gallows Bay 15, 65, 104, 106, 194, 203–206
Gallows Point 86, 88
Genti Bay 88
George Dog 169
Ginger Island 158, 160, 162, 194
Gorda Peak National Park 179
Gorda Sound 20, 171, 178, 181
Government Hill 64, 68
Grass Cay 82, 100
Grassy Cay 74
Great Camanoe 128, 130, 132
Great Carrot Bay 143
Great Cruz Bay 88, 89, 213
Great Harbour 15, 145–150, 157, 213, 214
Great Harbour Point 157
Great Lameshur Bay 88, 90, 92, 213
Great St. James Island 77, 86
Great Thatch Island 96, 137, 138
Green Beach 52
Green Cay 107–109, 145, 146, 149, 194, 205, 213, 214
Guana Island 128, 130, 132, 134, 213
Gun Creek 172, 174, 175, 179

H

Hamilton, Alexander 102, 103, 106, 112
Hannah Bay 142, 195
Hansen Bay 92
Hans Lollik Island 81
Hans Lollik Rock 82
Harbor Point 94
Harbour Spit 117, 118, 193
Hassell Island 65, 70
Haulover Bay 94, 96, 162, 213
Haulover Cut 70, 74
Havensight 64, 65, 68, 71, 83, 201–203
Hawksnest Bay 96, 98, 100, 213
Hawksnest Rock 100
Heritage Trail 112
HMS Astrea 185

Hodges Creek 125, 195, 208
Hog's Valley Point 118, 123, 193
Honeymoon Bay 72
Honeymoon Beach 172
Horse Shoe Reef 185
hurricane hole 20, 44, 125, 126, 177

I

Impact Beach 49
Indians, The 11, 132, 152, 154, 156
Inner Brass Island 82
Invisibles, The 82
Isabel Segunda 51, 52, 54, 212
Isla Chiva 54, 56
Isla de Culebra 26, 37, 39, 41, 47, 49
Isla de Culebrita 47, 48, 212
Isla de Palominos 35, 36
Isla de Vieques 25, 26, 49, 59, 191
Isla Palominotos 36
Isla Yallis 54

J

Jack and Burns Point 176
Jersey Bay 71, 74, 75
Johnson Reef 96, 98, 192
Josiah's Bay 144
Jost Van Dyke 115, 149

K

Katitche Point 169
Key Bay 154, 159
Key Cay 159
Key Point 159
Kingstown 123, 125
Kitchen Point 171
Knights of Malta 60, 103, 115
Krause Lagoon 112, 193
Krause Lagoon Channel 112
Krum Bay 70, 74

L

La Blanquilla 38
La Cordillera 34, 35, 37, 212
Lagoon Point 92, 94
Lana's Cove 39
Lang Bank 103
Lang Peak 104
La Pasa de los Cayos Lobos 39
Lark Bank 117, 118, 122, 123, 193
Las Cucarachas 34, 37
Las Hermanas 39

Index

Leduck Island 92
Lee Bay 128, 160
Leinster Bay 86, 96, 98–100, 137, 213
Lerkenlund Bay 82
Leverick Bay 172, 175, 179, 195, 208, 210
Limetree Bay Channel 111, 112
Little Camanoe 128, 130, 132
Little Dix Bay 116, 169, 179, 214
Little Fort National Park 177
Little Harbour 149, 154
Little Jost Van Dyke 145, 146, 214
Little Lameshur Bay 88, 90, 92
Little St. James Island 77
Little Thatch Island 60, 114, 137, 138, 213
Little Thatch Island Cut 137, 213
Lizard Rocks 82
Loblolly Bay 183
Long Beach 172
Long Point 63, 65, 92
Los Farallones 37
Los Galafatos 56
Los Gemelos 49
Lovango Cay 96, 99, 100
Luis Pena Channel 39

M

Magens Bay 82, 83
Maho Bay 99
Manchioneel Bay 158, 160–162, 213
Mandal Bay 82
Mandal Point 81, 82
Marina Cay 16, 127, 128, 130–132, 195, 213
Markoe Bay 158
Mary Point 98, 101
Maya Cove 20, 125–127, 143, 195, 208, 210, 213
Megan's Bay 81
Melones 39
Middle Passage 82
Millionaire Road 177
Mingo Cay 100
Mingo Rock 88, 192
Money Bay 154
Mongoose Junction 84, 87
Monkey Point 130, 134
Monte Pirata 51
moorings 10, 11, 13, 34, 44, 47, 49, 56, 65, 77, 82, 84, 86, 88, 92, 100, 104, 107, 109, 118, 123, 125, 127, 128, 132, 136, 138, 142, 146, 148, 150, 151, 153, 157, 159, 160, 172, 174, 177, 208
Moravian Point 88
Morningstar Bay 83

Mosquito Island 171, 172
Mosquito Rock 171
Mount Eagle 102
Mount Healthy National Park 134
Muller Bay 79
Muskmelon Bay 134

N

Nancy Point 96
Nanny Cay 20, 117, 119, 137, 139–143, 155, 195, 207–211, 213
Narrows, The 86
National Park moorings 155
Necker Island 82, 171, 172, 180
Newfound Bay 93, 94, 213
Norman Island 60, 114, 143, 152–156, 213
North Sound 16, 20, 114, 132, 163, 164, 171–177, 179, 180, 195, 214

O

Oil Nut Bay 176–178
Opuntia Point 176
Ornen Rock 82
Otter Creek 92
Outer Brass Island 82
Oyster Rock 175

P

Packet Rock 63, 65
Painted Walls 159
Palmas del Mar 35, 190, 197, 212
Paramatta 185
Paraquita Bay 20, 125–127
Pasaje Cucaracha 37
Pasaje de Barriles 39
Pasaje de Hermanos 39
Pasaje de San Juan 26, 37, 212
Patricia Cay 74, 75
Peace Hill 100
Pelican Island 152, 154, 156
Peter Island 16, 118, 127, 152, 154–160, 195, 208, 213
Picara Point 82
Piedra Stevens 49
Pillsbury Sound 77, 86, 192
Playa Zoni 47
Pomato Point 181, 183
Port Alucroix 112
Prickly Pear Island 171, 172, 176, 177, 180
Princess Bay 92
Privateer Point 92, 94

Prospect Reef 123, 162, 195, 207, 213
Protestant Cay 104
Puerto del Manglar 41
Puerto del Rey 35, 190
Puerto Ferro 26, 49, 56, 191, 212
Puerto Manglar 46
Puerto Mosquito 56, 212
Puerto Negro 56, 212
Puerto Real 15, 19, 50, 51, 56, 194, 212
Punnett Point 107, 108
Punta Aguila 36
Punta Aloe 44
Punta Arenas 52, 212
Punta Cabras 44
Punta Carenero 56
Punta Colorada 41, 44, 190
Punta Cruz 39
Punta de Maguey 44
Punta de Molinas 49
Punta Flamenco 47, 49
Punta Melones 39, 44, 190
Punta Mulas 49, 52, 54, 191
Punta Noroeste 49
Punta Pozuelo 194
Punta Soldado 39, 44
Punta Tamarindo Grande 39, 41, 49
Punta Tampico 41
Punta Tuna 35
Punte Este 54
Purcell Estate 140

Q

Queen Elizabeth Bridge 130

R

Radas Roosevelt 49, 52, 191
Rams Head 92
Recovery Hill 104
Red Hook 25, 77–79, 81–83, 86, 88, 194, 195, 202–206, 212
Red Hook Point 79
Red Point 74
Reef Bay 86, 88, 90, 92
Reef Bay Estate 92
Regis Point 72
Rendezvous Bay 90
Reseau Bay 82
Rhoda Bank 65
Rhone 119, 157, 159, 160, 172, 174
Road Harbour 115, 117–123, 125, 140, 193, 195, 209, 213
Road Town 12, 13, 15, 20, 114, 115, 117–121, 123, 137, 138, 140, 142, 143, 157, 162, 163, 195, 207–211
Roca Columna 39
Roca Cucaracha 54
Rocky Beach 172
Roger's Point 159
Rogers Point 154
Rotto Cay 74
Round Bay 92
Round Reef 103, 104, 192
Round Rock 161, 162, 165, 167
Round Rock Passage 162
Rupert Rock 65
Ruyter Bay 72

S

Saba Rock 172, 174, 176, 177, 195
Sabbat Channel 92
Sabbat Point 92
Sage Mountain 144
Sage Mountain National Park 144
Salt Island 119, 156–160, 162, 194, 213
Salt Island Bay 160
Saltpond Bay 91, 92, 213
Salt River Bay 102, 109, 213
Salt River Bay National Park 109
Salt River Point 109
Sanders Bay 94
Sand Pierre Bay 158
Sandy Cay 145, 146, 149, 214
San Ignacio 185
San Juan 194
Santa Maria Bay 82
Santa Monica Rocks 153
Sapphire Beach Marina 79, 81, 82, 203, 212
Savanna Bay 169
Schooner Channel 104, 192
Scotch Bank 104, 107, 108, 117, 118, 122, 123, 193
Scrub Island 127, 128, 213
Scrub Island Cut 127, 128, 213
Sea Cow Bay 139, 141, 142
Seal Dog 171
Setting Point 181, 183, 184
Settlement, The 183
Shark Bay 134
Shoy Point 107, 108
Signal Hill 64
Simpson Baai 163
Sint Maarten 163
Sir Francis Drake Channel 117, 122, 140, 143, 152, 153, 156, 162, 179
Skinny Dipping Beach 172

Skipper Jacob Rock 88
Skyworld 120, 122
Smuggler's Cove 143
Sonda de Vieques 26, 37, 52
Soper's Hole 9, 12, 96, 114, 117, 137, 138, 140, 143, 146, 193, 195, 207–211
South Haulover Bay 96
South Sound 177, 178
Southwest Cape 103, 193
Spanish Town 20, 164, 166, 177
Sprat Bay 157, 159, 195, 213
Sprat Point 130
Spring Bay 164
Spy Glass Hill 153
St. Croix 12, 15, 20, 23, 25, 51, 59–61, 63–65, 102–104, 106–110, 112, 113, 122, 153, 192, 193, 194, 201–206, 213
Steven Cay 79
St. John 11, 15–17, 19, 20, 25, 54, 59–65, 77, 79, 84–90, 92–94, 96, 99–103, 114, 137, 138, 152, 192, 194, 201, 202, 213
Stragglers, The 77
St. Thomas 12, 13, 15, 16, 20, 25, 49, 59–65, 67, 68, 70, 72, 74, 77, 81–84, 86–88, 102, 103, 106, 114–116, 138, 140, 191, 194, 202–207, 212
Sub Base 70, 72, 202–206
Sun Bay Beach 51, 58

T

Teague Bay 107–109, 194
Teague Point 109
Thatch Cay 82
Thatch Island Cut 137, 213
The Blinders 164
The Caves 152, 154
The Indians 156
The Settlement 183
The Walls 183
Tortola 12, 14, 15, 16, 20, 21, 23, 25, 26, 60, 96, 98, 114–120, 122–125, 127, 128, 130, 132–135, 137, 140, 142–144, 145, 152, 155, 156, 159, 166, 171, 180, 181, 193, 195, 207–211, 213
Treasure Point 155
Trellis Bay 128, 130–132, 193, 208, 210
Tropaco Point 82
Trunk Bay 11, 86, 96, 98, 100, 165, 213
Turner Point 94
Two Brothers 86, 192

V

Vanish Rock 160

Vessup Bay 79
Vieques 15, 16, 25, 26, 34, 35, 37, 49–52, 54, 56, 57–59, 191, 196, 197, 212
Virgin Gorda Valley 164
Virgin Gorda Yacht Harbour 15, 20, 163, 164, 166, 169, 177, 179, 214
Virgins Islands National Park 87
Virgin Sound 171, 180
Visibles, The 82
Vixen Point 172

W

Water Bay 81, 82, 92, 155
Water Island 63, 65, 70–72, 74
Watermelon Cay 96
Water Point 77, 155
West Dog 169
West Gregerie Channel 70, 74
Wharfside Village 87
Whelk Point 125
Whelk Rocks 77
White Bay 149
White Horseface Reef 82
White Horse Reef 109
White Horse Rock 109
Wickham's Cay I 118–120
Wickham's Cay II 118, 210
Willie T 154, 155
Windward Passage 96, 100
Wreck of the Rhone Marine Park 160

Y

Yawzi Point 88

Notes

About the Author

Photo Courtesy of Danielle Courteau

Stephen J. Pavlidis has been cruising The Bahamas and Caribbean since the winter of 1989.

Starting in the Exuma Cays, 20 years ago, Steve began his writing career with guides to the many fascinating destinations he visited. Many of his books stand alone to this day as the quintessential guides to the areas he covers.

His books are different from most other cruising guides in some very significant ways. All of the charts in Steve's books were created using data personally collected while visiting each area using a computerized system that interfaces GPS and depth soundings.

You can find out more about this exceptional author by visiting his Web site, www.Seaworthy.com, where there is current news and information about Steve's latest projects, as well as contact information.

Other books by Stephen J. Pavlidis:

Life at Sea Level, ISBN 978-1-892399-33-5

The Exuma Guide, 3rd Edition, ISBN 978-1-892399-31-1

A Cruising Guide to the Leeward Islands, 2nd Edition, ISBN 978-1-892399-36-6

The Northern Bahamas Guide, ISBN 978-1-892399-28-1

The Northwest Caribbean Guide, ISBN 978-1-892399-24-3

The Puerto Rico Guide, Third Edition, ISBN 978-1-892399-39-7

The Southern Bahamas Guide, ISBN 978-1-892399-29-8

A Cruising Guide to the Windward Islands, ISBN 978-1-892399-18-2

Where to Go for Hurricane Season

When hurricane season arrives most boaters in the Caribbean begin to move to safer waters although some take their chances and remain close to a hurricane hole for the season. Some head south to Trinidad, a popular destination at the bottom of the Windward Island chain. Others make their way to Venezuela and the ABC's where hurricanes don't threaten.

The Southwest Caribbean offers excellent protection in places like Columbia and Boca del Toros, Panama, both popular stops and out of the path of tropical storm systems.

The Northwest Caribbean, particularly Guatemala, has come into its own as a very popular destination for cruisers wishing to spend hurricane season with other like-minded crews. Both the SW and NW Caribbean are downwind from the Eastern Caribbean and that makes for some very good sailing.

As far as actual protection from hurricanes for cruisers in the Northwest Caribbean, the finest protection is on the *Río Dulce* in Guatemala. In fact, the *Río Dulce* is probably the finest hole in the entire Caribbean offering excellent protection, economical prices, and an eclectic group of gregarious cruisers. The marinas are well upstream, miles from the coast and the worst of any hurricane surge, and the surrounding hills go a long way in lessening the strength of the wind. Arguably this may be the best hurricane hole in the entire Caribbean because its location makes it very difficult for a hurricane to make a direct hit on the river without crossing a good bit of mountainous land that would only weaken the storm.

Whatever choice you make, whether to stay in the Eastern Caribbean, the Virgins, Puerto Rico, the DR, or head for better protection for the season, know where the best protection lies, how long it takes to get there, and be prepared to move early and quickly.

www.ingramcontent.com/pod-product-compliance
Lightning Source LLC
Chambersburg PA
CBHW080538300426
44111CB00017B/2784